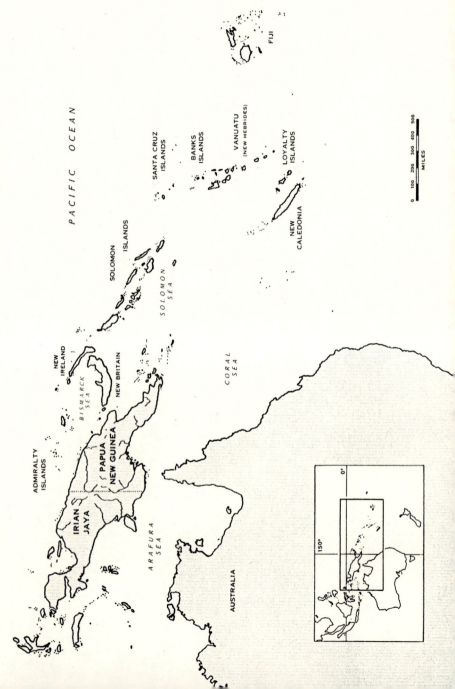

MELANESIA

PACIFIC OCEAN

FIJI

SANTA CRUZ
ISLANDS

BANKS
ISLANDS

VANUATU
(NEW HEBRIDES)

LOYALTY
ISLANDS

NEW
CALEDONIA

SOLOMON
ISLANDS

SOLOMON
SEA

NEW
IRELAND

NEW BRITAIN

BISMARCK
SEA

ADMIRALTY
ISLANDS

IRIAN
JAYA

PAPUA
NEW GUINEA

CORAL
SEA

ARAFURA
SEA

AUSTRALIA

0 100 200 300 400 500

MILES

0°

150°

Ritualized
Homosexuality
in Melanesia

Edited by

Gilbert H. Herdt

Ritualized

Homosexuality

in Melanesia

University of California Press

Berkeley • Los Angeles • London

University of California Press

Berkeley and Los Angeles, California

University of California Press, Ltd.

Oxford, England

First Paperback Printing 1993

Library of Congress Cataloging in Publication Data

Main entry under title:
Ritualized homosexuality in Melanesia.

Bibliography: p. 362
Includes Index.
1. Melanesians—Rites and ceremonies—Addresses, essays, lectures. 2. Melanesians—Social life and customs—Addresses, essays,
lectures. 3. Homosexuality, Male—Melanesia—Addresses, essays,
lectures. 4. Sex customs—Melanesia—Addresses, essays, lectures.
I. Herdt, Gilbert H., 1949–
GN668.R45   1984   306.7'662'0993   83-18015
ISBN 0-520-08096-3

Printed in the United States of America

The paper used in this publication meets the minimum requirements of
ANSI/NISO Z39.48-1992 (R 1997) (*Permanence of Paper*). ⊚

Contents

Maps

Introduction
to the Paperback Edition

In a little less than a decade the notion of ritualized homosexuality—made prominent in the first edition of this book—has become a significant perspective on Melanesian societies and the comparative study of sexuality at large. In 1982, when my review in the original introduction was completed, the concept of "ritualized" same-sex eroticism or "age-structured" homosexual relations hardly existed. As that text showed, "homosexuality" research was little developed in the anthropological literature on tribal societies, and was scarcely noticed in certain Melanesian and Australian Aboriginal tribes. What was known but ignored was—to use the early and insightful remark of Van Baal (1963:206)—that the "homosexual initiation cult [was] common to all these tribes." Since that time a small treasure of new ethnographic accounts and reinterpretations of older studies have appeared, especially in the work of Bruce Knauft (1985, 1987, 1990). The publication of this new edition provides the opportunity to update the cross-cultural review, expand upon the earlier critical analysis, and respond to certain interpretations (both positive and negative) of the research published herein that have appeared since the early 1980s.

Anthropology rests upon the twin purposes of translating Western folk ideas into cultural science and back-translating non-Western theories into ethnographies that reflect upon lifeways in all corners of our shrinking world. The cross-cultural study of sexuality is forever caught in the struggle between such purposes: the effort to chart local sexual practices and knowledge on their own terms, and the effort to represent these folkways in Western texts that "universalize" the forms from our own perspective. In the heyday of their main contributions to the anthropology of sexuality both Malinowski and Margaret Mead struggled with this issue (reviewed in Herdt and Stoller 1990). And the "sexual" continues to challenge our Western post-Enlightenment conception of the "natural" person and the "social" contract between the individual and polity.

Now all anthropological efforts can be thought of as either "lumping" or "splitting" strategies for comparison, and the domain of sexual culture (Herdt and Stoller 1990) is no different. Yet there is something bothersome to scholars about applying these strategies to the field of sexual study. Think, for example, about how notions and practices of the sacred—of worship, or of beliefs about the soul—vary widely across human groups, resulting in myriad forms of "religion" (Herdt and Stephen 1989). Westerners are not so uncomfortable about this idea as they were in the time of, say, William James and Sigmund Freud. Many do, however, feel more threatened by the notion that there are divergent sexualities, and even more uncomfortable with the suggestion that there are multiple homosexualities (and heterosexualities: Stoller 1985). Perhaps this is because sexuality is felt to be so close to our folk theory of "human nature."[1] Whatever the case, the structural trend in Western epistemology has been to collate, consolidate, and wrest from a comparison of Western sexuality with these other sexualities the supposedly shared common denominators of human sexual nature, suggesting to some that, ultimately, a rose is a rose no matter what its color.

The anthropology of sexuality has made progress on these general issues, but it was not until the early 1980s that a critical impasse ended (Read 1980). "Homosexuality" has been especially problematic for anthropology because we have remained divided over whether this is a universal or local condition of culture and "human nature" (Herdt 1990a, 1991a). It remains as controversial today as it was a decade ago, when this book was composed, in part because the AIDS epidemic has thrust itself into the cultural representation of same-sex relations.[2] Nonetheless, our society is more sophisticated than before, and scholarly work has clarified the conceptual relationship between different types of same-sex relations.

It is now clear that we must place the term "homosexuality" in quotation marks because its folk theory merges the distinction between kinds of cultural identity and types of sexual practice. What we once thought of as a unitary "it" entity—homosexuality—is, to use the metaphor of my original preface, not one but several "species" of same-sex relations. They differ not only in symbolic form but, I would claim, also in their deeper nature. Thus, the received category "homosexuality" in Western culture must now be represented as one of several different sociocultural types. It is argued by many experts that these "traditional" forms of culturally conventionalized same-sex erotic practices occur in clusters of culture areas of the world (Adam 1986; Greenberg 1988).

Indeed, four ideal types of same-sex practice can be contrasted in the category schema that I use (Herdt 1987, 1988): age-structured, gender-structured, role- or class-structured, and gay- or egalitarian-structured homosexualities.[3] In the Austro-Melanesian area, as the authors of *Ritualized Homosexuality* established, "age" is the key variable and defining factor in the same-sex relation between the boy and his sexual inseminator in this part of the world, as it was, by comparison, in ancient Greece and Tokugawa Japan. To refer to this practice as "homosexuality" seems now inelegant and unreflective (cf. Herdt 1981). I prefer to represent this symbolic type of same-sex practice as *boy-inseminating rites* (Herdt 1991b).

In the societies of New Guinea, the South Seas, and Australia in which these practices occur, age is a generalized and key organizing principle in many domains of culture and social action. The kinship and marriage systems are strongly marked by an age-graded principle of social hierarchy. Age also defines a critical aspect of the relationship between the partners in heterosexual marriage, in religious practices, and body substance beliefs. Ten years ago it was not known that age-defined same-sex practice was widely distributed in the tribal world. After all, no less authorities than Ford and Beach (1951:130), in their highly influential HRAF-type study *Patterns of Sexual Behavior*, could confidently state: "The most common form of institutionalized homosexuality is that of the *berdache* or transvestite." They were wrong. We now know that the age-structured form does not include genderized cross-dressing; that transvestism is rare in Melanesia. Indeed, the gender-reversed form of same-sex practice, especially the famous *berdache* custom, is geographically bound as a symbolic practice to North and South America and fringe areas of the Pacific Rim (reviewed in Callender and Kochems 1983; Greenberg 1988; Herdt 1991*a*; Murray 1987; Nanda 1990; Roscoe 1988, 1991; Williams 1986).

The comparative study of boy-inseminating rites is now faced with an embarrassment of riches owing to the creation of this new category of age-defined same-sex practice: a veritable explosion of analyses in anthropology, sociology, social history, and the classics. For instance, the Canadian sociologist Barry Adam has shown significant links between sexuality, kinship, social relations, and age in tribes, citing, for example, Evans-Pritchard's (1970) historical Azande data; along with studies of the archaic societies of ancient Greece, Japan, China; as well as contemporary ethnographic studies, most notably those from this book, after which he refers to a "Melanesian model" of homosexuality. The encyclopaedic study by David Greenberg, *The Construction of Homosexuality*, also contains a longish section on "transgenerational homosexuality" (1988:26–40) that highlights the function of "age" and kinship in the ethnographic analyses of *Ritualized Homosexuality in Melanesia* (see also the sociologist Murray, 1984:44–46). In classical studies, Sir Kenneth Dover's analysis of *Greek Homosexuality* (1978) brought an end to a long-implicit taboo among classicists on the topic (see Halperin 1990:4–5) and opened the way for a new series of controversial comparisons of boy-inseminating in archaic and Melanesian societies (Sergent 1986:40–54; and see Bremmer 1989; Cohen 1987). Recently, for example, Dover (1988) has compared Greek sexuality and ritual to the initiation practices of Melanesia and other tribal places; and Winkler (1990) compares contemporary and ancient Greek practices in the classics and anthropology to yield new and bold insights, as, for instance, the question of what constitutes "unnatural acts."

Of all these accumulating scholarly interests, however, none is more significant for cultural studies than the question of what is specifically "erotic" about boy-inseminating practices. The challenge is to understand both the "natural" properties and "cultural constructs" of boy-inseminating relations in the cultural reality of the actors themselves, as represented by ethnographers (Herdt and Stoller 1990; Parker 1991). No less a scholar than Michel Foucault (1986:221) has been absorbed with the meaning of homoerotic desire in these traditions: "To delight in and be a subject of pleasure with a boy did not cause a problem for the Greeks; but to be an object of pleasure and to acknowledge oneself as such constituted a major difficulty for the boy." Whether we may legitimately represent the "subjects" and "objects" of the ancient Greeks and New Guinea tribesmen by the Western cultural tropes for homoerotic "pleasure" and "arousal" remains a central problem in the anthropological study of sexuality.

Where this scholarly work on the anthropology of homosexuality began, however, is surely not the same as where it will end up. We have already had to reexamine our preconceptions of the phenomenon. As Marilyn Strathern (1988:11) has advised in another context: "All that can be offered is a prescription: one cure to the present impasse in the comparative anthropology of Melanesia might be to indulge less in our own representational strategies—to stop ourselves thinking about the world in certain ways."

THE HISTORICAL PRESENT

The anthropology of ritualized boy-inseminating owes its interpretative meanings to comparative studies and leftover controversies we are beginning to understand from the shadowy social history of homosexuality in the 19th and early 20th centuries (Herdt 1991*a*, 1991*b*; see also Greenberg 1988; Halperin 1990; Weeks 1985).

The cultural reality of sexual meanings, in a pluralistic and complex society such as our own, is a matter of politics, of competing social interests (Adam 1987; Foucault 1980; Hekma 1989). Nowhere has the contest been of more import than in social science studies of homosexuality, which have—often as not—been used to "prove" or "disprove" one or another claim, usually a biological claim, about "human nature," such as whether desire for the same sex is "natural" or "unnatural," with the cultural definition of "nature" here a struggle between the innate and social surround (DeCecco 1990; Gagnon 1988, 1989; Herdt and Boxer 1992; LeVine 1992; Whitehead 1985/86). In fact, the social history of homosexuality has seen the status of the entity change from a sin to a crime (either against nature or the state), then to a sickness or disease, and now to an alternative "lifestyle" on the margins of society (Bayer 1987; Boswell 1990; Money 1987).[4]

Such is the historical bridge to the present. It is generally argued that 1992 marks the 100th anniversary of the invention of "heterosexuality," a quintessence of modernity. Some associate the invention in 1892 with the sexologist Havelock Ellis and the cloying cultural ethos of late Victorian society (Weeks 1985). The invention of homosexuality, on the other hand, is usually credited to the German Benkert, about 1869, which becomes more widely identified as the fin-de-siècle "disease of effeminacy" popularized by the trial of Oscar Wilde (Herdt and Boxer 1992; Ellman 1987). Why, we might ask, did the category of deviance—homosexuality—precede that of heterosexuality—the "normal"—in the historical record? The answer rests with the structure of relations of power; with how conformity to a middle-class standard of reproductive sexuality was highlighted by sexology and medical science in the later 19th century; and with how the categorical "homosexual subject" became an "object," a matter of inverted "preference," a flaw in the assumptive heterosocial world of the day (see, e.g., Cain 1991; D'Emilio and Freedman 1988; Foucault 1980; Hekma 1989; Sedgwick 1990).

Much has changed since then, not only in the scientific constructs and folk theory of same-sex relations, but in the strategies that we in anthropology deploy in comparative analyses. Indeed, what we previously called "sexuality" is now recognizable as a bundle of entities and meaning systems. The new anthropological writing on sexuality thus suggests that comparative studies must both split as well as lump sociosexual constructs and practices (see, for instance, Parker 1991). Sexuality must be analyzed as part of a whole, contextual, social tradition, one that *embodies* cultural meanings and personal desires within the same ontological subject (see, for instance, Herdt and Stoller 1990; Schott 1988).

Such social and historical traditions create their own ontologies, and Melanesia is no different in this respect, except that in its immense cultural diversity, many and divergent cultural realities are contained within its vast social landscape. By cultural ontology I mean the sense in which reality is phenomenologically formed by active participation—"lived experience"—that defines the kind of a world it is; the categories of meaning that are formative of that world; and the kinds of persons who inhabit it. Such ontologies are critical in the effort to define the same-sex eroticism distinctive of a particular people (Herdt 1991a). We must resist the strong tendency in Western culture to dualize them: notice how easily our discourse converts subjects into objects in the Western tradition, as when same-sex practices of any kind, playful or committed, are labeled "homosexuality." By comparison, the form of same-sex desire in old China did not nominalize the subject or objectify the practice in the same way. The ancient Chinese spoke of what persons "do" or "enjoy" rather than what they "are" as essentialized objects (Hinsch 1990:7; Spence 1983, chap. 7). Here we find a familiar echo of the contemporaneous boy-inseminating rites of Melanesia.

What difference does the ontology make? It is critical to an understanding of sexual development and cultural identity, and on this score the putative *cause* of homosexuality in our Western folk theory is an enormously influential and much-abused issue of theory (Herdt 1989).[5] Take, for instance, the dominating-mother/absent-father complex of classical Freudian discourse. The relationship between absent fathers and the development of homosexuality has an important place in the study of ritual and sexual identity transitions in anthropology (see, e.g., Burton and Whiting 1961). The received Western folk theory predicts that where homosexuality is institutionalized we should find fathers absent from the childhood home. This is because our folk theory understands the ontology of sexuality to be vested in the lone child, rather than in relationships of a whole tradition. In Melanesia, contrary to the Freudian/Western ontology, we find instead that boy-inseminating rites occur *only* in societies wherein children live close to their fathers and mothers (e.g., the Sambia; Herdt 1981)! Surprisingly, in Melanesian societies in which fathers are absent from the childhood home (e.g., Gahuku-Gama, as studied by K. E. Read, chap. 5 in this volume) boy-inseminating rites are *never found*. Such interpretations challenge our ontological conception of "homosexuality" as a monolithic entity with common causes, developmental subjectivities, and functions in all cultures.[6]

"Homosexuality" is a dustbin of entities: it can no longer be used as an uncritical concept across cultures. Furthermore, it diverges ontologically and historically from the sociocultural system that we know today as "gay" in the meaning system and practices of many Westerners (Adam 1987; Herdt 1992; Weeks 1985). A simple historical contrast (Cain 1991), for example, suggests that "homosexuals" are hidden and fearful of disclosure, whereas "gays/lesbians" are socially open ("out") in many walks of their lives (e.g., home, work, school). Such a sociohistorical change demonstrates the enormously rich and rapidly changing cultural system of sexual meanings to which these identities and categories apply in the present (Herdt 1992; Sedgwick 1990).

Many scholars thus reject gross categorizations that lump, for instance, notions of "sodomy" with "pederasty," or refer to "homosexual" and "gay" as if these were interchangeable entities. Each of these is a distinct ideal type; and these are energized ideologies, modes of cultural reality. Or again, take, for instance, the lumping of "pederasty" with boy-inseminating rites. It remains confusing when scholars, even gay scholars (Boswell 1990), not to mention Western psychiatrists, speak of the nominalized "homosexual" (Lidz and Lidz 1989:195–199) as the same ontological type as the ritualized boy-inseminator in Melanesia: Bleibtreu-Ehrenberg (1991), Hage (1981), and Sergent (1986) continue to refer to such practices as "pederasty," a trope that owes its pejorative meanings to 19th-century clinical sexology, when all sexual variations were interpreted as disease (see Plummer [1991:246] on this point). Of course it is tempting to hedge on the matter and apply the Western concept of "bisexuality" (Davenport 1977) to these Melanesian forms, but this is inaccurate for reasons demonstrated below. Better to use a purely instrumental language than such imported concepts; and here we are wise to follow the lead of Schiefenhovel (1990), whose language is descriptive and speaks only of "ritualized adult-male/adolescent-male sexual behavior" in Melanesia.

From this perspective what I and other authors in our original 1984 collection labeled "homosexuality" was, I now think, a misnomer. To speak instead of boy-inseminating practices or age-structured homoerotic relationships is to open a far richer set of cultural worlds. One might object that the issue of adjectives and representations is at this point passé. After all, have not many ethnographers (though not me), including Margaret Mead (1930, who also used the trope "invert"), nominalized the Melanesian man's desire for a younger initiate with the representation "homosexual"? Indeed they have; and the continued reliance upon these tropes in the anthropological literature not only is confusing to scholars in other fields, but also smells of strong prejudices, including that nemesis of cross-cultural analysis, ethnocentrism. Melanesian sexual practices present, in my opinion, a different phenomenon than that of the "homosexual" subject of Western culture, though virtually all ethnographers in the Melanesian situation, myself included, have nominalized the local phenomenon as an "it entity" (Herdt 1991). It is time to mark a watershed in this conventional usage.

NEW ETHNOGRAPHIC CASES

Research over the past ten years has tended to confirm the speculations of my earlier analysis, based upon piecemeal linguistic, ethnohistorical, and ecological evidence, that boy-inseminating ritualized homosexuality in certain traditional societies of Melanesia is prehistoric, perhaps 10,000 or more years old (Feil 1987:176–177; Knauft 1987; Schiefenhovel 1990:410–411; and see Greenberg 1989:33 n. 44). Comparative scholars such as Greenberg believe that this tradition should be seen as a survival of a Paleolithic practice once widespread throughout the world (see also Sergent 1986:50–51).

Geographic diffusion between Australian Aborigines and certain New Guinea societies has also been reaffirmed (Feil 1987:189n.; Greenberg 1988:35–37). The additional Australian case (not available at the time of my original review) of the famous Tiwi of Northwestern coast affirms boy-inseminating practices among them.[7] More broadly, in a significant ethnological review, Hiatt (1987:98) concludes, "It is hard to escape the conclusion that man-making rites and their sequels, the ceremonial maintenance of universal fertility, were in some degree homoerotic."

Several significant scholarly reviews of "ritualized homosexuality" in New Guinea societies have appeared during the last few years, among which the anthropological analyses of Knauft (1986), Lindenbaum (1987), Feil (1987: esp. 176–199), Marilyn Strathern (1988: esp. 208–219), and Schiefenhovel (1990) are prominent. These scholars conceptualize boy-inseminating practices as thematic of Melanesian society and to culture theory at large. A new review of the sacred flutes in New Guinea (Hays 1986), and a fine analysis by Hauser-Schäublin (1989) of symbolic

procreation and insemination, are suggestive of how boy-inseminating rites lead to symbolic and sexual "reproduction" in Melanesia and Australia (Mead 1949; see also Bohle 1990;
M. Strathern 1988; Whitehead 1985–86).[8]

None have thought more carefully than Bruce Knauft (1986,
1990) about the conceptual issues in this book, and his superior
analyses display remarkable scholarship and insight.[9] Recently,
Knauft (1990) has reexamined the historical situation in Kiwai Island at the mouth of the Fly River, reviewing one of the most important 19th-century cases of Melanesian rites. His critical
reconstruction of the general pattern, distribution, and frequency
(in maps and estimates) of boy-inseminating rites among adjacent
societies along the southern coast of Papua is a tour de force.[10]
Knauft criticizes the inclusion of Kiwai Island culture among
groups that traditionally practiced boy-inseminating, and he systematically deconstructs each piece of ethnographic evidence on
the Kiwai set out in my original introduction. He builds a strong
case that Kiwai Islanders never practiced the custom. The main
effect of this effort is to establish that only the Keraki (Williams
1936) and other tribes *west* of the Fly River participated in the
practices (see the review in Busse 1987; and the unpublished dissertation of Ayres 1983, esp. chap. 3). Knauft (1990:208) then
concludes that "ritualized homosexuality was not as prevalent
along the New Guinea south coast as previously supposed."

The question of the frequency and pervasiveness of boy-inseminating rites has long dominated discussions of the phenomenon,
as mentioned in the original edition. In fact, we can never be sure
about the precolonial incidence of the rites in Melanesia, and the
facts are still open to question, much as they were in the time of
the first speculative theory on the matter, set out in Alfred Haddon's introduction to *The Kiwai Papuans of British New Guinea*
(1927). We do know that boy-inseminating rites, like the serial
male/female sexual relations of certain ritual occasions in Southwestern Papua, profoundly troubled many of the early white col-
onists (Godelier 1986; Herdt 1991*b*; Schiltz 1985; Van Baal
1966). It is difficult for us to adequately gauge the tremendous toll
that Western agents and missionaries have taken on these practices, including their suppression by force, and their subsequent
practice in secret. Still, Knauft is right to be skeptical of "misattri-

butions" of boy-inseminating rites; certainly "homosexual slanders" of a popular kind, mentioned in my review in this volume, continue at the present time.[11]

That boy-inseminating practice is less frequent than I had claimed must be examined at several levels of analysis (as Knauft [1986] quite rightly argues). Knauft's evidence on the matter is persuasive but inconclusive. As the reader will judge, I would concede that Kiwai tradition probably did not require boy-inseminating. How important is the actual number of groups and the size of the populations they contained? We are dealing with both statistical and normative phenomena, and it matters that we keep these separate. For the numbers, we lose the Kiwai as a case, but must add several new cultures to the ethnographic corpus originally cited for the region (see below). The difference in numbers of actual actors is a wash, though I doubt that this game of numbers has a level of significance to underscore. Though the numbers of groups are open to dispute, their importance for theory and the understanding of Melanesian area-wide cultural structure and ontology clearly is not (Knauft 1986; see also Herdt 1989, 1991*b*; M. Strathern 1988).

What Knauft is particularly concerned about is the "misattribution" of the ritual complex: he questions the "appropriateness of using ritualized homosexuality as an archetypal cultural feature of lowland south New Guinea in the pre-colonial era, as suggested by Shirley Lindenbaum and Daryl Feil" (Knauft 1990:190). It is misleading and ethnographically false to label whole traditions as "homosexual." The mention of "organization[s] of male homosexuality" as a generic categorization of the Big Nambas tribe of Malekula Island (Deacon 1934) and the use of the phrase "homosexual initiation rites" in reference to the immense Southwestern Papuan area bordering the Arufura Sea (Van Baal 1966) have created scientific and cultural stereotypes. Thus we find Andrew Strathern, in a book entitled *Mountain Papuans*, arguing that "homosexuality occurs in fringe societies" of New Guinea compared to its "complete absence" in "Central Highland cases" (1988:209; and see also Feil 1987). Such a sweeping assertion by a leading scholar raises troubling questions because it is not indexed to the ethnographic evidence or reviews in the literature. What troubles me and seems to pique Knauft (1990) as well is the

representation "homosexual cultures" used in reference to the entire culture area (Feil 1987, Lindenbaum 1987), an outrageous
trope that reifies the whole by the part (Herdt 1991*b*).

The best-documented recent case of traditional boy-inseminating comes to us from Bruce Knauft himself (1985, 1986, 1987,
1989, 1990), whose ethnography, more than that of any other recent writer, has taken seriously the social and symbolic problems
of ritualized boy-inseminating in the fabric of a New Guinea society. The Gebusi live in close proximity to the Great Papua Plateau
societies so well known for their boy-inseminating rites (reviewed
on pp. 33–37 of this volume). Knauft has demonstrated a symbolic
complex of a men's spirit cult including trancing, dancing, spirit
impersonation, homoerotic horseplay, and longer-term affectional
relations between older and young males. Among male pairs the
practice of oral intercourse was common. Among the findings of
his work are the demonstrations that cultural fantasies of desire
and attraction for the opposite sex permeate same-sex relations
and that Gebusi are sometimes compelled to break their own rules
of same- and opposite-sexual practice due to their passions (Knauft
1986, 1987).

In a new and significant study of the (Wamek) Boadzi people of
the Middle Fly River, Mark Busse (1987) has demonstrated vast
social change in the sexual practices of an area once made famous
for its boy-inseminating ceremonies (F. E. Williams 1936; Van Baal
1966). Today, Busse tells us, missionary activity has all but eliminated even the memories of such rituals. A few older informants
continue to hold beliefs regarding the magical power of semen as
an elixir for growth (reviewed in Busse, n.d.). The "medicine" not
only of semen but of the vagina is "very good for children," these
informants told him (1987:295).[12] Traditionally, boy-inseminating occurred under the aegis of the men's house. "When a boy's
beard begins to come in, his maternal uncles take him to the single
boys' house where he will live until he marries, an event which
usually takes place when a man is in his early or mid-twenties"
(ibid.:323). In fact, it was the prospective father-in-law of the boy
who might inseminate him, a cultural practice deeply entangled
with marriage exchange and bride-service to the older man.

Was erotic desire a potent motive in boy-inseminating here? To
anticipate my final discussion, I would cite an important myth collected by Busse entitled "The Boy Who Became Pregnant." This

traditional story describes a boy with a "girl's face" that was so "beautiful" that "all the . . . single boys fucked him all the time. As a result, he became pregnant. The boys hid him from the women." Later the myth tells that the inseminated boy died because he could not deliver the baby (Busse 1987:317; see also Ayres 1983). The myth is similar to those collected more than 70 years ago by Landtman (1917, on the nearby Kiwai Islanders) and it affirms an observation of Van Baal's regarding the Fly River area, that "among the people of the Trans-Fly, anal intercourse is believed to be necessary for boys' physical development" (Busse 1987:318). The Boazi men are reported to have viewed this ritual period as the "best time" in their lives, with hunting, comradeship, story telling, trysts with women, and the "option of homosexual relations with other males in the single boys' house" predominant themes of masculine culture (Busse 1987:323–324; see also Schieffelin 1982).

In a controversial book that describes same-sex practices, the popular writer Tobias Schneebaum (1988) provides a memoir of life with the Asmat people who inhabit a stretch of the coast of West New Guinea (Irian Jaya). As reported in the first edition of this book (pp. 29–30), Asmat were insinuated (but without documentation) by Van Amelsvoort (1964) to practice ritualized boy-inseminating. Schneebaum's personal account situates the Asmat in the general ritual complex of the area by reporting early initiation into opposite-sex relations (1988:84), important medicinal uses of semen, and the combinatory power of male and female fluids that are used for ritual production of masculine growth (ibid.:194). This part of his Asmat memoirs compares well to the ethnographies of the Marind-anim, Kimam, and related cultures as reported by Van Baal and Serpenti in their respective chapters below. The comparison is further strengthened by the fact that Van Amelsvoort himself had compared Asmat with the neighboring Jaquai tribe. And on the Jaquai, Boelaars (1981:60) has written: "Sodomy is the mentor's duty; it is his task to see to the boy's masculinization. Coming [from the initiation] . . . where he has been secluded like a girl, the boy is still girlish, and sodomy is the main means of making him strong and masculine and a good warrior." So far so good, in relation to the anthropological literature on boy-inseminating rites.

What is most controversial about Schneebaum's book are two sexual practices known only from one other group in Melanesia,

East Bay Island. First is his assertion that *both* anal and oral sexual practices occur within the same tradition and that such a combination occurs elsewhere only in East Bay (see pp. 16–18 below and Herdt 1989). But Schneebaum appreciates this novelty, and he properly compares it to Davenport's (1965) ethnography of East Bay. Second, and more problematical, is his report of an *egalitarian* mode of practice with exchange between same-aged partners. Asmat, he says, have a traditional concept of reciprocal sexual practice between peers as equals; they refer to it as *mbai*, a lifelong "friendship" of affection and sexual intercourse between males that is not entirely unlike heterosexual marriage (1988:43ff.). Asmat themselves, he continues, recognize the distinctive character of their homoerotic practices and they make their own inter-ethnic comparisons about it: "We know it is different with the Marind[-anim]. There are no *mbai*. There are no young men who have sexual intercourse together. There, it is *always a young boy with an older man*" (1988:194). The statement of this inter-tribal comparison on the part of the Asmat is remarkable, though not without precedent; however, such statements in themselves do not remove the suspicion of culture change in the matter. Such relations do not occur among women, the Asmat say; and the author feels that this is a time-honored tradition.

We cannot but wonder, nevertheless, given the long history of colonial contact and missionization among Asmat, whether this sexual culture was entirely indigenous, as Schneebaum believes, or was rather an effect of (in part or whole?) missionization and colonial control. When all the evidence is lined up, I am inclined strongly to the latter view, largely because these two novel features violate so many aspects of the cultural ontology of Melanesian sexuality and boy-inseminating in other tribes. Furthermore, the comparison with East Bay is telling, because, as I will show below, the situation there seems now to have been a product of social change.

From the study of a previously undescribed culture, the Kamula, Dr. Michael Wood (1982) describes ritualized boy-inseminating on the Papuan Plateau area south of Mount Bosavi. Kamula boys "receive semen through anal intercourse during initiation," Wood (1982:79) says, "and as a result are said to 'grow' and become 'big.'" The lad, at around age 9 or 10, becomes the object of ritual as well as sexual attention for years to come (1982:337). His ideal inseminator is his future wife's father or wife's brother (1982:80), a relationship that "concludes when the boy develops a beard. After this a man receives no more semen and in the remainder of his life can only lose semen in homo- or heterosexual intercourse." Here we find a ritual complex similar to that of the Kaluli tribe reported by Schieffelin (1976) not far to the north. Furthermore the resemblance to the Gebusi (Knauft 1987) is striking.

Besides this penetrative insemination, however, the Kamula tribe, like their neighbors the Onabasalu (Ernst 1984), rub semen on the bodies of the novices. Indeed, one account has it that the novices are masturbated and their own semen is smeared on them to make them "invisible to the eyes of their enemies during war" (1982:229). Kamula novices are referred to as the "wives" of the inseminators, an expression, both sexual and symbolic, that one finds among the Sambia and in several other societies described below (reviewed in Herdt 1981, 1982, 1989).

This new work on the Papuan Plateau gives added recognition to the long-neglected erotic meanings of these practices. We have already seen this in the Gebusi ethnography of Bruce Knauft. For the Kamula culture, Wood self-consciously struggles with various and competing explanations of the practices, including a straightforward power argument. He writes:

> Even including the sexual pleasure that senior men may derive from inseminating the novices I would still argue that the relationship between the novice and his inseminator is still skewed in favour of the novice who has acquired semen. I would suggest that his indebtedness to his inseminator persists for the rest of his life and provides an important basis by which his inseminator may later make claims to his labour, products and sociality, especially if the novice becomes a DHJ or (ZH) of his inseminator. Clearly the idea, found in the rites and certain myths, that killing the novices may be a means of reciprocating to the senior males is an effective means of dramatizing the nature of the novices' indebtedness to such men.
>
> (Wood 1982:251)

The Baruya provide another important addition to the ethnographic archives, one that was largely unknown at the time this book was written.[13] In the main, as Godelier makes clear, my work on Sambia coincides with his "findings concerning the Baruya"

(Godelier 1986:52), though our theoretical perspectives differ. The secrecy of Baruya homoerotism is very pronounced as it is among the Sambia, and may divide the Anga groups from others (cf. Feil 1987). Godelier sees the Baruya male cult as an organization of both production and domination, with sexual practices a key to the complete system.

The Baruya ethnography has provided something else quite remarkable: a report of *female* same-sex rites. These stroking and sensual practices—the so-called "lesbianism" (Lindenbaum 1987) of Baruya—is the focus of some discussion. Godelier's text suggests that there is a very intimate, though not necessarily erotic, meaning that occurs in the age-structured transmission of ritual knowledge and initiation between older women and girls. Yet its interpretation remains controversial; for instance, the Sambia do not report the existence of such practices, in spite of the fact that theirs is the most detailed ethnography of sexuality in Melanesia (Herdt and Stoller 1990). The degree of social change is a problem here again: the practice may have altered or its memory culture may be a bias. The fact that the report is based upon informants' accounts to an ethnographer of the opposite sex is certainly relevant. Nonetheless, if Godelier's report is borne out, this will be only the second instance (after Malekula Island) in Melanesia of female same-sex relations that are institutionalized (reported in the first printing).

In separate work among the Ankave Anga, Pierre Lemonnier (1990) and Pascale Bonnemere (1990) have provided new information on a distantly related lowlands Anga group. Their recent work is important because of their unpublished report that ritual homosexuality was not practiced traditionally among the Ankave (Bonnemere, personal communication). Here again we face the difficult interpretative issue of the effects of social change upon sexual practices. Perhaps the practice was not spread this far south or, if it was in precolonial times, it may have been abandoned over the past several decades, as it was, for instance, among the neighboring Yagwoia (Mimica 1981). However, we still do not know much of this ethnographic area, and this new report must serve as a warning not to overgeneralize even within distinct subculture regions such as the Anga tradition (Feil 1987; Knauft 1990).

In the first edition I considered "questionable" cases of boy-inseminating. One more has since emerged: the Hua tribe, who live near Lufa station in the Eastern Highlands, not too distant from the Sambia and the Baruya. As reported by Anna Meigs:

> The Hua admit to a belief in oral conception. There are, however, strong suggestions in an additional belief in anal conception. A direct connection between anal intercourse and pregnancy was suggested independently by two informants, who, in denying the existence of anal intercourse, said it would result in pregnancy and for this reason, among others, was not practiced (the Keraki beliefs about the relationship between homosexual intercourse and male pregnancy are similar).
>
> (Meigs 1984:54)

Hua beliefs are especially notable in view of the fact that men practice several forms of male menstruation, including nosebleeding, the eating of red foods, and concomitantly the ingestion of blood as a secret practice to dispel female pollution and blood clots (Meigs 1984:55–59). These notions, incidentally, are uncannily like those of Sambia.[14] What are we to make of a society in which a belief in anal conception occurs without the presence of ritualized boy-inseminating? Among other factors is the possibility that anal intercourse was practiced between men and women.[15] We cannot be sure that same-sex relations are absent, or, if they are present, if they are traditional. We cannot be sure that we are not dealing with exceptional or deviant informants, either; in the area of sexuality we are notoriously dependent upon a particular person's ideas and practices of the erotic (Herdt and Stoller 1990); that is, what constitutes sexual culture (Parker 1989; Parker et al. 1991). However, the existence of boy-inseminating practices among the Anga tribes to the south and the striking symbolic beliefs of the Gimi to the east (Gillison 1980) makes the Hua a possible candidate for inclusion in this survey.

THE PUZZLE OF EAST BAY

Ten years ago I noted that the study of "East Bay" island in the northeastern sector of Melanesia constituted a perplexing and seemingly unique form of same-sex relations. East Bay men were said to practice reciprocal relationships with egalitarian qualities; they take turns in masturbation and anal intercourse with each other (p. 17 below; Davenport 1977:155). This was the *only* such example known from the scholarly literature.[16] The account of Schneebaum on the Asmat, cited above, might be seen as another example of the same kind of egalitarian homosexuality. Davenport stated at the time:

> As boys reach late adolescence, they may also engage in mutual masturbation, but in the switch away from masturbation they may have anal intercourse with friends and trade off playing the active and passive roles. No love or strong emotional bonds are developed. ... It is considered to be part of the accommodations expected of friendship.
>
> *(Davenport 1977:155)*

It is equally extraordinary to note that two different erotic practices—masturbation and anal sex—co-occur in the same society (see Davenport 1965:201; p. 17 below). No other society in Melanesia contains this structural duality in the insemination techniques, as I pointed out in 1984 and again in a more recent study (Herdt 1989). I speculated that these East Bay anomalies might represent neocolonial cultural changes (p. 18 below). The new account by Schneebaum on the Asmat raises the question of change anew: Might not both of these "egalitarian customs" be a product of change rather than traditionalism?

New information now confirms the oddity of East Bay and suggests that we should not interpret the account as representing indigenous practice. Professor Davenport tells me in a recent letter of the full extent of these changes. Because of the importance of this material I must cite it at length.

> I am fascinated by your Melanesian cross-cultural finding of a complementary distribution between peer same-sex and age-structured practices. Obviously, the East Bay exception could be explained by culture change and overlap of patterns. Unfortunately, the data I have do not allow me to say, for certain, that the peer same-sex practices are a recent borrowing or invention.[17] ... Ten years after the field work for the original article was completed, age-structured practices had, virtually, ceased. During that intervening decade, there had been a strong and widespread social reaction against such practices. This was due to the inroads of Christian moral teaching, partly to the very vocal condemnation of them by one District Commissioner who had been greatly admired, and partly due to a reaction against a "old ways." ...

The fundamental institutional change had to do with the decline in importance of the men's house groups. They were dealt a severe blow, not by the Protectorate Government or Mission so much as by the decline in their importance with regard to the economics of specialized labor and inter-island trade. When the traditional economy was very strong—and there was a revival of this while the islands were cut off during World War II—the men's house groups were the organizers of production of special commodities and trade. That, of course, was how men obtained their wealth, prestige, and all the other accouterments of male hierarchy. The age-structured sex was linked to the concubine pattern. . . . With the decline in this male sector of the economy, and at the same time, the Government move against the holding of concubines (who were regarded as prostitutes, which they were in one sense, but still not aware . . . that they were a kind of slave as well) influential men moved away from holding concubines or boys as partners as demonstration of their success.

The Government move against the holding of concubines resulted in the killing of one man by the police, and at least three men were arrested and tried in connection with sex partnerships with young boys, and one of them died in jail. So, there were good reasons to be careful in that regard, and it is amazing, in a way, that the age-structured sex continued at all. However, in the last analysis, there was little success and prestige to flaunt anyway.

About this same time there was a marked increase in [outside labor] recruiting, and, of course, this favored the young and as yet not successful men. There is no question that homosexual partnerships were a very common aspect of life in the labor lines. On that I have all kinds of information from Santa Cruz Island and other Solomon Islands societies in the Eastern District. The question, then, is whether peer same-sex partnerships were introduced into Santa Cruz society at this time from the recruiting situation? It is quite true that that is what happened, but I don't have hard data to support such a reconstruction. It is also quite true that with the decline in traditional economics and the Government moves against concubinage and age-structured sex relations, the prestige and authority of successful men was greatly threatened, probably diminished. I have very bitter testimonies about this from several of my close, elder friends. . . . If younger men began engaging in peer sexual partnerships, the elder men would not have had the authority to stop them, even if they tried. The sequel to the whole process is that today Santa Cruz Island society has become, at least around East (Graciosa) Bay, very permissive as regards extramarital heterosexual relations, and despite a great deal of public indignation about this, the traditional sanctions against such permissiveness cannot be applied. Both Government and Church, oddly, have worked hard and successfully against the application of severe sanctions against heterosexual offenses (fornication and adultery). It is my impression that with this permissiveness toward extramarital heterosexual relations, there has been a distinct decline in peer same-sex relations.

So, it is possible that the peer same-sex relations were borrowing from experiences in the labor lines; they were permitted to go on as long as the sanctions against extra-marital offenses were maintained; but as the latter have been given up, peer same-sex relations are now in disfavor.

(Davenport, letter, September 1987)

We are indebted to Professor Davenport for this communication, which helps to establish two points. First, East Bay practice must be interpreted in the context of great social change, and the prior report of reciprocal sexual practice between peers must be understood as an innovation. Thus, no traditional society in Melanesia could now be said to have had an institutionalized form of same-sex relationships that was not age-structured. An even stronger doubt must now be cast upon the traditionalism of Asmat practice. Surely East Bay and Asmat had boy-inseminating, but their precolonial forms were not unlike those of the numerous other societies first reported in the 1984 collection. Second, with the advent of culture contact and modernization, including Christian missionization, same-sex relations in the tradition-bound ways of Melanesian ritual seem to fall. As I have suggested in a more detailed critique of these issues elsewhere (Herdt 1991), what is at stake, in cultural lifeways such as those of New Guinea or the North American Indian *berdache*, is an ontology, a cultural reality, so at odds with that of Westerners (and acculturation to Western norms) that the boy-inseminating practice is quickly buried. In the absence of structural support, then, it falls upon the individual to express personal desires and tastes, which become increasingly privatized and removed from the broader cultural tradition. Among the things most abhorrent to the Western view is the erotic aspect of the practices, and for a reconsideration of this we must turn to a final section.

THE DESIRES OF BOY-INSEMINATING

No issue in recent reviews has inspired more debate than the basic question of whether—or to what extent—sexual feelings and erotic desires are motives or consequences of these cultural practices.

Does the boy desire sexual intercourse with the older male? Is the older male sexually attracted to the boy? Indeed, what does "erotic" or "sexual" mean in this context, and is "desire" the proper concept with which to gauge the ontology? Or do other factors, such as power or kinship, produce the sexual attraction and excitement (conscious or unconscious) necessary to produce arousal and uphold the tradition (Herdt 1991*b*)?

Ritualized boy-inseminating challenges the anthropology and history of sexuality with the social problem of explaining how the production of adult relationships—of marriage and sex with women—results from first having sex and social relations with boys. That the youths are in a state of symbolic "marriage" with older males suggests that persons and groups invest energy and interest in these rites. Such a perspective links erotic desire to social exchange and group formation in the Melanesian historical context. It is this perspective from which we begin the study of how erotic desire is related to social exchange and group formation in Melanesia. As Bruce Knauft (1987:157) rightly points out in a meticulous review of the 1984 book, the ethnographers wrote "unconvincingly [of] the 'sex' in Melanesian homosexuality" (see also Tuzin 1991).

The omission of sexual desire, attraction, and sexual relations from ethnographic study seems more glaring than ever.[18] Many anthropologists in the past, as Robert Stoller once remarked, seem to assume that when sexual desire or excitement is needed, the "culture" will somehow supply "it" automatically in the minds and bodies of the actors (Herdt and Stoller 1990), a position that ultimately embraces an essentializing folk theory of human nature that vests the sexual in the biology of the body. Few ethnographers have had the theoretical interest, training, or opportunity to undertake the kind of study that is necessary to provide the missing data. Such ethnographic accounts, whether for the Sambia or the Gebusi, continue to be rare in Melanesia.

Consider the theoretical question of how boy-inseminating rites are related to marriage practices. The earliest conceptual interest in the problem comes to us from John Layard (1959), who suggested that boy-inseminating was caused by incest avoidance under the influence of the Oedipal complex. The issue has stirred interest: among the commentaries that consider the link between the rites and symbolic exchange are, in particular, reviews that examine how wealth, prestige, and trade are used to consummate the symbolic marriage of men to boys and the resulting social reproduction (see chap. 4 of this volume; Lindenbaum 1987; M. Strathern 1988:227f.). The idea fans out further: why does boy-inseminating occur with sister-exchange marriage (Feil 1987; Lindenbaum 1988:227f.), and how or why is the ideal inseminator the older brother-in-law in many of these societies (my comments in the original introduction are reviewed in Lindenbaum 1987:227–233).

In the words of M. Strathern (1988:209), for example, "Semen can be seen as an analogue of bridewealth." But how? Some writers, such as Whitehead (1985–86), contrast the lowlands and highlands of New Guinea as symbolic prototypes (cf. Feil 1987). She refers to these as "manhood" (Lowlands) vs. "clanhood" (Highlands) ideologies, which have meaning for how social identities are produced and "consumed" in these groups. These are clever metaphors, but how literal are they, and at what levels of meaning—personal symbol or group representation—are they meant to be interpreted?

A strong tendency to disembody the sexual from the social, and to metaphorize "experience" to the point of a loss of perspective on the lives of real actors, continues to haunt such work. The basic question of how desire and sexual excitement are generated out of social life is thus ignored. Whitehead's (1985–86) is a prime example of the process in the Melanesian literature. As the noted sociologist of sexuality, David Greenberg, has recently put it in his review of the age-structured practices in Melanesia:

> [Erik] Schwimmer and [Shirley] Lindenbaum explain transgenerational male homosexuality by the functions it serves for men—in helping them dominate women, or secure wives. What these explanations lack is any account of erotic attraction. They simply assume that if male homosexuality is needed to strengthen male solidarity or to make marriage obligations more secure, it will spontaneously appear and be institutionalized. Questions of how homosexuality is produced, and why it is not resisted, are not raised.
>
> *(1988:37)*

I agree. Of course, desire and sexual practice must also be seen as products of ideology and of power relationships, at both the "experience near" and "experience far" levels of the actor. Such has more recently concerned Foucault (1986), for instance, and this has been highly important to sexuality studies. But notice that even Foucault does not address the question of where desire is located, and his framework is largely bereft of an explanation for individual and cultural experience. For instance, with Foucault, the anthropologist Shepard suggests that the Western sexual invert is viewed as a political subversive who challenges the wider patriarchal order (1987:264–265). How different is the Melanesian situation where, as Michael Allen shows in this volume, homosexual imagery and hoaxes are used as the very foundation of the social order, to place political power in support of the status quo and, *mutatis mutandis*, to reproduce the total system of the sexual and the social within the individual.

Take, as one account of the kind of whole system I mean, the way in which the Sambia of Papua New Guinea create extraordinary conditions for the social conditioning of sexual excitement. As I show below, Sambia especially value semen and its equivalents—which include mother's milk and certain white tree saps. The adult man can be aroused by the sight of a woman's breasts or the act of her nursing a child. The dangerous and the forbidden are a major source of excitement in Sambia sexual culture and sexual nature. Women are roped off to the initiates for many years, and their interest is transferred to bachelors. "Suckling" is a major metaphor of the erotic for older unmarried bachelors who inseminate boys after their initiation into the men's secret society. Homosexual fellatio is the only form of this and it is conceptualized as a latter form of penis "suckling" which men do to "grow" boys into manhood. The bachelors thus "grow" boys, as their mothers once "grew" them, to make them strong warriors; and the men inseminate their wives, first through fellatio, and then in genital sex, in order to "grow" her breasts and make her a strong mother. These acts of insemination are, however, depleting, like the Hua conception cited above, and since Sambia men fear the loss of semen as a vital essence, they require replenishment of the fluid from a secret white tree sap, always consumed after sex (with boys and with women) to stay healthy. Genital intercourse between the sexes is also polluting to the man, because menstrual blood and vaginal fluids are deadly. The basic conditions of social life thus generate interest and energy "commitments" in certain images, substances, and practices; their production essentializes and even fetishizes the fluids, both by what is unlearned and newly learned.

The question of how the erotic links to society and power emerges in two other issues in the literature. One is a persisting tendency in some writers to locate the cause of boy-inseminating in a purely materialist factor, such as population shortage. Some authors have a kind of "heterosexual drive" model that indicates same-sex relations occur only in the context of female shortage or frustration of male/female relations. (Davenport's [1977] analysis of East Bay comes closest to a pure expression of such a folk model.) However, the old view still prevails, for instance, in no less an authority than Andrew Strathern (1988:209), who states: "Homosexuality may thus be interpreted as a form of bonding behavior that deflected men away from frustrations associated with heterosexual desires." (He says that the "structural significance" of homosexual practices is "well known" though he cites neither authorities nor reasons why he thinks so.) The functionalism of this view, combined with a boiler model of the frustration-aggression hypothesis (see Langness 1967), should be noted. We find a more thoughtful version of the same notion in Schiefenhovel's (1990:417) work, which sees the shortage of women as being expressed symbolically in "a shortage of semen that must be overcome if the society is to flourish." Here is a property of the local ontology that helps us to make sense of action "on the ground" (and see M. Strathern 1988).

An entirely different muddle occurs when anthropologists accept the erotic component of boy-inseminating but then interpret it as derivative of "bisexuality." This is the model provided by Davenport's (1977) well-known study cited and clarified above. As I have shown in a critical analysis, he represents East Bay same-sex relations as an "accident" of culture, or, if one prefers, an interruption of human nature (Herdt 1991b). At the same time, however, his account presents East Bay not as constitutive of our "it entity" homosexuality—in either the masculine/bisexual or effeminate/invert tropes. Rather, the "it" of Davenport's representations emerges as an essentialized and individualized sexuality, much like Freud's concept of libido and Kinsey's "sex drive," the expression of which—in sexual interaction—seeks the path of least resistance to its "gratification." The East Bay man cares less than he should about his partner's gender or the orifice of penetration—if, that is, the subject/object split of Western morality and sexual ideals hold. The age-structured relationships of East Bay males are also pictured as emotionally flat and loveless, materialistic, and opportunistic, in Davenport's sketch. The homoerotic is here seen as an immature, bide-your-time substitute for the more truly desired heteroerotic (see, for instance, Schieffelin 1982): "institutionalized bisexuality" by default. These interpretations are unfaithful to much of what is known about Melanesian tradition.

The precolonial form of East Bay same-sex practice was pretty much the same as boy-inseminating practice in other areas of New Guinea and the off-lying islands. It is Davenport's theory and imported Western ideology that is at issue. He states that the practice in East Bay is a "fundamentally different phenomenon" compared to "Western preferential or exclusive homosexuality." He ascribes the difference between these two cultural forms not to the presence of something within East Bay but to the *absence* of the ontological homosexual of the West: the "exclusive homosexual" derives from "an inversion of the individual's motivational and cognitive organization" due to biology or early childhood experience or both. Thus the representational contrast set that inspired Davenport's interpretation is East Bay bisexuality/Western inversion. We can see the conundrum Davenport faced, writing as he did before age-structured homosexuality emerged as an alternative construct. If the ideology of "inversion" homosexuality is required, no such effeminate homosexuals in the Western sense are present in East Bay. By contrast, the North American Indian *berdache* was closer to the Western "inversion" stereotype, since same-sex relations were cast as gender-reversed and effeminate transvestism. Thus, the *berdache* symbolic system delivers a form of "homosexuality" more akin to Davenport's model, whereas East Bay men with their rites of boy-inseminating and rugged masculinity did not (see Herdt 1991*a*). In all these cultural systems "homosexuality" is lacking; but that does not mean East Bay men practiced "bisexuality." As Walter Williams has commented on the contrast between Melanesia and North American Indian *berdache:*

Because a boy is expected to engage in these sexual acts with older males does not mean that he will become a lifelong exclusive ho-

> mosexual. . . . He does not have a "gay" lifelong pairing with a man of similar age. We cannot even properly call him lifelong bisexual, because he is homosexual at one stage of his life, followed by a period when he is bisexual, and then (in some societies) ends up as heterosexual in his later years.
>
> *(1986:263)*

We have already seen that the egalitarian mode was likely to be a cultural import of modernization. Thus, shorn of a symbolic space for either ritualized boy-inseminating or for the "homosexual," the work of Davenport on East Bay portrayed these entities as inconsequential and driven from inside the individual, not from social and cultural forces outside. This seems to me a miserly view and I offer another interpretation. Through successive sexual experiences with males and females, I would guess, first only with males—and later with younger boys in addition to marital sex—the East Bay man becomes a whole social and sexual person. It is a sexual course of life, incidentally, that never alters until death, since East Bay adult men, after they are married, and even as grandfathers, may continue inseminating boys.

We are dealing, in Melanesia, with one of the most complex and intricate sexual systems in culture that has ever evolved. These are ontologies in which adult men develop multiple desires that are approved by their societies; hence they develop more than one sexual subject/object relationship, which is quite different from the Western norm. It is an elaborate ritual and mythological tradition that defies any easy categorization of functions and causes, pitting psyche against culture, as some theorists might like. In his study of the Gebusi tribe of central New Guinea, Knauft has come closest to capturing the scope of the system at play.

> In early adolescence (ages 11–14) boys extend their affection to older unrelated males in the community by establishing homosexual relationships with them—i.e., being their fellators. Rather than being based on subordination or domination, these relations tend to be coquettishly initiated by the young adolescents themselves. The ideological reason for insemination is to "grow" the boys into men, but homosexuality appears for all practical intents and purposes to be grounded in personal affection rather than obligation.

Such affection is not apart from social life or personal experience, and though it is neither wholly asexual nor erotic, it is certainly not nonerotic. In a few years, we may safely conclude, it will be erotic for most of these males as adults; perhaps for some of them it may even be *homoerotic*, in the sense that they might prefer inseminating boys over women (Herdt and Stoller 1990). Such a system of social desires and sexual desires belongs to an ancient tradition that was once self-reproducing.

To close: These studies provide the critical analyses to understand, represent, and engage in anthropological comparison of sexuality and same-sex erotic relations. We see now the difficulties of generalizing about sexuality in the absence of good ethnographic information. We see also the problems left over from constructs and paradigms that were assumptively loaded with Western notions and ideologies: an implicit folk model of sexual nature and sexual culture exported to New Guinea in another time. As a result of this review on how age structures social and sexual relations in Melanesia, we have good reason to conclude that egalitarian sexual relations between persons of the same gender occur only in the modern and early premodern period, not in the traditional context of island cultures of the Pacific. Today, largely through the work of a small host of scholars, the notion of age-structured same-sex relations is generating new theory and insights, and *Ritualized Homosexuality in Melanesia* has no doubt played a decisive role in this new anthropology of sexuality.

G.H.H.
Chicago
1992

NOTES

Some of the ideas contained within this review were originally developed in my article "Representations of Homosexuality: An Essay on Cultural Ontology and Historical Comparison," Parts I and II, in the *Journal of the History of Sexuality* (Herdt 1991a, 1991b). My thanks for feedback on prior works related to this paper go to Jan Van Baal, Mark Busse, Stephen Murray, Erik Schwimmer, the late Robert J. Stoller, and Donald Tuzin. I am very grateful to my Spanish colleague Jose Nieto for his support of the project. I am especially indebted to Bruce Knauft for his critical review and insights on my work, and I salute the originality and scholarly significance of his own.

1. I suspect that further we may trace this desire for a common form (that is like the Western form) to our long-standing Western preoccupation with shared "psychic unity" and human nature (Herdt 1990a, 1990b; Spiro 1982).

2. See, especially, Herdt and Lindenbaum, eds. (1992), on AIDS and gays.

3. See, for a history of these typologies, the works of B. Adam, S. Murray, and more recently D. Greenberg, reviewed in Herdt (1990a, 1991a).

4. Homosexuality remains a crime or a disease in many parts of the world; in the United States, for example, many states maintain laws that make "sodomy" a crime, including consensual relations between adults in private.

5. Why, you might ask, does the question of the cause of homosexuality matter anyway? Boxer and Cohler (1989), in reviewing the question, have found that in the history of sexuality research, theorists invariably asked what caused homosexuality but not what its (especially positive) outcomes were, while, conversely, the study of heterosexuality was always centered on its outcomes (e.g., marriage) but never on its causes (usually assumed to be in nature).

6. It also requires a reconsideration of the Oedipal complex and its contribution to sexuality, as Spiro (1982) suggested in his review of Melanesian ritual homosexuality. My view is that the Melanesian corpus shows strong and complex rivalries and alliances between fathers and sons that take a different form from those in Western culture (cf. Langness 1990).

7. Arnold Pilling writes, "Not long after puberty, a Tiwi male took a regular male sexual partner from the males who might become his brother-in-law, preferably his actual sister's husband" (1990:5). This quote suggests that the Tiwi form of boy-inseminating was structurally similar to that of Melanesian cultures such as the Etoro, Sambia, and Baruya, whose sister-exchange marriage practices involved semen transactions as a form of marriage service (chap. 4 below; Lindenbaum 1987).

8. A contrary view occurs in Weiner's work on sickness and the male cult among the Foi of New Guinea: he challenges the very idea of male rituals serving to address what he calls "male vulnerability to female influences" (1987:274). Clearly, we need to rethink the symbolic bases of such folk beliefs, but the link between male cults and such ethnopsychologies is so long and powerful in the Melanesian literature that a documented and compelling critique is required beyond that of Weiner's.

9. Knauft's writings are highly recommended to the interested reader; because I am not able, in a short space, to do them justice, his emerging work should be studied as a critique of the whole body of this book.

10. Knauft (1990:189) claims, in fact, that the total population related to the precolonial practice of boy-inseminating was 39,768 individuals—itself a remarkable figure; how accurate this is I cannot judge. Some writers, such as Schiefenhovel (1990:411), also provide different estimates of the incidence of total ethnic groups that practiced the custom in Melanesia; he uses my 1984 figures to estimate 3% of all cultures, based upon an arbitrary number of 1000 cultures, but then he explains that the "real" figure was probably much higher. Why he thinks this is unclear. The point is that these are all educated guesses, mine included, and we should not place too much credit in them due to the lack of accurate historical information.

11. Popular assertions of homosexuality still occur in the literature. For instance, in a memoir of the old colonial days, the former Australian patrol officer Ian Downs reports that "sodomy is a common practice in the Sepik area Aitape villages . . . (especially west of Wewak!)" (1986:57), but not a shred of documentation or a concern with evidence graces this assertion, any more than in those of like kind I listed here years ago.

12. This and other numerous rich asides make this unpublished dissertation a significant contribution to the literature which I cannot do adequate justice to in this review.

13. Godelier's ethnography (1986) was not published at the time of the first printing; he had not published data on same-sex relations prior to that publication.

14. On male pregnancy (oral, not anal, conception), see Herdt 1981, and on nose-bleeding, see Herdt 1982; reviewed with regard to inseminating rites in Herdt 1989.

15. In the Trobriand Islands a similar category question occurs; that is, a Trobriand category term for anal intercourse occurs but not the sexual practice itself, according to cultural ideals (Malinowski 1929).

16. See, however, the discussion in Schneebaum 1988 and also my own comments in the original introduction.

17. Professor Davenport continues: "The whole truth of the matter is that I never asked the older informants that question. It did not occur to me then to do so. Even some years later, after I published the original article, I did some questioning there with regard to the rapid disappearance of the age-structured practices, but I did not pursue questioning about the peer practices, because it had become a very touchy subject among the younger men with whom I never had the chance to establish close rapport" (Letter, September 1987).

18. We have seen how woefully inadequate the position of anthropology is in relation to such gaps and the problems they pose for the construction of culturally sensitive AIDS education and prevention (Herdt 1992).

REFERENCES

Adam, B. D.
1986 Age, structure, and sexuality: reflections on the anthropological evidence on homosexual relations. *J. of Homosexuality* 11:19–33.

1987 *The Rise of a Gay and Lesbian Movement.* Boston: Twayne Publishers.

Amelsvoort, V. F. P. M. Van
1964 *Culture, Stone Age and Modern Medicine.* Assean, The Netherlands: Van Gorcum.

Ayres, M. C.
1983 This side, that side: locality and exogamous group definition in Morehead area, southwestern Papua. Ph.D. dissertation, The University of Chicago.

Bayer, R.
1987 *Homosexuality and American Psychiatry.* New Brunswick, NJ: Rutgers University Press.

Bleibtreu-Ehrenberg, G.
1991 Pederasty among primitives: institutionalized initiation and celtic prostitution. *J. of Homosexuality* 20:13–30.

Boelaars, J. H. M. C.
1981 *Head-hunters about Themselves.* Verhandelingen van het kon. Instituut voor Taal-, Land- en Volkenkunde, no. 92. The Hague: Martinus Nijhoff.

Bohle, B.
1990 Ethnoligische Untersuchung zur "Konstruktion" von "Männlichkeit" und "Weiblichkeit" in Gesellschaften mit ritualisierter Homosexualität in den Randgebieten von Neuguinea. Univeröffentlichte Magisterarbeit, Universität Wien, GruWi-Fak., Institut für Völkerkunde.

Bonnemere, P.
1990 Considérations relatives aux représentations des substances corporelles en Nouvelle-Guinée. *L'Homme* (April–June) 30:101–120.

Boswell, J.
1990 Sexual and ethical categories in premodern Europe. In *Homosexuality/Heterosexuality*, edited by D. P. McWhirter et al., pp. 5–31. New York: Oxford University Press.

Boxer, A., and B. J. Cohler
1989 The life course of gay and lesbian youth: An immodest proposal for the study of lives. In *Gay and Lesbian Youth*, edited by G. Herdt, pp. 315–355. New York: Harrington Park Press.

Bremmer, J.
1989   Greek pederasty and modern homosexuality. In *From Sappho to De Sade: Moments in the History of Sexuality*, edited by J. Bremmer, pp. 1–14. London: Routledge.

Burton, R. V., and J. W. M. Whiting
1961   The absent father and cross-sex identity. *Merrill-Palmer Quarterly of Behavior and Development* 7:85–95.

Busse, M.
1987   Sister exchange among the wamek of the Middle Fly. Ph.D. dissertation, University of California, San Diego.
n.d.   Continuities and discontinuities in the transition from adolescence to marriage among the Marind-Anim and Boazi of southern New Guinea. In *Adolescence in Pacific Island Societies*, edited by G. Herdt, Princeton Press.

Cain, R.
1991   Disclosure and secrecy among gay men in the United States and Canada: A shift in views. *J. Hist. Sexuality* 2:25–45.

Callender and Kochems
1983   The North American Indian Berdache. *Current Anthropology* 24:443–470.

Carrier, J.
1980   Homosexual behavior in cross-cultural perspective. In *Homosexual Behavior: A Modern Reappraisal*, edited by J. Marmor, pp. 100–122. New York: Basic Books.

Cohen, D.
1987   Law, society and homosexuality in classical Athens. *Past and Present* 117:1–21.

Davenport, W. H.
1965   Sexual patterns, and their regulation in a society of the southwest Pacific. In *Sex and Behavior*, edited by F. A. Beach, pp. 164–207. New York: John Wiley.
1977   Sex in cross-cultural perspective. In *Human Sexuality in Four Perspectives*, edited by F. A. Beach and M. Diamond, pp. 155–163. Baltimore: Johns Hopkins University Press.

Deacon, A. B.
1934   *Malekula: A Vanishing People in the New Hebrides*. London: George Routledge.

DeCecco, J. P.
1990   Sex and more sex: A critique of the Kinsey conception of human sexuality. In *Homosexuality/Heterosexuality*, edited by D. P. McWhirter et al., pp. 367–386.

D'Emilio, J., and E. Freedman
1988   *Intimate Matters*. New York: Harper & Row.

Devereux, G.
1937   Institutionalized homosexuality of the Mohave Indians. *Human Biology* 9:498–527.

Dover, K. J.
1978   *Greek Homosexuality.* Cambridge, Mass.: Harvard University Press.
1988   Greek homosexuality and initiation. In K. J. Dover, *Greeks and Their Legacy.* Volume II: Prose Literature, History, Society, Transmission Influence. Oxford: Oxford University Press.

Downs, I.
1986   *The Last Mountain.* St. Lucia: U. Queensland Press.

Ellman, R.
1987   *Oscar Wilde.* New York: Alfred Knopf.

Evans-Pritchard, E. E.
1970   Sexual inversion among the Azande. *American Anthropologist* 72:1428–1434.

Ernst, T. M.
1984   Onabasulu local organization. Ph.D. dissertation, University of Michigan, Ann Arbor (UMI).

Feil, D. K.
1987   *The Evolution of Highland Papua New Guinea Societies.* New York: Cambridge University Press.

Ford, C. S., and F. Beach
1951   *Patterns of Sexual Behavior.* New York: Harper and Bros.

Foucault, M.
1980   *The History of Sexuality.* Trans. by Robert Hurley. New York: Vintage Books.
1986   *The Use of Pleasure*, Vol. 2. Trans. by R. Hurley. New York: Vintage Books.

Gagnon, J.
1988   Sexuality across the life course in the United States. In *AIDS Sexual Behavior and Intravenous Drug Use*, edited by C. F. Turner, H. G. Miller, and L. E. Moses. Washington, D.C.: National Academy Press.

Gagnon, J. H.
1989   Disease and desire. *Daedalus* 118:47–77.

Gillison, G.
1980   Images of nature in Gimi thought. In *Nature, Culture, and Gender*, edited by C. MacCormack and M. Strathern, pp. 143–173. Cambridge: Cambridge University Press.

Godelier, M.
1986   *The Production of Great Men.* Trans. by R. Swyer. Cambridge: Cambridge University Press.

Greenberg, D. F.
1988   *The Construction of Homosexuality*. Chicago: University of Chicago Press.

Haddon, A.
1927   Introduction to *The Kiwai Papuans of British New Guinea*, by G. Landtman, pp. ix–xx. London: MacMillan and Co.

Hage, P.
1981   On male initiation and dual organization in New Guinea. *Man* 16:268–275.

Halperin, D. M.
1990   *One Hundred Years of Homosexuality*. New York: Routledge.

Hauser-Schäublin, B.
1989   The fallacy of "real" and "pseudo" procreation. *Zeitschrift für Ethnologie* 114:179–194.

Hays, T. E.
1986   Sacred flutes, fertility, and growth in the Papua New Guinea Highlands. *Antropos* 81:435–453.

Hekma, G.
1989   Sodomites, platonic lovers, contrary lovers: The backgrounds of the modern homosexual. *J. of Homosexuality* 16:433–455.

Herdt, G. H.
1981   *Guardians of the Flutes: Idioms of Masculinity*. New York: McGraw-Hill.

1982   *Rituals of Manhood: Male Initiation in New Guinea*. Berkeley: University of California Press.

1987   *Sambia: Ritual and Gender in New Guinea*. New York: Holt, Rinehart and Winston.

1988   Cross-cultural forms of homosexuality and the concept "gay." In "Sexuality and Homosexuality": Special Issue, *Psychiatric Annals* 18:37–39.

1989   Father presence and ritual homosexuality: Paternal deprivation and masculine development in Melanesia reconsidered. *Ethos* 18:326–370.

1990*a*   Developmental discontinuities and sexual orientation across cultures. In *Homosexuality/Heterosexuality: Concepts of Sexual Orientation*, edited by D. P. McWhirter el al., pp. 208–236. New York: Oxford University Press.

1990*b*   Mistaken gender: 5-alpha reductase deficiency and biological reductionism in gender identity reconsidered. *American Anthropologist* 92:433–446.

1991*a*   Representations of homosexuality in traditional societies: An essay on cultural ontology and historical comparison, part 1. *J. of History of Sexuality* 1:481–504.

1991*b*   Representations of homosexuality in traditional societies: An essay on cultural ontology and historical comparison, part 2. *J. of History of Sexuality* 2:603–632.

1992   *Gay Culture in America.* Boston: Beacon.

Herdt, G., and M. Stephen

1989   *Varieties of the Religious Imagination in New Guinea.* New Brunswick: Rutgers University Press.

Herdt, G., and R. J. Stoller

1990   *Intimate Communications: Erotics and the Study of Culture.* New York: Columbia University Press.

Herdt, G., and A. Boxer

1992   Introduction to *Gay Culture in America*, pp. 1–28. Boston: Beacon Press.

Herdt, G., and S. Lindenbaum

1992   *The Time of AIDS.* Newbury Park: Sage Publications.

Hiatt, L. R.

1987   Freud and anthropology. In *Creating Culture*, edited by D. J. Austin-Broos. Sydney: Australia.

Hinsch, B.

1990   *Passions of the Cut Sleeve.* Berkeley: University of California Press.

Knauft, B. M.

1985   *Good Company and Violence: Sorcery and Social Action in a Lowland New Guinea Society.* Berkeley: University of California Press.

1986   Text and social practice: Narrative "longing" and bisexuality among the Gebusi of New Guinea. *Ethos* 14:252–381.

1987   Homosexuality in Melanesia. *The Journal of Psychoanalytic Anthropology* 10:155–191.

1989   Bodily images in Melanesia: Cultural substances and natural metaphors. *Fragments for a History of the Human Body*, edited by M. Feher et al., Part 3, pp. 190–279. New York: Urzone.

1990   The question of ritualized homosexuality among the Kiwai of South New Guinea. *The Journal of Pacific History* 25:188–210.

Landtmann, G.

1917   *The Folk Tales of the Kiwai: Papuans.* Acta Societatis Scientarum Fennicae 47. Helsinki: Printing Office of the Finnish Society of Literature.

Langness, L. L.

1967   Sexual antagonism in the New Guinea Highlands: A Bena Bena example. *Oceania* 37:161–177.

1990   Oedipus in the New Guinea Highlands? *Ethos* 18:387–406.

Layard, J.
1959   Homo-eroticism in a primitive society as a function of self. *J. of Analytical Psych.* 4:101–115.

Lemonnier, P.
1990   *Guerres et festins.* Paris: Editions de la Maison des Sciences de L'Homme.

LeVine, M. P.
1992   Life and death of gay clones. In *Gay Culture in America,* edited by G. Herdt, pp. 68–86. Boston: Beacon.

Lidz, T., and R. W. Lidz
1989   *Oedipus in the Stone Age.* Madison, Conn.: International Universities Press, Inc.

Lindenbaum, S.
1987   The mystification of female labors. In *Gender and Kinship,* edited by J. F. Collier and S. J. Yangisako, pp. 221–243. Stanford, CA: Stanford University Press.

Malinowski, B.
1929   *The Sexual Life of Savages in North-Western Melanesia.* New York: Harcourt, Brace & World, Inc.

Mead, M.
1930   *Growing up in New Guinea.* Harmondsworth, England: Penguin Books. Reprint 1968.

1949   *Male and Female: A Study of the Sexes in a Changing World.* New York: William Morrow & Co.

1961   Cultural determinants of sexual behavior. In *Sex and Internal Secretions,* edited by W. C. Young, pp. 1433–1479. Baltimore: Williams and Wilkins.

Meigs, A.
1984   *Food, Sex, and Pollution: A New Guinea Religion.* New Brunswick: Rutgers University Press.

Mimica, J. F.
1981   Omalyce: An ethnography of the Ikwaye view of the cosmos. Ph.D. dissertation, Australian National University.

Money, J.
1987   Sin, sickness, or society? *American Psychologist* 42:384–399.

Murray, S. O.
1984   *Social Theory, Homosexual Realities.* New York: Gaisabre Monographs.

1987   Male homosexuality in Central and South America. New York: Gaisaber Monograph 5.

Nanda, S.
1990   *Neither Man nor Woman: The Hijras of India.* Belmont, CA: Wadsworth Publishing.

Parker, R. G.
1991   *Bodies, Pleasures and Passions.* Boston: Beacon.

Parker, R. G., G. Herdt, and M. Carballo
    1991   Sexual culture, HIV transmission, and AIDS research. *Journal of Sex Research* 28:75–96.

Pilling, A. R.
    In press   Homosexuality among the Tiwi of North Australia. In *Oceanic Homosexualities*, edited by S. O. Murray. New York: Grove Press.

Poole, F. J., and G. Herdt
    1982   Sexual antagonism, gender and social change in Papua New Guinea. Special issue of *Social Analysis*, no. 12.

Plummer, K.
    1991   Understanding childhood sexualities. *J. of Homosexuality* 20: 231–247.

Read, K. E.
    1980   *Other Voices.* Novato: Chandler and Sharpe.

Richardson, D.
    1983   The dilemma of essentiality in homosexual theory. *J. of Homosexuality* 9:79–90.

Roscoe, W.
    1988   Strange country this: Images of berdaches and warrior women. In *Living the Spirit: A Gay American Indian Anthropology*, pp. 48–76. New York: St. Martin's Press.

Schiefenhovel, W.
    1990   Ritualized adult-male/adolescent-male sexual behavior in Melanesia: An anthropological and ethological perspective. In *Pedophilia: Biosocial Dimensions*, edited by J. R. Feierman, pp. 394–421. New York: Springer-Verlag.

Schieffelin, E. L.
    1976   *The Sorrow of the Lonely and the Burning of the Dancers.* New York: St. Martin's Press.
    1982   The Bau'a ceremonial hunting lodge: An alternative to initiation. In *Rituals of Manhood: Male Initiation in Papua New Guinea*, edited by G. Herdt, pp. 155–200. Berkeley: University of California Press.

Schiltz, M.
    1985   Review of *Ritualized Homosexuality in Melanesia. Research in Melanesia* 9:68–71.

Schott, R. M.
    1988   *Cognition and Eros.* Boston: Beacon.

Schneebaum, T.
    1988   *Where the Spirits Dwell.* New York: Grove Press.

Sedgwick, E. K.
    1990   *The Epistemology of the Closet.* Berkeley: University of California Press.

Sergent, B.
    1986   *Homosexuality in Greek Myth.* Boston: Beacon.

Shepherd, G.
1987   *The Cultural Construction of Sexuality*, edited by
            P. Caplan, pp. 240–270. London: Tavistock Publications.
Spence, J. D.
1983   *The Memory Palace of Matteo Ricci*. New York: Pen-
            guin Books.
Spiro, M. E.
1982   *Oedipus in the Trobriands*. Chicago: University of Chi-
            cago Press.
Strathern, A. J.
1988   Conclusions: Looking at the edge of the New Guinea
            Highlands from the center. In *Mountain Papuans*, edited
            by James F. Weiner, pp. 187–212. Ann Arbor: University
            of Michigan Press.

Strathern, M.
1988   *The Gender of the Gift*. Berkeley: University of Califor-
            nia Press.
Stoller, R. J.
1985   Psychoanalytic "research" on homosexuality: The rules
            of the game. In *Observing the Erotic Imagination*, pp.
            167–183. New Haven: Yale University Press.

Tuzin, D.
In press   Sex, culture, and the anthropologist. *Social Science and
            Medicine*, forthcoming.

Van Baal, J.
1963   The cult of the Bull-Roarer in Australia in Southern New
            Guinea. *Bijdragen tot de Taal-, Land-, en Volkenkunde*
            119:201–214.
1966   *Dema, Description and Analysis of Marind-anim Cul-
            ture*. The Hague: Martinus Nijhoff.
1982   *Jan Verschueren's Description of Yei-Nan Culture*. The
            Hague: Martinus Nijhoff.

Weeks, J.
1985   *Sexuality and Its Discontents*. London: Routledge & Ke-
            gan Paul.

Weiner, J. F.
1987   Disease of the soul: sickness, agency and the men's cult
            among the Foi of New Guinea. In *Dealing with In-
            equality*, edited by Marilyn Strathern, pp. 255–277.
            Cambridge: Cambridge University Press.
Whitehead, H.
1985–86   The varieties of fertility cultism in New Guinea: Parts I
            and II, *American Ethnologist* 12–13:80–99.
Williams, F. E.
1936   *Papuans of the Trans-Fly*. Oxford: Clarendon Press.

Williams, W.
1986   *The Spirit and the Flesh*. Boston: Beacon.
Winkler, J. J.
1990   *The Constraints of Desire*. New York: Routledge.
Wood, M.
1982   *Kamula Social Structure and Ritual*. Ph.D. dissertation, Macquarie University, Australia.

Editor's Preface

What system of factors, synergistically interacting, result in the creation and maintenance of institutionalized homosexual practices in whole societies? Why should one culture area manifest more institutionalized homosexuality than others? Why, that is, are many such groups found in Melanesia, a vast tribal world of preliterate, technologically simple societies that includes the island of New Guinea, the New Hebrides (Vanuatu), Fiji, and many other island peoples? This book is concerned with these questions. In new and original essays, leading anthropologists examine ritualized homosexual behavior in its indigenous cultural contexts: seven different traditional societies, and many other neighboring ones, spread over the Southwestern Pacific. Our concern is not merely with homosexual behavior but with its *meaning* for individuals and groups. And when this meaning is studied through variations in environment, social structure, myth, and ritual symbolism, both the form and content of homosexual activity take on new meaning in contrast to past and present views of homosexuality in the West. The comparative-historical survey and empirical studies collected here are thus a double contribution: they not only represent the first collection of systematic anthropological studies on homosexual behavior in Melanesia or any other non-Western culture area but they also provide a very important chapter in the cross-cultural study of sex and gender at large.

This book may contain some surprises for general readers and specialists alike. Readers may be puzzled at the thought that societies prescribe obligatory homosexual contacts for all males. "Indeed," as Robert A. LeVine (1981:ix) wrote elsewhere, "from a Western perspective it may seem unimaginable that any society would risk universal homosexuality among young males without endangering its survival." Yet the fact that the societies reported on below do so and, moreover, to quote LeVine (1981:x) further, that they "have created a symbolic environment in which it seems natural, normal, and necessary is convincingly demonstrated" in these Melanesian case studies. For sex researchers, then, "this fact poses a fundamental challenge to developmental theories of gender identity, which will have to be rewritten to encompass it" (ibid.). For Pacific and Melanesian specialists as well, the historical, geographic, and sociocultural depth and extensiveness of ritualized homosexuality both in old reports and in these new ones may come as a different surprise, in view of past ignorance of, or disregard for, the topic and this impressive literature.

Sex researchers and anthropologists interested in the comparative study of sexual behavior will find this volume a welcome addition to a literature dominated by sketchy and uneven reports that have skimmed the surface (out-of-context), ignored cross-cultural variations, or covered such widely divergent groups that controlled comparisons were previously difficult to make. Here is the grist, then, for a new and much needed cross-cultural survey in the tradition of Ford and Beach (1951). Earlier reviews have addressed aspects of the cross-cultural context, frequency, and social attitudes about homosexuality (Ashworth and Walker 1972; Carrier 1980a; Cory 1956; Davenport 1965, 1977; Hooker 1968; Landes 1940; McIntosh 1968; Mead 1961; Opler 1965; and others reviewed in Murray, n.d.). Some of these reports drew directly on Melanesian data, sometimes in ways unflattering to the perspectives of social anthropology (see Herdt, this volume, chap. 1). Yet in spite of these reviews, scattered ethnographies (e.g., Williams 1936c), and occasional hints that ritual homosexuality was more common in Melanesia than we had thought (e.g., Haddon 1936; Layard 1959; Wagner 1972; Van Baal 1963, 1966), the literature and its puzzling pattern went unstudied. It was not until Dundes (1976) that an anthropologist seriously tackled the Melanesian material. Moreover, no survey considered homosexuality as a structural theme in the study of gender roles, sexuality, male cults, or initiations in the area; instead, these customary Melanesian behaviors were seen as "absent," "rare," or as a "tangential curiosity" to be empirically and theoretically neglected.

A more general stumbling block to the comparative study of

homosexuality has been its definition and interpretation. Here, enormous historical and cultural variation and controversies between viewpoints must be confronted. The Western, post-Renaissance attitude, still current in some respects, is that those who engage in homosexual behavior become exclusive "homosexuals," and, since "homosexuality" is by definition unnatural and perverse, so are such persons. Thus the dual "social problems" of "the homosexual" and "homosexuality as perversion" and their associated stigma. Psychiatry and psychoanalysis have been justly criticized for propagating this ethnocentric view (Foucault 1980), and certain analysts now recognize this point. Rado (1965), for instance, wrote that "the term 'homosexual' has been so stretched as to become almost meaningless," and the related notion of "bisexuality" has had "deplorable consequences" in analytic therapy and theory (Rado 1965:186; see also Stoller 1977, 1980). Particularly unfortunate is the Western folk model that homosexual acts are always or mostly effeminate or passive behaviors associated with cross-gender behavior or dressing, paranoia, or other forms of social deviance or psychopathology. This ethnocentric stereotype is not shared by all other human societies, Melanesian groups being a case in point. Even more, recent studies raise new questions and inconsistencies with this folk view *within* Western culture (reviewed in Murray, n.d.). We need a different model of homosexuality that draws on other cultures.

The view that I take in this book regards the homosexualities of the West as a different species than that of ritualized homosexuality in Melanesia. Perhaps they are two species of the same genus, with similar but distinct developmental antecedents or consequences; but perhaps not: it is premature to classify until more empirical and historical research is done. The traditional rhetoric has characterized all homosexual behavior as abnormal or, at the least, aberrant. The Western social norm, that is, *pro*scribes homosexual activity and *pre*scribes only heterosexual (fantasy and) intercourse, depending upon one's class, ethnic group, social situation, and historical period. However much individuals conform to this norm, it is not universally valid. And in cross-cultural interpreting, it is "singularly unhelpful when projected onto cultures in which the equation of homosexuality and effeminancy is not made, and/or the homosexual role is positively valued, and/or family structure differs from the form of Western nuclear families" (Murray n.d.:1). Of course, to equalize the complaint, the view of the new rhetoric—to project into history (Boswell 1980) or onto other cultures the identity-category "gay"—is also fallacious (Carrier 1977; Weeks 1981). In Melanesia, our Western norm does not apply; males who engage in ritual homosexual activities are not "homosexuals," nor have they ever heard the concept "gay."

In other words, to follow Stoller (1980), we can distinguish between outward sexual behavior and internal identity; *homosexuality,* as we customarily use the term, lumps both these aspects together. *Identity* includes feelings, ideas, goals, and sense of self. Homosexual behavioral contacts do not necessarily entail any particular mental traits or intentions, aside from the doing of the acts. Individuals may engage in homosexual acts in sexually segregated institutions in the West, such as in the armed services, gangs, prisons, or as experimentation in childhood, adolescence, or adulthood, even frequently (Kinsey 1948), and yet they may still prefer opposite-sexed sexual objects, marry, and have children. They are not, then, life-long "homosexuals" whose sense of self habitually compels them to prefer same-sex contacts. In other words, sex contacts are not reducible to any single identity type, whether the contacts are with the same or opposite sex, or both. The case of Melanesian cultures well illustrates these distinctions.

Homosexual behavior in Melanesia may be understood at several levels simultaneously. These levels depend first upon sociocultural principles and contexts that define for the group the meaning of *all* sexual acts. What organizes these principles? In the typology of Trumbach (1977), which includes (1) age, (2) gender, and (3) profession as distinct categories, age clearly serves as the key organizational principle in Melanesia. Typically, males of different ages only (preadolescent/adolescent, pubescent/adult) are permitted homosexual contacts with one another, the older partner always serving as the sexual insertor. "Gender" traits do not grossly organize these homosexual contacts: there is no erotic cross-gender or cross-dressing behavior reported from Melanesia. Yet the chapters below question whether "masculinity" and "femininity," as broad cultural categories of gender-related behavior, do not diffusely organize the homosexual behavior and experience of the participants. "Profession" is not an organizing principle either, except in the broadest sense of being a warrior/hunter involved in the ritual activities (that exclude women and children) leading to homosexual contacts. Social status, both in kinship and ritual terms, is a more important principle. Another level of same-sex contacts rests upon the meaning of pervasive cultural assumptions about semen as a "scarce" resource, and the nature of its influence on individual "biological" growth and intergroup relations in many Melanesian societies.

To take the case of the Sambia of Papua New Guinea (Herdt 1981), for instance, we may ask: How do Sambia valuate other persons or groups (e.g., sexual, familial, kinship) as semen donors or recipients? How do homosexual and heterosexual semen transactions differ in such relationships? Or we may ask: How do semen transactions define who is related as kin or affines and, thus, who may serve as homosexual partner, and what are the nature of those social bonds? Since sexual intercourse may be defined by Sambia as either work or play, we may ask: Is it semen flow that registers the difference between sexual exchanges being work or play? And why do they regard homosexual activity as play? If semen is a scarce resource—a means toward the social reproduction of babies and hence heirs, gardeners and hunters, females for marriage exchange, warriors for group production—who or what regulates this commodity in Sambia culture? Ultimately, I think, the societal and symbolic value of semen informs both what Weiner (1980) has called the "reproduction" of meaningful acts of production (i.e., heterosexual intercourse cements marriages and semen is believed to create offspring) and the "regeneration" of the meaning of entities (homosexual intercourse strengthens members of a warriorhood) being reproduced. (I am here using Weiner's [1980] distinctions with a somewhat different focus and concern than she has used them. In chapter 4, I return to them again.) Observers might interpret the *structure* of semen value in heterosexual and homosexual relationships as a product of unconscious drives (Freud), or as a mystification of political economy (Marx), or as an expression of *conscience collective* (Durkheim). But whether psyche, economy, or society are emphasized, one's analysis cannot ignore the relation between cultural meaning and social action in these sexual acts (see also Whitehead 1981).

There are several powerful reasons for adopting this symbolic point of view in studying ritualized homosexual behavior in Melanesian societies. First, of course, homosexuality must be understood in psychocultural context: its patterns of symbolic interaction in Melanesia are quite different from those of Western cultures. Second, we need to shake ourselves of some deeply entrenched Western assumptions surrounding sexuality, to reiterate what I said above. Third, there are other cultural and contextual principles aside from those already mentioned (e.g., age, gender, profession) that help clarify all sexual acts in Melanesia. Three modes of defining sexual contacts will help orient readers:

1. Sexual contacts may be culturally and/or individually organized and defined exclusively by the choice of the *sex of one's partner.* In Melanesian societies, as noted in this book, the situation is more complex and, I think, more fluid. In such societies, males have sexual contacts with both males and females during the normative life cycle. These sexual contacts are of course organized by cultural standards: rules, taboos, expectations, and rituals. However, the capacity to have sexual contacts with both sexes conditions the individual's awareness of sexual behavior throughout. The choice of the sex of one's partner is a *mode of thought* that more fully and consciously pervades the meaning of sexuality. (See Davenport 1977:156 for a similar point.) The social acceptance of same- and opposite-sex contacts introduces the experiential element of subjective comparison—the feelings and consequences of homosexual versus heterosexual contacts—in organizing sexuality, which is alien to most Westerners' experience (the "problem" of erotic bisexuality). This dual sexual regime makes homosexual and heterosexual relationships far more open to self/other evaluations. Thus, it is erroneous in these societies to define sexual contacts except in reference to the whole semiotic system: *heterosexual and homosexual relationships,* their signs and symbols.

2. Sexual contacts may be defined and organized according to their *social purpose.* Here we may distinguish between motives, functions, and outcomes. Individuals may be consciously *motivated* to engage in sexual intercourse for pleasure, recreational enjoyment, social status, and so forth. (They may be unconsciously motivated by other factors, too, but in this book that problem is ignored.) Sexual contacts may be a *manifest function* of marriage or social status. Or homosexual intercourse may be a *latent func-*

tion of the shortage of available women. These and other social functions of sex are also related to the consequences of social relationships as psychosocial *outcomes:* ritual incorporation into a men's society, which implies symbolic and social approval and domination, life cycle transitions and concomitant feelings of self-esteem. All these factors influence one's social position in society; some apply to both Western and Melanesian groups. Where the latter differ, however, is in their cultural view of the role sexuality plays in biological maturation. Many Melanesian groups hold that sexual and gender differentiation continues for years into adolescence and early adulthood. Postnatal development merely marks the beginning of personality formation and psychosexual differentiation into adulthood. Insemination of every person's body, in childhood and/or adolescence, is vital for the "finishing off" of growth (Herdt 1980, 1981). Although this folk model is alien to Western ideology, it is widespread throughout the Melanesian groups studied below, and it even resembles that of ancient Greece (Dover 1978).

3. Sexual contacts may be defined according to the acquisition of a *scarce commodity* (e.g., semen). Westerners are not inclined to see sexuality in this way, at least consciously. Yet our own cultural transformation from "lover" to "wife" touches upon this issue. More obvious is the big business surrounding prostitution and pornography, in which *erotic access* to someone's body becomes an article of utility that can be fetishized like other valued products of labor, in Marx's (1977) terms. (Sex as commodity is symbolically defined in America, I think, not by content as much as by form: *erotic access to another's body which has been paid for.* Access may mean: paid to be able to look sexually [pornographic magazines, movies, nude shows]; or paid to be able to "experience" sexually [penetrate; suck, be sucked; beat, be beaten; touch, be touched; kiss, fondle; urinate or defecate on, or vice versa; or simply to sit in a room and watch or talk to someone, [i.e., erotically].) The traffic in women (Rubin 1975)—as producers (e.g., housewives, gardeners) or reproducers (e.g., baby-machines, breast-feeders, babysitters)—shows that in many societies females are regarded as among the scarcest commodities by males, for procreation, recreation, and conspicuous consumption, social facts that organize the manner and meaning of sexual contacts.

Beyond this, in Melanesian societies, semen (and its symbolic equivalents, e.g., mother's milk) is clearly treated as a scarce commodity. Sperm not only conceives babies, it is believed to magically build the embryo's body, to be transformed into breast milk, to produce postnatal physical strength, and to precipitate puberty and biological reproductive competence, that is, adult personhood. These tangible achievements, and their religious consequences, are the valued product of taking in semen, which is itself believed to be in scarce supply. On the one hand, such cultural beliefs and values unite this aspect of sexual contacts with the second one described above, for individuals are socially directed and psychologically motivated to acquire from men the semen needed to make and complete themselves as human beings. On the other hand, though, semen is treated as a scarce resource that is *circulated* through group exchanges as a commodity within the total societal pool. Therefore in native thought, the signs, symbols, and cultural contexts of sexual contacts are also defined in reference to "circulating" semen as part of a constructed social reality.

In all three of these modes of defining sexual contact people's meanings in certain instances of sexual intercourse are influenced by a range of social and personal attributes brought to the specific situation. Kinship and marital status, age, the sex of one's partner, gender identity, and other variables thus contextually define sexual behaviors. Yet, ritual status and the generational position of the partners in the developmental cycle of the group are especially significant contributing factors in Melanesia. Because age and ritual status change, it is therefore a mistake to believe that individuals do not alter their interpretations of sexual contacts as they acquire experience and pass through the life cycle. Especially in societies where elaborate ritual initiations punctuate social development, sexual experience undergoes changes in response to successive ritual teaching about erotics, access to appropriate sexual partners, and the achievement of sociopolitical power and the privileges of adulthood.

What are the contours of this culture area called Melanesia, and how do the following studies make sense of it? The late Gregory Bateson commented recently that neither his nor Margaret Mead's New Guinea works had taken "full advantage of the fact of the culture area" (Bateson 1978:77). He argued further that "the notion of a culture area is that all the pieces of culture used by" one group "have been available to" others, and vice versa: "Each culture supposedly made its specific picture out of the same jumble of pieces of the jigsaw puzzle" (ibid.). Melanesia, in this sense, is certainly a very big jigsaw. Its geographic territory covers tens of thousands of square miles, spread from Fiji in the east, to the offshore islands of Irian Jaya far to the west. Reasonable estimates place the number of different cultures at between 700 and 1,000, while the number of languages is well over 2,000. Such numbers indicate tremendous regional variation, perhaps greater than in any other world culture area. And yet, at the same time, cultural patterns such as warfare, patrilineal descent, male initiation rites and/or ceremonial exchange systems, animistic religion and beliefs about spirits, and a discrete set of variations on symbolic themes concerning the body, gender, work, marriage, and personhood seem pervasive throughout the region. Such variations make a difference in some but not in all areas of research. How do we handle variations in sexuality and ritual when we "come down to the business of making anthropology out of fieldwork" (ibid.)?

When I initiated this volume in 1980, I could think of only two reasonable ways to handle this problem. The first was to invite as many different anthropologists as possible to contribute studies on Melanesian cultures in which ritualized homosexuality was already known or probable. The second was for me to survey the ethnographic literature. The immensity of cross-cultural variation in this Melanesia material seemed at first overwhelming. Two years later the variation seemed less, and I am now more impressed by area-wide similarities than by differences. It is likely that ancient population migrations and subsequent cultural diffusion have played a tremendous part in shaping culture-area variations in sexual customs within Melanesia. The full extent of this culture history, including recent colonial history, shall never be fully known. Nonetheless, using the available data, I speculate below that an unequally distributed and ancient ritual complex has shaped some of the "deep structure" elements associated with strikingly similar forms of ritualized homosexuality scattered across a vast area of Melanesia.

Letters of invitation to contribute to the volume went out. The responses (as with any such endeavor) varied. Time was of the essence: most groups that practiced ritualized homosexuality have long since been pacified and colonialized, with dire effects upon their traditional cultures, particularly upon this form of homosexuality (which missionaries, and in some instances, government authorities, eliminated first of all). Some of the key early ethnographers, whose studies were primary, had passed away (e.g., F. E. Williams, John Layard). Several young ethnographers who had data also could not contribute for political reasons, fearing that publication of their material on homosexuality would be resented by village people among whom they had worked (a sensitive issue that cannot be underestimated in today's postcolonial world). But others responded affirmatively, as shown by the excellent chapters below.

The anthropologists who have contributed to this volume are among the most distinguished living Melanesianist scholars. Professor J. Van Baal (Holland), the world's greatest authority on the peoples of Irian Jaya, has contributed a critical essay on the Marind-anim (Southwest New Guinea) whose culture, he writes, "now belongs to the past." Professor Kenneth E. Read (U.S.A.), who published the first anthropological reports on Highlands Papua New Guinea, contributes a retrospective essay on the Gahuku-Gama (Eastern Highlands Province). Professor Michael Allen (Australia) writes on the comparative situation in Vanuatu (formerly the New Hebrides); his major study on male cults, and other papers, are well known to specialists. Professor Eric Schwimmer (Canada), whose studies on Melanesian exchange and semiotics are well known, writes on the Orokaiva (the Northern Province, Papua New Guinea). Professor Laurent Serpenti (Holland), best known for his study of Kimam culture (Frederik Hendrik Island, Irian Jaya), contributes a much needed new study on that group. Professor Shirley Lindenbaum (U.S.A.) has provided an important theoretical overview, following many early and important papers on Papua New Guinea. Dr. Arve Sørum (Norway), writes the first focused essay on initiation and homosexuality among the Bedamini of the Great Papuan Plateau (Southern Highlands Province, Papua New Guinea) which extends his earlier work. And I write on unreported aspects of Sambia (an Anga group), Eastern Highlands Province, Papua New Guinea), complementing earlier papers.

The geographic spread of these papers is thus impressive, and it covers virtually all of the extant areas on which ritualized homo-sexuality has ever been reported: the New Hebrides; the Anga peoples of fringe-area Eastern Highlands; the Great Papuan Pla-teau; the Northern Province; and Southwestern Irian Jaya.

These essays are introduced by my own historical survey of the Melanesian literature, which traces and analyzes reports of rit-ualized homosexual practices over a period of more than a century. This regional survey is the first of its kind, and it summarizes the literature up to the present. Various theoretical and ethnographic factors permeate the review, which organizes the literature—vast, checkered, and contradictory as it is—in order to make sense of culture-area patterns of homosexual behavior. But I have not pro-vided a systemic regional model, a larger project that would entail another book.

Professor Shirley Lindenbaum's concluding chapter does provide a much needed framework, however, both for addressing common ethnographic themes in these papers as well as for conceptualizing them. She brings to this scholarly task extensive ethnographic experience in New Guinea and long interest in sex and gender, women's roles, and social ideology in Melanesian studies. I wish to thank her again for such an insightful and excellent synopsis which helps bring intellectual closure to our joint endeavors.

For their extremely generous and thoughtful reviews of this volume I am very indebted to Professors Jan Van Baal, Fitz John P. Poole, and Donald F. Tuzin.

Finally, I gratefully acknowledge the assistance of the Depart-ment of Anthropology, Stanford University, for institutional sup-port in the preparation of this volume.

G. H. H.
Stanford, California
1982

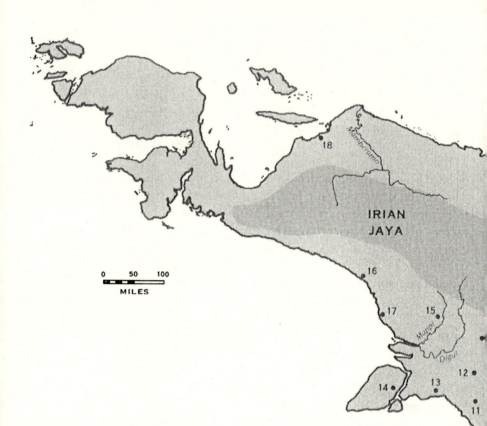

SOCIAL UNIT

1. Fiji
2. New Caledonia
3. New Hebrides
4. New Britain
5. Duke-of-Yorks
6. East Bay
7. Kiwai Island (+ Bugulai)
8. Keraki
9. Suki
10. Boadzi
11. Kanum
12. Yei-anim
13. Marind-anim
14. Kimam (Fr. Hen. Is.)
15. Jaqai

16. Asmat
17. Casuarina Coast
18. Humboldt Bay
19. Bedamini
20. Etoro
21. Kaluli
22. Onabasalu
23. Gebusi (Nomad River)
24. Sambia
25. Baruya
26. Jeghuje
27. Other Highlands — Anga groups
28. Lowlands — Anga groups
29. Ai'i

MAP 1
NEW GUINEA AND ADJACENT ISLANDS

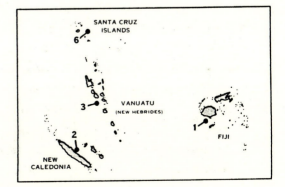

1

Gilbert H. Herdt

Ritualized Homosexual
Behavior in the Male Cults
of Melanesia, 1862–1983:
An Introduction

INTRODUCTION

Melanesia has long provided a rich stomping ground for anthropological studies of initiation rites, secret societies, sex-related principles of social grouping and, more recently, gender ideologies. The numerous studies of male/female relations and "sexual antagonism" (Brown and Buchbinder 1976; Langness 1967; Meggitt 1964; Read 1954; reviewed in Herdt and Poole 1982) alone distinguish Melanesia as a culture area. Considering this intersection of ritual and sexuality, it is puzzling how little has been written on the institutionalized aspects of eroticism in Melanesian societies, particularly since Melanesianists such as Haddon (1917:351) long ago argued that throughout New Guinea, "initiation ceremonies are not merely the promotion of the no-vitiates, but also their introduction to the sexual life." But even more puzzling is the virtual evasion of a psychosocial phenomenon that is of patent anthropological interest and one that now appears more common than once thought: ritualized homosexual behavior.

1

I reached this conclusion when summarizing a study of such sexual practices and their gender symbolism among the Sambia, a hunting and horticultural society of the Eastern Highlands, Papua New Guinea (Herdt 1981). In reviewing the Melanesian literature of the past 100 years or so, it surprised me that similar practices are more widespread and significant than one would ever suspect from contemporary Melanesian studies (e.g., Allen 1967).[1] Moreover, cross-cultural surveys of initiation and sexuality, which invariably draw upon Melanesia, ignore ritualized homosexuality (see, for example, Cohen 1964; Stephens 1962; Whiting et al. 1958; Whiting and Whiting 1975). By thus neglecting the data cited below, previous surveys and models of social and symbolic variation in initiation rites and relationships between the sexes and gender roles are lacking, and the incidence and meaning of ritualized homosexual practices in these groups remains obscure.

The aim of this introduction is to review the extant Melanesian literature and to explore the linkages between institutionalized homosexuality and certain sociocultural arrangements in Melanesia as a whole. My thesis is that systems that incorporate ritualized homosexuality can be seen as representing the extremes to which sexual polarity extends in a range of Melanesian societies. Rather than ignore homosexual practices as a tangential curiosity, we may look to their distribution, elaboration, and cultural meaning in helping to sort out cross-cultural variation in sexual behavior and gender ideologies in these groups. My review concludes with the possibility that there is a geographic-historical nexus of ritualized homosexuality between these Melanesian groups which is further substantiated by correlations of related sociocultural patterns among them.

What is the current state of the cross-cultural survey literature on homosexual behavior in Melanesia? The view outside of Melanesian studies is plainly muddled, a confusion that invites comment before sorting out the ethnographic texts. Opler (1965:121), for example, in a widely read textbook on human sexuality, denies the existence of institutionalized homosexual practices:

Clubs and societies have on occasion been sex limited, as in Melanesia, but there is no reason to believe that this limitation has promoted homosexual behavior in these social, economic, or some-times ritual settings—or indeed that such behavior exists at all in such instances.

Several years later, Minturn et al. (1969), in a Human Relations Area Files cross-cultural survey on sexual beliefs and behavior, coded homosexual behavior as being "absent" in New Guinea societies, but present in Australia. Yet Hiatt (1971:87), speaking in the context of Róheim's early accounts of Australian aboriginal rites, states, "It would be hard to find empirical grounds for rep-resenting these rites as 'guilty homosexual secrets.'" Where Aus-tralian and Melanesian materials bear comparison in this matter, Hiatt's view seems inadequate (see below). And as recently as 1976, Parratt, in a literature review of F. E. William's (1936c) Keraki work, writes:

> The trans-Fly Papuans appear to have been unique among Mela-nesian peoples in that novices were initiated also into the practice of sodomy, which was thought to contribute to the physical de-velopment of the youths.
>
> *(1976:65)*

Here we find homosexual practices either denied, coded as absent, or treated as unique. Why should scholars have developed such views?

There are several reasons. One is that many of the Melanesian references on ritualized homosexuality are skimpy, single-line al-lusions that do not inspire much confidence. Another is that sex remains one of the "taboo" subjects in anthropology (Marshall and Suggs 1971). Anthropologists, including Melanesianists, have not in general provided good descriptive accounts of sexual be-havior, homosexual activity in particular. A third factor is a ten-dency for writers still to view homosexual behavior as universally deviant, unnatural, or perverse, not seeming to recognize that such practices are relative to particular cultural contexts and therefore invite analysis like any other form of social behavior.[2] Fourth is the related matter of "authorities" who have tended to regard only heterosexuality as prevalent or "normal." Malinowski is a case in point. In his early literature review on *The Family Among the*

Australian Aborigines, he paid no attention to ritual homosexuality, though he used Australian sources that had mentioned it (see especially 1913:262–269). Later, in his writings on the Trobriand Islands he denied the existence of homosexual activity except as "perversion" (1929:448–453, 468, 472–473), arguing that the *natives* saw "sexual aberrations as *bad* because a natural law has been flouted" (1929:468, emphasis mine). (He does not, incidentally, account for why Trobrianders should have a category for anal intercourse.) Elsewhere, he argued ironically: "Homosexuality is the rule among those upon whom white man's morality has been forced in such an irrational and unscientific manner," adding, however, that such indigenous "perversions" are "much more prevalent in the [nearby] Amphlett and d'Entrecasteau Archipelago" (Malinowski 1927:80; cf. Róheim 1950:174). Needless to say, no one has ever investigated that latter suggestion.

In his own day, when generalized to all of Melanesia, Malinowski's view was overdrawn. To illustrate, Havelock Ellis[3] (1936: Pt. II, 8–21), whose *Psychology of Sex* was widely read, cited various ethnographic examples of institutionalized homosexual practices in Melanesia and Australia. So did Westermarck (1917:459ff.) in another book of similar popular currency. Malinowski's teachers—Seligman (1902) and Haddon (cited in Ellis 1936:9)—also referred to such sources. Van Gennep in his classic study *Les Rites de Passage* (1960:170–171), specifically argued that the use of heterosexual coitus as a final "rite of incorporation" held "equally true for those of homosexual nature," and he quoted Parkinson's (1907) New Britain ethnography to make his point. Moreover, the early Freudians, always quick to exploit new ethnographic data, specifically compared the manifestations of ritualized homosexuality in Austro-Melanesian groups (e.g., see Reik 1946; Róheim 1926:70).

Since the days of such old-fashioned ethnological scrapbooks, other scholars have unsystematically used various works cited below. They have ranged from eminent sex researchers (Ford and Beach 1951:132; Money and Ehrhardt 1972:132–139), to cross-cultural psychiatrists (Foulks 1977:12–13), classicists (e.g., Bremmer 1980:280f.), the indefatigable German ethnologists (Baumann 1955:210–229; Bleibtreu-Ehrenberg 1980; Karsch-Haack

1911:92–115), Jungians (Eliade 1958:26–27), Freudians (Bettelheim 1955; Vanggaard 1972), social historians (Trumbach 1977:26–27), biologizers (Tiger 1970:126–155) and popularizers (Kottak 1974:287–288; Tripp 1975:64ff.). Each of these writers, in terms not altogether congenial to social anthropology, have variously argued for, and used, Melanesian materials on ritualized homosexuality to make one or another point about universals of normality and variation in human sexual behavior. Throughout this long period, however, no one ever systematically studied the phenomenon; the ethnological comments of Haddon (1936) and Layard (1959) are notable exceptions, and they appeared, unfortunately, in obscure places. Allen's *Male Cults and Secret Initiations in Melanesia*, still the chief source book on the area, only mentions ritualized homosexual practices (1967:96–99). Not until Dundes' (1976) discussion had an anthropologist studied and challenged this literature to interpret Melanesian sociocultural systems. In sum, there are ample reasons for non-Melanesianists to be confused about the Melanesian materials on ritualized homosexuality. The remainder of my chapter is devoted to clarifying both what we do and do not know about it.

To ensure the fullest measure of control over the ethnographic material, I shall only examine ritualized homosexuality in Melanesia, especially the island of New Guinea. This culture area involves an immense literature that is thick and uneven, with the older sources in several different languages, published in obscure and inaccessible, often defunct journals, and often referenced to outmoded ethnographic names; but this material I know best. Similar phenomena are reported from elsewhere in the tribal world; perhaps, beyond Australia, the Amazon Basin is closest to the Melanesian situation (see Keesing 1982).[4] Regretfully I cannot review the Australian Aboriginal material, which properly should be considered alongside of Melanesia, as Róheim (1926:70; 324–337 and passim) and later Van Baal (1963) have argued. Thus, I leave it to others to make sense of the following *explicit* references to ritualized homosexual practices in the Australian literature, especially on the Kimberley Mountains and Central Desert tribes (see Berndt and Berndt 1951:67; Hardman 1889:73–74; Kaberry 1939:257; Mathews 1896:334–335; 1900:635–636; Meggitt

1965*a*:183; Purcell 1893:287; Ravenscroft 1892:121–122; Ró-heim 1926:70; 1929:189; 1932:51; 1950:118–119, 122; 1974:243–244, 247–248; Spencer and Gillen 1927, 2:470, 486; Strehlow 1913:98–122).[5]

TERMS • Part of the difficulty in the anthropological literature on sex and gender stems from a plethora of confusing terminology which finds scholars arguing whether something is present or absent without first defining what that something is. The questions surrounding the Omani *xanith* (Wikan 1977) belong to this confusing morass (see Carrier 1980*b*). It is therefore crucial at the start to define the parameters of our subject as precisely as possible.

The subject of these essays is restricted to *ritualized* homosexual (RH)* practices and behavior. I myself prefer the adjective *ritualized*, despite its ambiguous and exotic connotations, over other imprecise terms such as *ceremonialized*, which is weaker and incidental. (Devereux's [1937] classic paper on Mohave homosexuality utilizes these modifiers and many more.) *Ritualized* as a modifier applies best to the Melanesian situation because: (1) homosexual practices are implemented usually through male initiation rites, having (2) religious overtones, as well as being (3) constrained by broader cultural rules and social roles, for which the full moral and jural force of a society, or a secret men's society, not only condones but often prescribes sexual intercourse among certain categories of males; and (4) various age-related and kinship taboos define and restrict the nature of this male/male sexual behavior. Ritualized homosexuality is thus a Melanesian type of institutionalized homosexual activity in the broader sense found elsewhere in the world.

Several other general points will help indicate the terms of the following review. First, the Melanesian literature advises that ritualized homosexual behavior is almost exclusively a *male* phenomenon (cf. Ford and Beach 1951). Institutionalized female homosexuality is very rare (cf. Hooker 1968:230), and little is known of the few reported cases (see below). Second, the males who are involved are usually of markedly different ages; they are

---

*I will at times use (RH) to indicate ritualized homosexual behavior or groups with such practices, to avoid too bumpy reading.

forbidden to reverse sexual roles (inserter/insertee) with *each* other, meaning, in effect, that they are in age-ranked, asymmetrical status relationships. Third, these homosexual contacts are culturally focused virtually everywhere on semen transmission. Fourth, as far as is known, Melanesian homosexual behaviors do not involve fetishistic cross-gender dressing or eroticized transvestism of any sort, individual or institutional (see Davenport 1977:155). Although nonerotic ceremonial transvestism is known from Melanesia, it seems infrequent and not strongly correlated with ritualized homosexuality,[6] (see Schwimmer, chap. 6 below). Nor is there any evidence that primary male transsexualism (Stoller 1968, 1975) is involved.[7] Fifth, in these societies males are involved in homoerotic contacts first as insertees, then as inserters, being often steadily involved, after initiation, for months or years. Yet in all known cases, they are later expected to marry and father children, as is customary. Their psychosexual involvement (to use a comfortably neutral term) does not make them into "homosexuals," in the sense that this noun connotes (life-long habitualized sexual preference for members of the same sex) in Western culture (Stoller 1980). In other words, to engage in initiatory or secular homosexual acts (behavior) does not necessarily mean that one is or becomes "homosexual" in habitual sexual motivation or sex object choice (identity). This analytic distinction is reviewed in my summary. Finally, if these acts are not performed by "homosexuals," then why use the adjective *homosexual*? It might be objected that their initial ritual context places these sexual contacts in a category different from that with which Westerners mark off "homosexual." While this objection holds truth in a sense, we should not forget that sexual acts, ritualized or not, always entail erotic arousal, at least for the inserter. Moreover, as a simple modifier, *homosexual* is preferable and more accurate than any other, since these societies permit sexual penetration and insemination between people of the same sex.* *Bisexual* is therefore inaccurate to describe these people or their homoerotic acts: typically, (RH) groups often forbid heterosexual contacts during the *same* period when boys

---

*Wherever possible below I shall use "ritualized homosexual behavior" or (RH) in this sense; where I slip into using "homosexuality" it is for stylistic economy, and it should be understood in the fuller sense.

are being inseminated by older males; and the younger insertees are strictly separated from females and are only allowed sexual contacts with superordinate males after initiation.

In these terms I thus exclude from this survey all of the following phenomena: individual (aberrant) or noninstitutionalized homosexual behavior; homosexual behavior as reported from acculturated settings such as plantations or prisons;[8] all fetishistic cross-gender dressing or eroticized transvestism; transsexualism; psychotic behavior or any other form of social deviance as defined by the natives. We shall only be concerned, then, with ritualized homosexual behaviors supported by customary sociocultural arrangements.

Finally, I wish to make it explicitly clear that I am *not* asserting (or even hinting) any of the following: that all ritual involves homosexual activity, latent or manifest, in Melanesia or elsewhere; that all Melanesians are prone to engage in homosexual activity; or, to reiterate, that these homoerotic activities make the practitioners into "homosexuals." The patterns of (RH) examined below are clearly known from only a small number—perhaps 10 to 20 percent—of all Melanesian groups that have been studied. What matters is not the gross numbers of these societies or their total populations but rather their psychosocial and symbolic meaning when viewed against broader trends of sexual polarity and gender ideology in Melanesia.

Because of its historical depth and unevenness, I have organized the literature review geographically, then by the date of ethnographic reportage and by cultural subarea (e.g., Eastern Melanesia, Western Papua, etc.). The unfolding survey may be read as a story—of increasing allusions followed by fuller accounts of ritual homosexuality, the accumulation of which provides understanding of the pieces of a puzzle widely scattered and still not entirely unscrambled.

Comparisons between these texts involve huge problems concerning the comparability of social units. In some ethnographic reports (e.g., Chalmers's [1903a] note on the Bugi, see below), tiny communities are described; in others, there are far larger populations (e.g., the Marind-anim [Van Baal 1966]), tribes whose total numbers run into the thousands, scattered over vast areas. Then there is the question of considering related social units as discrete and historically unrelated (i.e., Galton's problem). This issue raises difficulties in the entangled Melanesian literature. My solution is to be conservative: in doubtful cases of geographically close groups (e.g., the Bugi [Chalmers 1903*a*] versus Kiwai Islanders [Landtman 1927]) I will assume social linkage. When dealing with whole subregions (e.g., Southeastern Irian Jaya), I count groups as different (e.g., Marind-anim versus Jaquai) when there is evidence sufficient to justify their classification as separate units. But such classifications do not mean that these peoples necessarily belong to different subregional cultural traditions. We can thus identify a people both as constituting a separate *social unit* as well as belonging to a broader *cultural tradition* in a geographic subregion of Melanesia. In this survey we shall examine eight different subregions which vary in size and in the number of their constituent social units (see table 1.1). Then I shall briefly reconnoiter several questionable cases. Each subregion will be treated separately; clear statements about ritualized homosexual behavior is the organizing theme. Finally, I have tried also to assess the quality of these reports where possible and to substantiate early reports with later ones, either in the same society or elsewhere from the same cultural tradition.[9]

The ethnographic material from the earliest historical period is often thin, diverse, and difficult to interpret. It covers the widest possible geographic and ethnological spectrum, from Eastern Melanesia (Fiji, the New Hebrides,* and New Caledonia), the off-lying islands of old German New Guinea, and the Papuan Gulf at the Fly River, to disparate parts of North and Southeast Dutch New Guinea (see endpaper map). It is also checkered, being an unreliable mixture of reports from travelers, missionaries, and early anthropologists. (Some early travelers' reports are fantastic—"a stimulus for jaded imaginations": Whittaker et al. 1975:271ff.)

EASTERN MELANESIA

FIJI • Our earliest hints of ritualized homosexuality come from the extreme easternmost part of Melanesia, Fiji, which was colonized before island New Guinea. These data suggest the presence

---

*The New Hebrides will be used here to conform to the older literature references; however, it covers the New Hebrides Archipelago, the Banks Islands, Torres Straits, and other islands now incorporated in the new nation of Vanuatu.

TABLE 1.1

The Distribution of Ritualized Homosexuality in Melanesian Groups

Geographic Subregion	Social Unit (referred to in text)	Related social units (not referred to in text)	Language type*
I. Eastern insular Melanesia	1. Fiji		A
	2. New Caledonia		A
	New Hebrides:		
	3. Malekula Island		A
II. Northeastern insular Melanesia	4. New Britain		
	5. Duke-of-Yorks		
	6. East Bay		
III. Western Papua	Lower Fly River:		
	7. Kiwai Island (+ Bugilai)		
	Trans-Fly Delta:		
	8. Keraki	Karigare[1]	N
		Yarne	N
		Kaunje	
		Wekamara	N
	9. Suki		N
	10. Boadzi		N
IV. Southeastern Irian Jaya	11. Kanum		N
	12. Yéi-anim		N
	13. Marind-anim	Maklew-anim[2]	
		Yab-anim	
		Kurkari-anim	
	14. Kimam (Fr. Hen. Is.)		N
	15. Jaquai		N

V. Northeastern Irian Jaya	16. Asmat	N
	17. Casuarina Coast	N
	18. Humboldt Bay	N
VI. Great Papuan Plateau	19. Bedamini	N
	20. Etoro	N
	21. Kaluli	N
	22. Onabasalu	N
	23. Gebusi (Nomad River)	
VII. Anga (Kukukuku)	24. Sambia	N
	25. Baruya	N
	26. Jeghuje	N
	27. Other Highlands Anga groups	N
	Usarumpiu	
	Wantukiu	
	Aziana	
	Lohiki[3]	
	Kapau	
	Ivori	
	Mbwei	
	Yagwoia	
	Ampale	
	Langamar	
	Menya	
	Katje	
	28. Lowlands Anga groups	N
VIII. Northern Province	29. Ai'i	N

Total: 29 societies   Total: 19 related societies

* Austronesian = A
Non-Austronesian = N
[1] From Williams (1936c:208)
[2] From Van Baal (1966:maps)
[3] From Gajdusek et al. (1972)

of ritualized homosexuality, but they are highly questionable (see, for example, Seemann 1862:160–162, 169–170; and Waterhouse 1866:341, 345). Nonetheless, in the late 1920s, the authority A. M. Hocart speculated that "sodomy [anal intercourse] was once recognized between cross-cousins" among the hill tribes of Fiji (quoted in Layard 1942:491). Hocart linguistically compared the pertinent Fijian terms of address with those associated with anal intercourse in ancient Hawaii (cf. Remy 1862:xliii; and see below on Malekula Island). For Fiji, then, the case for ritual homosexuality is thin.

NEW CALEDONIA • Foley's (1879) report is the earliest definite mention of (RH). Comparing the New Caledonian villagers to the ancient Greeks, Foley states: "It is true that this military club is complicated by pederasty" (ibid.:606). Arguing that the warriorhood is opposed to "the uterine club," he also remarks, "Women are the enemies of pederasty" (ibid.). Collaborative sketchy reports can be found in De Rochas (1862:235) and in Jacobus X. (1893:330–331; 1898, 2: 359–360). New Caledonia is culturally similar to New Hebrides societies, where homosexual activities are much better described.

MALEKULA ISLAND (NEW HEBRIDES)* • The first major source for Malekula is A. B. Deacon, a Cambridge-trained anthropologist who carried out intensive fieldwork in Seniang district, South West Bay area, and who also collected valuable survey data on other Malekula communities (see map 2). Though the most elaborate forms of ritualized homosexuality occur in the northern districts, especially among the Big Nambas tribe, related elements of the same complex occur elsewhere on Malekula as well as on neighboring islands. The characteristics and possible interrelations of this complex are delineated in Allen's important paper below (see chap. 2). Outside the Big Nambas area, "homosexuality is apparently very rare" (Deacon 1934:156), though among prepubertal boys masturbation and heterosexual play are "common." In other, more northerly areas, male homosexual practices are "occasional and sporadic," whereas lesbianism is "com-

*I am very grateful to Professor Michael Allen for clarifying the ethnographic data provided in this section.

mon" (Deacon 1934:170).[10] Elements of the same ritual complex—including a belief in heads (both penis heads and mens' heads) as loci of male power, the use of elaborate headdresses to represent spirit beings, the symbolic importance of sharks, and the performance of painful initiation rites with long periods of seclusion—are found in varying combinations throughout much of the northern New Hebrides and Banks Islands (Layard 1942:493–494; Allen 1981).

The main features of the traditional North Malekula case can be roughly sketched as follows.[11] These groups tend toward chieftainship, the highest form being attained among the Big Nambas. Here, too, ritualized homosexuality is the most prominent. Layard (1942:489) describes the Big Nambas as "an extreme form of patrilineal culture . . . exceeding all other New Hebrides tribes in the very low status which they accord to women." Boys are initiated at an early age and thereafter stringently avoid women. Circum-incision* accords them masculine status; and it is positively correlated with "organized homosexuality" (Layard 1942:486–488). Thus, while homosexual contacts may have traditionally existed in other parts of Vanuatu, they are most highly elaborated among the Big Nambas, where circumcision is practiced (Allen 1967:96–97). Is demography a relevant consideration? Here as elsewhere in New Guinea, there is a sex ratio disparity (126 males per 100 females [Layard 1942:745]), exacerbated by the chiefly system, which enables the Big Nambas chiefs to hold a virtual monopoly of the women (Layard 1959:109). Is cultural belief related? Yes: the natives see homosexual intercourse as a way to strengthen the boy's penis (Deacon 1934:260–262)—which Layard (1942:489) believes to be a "transmission of male power by physical means"—for the penis is held in "high esteem" and the glans penis is accorded "extreme reverence."

Finally, the New Hebrides complex reveals a symbolic relation between living and dead kinsmen and male gender ideology. Homosexual partners refer to each other as husband and wife, the initiate calling his man-lover "sister's husband" (Deacon 1934:261; Layard 1942:488–489), terms that indicate the close affinal, sex-

---

*A rare and complex form of circumcision found here which Layard has described in detail and Allen (chap. 2) mentions below.

ual, and perhaps economic interrelation between these males. Layard speaks of homosexual anal intercourse as symbolizing "continuity with the ancestral ghosts in the male line," especially in areas, such as the Small Islands, wherein mystical anal penetration as a ritual hoax supplants actual homosexual coitus (Layard 1959:111). We see similar symbolic themes of spiritual insertion elsewhere in Melanesia (see Summary and Analysis). This same culture complex, minus circumcision and ritual homosexuality, is found in a wide area extending through Malekula, Raga, and the Banks Islands (Layard 1942:493–494). Deacon was so struck by the similarities between this cult and a structurally similiar initiatory complex (with circumcision, devouring ritual spirits, bullroarers, etc.) found in the Finschhafen area, near the Markham River on mainland New Guinea, that he argued for a historical connection through diffusion from a common source, most probably located in Eastern Indonesia (Deacon 1925, 1934:268–269).[12]

If Layard found mystical support for patrilineal descent in the New Hebrides, he also saw symbolic connections between homosexuality, marriage, and masculinity. Drawing speculative parallels between Malekula, Fiji, and Western Australia, Layard (1942:494) states: "Among the Big Nambas a man took as his boy lover a member of his wife's marriage section, and it was only later that this love-relationship turned into one of joking and mutual violence." Further, Layard (1942:489–490) advanced a rather sophisticated argument about the causes of (RH). He believed that social forms (sexual polarity, chieftainship, sister exchange), created by the religious rationalization of male descent and affiliation (e.g., circum-incision and ancestral "mythical homosexuality"), gradually resulted in homoerotic contacts "as an everyday practice." In other words, ideology and social structure historically produced ritual homosexual contacts that became as regularly institutionalized as heterosexual contacts. I shall return to this historicist argument in the summary.

NEW BRITAIN AND NORTHEASTERN MELANESIA

If we now look north (see map 1), we may trace a series of ethnographic cases including New Britain and the nearby Duke-of-York Islands (formerly German New Guinea), and East Bay.

NEW BRITAIN AND THE DUKE-OF-YORKS • The German ethnologist Richard Parkinson wrote a massive early text which, though in German and little read, remains the classic source on the area. He describes men's secret societies among the Tolai people of the Gazelle Peninsula area of New Britain island. Ritualized homosexual practices are present in the special Ingiet cult there.

> When candidates are admitted in the Ingiet, sodomy [anal inter-
> course] is committed before the eyes of all present. An older Ingiet
> leaves the *balana marawot* [cult house] and returns quite naked
> and smeared with lime from top to toe. He holds in his hand the
> end of a coconut mat, the other end he offers to one of the novices.
> The two of them scuffle around with it for some time, and then
> fall over each other and the abomination takes place. Each initiate
> in turn must submit to this procedure. In extenuation of this, how-
> ever, I will remark that paederasty is no crime in the eyes of the
> native, who regards it merely in an amusing light.
>
> *(Parkinson 1907:544)*

Shortly later, no less an authority than Van Gennep (1960:171) used this passage as an example of homosexual "rites of incor-poration" in *Les Rites des Passage*. It is unclear how widespread this practice was in the Bismarck Archipelago of that day, but it may have been restricted to the Ingiet secret society.

The lime-coated figure may here symbolically represent a "spirit woman," which Parkinson (1907:537) tells us the fully initiated elder can "turn himself into." If so, it would exemplify what Lay-ard (1942:474) called a "mythical" symbolization of homosexual practices. Whether similar practices existed in the related Duk-Duk men's cult (Rickard 1891) is unclear, but Richard Salisbury (personal communication) thinks not. On the Ingiet cult, however, Parkinson pointedly (1907:544) reassures us that his sexual in-formation is reliable.[13]

No further reports even mentioned ritual homosexuality in New Britain for almost seventy years.[14] Presumably, the practice is now long since abandoned. However, Epstein (1977:178–179) refers to fragmentary evidence indicating the traditional practice of anal homosexual intercourse among the Tolai. And Errington (1974), whose work on the neighboring Duke-of-York Islands is the first since Parkinson's (1907:545), has supplied important confirmation of ritualized homosexual practices in the wider New Britain area. In the contemporary context of initiation on the Duke-of-Yorks, he notes:

> One man, a volunteer, not otherwise important in the ritual, lay on his stomach without his waistcloth in order to expose his anus to the boy. An informant of sixty said that in the past a boy going to the *taraiu* for the first time had to perform fellatio* on one of the adult men. Another informant, a young man about thirty-five, was shocked when I asked about this practice. . . . [Errington here cites Parkinson. Thus, these practices suggest . . .] homosexual submission when a boy is separated from the society of women and incorporated into the society of men.
>
> *(Errington 1974:84)*

The New Britain material clearly indicates homosexual practices in secret initiation. But we do not know whether (RH) occurred after initiation in secular life. And in contrast to Malekula and Papua (see below), no evidence of native ideas about "growth" is evident. (I take up Errington's suggestion about "homosexual submission" later.)

No other definite reports are known from the off-lying islands north of New Guinea. The nearby island of Buka may be a candidate, "for homosexuality is actually found among these people, but is rare, and is regarded with intense disfavour" (Blackwood 1935:128). The channel islands and Vitiaz Straits groups, together with the lowlands' Northeastern New Guinea mainland communities seem similar in cultural form to New Britian and the Duke-of-Yorks, but again the relevant ethnographic materials, often collected by missionaries, are difficult to assess (e.g., Neuhauss 1911).

EAST BAY • The only new report of homosexual activity in an off-lying island society here is that of Davenport (1965, 1977).[15] Although he (1977:155–157) refers to "institutionalized male bisexualism" in an acculturated community, we may safely include East Bay in our sample.

---

*Note the presence of contrary sexual techniques—anal intercourse in the Ingiet society, and fellatio among Duke-of-Yorks—in such closely related areas. Cf. below on the Great Papuan Plateau.

It is particularly interesting that two contrary modes of homosexual relations exist side by side in East Bay. The first is *reciprocal* and egalitarian sexual satisfaction between peers (even "brothers"; Davenport 1965:199) or friends: each must please the other in return.

> As boys reach late adolescence, they may also engage in mutual masturbation, but in the switch away from masturbation they also may have anal intercourse with friends and trade off playing the active and passive roles. No love or strong emotional bonds are developed. . . . It is considered to be part of the accommodations expected of friendship.
>
> *(Davenport 1977:155)*

This type of homosexual contact between peers is apparently rare in Melanesia (but cf. below, and Hogbin 1970). It opposes the normative distinctions between inserter and insertee so common in (RH) groups. The other mode was *asymmetrical* homosexual contacts between East Bay men and boys, which is common.

> Another substitute for older men was young boys, and they did take boys as passive partners for anal intercourse. Before a boy could be induced into such a partnership, permission had to be obtained from his father.[16]
>
> *(Davenport 1977:155)*

It is not clear if transmission of semen is here involved in "strengthening" boys, but it seems a likely possibility because of traditional initiation rites. The boy would receive small presents in return for his sexual favors.

Essentially, Davenport (1977:155) sees asymmetrical homosexual activities as a substitute sexual outlet for heterosexual relationships before marriage (for adolescents) or during postpartum taboos after marriage (for men). Ritual homosexuality was also associated with male initiation (Davenport 1965:205–206), at least in its men's-house variety. Homosexual activities are sporadically engaged in for years, along with heterosexual contacts, even in adulthood. It is also unusual that two erotic modes (i.e., mutual masturbation and anal coitus) coexist in East Bay, while others (e.g., fellatio; see Davenport 1965:201) are considered "ridiculous." Much social change has occurred in East Bay. Homosexual practices, for example, are no longer secret. One wonders whether the more-or-less egalitarian mode of mutual masturbation does not represent cultural change. If so, it would help to explain the sexual mutuality of peers resulting from changes in the power relationships underlying customary asymmetrical (RH). Davenport (1977) has recently advanced an important idea about how "gender segregated communities" led to (RH) in Melanesia, to which I shall return in the summary.

WESTERN PAPUA

This area is vast and includes many different social groups that essentially belong to the same subregional cultural tradition. They were the first mainland New Guinea groups reported to have ritualized homosexuality.

THE LOWER FLY RIVER • Initial reports in this area came from the Fly River delta and Kiwai Island, which lies at its mouth. These small tribal groups were once fierce warriors. All males were initiated into a secret cult, the various forms of which extended west throughout the Morehead District. The status of women was low (see Landtman 1927; Williams 1936c). Beardmore (1890:464), a missionary, first mentioned that "sodomy [anal intercourse] is regularly indulged in" on the left bank of the Fly (see also Haddon 1890:315).

The next overt references came from James Chalmers, a better-known missionary, on two closely related peoples: the Bugilai, again of the left bank of the Fly (see Williams 1936c:32n), and the nearby Kiwai Islanders. Of the Bugilai, Chalmers (1903a:109) states: "At the initiation of young men, they practice sodomy, but not bestiality as some other tribes do." (No further explanation!)

On the Kiwai Islanders, Chalmers's often sympathetic view turned cold even when it came to their heterosexual life. "Fornication is rife, rife here and the old men are the greatest sinners" (quoted in Langmore 1978:22). (When Chalmers [1903b:123] alluded to heterosexual arousal in the *Journal of the Royal Anthropological Institute,* the editors placed the crucial passage entirely in Latin, presumably out of censorship.) And Langmore (ibid.), quoting

Chalmers's unpublished papers, cites him thus on ritual homosexuality:

> The festival which so incensed him was the *moguru:* the series of ceremonies which initiated the young men. Chalmers opposed it partly because it emptied his classrooms for four months of every year, but more fundamentally because of its nature. It was "abominably filthy" he wrote. "The lads are prostituted by the men for quite a long time and soon become so diseased* that they never recover."

Chalmers was heartened when they did "recover" from their heathen ways by dropping these cult ceremonies in around 1898 (ibid.).

Censorship is apparent again with Baxter-Riley's (1925:216, another missionary) work on Kiwai, for he obliquely refers to an "unprintable ritual" (cf. also Beaver 1920:158 on "sexual crimes," and Strachan 1888:148, 155). In such instances we see what was seemingly common censorship practice vis-à-vis ethnographic reports on sexuality, at least until recently; at any rate it is clear from Haddon that Baxter-Riley was referring to ritualized homosexuality.[17]

The richest ethnography of Kiwai came from the Finnish ethnographer Landtman. In 1917 he noted that anal intercourse, sanctioned by myth, was believed to promote the physical growth of initiates (see Landtman 1917:78–80, 293–295). Later, in *The Kiwai Papuans of British New Guinea* (quaintly subtitled "A nature-born instance of Rousseau's ideal community"), Landtman (1927:237) writes:

> In connection with the initiation of youths at Masingle [Kiwai village], these have to practice sodomy in order to become tall and strong. Mr. E. Beardmore, who stayed in Mawata in 1888, states that "sodomy is regularly indulged in". . . . I did not come across any traces of it at Mawata as a general or ceremonial practice, but think it quite possible that the customs of the people, changing as they are, may have altered in this respect since Mr. Beardmore's time.[18]

*Metaphorically.

In the Kiwai case, we see a set of cultural themes which extend throughout the Western Papuan Gulf: a ritual cult feeding into a warriorhood; ritual seclusion and separation from women; and homosexual practices instituted through initiation to spur boys' masculine development.

It is worth underlining in general effects of social change on sexual customs as illustrated by the differences between the reports of Beardmore and Landtman. By 1910, when Landtman first worked, some twenty-two years had elapsed since Beardmore's work: undoubtedly, after pacification and missionary activity, social change had led the natives at Mawata to drop ritual homosexual practices. It is certain that for decades a similar historical process has been at work elsewhere in Melanesia: by the time an anthropologist arrived on the scene, trailing behind government and mission, (RH) activity, which was traditionally secret and hidden from the uninitiated in many areas, had been abandoned or suppressed owing to European authorities. (For striking examples of the political suppression of such homosexual practices, see the rare reports of Parkinson [1907:530n, 543–544], on German New Guinea, and Van Baal [1966:492–493], on Dutch New Guinea.) Thus, its presence was actively hidden from the anthropologist (see, for example, Williams 1936c:158), and/or the practice was defunct and unknown to younger natives themselves, so descriptions had to be salvaged from oldster's memories (e.g., Errington 1974, quoted above).

THE TRANS-FLY RIVER DELTA • We have already examined early reports from the mouth of the Fly River. Beginning in the 1920s, government anthropologist F. E. Williams immeasurably added to the ethnography of this cultural tradition, which extends up to the Fly headwaters, throughout the Morehead district, and west beyond the international border. Williams's classic studies of the Purari Delta, Keraki, Elema, Orokaiva, and other societies provide rich material for an emerging ethnology of the Papuan Gulf and Southern Irian Jaya (cf. Haddon 1927, 1936; Parratt 1976; Wagner 1972; Van Baal 1966). The Lower Trans-Fly Keraki are also the most famous Melanesian example of ritualized homosexual behavior cited in cross-cultural studies (e.g., Ford and Beach 1951). Williams was usually careful to record notes on sexual behavior—along with his biases about them (see n. 2). Until recent years, the Keraki were also the best described Papuan case of ritualized homosexual (anal) intercourse (see Williams 1936*a*:33n; 1936*c*:158–159, 194, 202, 294, 308–309). They were but one of several small tribes, numbering only a few hundred people, whom he believed to be nearly identical in culture and social organization.

The following passage best illustrates the main features and context of Keraki homosexual practices:

It was frequently maintained that *setiriva*, or bachelors, remained truly celibate until they entered upon sexual relations with their own wives. Without giving too much credence to this statement, we may note that the hospitable exchange above noted was nominally restricted to married adults. Some informants maintained that *setiriva* could secure the favors of married women at feast times, but it seems evident that this was not definitely sanctioned.

The bachelors had recourse to sodomy, a practice which was not reprobated but was actually a custom of the country—and a custom in the true sense, i.e., fully sanctioned by male society and universally practiced. For a long time the existence of sodomy was successfully concealed from me, but latterly, once I had won the confidence of a few informants in the matter, it was admitted on every hand. It is actually regarded as essential to the growing boy to be sodomized. More than one informant being asked if he had ever been subjected to unnatural practice, answered, "Why, yes! Otherwise how should I have grown?"

The ceremonial initiation to sodomy and the mythological antecedents to it will be spoken of elsewhere. . . . It is enough to note that every male adult in the Morehead district has in his time constantly played both parts in this perversion. The boy is initiated to it at the bull-roarer ceremony and not earlier, for he could not then be trusted to keep the secret from his mother. When he becomes adolescent his part is reversed and he may then sodomize his juniors, the new initiates to the bull-roarer. I am told that some boys are more attractive and consequently receive more attention of this kind than do others; but all must pass through it, since it is regarded as essential to their bodily growth. There is indeed no question as to the universality of the practice.

It is commonly asserted that the early practice of sodomy does nothing to inhibit a man's natural desires when later on he marries; and it is a fact that while the older men are not debarred from indulging, and actually do so at the bull-roarer ceremony, sodomy is virtually restricted as a habit to the *setiriva*.

(*Williams 1936c:158–159*)

These general patterns can thus be adduced on Keraki: Homosexual anal intercourse was (1) universal among all males, (2) obligatory, (3) implemented through ceremonial initiation, (4) secret and hidden from women and children, (5) culturally sanctioned by myth (Williams 1936c:194, 308–309), and (6) by the native belief that semen masculinized the initiate. The last notion is elaborated remarkably to the extent of fearing homosexual impregnation, which certain rites protect against (Williams 1936c; and cf. Meigs 1976). Trans-Fly homosexual contacts were also—as nearly everywhere else in Melanesia—(7) age graded and asymmetrical, so that bachelor youths inseminated younger males, who could not situationally reverse roles. (8) The Keraki initiate is inseminated by males of the opposite moiety, specifically his older cross-cousins (Williams 1936c:128), who have already been initiated and treated likewise by the initiates' older male clansmen (F E1.B., FB, FBSo). Hage (1981) has made much of this dualism (see my summary), following the important analysis of Rubel and Rosman (1978). It is likely, as Layard (1959:112–115) and Van Baal (1966:493–494) have argued, that this customary homoeroticism between groups that exchange wives—potential brother-in-laws—is a symbolic underpinning of semen exchanges between structurally related affines (see Herdt, chap. 4, and Lindenbaum, chap. 9, this volume). Finally, (9) Keraki homosexuality is practiced by unmarried males who eventually marry, as Williams noted above. These themes are discussed from a different perspective in Schwimmer's chapter 6.

Ethnographic data on other parts of the Fly River, Western Province, and eastern Gulf Coast are sketchy, but they should be mentioned here.* First, ritualized homosexuality is absent from the coastal Papuan societies east of the Fly River (Williams 1940a:428 n. 3), aside from the Ai'i and the probable exception of the coastal Anga peoples (see below). For example, the Elema people, in spite of symbolic and structural similarity to the Irian Jayan Marind-anim tribes, do not practice institutionalized homosexuality (Williams 1939:368 n. 3). (RH) also seems absent from

---

*I am greatly indebted to Professor J. Van Baal for information in the following two paragraphs and for many substantive remarks in the following section on Irian Jaya.

the Lake Kutubu area (Williams 1940*b*), as seems true for the eastern Motuan groups. Barker (1975), however, reports (RH) among the Ai'i, a people south of Orokavia, which Schwimmer discusses below. (RH) was absent from the Massim area, as noted above, and was probably absent from Normanby Island (Róheim 1950). And ritual homosexuality is not explicitly reported for any of the off-lying islands of the Papuan Gulf (see Haddon 1890, 1936). For the Torres Straits, there is a hint that Waiat cult leaders, impersonating spirits, may have on occasion perpetrated homosexual acts (see Haddon in *Reports* [1910, vol. 6], pointed out by Jeremy Becket, personal communication; see also Ellis 1936:9).

West of the Fly the situation is clear. Williams (1940*a*:492 n. 2) tells us that ritual homosexuality extended west throughout all villages of the left bank of the Lower Fly (e.g., including the Bugilai [Chalmers 1903*a*] noted above). Farther west the same practices are found. Culturally closely related to the Keraki are the most eastern tribes of the lowlands of Irian Jaya just across the international border. These include two distinct tribes, the Kanum peoples in the savannah east of the Lower Maro River, and the Yéi-anim (or Yéi-nan) of the Upper and Middle Maro River (see map 3). Their languages are closely related to those of the Trans-Fly. Information on the Kanum is very limited, though we know that some were yam-growers, that they are small in population, and that they practiced anal homosexuality, at least in the context of Sosom cult rites.* The Yéi-anim also live in small groups, and although sago-eaters like the Marind-anim, they consume tubers as daily food (like the Marind). The Yéi seem very similar to the Keraki: their totemism and moiety dualism match Keraki, and they identify the male sex with bull-roarer and *pahui* (ceremonial head-hunting clubs). More importantly, they practice quite similar anal homosexual intercourse, with young boys as insertees and bachelors (and some younger mature men) as inserters, for the purpose of "growing" the boys (Van Baal 1982).

To the north of Keraki, ritualized homosexuality of a like form has been reported from the Suki people on the Lower Middle Fly (Nieuwenhuijsen-Riedeman 1979), and from the Boadzi, a tribe

---

*In this area and among the Marind-anim peoples (discussed next), two elaborate and widespread ritual cults, referred to as Sosom and Mayo, utilized (RH).

inhabiting both sides of the international border where it meets the Fly River (see below). Farther to the north, recent anthropological work at the Fly headwaters, bordering the Telefomin area (see below), has revealed no ritualized homosexuality (Barth 1971).

IRIAN JAYA (formerly Dutch New Guinea)

The ethnography of Irian Jaya is not presently well integrated into Melanesian studies for several reasons, and since most ethnographic research there halted after Indonesia's annexation in the early 1960s, our contemporary knowledge is limited. Fortunately, we have Professor Van Baal's essay below (chap. 3) on the Marind-anim peoples, who are, next to the Keraki, the best known and probably the most flamboyant case of ritualized homosexuality known from Melanesia. Two areas of Irian Jaya are definitely known to have (RH): essentially the entire southern area, from the international border to Frederik Hendrik Island, extending north along the Irian Jaya coast in some groups; and in the extreme north, at Humboldt Bay.

THE MARIND-ANIM TRIBES • The Marind-anim groups numbered some 7,000 people (as of the most recent census; Van Baal 1966:33–37), dispersed in coastal villages, inland villages, and those on the Upper Bian River. They were sago-eaters, and though ecologically adjusted, they were demographically declining. Despite their relatively small numbers, they were unquestionably the fiercest headhunters throughout the Papuan Gulf (e.g., Beaver 1920:106ff.). They speak different dialects but are fairly homogeneous culturally. Linguistically, they are closely akin to the Boadzi, who also share in their traditions of head-hunting and ritualized homosexuality. Van Baal (1966:99–104) has shown affinities between the Boadzi of the Central Fly area around Lake Murray and the Marind-anim. Indeed, he (1966:214, 218) suggests the Middle Fly as the precursor cultural tradition of the Marind. Furthermore, as with the Marind, "sodomy has an important place in [Boadzi] life. The men indulge in it both in the men's house and in the bush" (Van Baal (1966:595). It had numerous magical functions in ritual, myth, and warfare.

First reports of the Marind came from Haddon (1891) and

others, but it is to Wirz (1922–1925) that we owe the first systematic study. Though published in German and not widely circulated, Wirz's dissertation contained rich mythological and ritual material on the Mayo and Sosum (bull-roarer) male cults of the Marind-anim. Wirz was cited by specialists (cf. Haddon 1927, 1936; Mead 1949:228–229; Williams 1936c), especially before Van Baal's (1966) work was available. Wirz (1922:39) noted, for instance:

> This is a secret society whose ceremonies consist, above all, of sexual orgies and end up with cannibalism.*. . . According to the natives, the abstinence of the novices from nutrition and administering of certain dishes that are garnished with sperm are supposed simply to excite the [sexually dominant] youth, in the usual *festivals,* so that the feasts get all the more obscene.

Some years later Haddon (1936:xxvi) summarized Wirz's data, in relation to ritual homosexual practices, thus:

> When a boy leaves the village and resides in the youth's house he comes under the care of the man to whom he is under complete obedience, and with whom he sleeps at night. There is sexual jealousy among the guardians, but when *Sosom* [spirit being] comes these proprietary rights vanish (as at ordinary feasts in the case of the women) and unrestricted sodomy prevails.

The Marind-anim material thus indicated the first glimpse of a widespread "homosexual initiation cult" (the phrase is Van Baal's [1963] extending from the Trans-Fly River tribes in the east to the Trans-Digul River Jaquai in the west.

The following general points will serve to introduce the Marind groups, which Van Baal's own essay below develops far more fully. The main point: ritualized anal homosexual practices are institutionalized on a widespread scale throughout the entire Marind area. They are associated with the Sosom cult, in particular, which is identified with the mythological figure of Sosom, an ancestral giant (Wirz 1922; Van Baal 1934, 1966:248). Homosexual anal intercourse is begun in male initiation for boys between the ages

---

*See Van Baal (chap. 3), who sees this cannibalistic act as a symbolic, rather than literal, practice.

of seven and fourteen years (Van Baal 1966:143–144). Afterward, boys live in the men's clubhouse for some six years, avoiding females and regularly engaging in anal intercourse. Initial promiscuous homosexual contacts, jealousies, and more extended liaisons are with members of the opposite moiety. Later sustained contacts are with the boy's appointed "mentor" or *binahor-evai*, who is usually his mother's brother (Van Baal 1966:113–115; 493). But, unlike with the Kimam of Frederik Hendrik Island (Serpenti 1965), there is no evidence at all that the *binahor* father—the (RH) inserter—cedes his daughter in sister exchange to the younger male.

As elsewhere, homosexual insemination here is seen as crucial to a boy's physical masculine development. Verschueren wrote early on: "In our studies of the notions underlying the [homosexual] practice F. Boelaars and I found that, everywhere, the act is seen as a necessary condition for the completion of a boy's physical development" (quoted in Van Baal 1966:494).

Compared to other (RH) groups, homosexual practices here are less secret, and women apparently know of their existence. This fact seems anomalous, considering the elaborate sexual polarity of Marind-anim society, a point pursued in my summary below. However, it may be, as Van Baal (1966:948ff.) argues, that the "phallic religion" of Marind symbolically concerns this oddity.

> The secret of the great cults is that the men must submit to the women, caught *in coitu*, powerless. . . . The source of all life, sperma, is effective only—at least, in principle—if produced in [heterosexual] copulation. These self-sufficient males need the females and they know it; only, they do not care to admit it.
>
> *(1966:949)*

Here is a very dramatic characteristic found only in Southern Irian Jaya: the efficacy of sperm used for certain (RH)-related activities must come from *heterosexual* intercourse. Homosexual activity is distinct from that, but as Van Baal (chap. 3) argues below, both types of sexual relationships must be seen as counterparts of each other.

The discrepancy between men's wanting to be self-sufficient yet needing women is associated with the act of head-hunting, which was so important in Marind-anim social reproduction. We know that head-hunting was the final incorporating initiatory rite of the Mayo cult (Van Baal 1966:740–742), and that it legitimized male adulthood. Van Baal (1966:949) goes beyond cultural facts, however, and sees a psychosocial dynamic in the men's ritual denial of women's power.

> In secret, in the celebration of the rites, they will allow their dependence and immediately afterwards go out headhunting. It is as if by that time their rage had mounted to such a pitch that they have to find an outlet for it. . . . It is fairly probable that these pent-up feelings of discomfort are, indeed, a major source of aggressiveness.[19] It is aggressiveness directed toward the innocent. Somebody has to be killed and there is no real motive for the act.
>
> *(1966:949)*

The Marind-anim were certainly regarded as among New Guinea's most ruthless headhunters from the earliest period of contact (see Haddon 1891; Baxter-Riley 1925; Wirz 1934).

Ultimately, Van Baal (1966:950–954) sees the meaning of Marind-anim ritual homosexuality as being caught up in the contradictions of their heterosexual relationships. Theirs was a society with an "ineffective" sexual segregation, with some freedom of marital choice nevertheless curtailed by sister exchange, and with promiscuity and wife-beating. And yet, "couples seem strongly attached to each other"; even in the male initiation rites, women took a part, while at other times, the sexes ceremonially battled. Other social facts inform, such as the kidnapping of children; and the associated "alarmingly low fertility rate of women. . . . [is] an indirect, but nevertheless convincing symptom of a serious imbalance in their sexual life" (Van Baal 1966:950). These conditions, in addition to the fact that men continue having homosexual intercourse throughout life, even into old age (unusual in Melanesia) suggest that "relations between the sexes are beset with [personal] conflicts and institutional controversies" (Van Baal 1966:949). The Marind-anim and related cultures thus show a complex system of variables that defy any simple causal explanation, psychological, ecological, or structural.

West of the Marind-anim, among groups occupying Frederik Hendrik Island, the north part of the Lower Digul River, and the Jaquai of the Mappi River basin, we are again confronted with

27

ritualized homosexuality. In contrast to the Marind and Boadzi, however, who are organized in patrilineal clans and moieties, these are nonunilineal descent groups. In other respects they seem like the Marind.

First to the Kimam of Frederick Hendrik Island, who lie directly west of the Marind: Serpenti (1965) has already reported pronounced ritualized anal homosexual practices among them, and his chapter 7 below is an important addition to the literature. Here I will simply place the Kimam in a broader framework. Upon initiation, a boy was placed under the charge of an older youth, who "adopted" him as his "mentor" (Serpenti 1965:162). They regularly practiced homosexual anal intercourse. "This 'mentor' is usually a classificatory elder brother from the same *pabura* (village-sector)" (Serpenti 1965:162–163). But this remarkably close relationship was unusual; mentors were often mother's younger brothers or cross-cousins, too (biological brothers were excluded). At least some aspects of ritual homosexuality and initiation were secret (ibid.:171). The magical and medicinal employment of sperm here was central to cult activities: "Everywhere on the island sperm is believed to contain great powers" (ibid.:164). Sperm is rubbed all over an initiate's body, particularly into incisions made by his mentor, to make boys "big and strong" (ibid.:165n.). Serpenti compares Kimam to Marind-anim and Keraki in these respects (see also Landtman 1927).

Kimam culture reveals the clearest relationships between sister-exchange marriage and ritual homosexuality.

> For the purpose of arousing the sperm the "mentor" has to put his betrothed [wife] at the men's disposal.[20] Immediately after the betrothal the girl goes to live with her father-in-law. At the same time the boy goes to the [men's house], for he is not allowed to see the girl. Sometimes he does not even know who she is. At this stage, however, the girl is not yet sexually mature. The [mentor's] betrothed, on the other hand is mature, but the [mentors] are not allowed to have sexual intercourse with women. As a compensation for the use of his betrothed, the [mentor] has sexual claims on the [first-stage boy-initiate] for whom his betrothed is used [i.e., older men copulate with her to collect semen to anoint this boy's body, helping to strengthen him]. Only contact with women is considered dangerous at this critical period of their lives.
>
> *(Serpenti 1965:164)*

Here we see a complex exchange of: the right of the superordinate men to have sexual intercourse with the bachelor's betrothed woman; sperm collected from her through these contacts to "grow" younger initiates; and the bachelor-mentors' right of sexual intercourse with an initiate in return. (Wives are often MBD or FZD; Serpenti 1965:124–126.) Older men continue having homosexual relationships as well as heterosexual access to the bachelor-mentor's betrothed (ibid.:167). We shall see similar cases of structural relation between marriage and (RH) below.

Next are the Jaquai, reported on linguistically by Boelaars (1950:1, 60). They are linguistically closely related to the Marind but differ from them in social organization. The Jaquai (like tribes of Frederik Hendrik Island, the Asmat, and the Mimika) are organized in nonunilineal descent groups, the Marind in patriclans. They are separated by the lower Digul River area (see map 2). We can locate the Jaquai along an affluent of the Digul River north of its right bank, whereas the Marind-anim live at some distance south of its left bank. In spite of differences in social organization, though, among the Jaquai, (RH) is prominent. We are safest to quote Boelaars's (1981:84) most recent report:

> A father can order his son to go and sleep during the night with a certain man who will commit pederasty with him. The father will receive compensation for this.[21] If this happens regularly between a man and the same boy, a stable relationship arises, comparable to that between a father and son, *mo-e* or anus father and *mo-maq*, anus son (father = *nae*, son = *maq*). Such a boy is allowed to consider that man's daughter as his sister and she will be "awarded" to him as his exchange sister for his future marriage.

Here we have perhaps the most extreme instance of an (RH)/ marriage correlation known in Melanesia: the insertee has the right to use his male partner's daughter for marriage exchange. In the marriage game, therefore, we can identify the Jaquai and the Kimam as being culturally very similar. Yet again, in significant aspects of social organization, both groups differ from the Marind groups even though all practice ritualized homosexuality.

What do we find north of these westerly Irian Jaya groups? The data are mostly useless. Along the western coast, only one group, the Asmat, is definitely known to practice homosexual activities.

But even here the situation is cloudy. Although the allusion is skimpy, Van Amelsvoort (1964:43) states of the Asmat: "Homosexual relationships are [present but] less institutionalized than among the neighboring Jaquai people." The same is probably true for the Casuarina Coast peoples. Nothing else is known, except that the northern neighbors of the Asmat—the Mimikans—do not practice ritualized homosexuality (J. Pouwer, personal communication to J. Van Baal; see also Pouwer [1955]).

Farther north and inland east, ritualized homosexuality is also absent. It is not found in the Wissel Lakes area among the Kapauku (Van Baal, personal communication). Farthest north at Vogelkop (the Bird's Head), Elmberg (1955:88) states that there is "no homosexuality" among the Mejbrat tribe. Likewise, at Geelvink Bay among the Waropen people, Held (1957:87–88) notes: "Among men anal sodomy also occurs, but according to my informants this only happens when they are drunk." All available information confirms that Held's statement refers to homosexuality being treated as a culturally standardized attribution of deviance (e.g., like madness) which should be taken on face value. The Waropen do not have *ritualized* homosexuality.[22]

Finally, Highlands Irian Jaya: It appears certain that ritualized homosexuality is completely absent here. Heider (1979:79) notes: "There is no sign at all of homosexual relations" among the Grand Valley Dani. In the Star Mountains to the east, extending to the international border, ritualized homosexuality is clearly absent (Hylkema 1974). (Here we see confirmation of the absence of RH in the adjacent Telefomin tribes, noted below.) Moreover, there is no indication of institutionalized homosexuality in the hill-dwelling tribes south of these mountains (J. Van Baal, personal communication).

NORTHEASTERN IRIAN JAYA • The only other reports of institutionalized homosexuality come from the northeastern part of the territory. The one clear and unequivocable report concerns the Humboldt Bay villages, due east of the Waropen. Ritual cult houses (*Karawari*) are prominent here. K. W. Galis confirmed older reports of ritualized homosexuality there:

> The boys [initiates] receive food once a day, at 9:00 P.M. They have to wait for it, and all the time they are teased. An important part

is played by a boy's mother's brother. He has the right to let the boy take any thinkable posture and to let him stand that way. He also has the right to commit sodomy with the boy, which he does openly and apparently repeatedly. The act is, obviously, an important part of the initiation ritual (it is said, inter alia, that it is done to let the boys grow). Another pastime is that the older men walk around in the temple [the *Karawari* house] playing with their genitals [masturbating?]. The novices are forbidden on pain of death, to laugh.

(*Galis 1955:190*)

Interestingly enough, Galis also noted that these ritual activities are necessary for the boys to learn how to play ritual flutes (see Herdt 1982*a*). The Humboldt Bay complex strikingly compares with that of other groups already described.

Yet, the combination of the Karawari cult houses and homosexual activity is limited to this group. Karawari houses are found as far away as the Sentani Lake area, much farther east. However, Wirz (1928) wrote that no form of homosexuality played a role in initiation there. The same is true of the Sarmi people, somewhat west of Humboldt Bay, whose Karawari cult houses are found as far west as the right bank of the Mamberao River (J. Van Baal, personal communication).

The Mamberamo River tribes are the only remaining Irian Jaya case. The situation in the early literature is murky. M. Moszkowski, an amateur explorer and ethnographer, lived for some eight months with the Kaowerawédj, one of the hill tribes of the Mamberamo River. Moszkowski (1911:339) claims to have seen the initiations, and he states that boys are initiated into the cult house at age ten. His astonishing report reads in part as follows:

Unmarried men live together in the men's house. The origin of the men's house is apparently to be found in certain efforts on the part of the men to emancipate themselves from the tyranny of women. One immediate consequence of these efforts is that the worst orgies of a homosexual kind are celebrated in the men's house. The Papuans seem not to have the slightest modesty in this regard. Not only were obscenities uttered in our presence . . . but also mutual masturbation was directly marked and homosexual acts were indulged in.

(*Moszkowski 1911:339*)

31

This paper and this particular passage, which has such an absolute ring of factuality about it, was cited by the old sexologists as fact (see Ellis 1936:20; Karsch-Haack 1911:528–529; Reik 1946:155). But Moszkowski's data, coming from one who *was* a popularizer (and who was probably stimulated by the earlier sensation of the Russian Mikloucho-Maclay's [1975] work), has never been confirmed.

Moszkowski's findings were disputed by J. P. K. Van Eekhoud who investigated the Kaowerawédj in 1939. The natives denied the occurrence of ritualized homosexuality not only among themselves but also among their friendly neighbors and enemies (Van Eekhoud 1962:50f.). Furthermore, in more recent, related work, G. Oosterwal has never mentioned ritualized homosexuality, neither east among the nearby Tor, a coastal people northwest of the Mamberamo (Oosterwal 1961), nor among the Upper Mamberamo villages (Oosterwal 1967). I think Oosterwal's report suggests the absence of (RH) here: he noted important facts such as the ritual use of transvestism (cf. the Mejbrat, Marind-anim, etc.) and the months-long supervision of initiates under their mother's brothers' supervision (Oosterwal 1961:241–242; 1967:184, 188). Although we cannot completely rule out the possibility that social change had eliminated homosexual activities in the area, the total evidence makes that unlikely. At the very least, then, Moszkowski's observations about male emancipation and female tyranny uncannily mirror the popular ideology of his day.[23] At the worst, his reports were fabrications. We may assume that (RH) simply does not here occur east of Humboldt Bay.

But how far east is it absent? Ritual complexes that seemingly parallel Humboldt Bay Karawari cults traditionally extended along the north coast of Papua New Guinea. Yet the occurrence of homosexuality is not known. Should not we expect historical and cultural continuities here, say, along the lines of Wurm's (1975:940–953) Trans-New Guinea Phylum migrations? Unfortunately, the concrete evidence for ritualized homosexuality must be culled from poor sources (e.g., Neuhauss 1911). And what of the Sepik River region? We shall later examine these questionable cases.

To summarize: Ritual homosexuality in Irian Jaya is a lowlands phenomena, concentrated along the southern coast. The related social units are numerous; they represent tremendous linguistic and cultural diversity. Yet, we are on safe ground in arguing that ritualized homosexuality, as part of a pervasive ritual complex, is virtually universal west of the Trans-Fly River, throughout the Morehead district, across the international border, to Frederik Hendrik Island, including the adjacent coastal fringe areas. Initiation rites and head-hunting (usually including cannibalism) were also pervasive among these groups. Though they can be defined essentially as culturally cognate societies, we cannot ignore differences among them. For instance, the Marind-anim: Van Baal (personal communication) believes they were "unique in Southwest Papua; that they have more in common with the cultures of Arnhem Land [Australia] than with others of New Guinea, except, possibly, the Elema of the Papuan Gulf" (e.g., see Williams 1940a). Again, this Australian parallelism has long been advocated (Van Baal 1963).[24] I shall later return to the diffusionist arguments for Melanesia. For the moment, let us ignore these infraregional cultural differences, however, and refer to this vast area as but one cultural tradition, the Southwestern New Guinea coastal fringe (or SWNG).

RECENT PAPUA NEW GUINEA WORK

The ethnography of the 1970s has revealed two new subregions in which ritualized homosexuality is prominent and probably universal. The Great Papuan Plateau (politically located in the southern Highlands Province of Papua New Guinea) saw anthropological work begin only in the mid-1960s. The plateau is relatively small, with small populations numbering only in the hundreds, who live in close proximity. They are "fringe-area" peoples, who hunt and exploit sago. These groups belong to one cultural tradition, however, and I think it may be argued that they should properly be considered cognate to the Southwestern New Guinea ritual complex (e.g., Boadzi, Marind-anim). The other new reports come from the Anga peoples (formerly called "Kukukuku"; politically located in the Eastern Highlands and Gulf provinces). They are diverse, with nine different languages and at least thirteen different tribal groups spread across a vast area numbering perhaps 100,000 people (see Gajdusek et al. 1972; Lloyd 1973). The Anga may eventually be seen as a cognate tradition of the SWNG systems too.

GREAT PAPUAN PLATEAU • On the plateau itself, four groups have been reported upon: Etoro, Kaluli, Onabasalu, and Bedamini. The Kaluli are best known from the works of E. L. Schieffelin (1976, 1982), who has written on their homosexual practices. The Etoro (Kelly 1976, 1977), are less documented in this regard. Thomas Ernst has not as yet published on homosexual activities among Onabasalu. Arve Sørum (1982) has mentioned homosexuality before on the Bedamini, and his chapter below is a new and important addition to the literature. Here, I shall examine the general relationship among these groups, highlighting the Kaluli in particular.

Raymond Kelly (1977) has provided a valuable schematic contrast between the Plateau tribal groups in terms of ritual and sexual techniques. I cite it in full:

> The Etoro, Onabasulu, and Kaluli culturally differentiate themselves from each other in a number of ways, but most particularly by their customs of male initiation. All three tribes share the belief that boys do not become physically mature men as a result of natural processes. Growth and attainment of physiological maturation is contingent on the cultural process of initiation, and this entails insemination because it is semen which ensures growth and development. According to the Etoro, semen does not occur naturally in boys and must be "planted" in them. If one does not plant sweet potato vines then no sweet potatoes will come up in the gardens and, likewise, semen must be planted in youths if they are to possess it as men (and indeed they do not possess it as boys). Moreover, all aspects of manliness are consequences of this acquisition. Although all three tribes share roughly similar views concerning the necessity of insemination, each differs from the others concerning the appropriate mode of transmission. The Etoro achieve this through oral intercourse, the Kaluli through anal intercourse, and the Onabasulu through masturbation and smearing of the semen over the bodies of the initates . . . (Ernst, personal communication, 1972). Inasmuch as the members of each tribe become men in different ways, they are preeminently different kinds of men, culturally distinct beings at the most fundamental level. The Kaluli are traditional enemies of the Etoro, and the Etoro particularly revile them for their initiatory practices which are regarded as totally disgusting. (The feeling is probably mutual.) The Onabasulu, on the other hand, are closer to the Etoro in this area of belief and some boys of that tribe have undergone initiation at Etoro seclusion houses. Ernst (personal communication, 1972) reports that the Onabasulu pre-

viously followed Etoro custom and have distinguished themselves in this respect only in recent generations.

(Kelly 1977:16)

The neighboring Bedamini also practice homosexual fellatio (Sørum, chap. 8), which is relatively rare (cf. below on Anga groups).[25] Cultural variation in these homosexual techniques is clearly related to the organization of ethnic identity, as Kelly hints. But it is not obvious how cultural arrangements and beliefs are functionally or symbolically correlated with such divergent homoerotic modes. Here is a research problem worthy of comparative study.

Both Kaluli and Etoro emphasize the need for boys to be inseminated to grow and become masculine. Yet they appear to vary considerably in the duration and cultural timing of these activities. Among the Etoro, "a youth is continually inseminated from about age ten until he reaches his early mid-twenties" (Kelly 1976:45). This long period follows from the belief that males do not "naturally" make semen and "moreover, all aspects of manliness are seen as consequences of this acquisition" (Kelly 1976:45).[26] Kaluli initiation and homosexual activities, in contrast, seem more truncated:

> Semen is also necessary for young boys to attain full growth to manhood. . . . They need a boost, as it were. When a boy is eleven or twelve years old, he is engaged for several months in homosexual intercourse with a healthy older man chosen by his father. (This is always an in-law or unrelated person, since the same notions of incestuous relations apply to little boys as to marriageable women.) Men point to the rapid growth of adolescent youths, the appearance of peach fuzz beards, and so on, as the favorable results of this child-rearing practice.
>
> *(Schieffelin 1976:124)*

Here we see that the duration of homosexual practices in the male life cycle of these two groups is quite different. We can certainly guess that the effects of this difference—years versus months of (RH) activity—would be significant, both in institutional and individual terms. (It is too bad neither ethnographer has addressed the meaning of this difference in comparative or regional study.)

What conclusions can be drawn from the Papuan Plateau case? Here again the ethnographers differ. While Kelly (1977:16) and

Sørum (1982) argue that homosexual practices should be seen as part of the "cultural process of initiation" in Plateau groups, Schieffelin (1982) has recently described the Kaluli context, the *bau a* ceremonial lodge, as an "alternative to an initiation program." He also says of their homosexual practices: "Certainly there is no ritualization about the act itself" (Schieffelin 1982:177–178), by which he seems to mean that the homoerotic acts are not framed by ritual or they occur also in secular situations. One fact that apparently supports this view is the nonobligatory character of homosexual practices: only certain males engage in them, and Kaluli stress choice in the matter. Here we have a distinct contrast with most groups reported on in this book, though I would argue that Kaluli are but a variant of the (RH) pattern.[27] In these groups, warfare also reinforces an aggressive ethos among men. Schieffelin's (1982) analysis sees hunting and homosexuality, and symbolic relationships to spirit beings, as interrelated elements in the social control of male transition from adolescence to the assumption of adult marital and sexual bonds in Kaluli society. He thus argues that "homosexual activity seems to have a certain aura of the profane or impure about it" (ibid.:178). On marriage, Etoro reveal a pattern strikingly similar to that of SWNG groups. "The ideal [homosexual] inseminator . . . is a boy's true sister's husband or her betrothed; brother and sister will then receive semen from the same man (ideally a FMBS) and be, in a sense, co-spouses to him" (Kelly 1976:52). (See also my summary, chap. 4, and chap. 9.) In Papuan Plateau groups, then, the male belief in the magical growth-power of homosexual insemination is stressed and symbolically elaborated in other domains, consistent with the above material on Southwestern Papuan groups.

Finally, the Nomad River area should be mentioned here. This region extends in both directions south of the Papuan Plateau, in the watershed of the Strickland gorge. Since it is geographically intermediate between the Plateau and the Upper Fly River area and has similar ecological parameters, we should expect to find similar homosexual practices. This area is still poorly described, though Shaw (n.d.) mentions "homosexual joking" among the Samo people. Nonetheless, it seems unclear whether actual homosexual contacts occur among Samo. Southwest of the Nomad area, however, Bruce Knauft describes widespread and obligatory male homosexual activity among the Gebusi people very similar to that of the Great Papuan Plateau,[28] for example, in the context of bawdy joking at spirit seances and ritual feasts (cf. Sørum, chap. 8). Homosexual fellatio "occurs for all males between 14 and 25 years of age." And Knauft explains: "The explicit reason for insemination is 'to make boys become big' *(wa kawala)*, so that they can be initiated. Indeed, this same term is the proper name of the initiation ceremonies, these being the public celebration of the 'bigness' the young men have attained." I expect that eventual publication of the Gebusi ethnography will confirm their similarity to cultural traditions of the Papuan Plateau, the Bedamini and Etoro in particular.

ANGA SOCIETIES • The Anga are a congeries of tribes spreading from the Papuan Gulf through the Eastern Highlands ranges of the Kratkes, east of the Lamari River. Some of these groups number into the thousands, and most of them are unstudied (see table 1.1). B. Blackwood (e.g., 1939) did the first ethnographic work in the Papuan hinterland near Menyamya in the 1930s; H. Fischer (1968) next worked farther inland in the 1950s. But the work of neither is well known. Colin Simpson, a flashy journalist[29]—wrote a popular account in the fifties (Simpson 1953). New Guinea folklore depicted the Anga generally as fierce headhunters, thieves, and homosexuals. Little else was known about this region[30] until the work of M. Godelier on the Baruya (1971, 1976), and my work on the Sambia, neighboring Eastern Highland fringe-dwelling groups, both immigrant groups from the Menyamya area who fled a great war, they say, some 150 to 200 years ago (Godelier 1969; Herdt 1981:22–23). Along with Lloyd (1973) and Gajdusek et al. (1972), I would argue that the Anga comprise many different social units of the same cultural tradition. They were all enmeshed in war; hunting and shifting tuber agriculture were pervasive; and initiation was obligatory.

Blackwood's early work on the Langimar and Nauti of the Upper Watut River* illustrates the complexities of superficial reports on sex in New Guinea and the difficulties in reinterpreting them. She

---

*Edited by Hallpike (1978).

described these groups as evincing "greater secretiveness" compared with the Buka whom she had previously studied (B. Blackwood 1935), adding that "sexual interests play a minor part" for Anga, "whose main concerns are food and fighting" (Hallpike 1978:153). Although Hallpike (1978:153 n. 62) approvingly footnotes Fischer's (1968) account of the Western Jeghuje—a neighboring people—in support of these views, Mimica (1981) questions its applicability to the Central Jeghuje (and, I would also add, to the Eastern Jeghuje, bordering the Sambia, based on my reconnaissance fieldwork there). Blackwood tried also to learn if homosexual practices occurred during the ritual seclusion of boys in the forest after initiation. Mimica (1981:226), in review of a relevant passage, derides Blackwood:

> Miss Blackwood was limited by her sex and bold naivety in approaching the matter of the male secret cult. The following immortal passage rather aptly expresses it: "In answer to the direct question, whether sodomy[31] occurred between the boys and their 'big brothers' while they were in the bush, they said that it did not"
> (Hallpike, p. 127).

Did these groups thus practice ritualized homosexuality? Mimica (1981) hints that they did. Hallpike (1978:127 n. 45) cites D. C. Gajdusek to the effect that "initiates" (groups unspecified) engage in homosexual practices because of prolonged periods of isolation from women. (Regarding the purely behavioral explanation of these practices, see the summary.) Yet Hallpike (1978:153 n. 62) later reaffirms Blackwood's remark about absent homosexuality, this time by citing Fischer (1968)—who has not reported it[32]— and concludes that Gajdusek's earlier report seems "uncharacteristic of the Kukukuku as a whole." No real evidence is thus cited in support of this claim. It is certainly false.

Godelier's work among the Baruya began in the late 1960s. In an important recent essay he describes social and sexual aspects of Baruya homosexuality:

> In the men's house, initiates live in pairs of different ages. They stroke each other, masturbate, suck each other; but sodomy [anal coitus] was unknown until the arrival of policemen and soldiers belonging to tribes that practiced it. Girls stroke each other, but

we know little about what actually goes on among them.* Homosexuality apparently disappears after marriage.

(Godelier 1976:15)

He describes further the intricate ideas and customs that inform
reproduction and male/female relationships. The Baruya view heterosexuality as a force that potentially threatens the entire social
order.

> Sex is dangerous, but the danger comes mainly from the woman,
> who constantly threatens to rob man of his integrity and above all
> of the synthesis of all his virtues which he calls strength. But the
> woman is dangerous too because, whether she likes it or not, she
> serves as a vector for the evil powers and hostile forces that populate
> the invisible side of the world. What is in fact threatened is the
> entire social and cosmic order. Sexual intercourse, therefore, is an
> evil under any circumstances, but a necessary evil, since homosexual
> relations are fruitless.
>
> *(Godelier 1976:20)*

How do these views of homosexuality and heterosexuality cohere?

Godelier's report provides important symbolic contextualiza-
tion of homosexual activites in another Anga tribe. I would argue,
however, that Godelier here blurs the natives' and observers' viewpoints on sexual contacts. It is true that homosexual contacts are
"fruitless" in the procreative sense, since sperm does not create
offspring in boys. But his observer model does not fully account
for homosexual practices from the natives' point of view: they *are*
fruitful given the belief in the magical power of semen to "grow"
and "strengthen" boys, who will socially reproduce the village
warriorhood in the next generation (Herdt, chap. 4; cf. Godelier
1982*a*). Given the symbolic power of male/male insemination in
facilitating boys' reproductive competence, the "dangers" of women
take on a new meaning. If we turn now to the nearby Sambia,
certain contrasts will help fill out what can presently be said of
the Anga case. Since my work is recent and sketched in chapter
4, I shall cover general themes here.

Among the Sambia, homosexual activities are believed vital to
psychosocial and biological development. All males are initiated

---

*See also Godelier (1982*a*:80ff.).

into an age-graded secret society, coordinated with local patrilineal descent groups. Through prolonged homosexual fellatio, sperm creates growth and strength in males between ages seven through fourteen. Only older and younger unmarried males engage in homosexual intercourse, which is tied to the symbolic meanings of sacred flutes (Herdt 1982*a*). In this symbolic system, flutes are equated with mothers' breasts and penises, and semen is compared to breast milk. All homosexual contacts are asymmetrical, and boys must not situationally reverse roles. At puberty, they are elevated through initiation into the fellated-bachelor role, when they appropriately inseminate younger males until marriage in their late teens or early twenties. But after they have fathered a child, men are expected to give up homosexual activity, and most of them do so, preferring heterosexual activites with their wives (cf. Herdt 1980). Homosexual activities among females are unknown.

Several broad patterns link Sambia to other (RH) groups noted throughout this chapter. First, as an institutional complex, Sambia practice intitation as a means of sex-role socialization, and induction and recruitment into village-based warriorhoods. Warfare has been widespread and destructive within and between Sambia, Baruya, and their neighbors. Warfare and hunting are the chief secular contexts of public masculine performance. Initiation is the main sacred and secret context for demonstrating male "strength." Second, sexual polarity is intense and permeates virtually all social arenas and cultural domains. There is a concomitantly strict sexual division of labor. Third, residential arrangements separate all initiates from all females, initiates residing in men's houses, married men, women, and children living in women's houses (albeit divided into "male" and "female" spaces). Children are primarily socialized by their mothers and other caretakers until initiation (males) or marriage (females). Fourth, women have low social status, and men dominate public affairs. Fifth, Sambia emphasize patrilineality and patrifiliation at the expense of other kin and social bonds, which include all sexual relationships. All persons outside the natal hamlet are seen as potentially hostile. Hence, women are imported for marriage, and homosexual partners are from hostile hamlets. Sixth, men fear both depletion and pollution from their wives and, in general, from all reproductively active females. Seventh, sexual intercourse is carefully regulated and monitored through numerous taboos, institutional arrangements, values, and norms, including long postpartum taboos that result in prolonged mother/infant attachment bonds. Finally, semen is treated as a scarce resource that circulates in the population pool through both homosexual and heterosexual contacts. The "value" of semen thus rationalizes—"naturalizes" and "mystifies"—all sexual relationships (cf. Keesing 1982). Marriage and homosexual activities are therefore inseparably linked through semen exchange, in a manner paralleling that of Kimam, Etoro, and others (Herdt, chap. 4). Ultimately, the low population density of the Sambia and their warring relationships must be seen as the behavioral conditions that contributed to this cultural patterning of semen ingestion and (RH).

My impression is that this complex of factors applies in similar systemic relationship to all Anga groups of the Eastern Highlands, which includes many different tribes. Furthermore, this same ritual complex apparently occurs through the Menyamya area and probably extends south to the Papuan coast (although this latter suggestion must remain a conjecture for the present).[33]

QUESTIONABLE CASES

It seems clear now that ritualized homosexual practices are absent from the New Guinea Highlands, except among the fringe-area Anga groups just described. (Remember, though, that these mountain Anga groups are immigrants from the Papuan hinterland who should be seen as shareres in SWNG cultural traditions.) No homosexual activity is known from the Western Highlands or adjacent Chimbu areas, which encompass many different social units of different cultural traditions (see Lindenbaum, chap. 9). Likewise, it is absent among the Maring (Buchbinder 1973:85). K. E. Read (1980b), the key early ethnographer of Eastern Highlands groups, reported only ostentatious ritual masturbation in the context of nosebleeding ceremonies. More recently, he has questioned whether individual homosexual activity occurred among the Gahuku Gama; but it seems clear that it was not institutionalized (Read 1980b, app. I). He extends his observations and relates them to (RH) groups in a retrospective account below (see below, chap. 5). Meigs (1976) has noted a male ideology of male pregnancy and related beliefs among the Eastern Highlands' Hua, though no mention is made of homosexuality. Even among the Awa and Tairora groups bordering the west bank of the Lamari, near Anga groups, ritualized homosexuality is absent (Terence E. Hays, David Boyd, personal communications). The nearby South Fore may have secretly practiced (RH), though it is not reported anthropologically, so this suggestion remains doubtful.[34] (Keesing [1982:10], however, reports that one ethnographer in this central part of the Eastern Highlands has noted homosexual practices but has not published these data in respect of local people's wishes.)

The only report of *any* Highlands homosexual activity is from DuToit (1975), on the Eastern Highlands' Akuna.

> We do find a form of homosexual play. This is referred to as *iyer-anenu*, meaning simply "play," as children play with marbles or any other objects. In this homosexual play among boys, one will assume the active and another the passive role, while the first places his penis in the anus of the other. This seems to be relatively common among boys as they become increasingly segregated from their female age-mates, and informants explain that it usually continues until the sixteenth or seventeenth year of life. Among girls there is something similar, in which two girls associate intimately with one another caressing and petting the breasts and genitals of the other. In this homosexual play they assume the position of intercourse with one lying on the other. In neither case, it seems, is orgasm reached.
>
> *(DuToit 1975:220)*

We are informed that Akuna parents disapprove of homosexual play, which is regarded as "dangerous," though we are not told why. These activities occur out of sight of adults, who can only warn against them. Nothing else is said about their context or meaning. Nonetheless, if DuToit's report is taken at face value, it compares with that of East Bay (Davenport 1965, 1977) and indicates a form of homosexual activity that is an ad hoc, if illicit, pattern in Akuna sexual development. The Akuna are doubly aberrant because females also engage in homosexual activities (even if orgasm reportedly does not occur).

DuToit's report is anomalous; and Akuna homosexual practices are not supported by any institutional forces. This fragment thus reveals homosexual activity in Akuna but, until data are shown otherwise, not ritualized homosexuality.

No other Highlands instances are known, supporting the generalized and strong correlation between lowlands groups and ritualized homosexuality.

ADMIRALTY ISLANDS (MANUS) • The Manus Island case is dubious, but Margaret Mead's (1968) remarks are sufficiently suggestive to merit mention. Her data fall under the domain of what she called "variations of the sexual picture."

> Homosexuality occurs in both sexes, but rarely. The natives recognize it, and take only a laughing count of it, if it occurs between unmarried boys, in which cases it is sometimes exploited publicly in the boys' houses. Sodomy [anal intercourse?] is the only form of which I received any account.
>
> *(Mead 1968:126)*

This passage seems puzzling. For the natives to "recognize" homosexual practices and "laugh" at them (in public?) among bachelors—who nonetheless "publicly exploit" them—is somewhat inexplicable.

We can speculate about the historical context of such statements. Let us remember that Manus had sustained years of pacification and missionary activity well before Mead's fieldwork in the 1920s. Perhaps, then, seen as statements by acculturated natives to a European woman, the above passage might be interpreted as a means of admitting, yet simultaneously denying, homosexual practices, which were formerly practiced but then stopped (see below, on the Sepik Iatmul).

This suggestion remains purely speculative, however. No evidence suggests *ritualized* homosexuality. It is only the broader cultural pattern of explicit reports on (RH) in distant off-lying islands such as New Britain or the Humboldt Bay area that should make us question Manus Island in relation to Northern New Guinea as a whole.

THE SEPIK • The case for ritualized homosexuality in the vast Sepik River area is weakest of all. For others (see Keesing 1982:11n.) as for me, the great Sepik with its numerous anthropological studies for over sixty years remains an enigma in regard to the presence or absence of such practices.[35] Despite contemporary stories from New Guineasts[36] and the folklore of New Guineans themselves to the contrary, I have not been able to uncover a single clear-cut ethnographic report of (RH) from the entire area. Nevertheless, my doubts persist; so I shall here risk a reinterpretation.

Consider the following fragment from Bateson's (1958) classic *Naven,* which remains (along with the texts of Thurnwald [1916] and Mead [1935]) a well-known work from the Sepik.

> During the early period of initiation when the novices are being mercilessly bullied and hazed, they are spoken of as "wives" of the initiators, *whose penes they are made to handle.* Here it seems that the linguistic usage indicates an ethological analogy between the relationship of man and wife and that of initiator and novice.
>
> *(Bateson 1958:131, my emphasis)*

What does Bateson's observation suggest? My first question concerns the kind of data it represents. We know (Bateson 1932, 1958) that Iatmul initiation was gone by the time Bateson arrived; therefore, this passage must be from an informant's retrospective account. In the absence of ritual observations, then, should we interpret the boy's "handling" of the initiator's (probably MB) penis as an allusion to sexual, not merely symbolic, behavior? Perhaps; and here follows a speculative rethinking of the Iatmul case.

The *naven* ceremony itself, as is well known, concerned the mother's brother's "demeaning" act of "rubbing the cleft of his buttocks down the length of his *laua*'s [sister's son's] leg, a sort of sexual salute" (Bateson 1958:13). Such public displays required prestations in return. Does this act also represent or signify a homosexual component? Possibly: we know that sexual polarity and the subordination of women was marked in Iatmul society, that men were traditionally fierce headhunters concerned with maintaining a warriorhood and, through initiation, with instilling pride in the male ethos. We know also that boys had to stringently avoid women by hiding in capes after initiation (Bateson 1932:438). Furthermore, the fearsome gate to the initiation enclosure, represented by a crocodile jaw, was called "clitoris gate" (Bateson 1932:282), and men routinely referred to an "anal clitoris, an anatomical feature frequently imagined by the Iatmul" (Bateson 1932:279; see also Hauser-Schaeublin 1977).

A few years later, Margaret Mead described the Iatmul scene (from 1938 fieldnotes) in these ambiguous terms:

> In the men's group there is loud, over-definite masculine behavior, continuous use of verbs that draw their imagery from phallic attack on men and women alike. But there is also a very strong taboo on any display of passivity, and there is no development of male homosexuality within the society. The slightest show of weakness or of receptivity is regarded as a temptation, and men walk about, often comically carrying their small round wooden stools fixed firmly against their buttocks. A male child from any outside village or tribe becomes a ready victim, and Iatmul work-boys are said to become active homosexuals when they meet men from other tribes away at work. But within the group, the system holds . . . so that his capacity and temptation to introduce sex into his relationship with other males is very strong and yet kept closely in control.
>
> *(Mead 1949:95–96)*

How shall we view this report? Since Bateson has stated that the Iatmul male cult was in a state of "decay" by 1930, the men "fatalist" that "the mechanism of initiatory age grades had broken down" because "all the available young men had left the village to work for Europeans" (Bateson 1932:275), we wonder how Mead judged that there was "no male homosexuality." A possibility is that Iatmul had *secret* homosexual practices that were never revealed to ethnographers or had been already abandoned by the time Bateson and Mead arrived. Another problem is definitional: Mead ethnocentrically saw "homosexuality" as passive, effeminate, and deviant lifelong sexual contacts with the same sex.[37] On these terms one finds virtually no homosexual behavior anywhere in Melanesia. If the Iatmul practiced secret homosexuality, it almost surely did not take Mead's form.

The Iatmul may have thus practiced secret homosexuality in the context of traditional initiation (see also Layard 1959:107); moreover, there are two additional points made by Bateson (for other purposes) that support this view.

First, Bateson (1958:81–82) suggested that the structural and symbolic aspects of Iatmul marriage explained the "sexual gesture" in the naven act. Why should MB present buttocks to ZSo?

> Such conduct is of course not characteristic of a mother, but I have a casual mention in mythology of *a man who rubbed his buttocks on the leg of the man who was marrying his sister.* If we bear in mind the identification of a man with his sister, this conduct is comprehensible. . . . The man expressed his relationship to his sister's husband by ritually making a sexual gesture in which he identified himself with his sister. . . . For the sake of clarity we may state these identifications as if mother's brother were speaking, viz. "I am my sister" and "my nephew is my sister's husband." If now we consider these two identifications simultaneously it is perfectly "logical" for the *wau* to offer himself sexually to the boy, because he is the boy's wife. . . . Upon this hypothesis the *wau's* exclamation, *"Lan men to!"* "Husband thou indeed!" becomes understandable.
>
> *(Bateson 1958:81–82, emphasis mine)*

The subordinate position of being a prospective younger brother-in-law is converted via ritual action into a symbolic game. This game—the naven—denies the shame and submission of ZSo (Bateson 1958:270). Whether naven is merely ritual play seems debatable; but as Handelman (1979:181–182) argues convincingly, it seems like a superb mechanism for maintaining "the correctness of the complementary mode" between MB and ZSo. The wife-taker's shame-laden position is stressed in Bateson's (1958:132) remark, "Each of these elements of culture is based upon the basic assumption that the passive role in sex is shameful." I would go further than Bateson and argue, *mutatis mutandis,* that the symbolic structure of naven disguises the probability that the MB provides a wife for ZSo who, in the context of initiation, provides homosexual service to his "uncle." The shame-filled submission of that secret homosexuality is symbolically inverted and thereby expressed through the naven act in public. The *wau's* "sexual gesture" may be limited to the Sepik area, as Bateson (1958:82) thought. Yet the occurrence of homosexual service to the wife-givers by the younger initiate seems marked elsewhere (e.g., Kimam, Jaquai, Etoro, Sambia, etc.), in line with this reinterpretation.

Second, early on Bateson noted a cultural parallel that is germane to my reinterpretation. He believed that tribes of the Lower and Middle Sepik and of the Fly River all showed a "broad similarity of culture" (Bateson 1932:255). He names the Kiwai, the Marind-anim, and the Banaro,[38] suggesting parallels between because they all had large villages, were headhunters, initiated, and built great ceremonial cult houses. It is interesting to note that these groups (should we exclude the Banaro?) practiced (RH). In the summary, I will return to the Iatmul as a possible instance of "mythical homosexuality," in Layard's sense.

Elsewhere in the Sepik region, only two other groups are worth mentioning as questionable cases. Wogeo Island lies just off the Sepik mainland, and its ritual cult is similar to those of Iatmul, New Britain, and perhaps Humboldt Bay. Male initiation involved ordeals, sacred flutes, and spirit impersonations. Male fears of female menstrual pollution, with associated sexual polarity, were intense. In relation to these thematic features we are told:

> The popular attitude might well be thought to encourage homo-sexuality, especially as this is allegedly common among neighboring peoples of the [Sepik area] mainland.* Yet in fact homosexual relations, apart from mutual masturbation by pairs of youths, are rare in the village.
>
> *(Hogbin 1970:90)*

The extensiveness, meaning, or cultural context of such "mutual masturbation" is not clear from this report (nor from earlier Hogbin [1945–1946]). Is such reciprocal male/male sexual contact like the East Bay situation (Davenport 1965) noted above? We cannot know; so these fragments are insufficient to include Wogeo in our (RH) distribution.

One other Middle Sepik people, the Kwoma, merit a side note. Whiting (1941:51) states that they did not practice homosexuality, despite homosexual "games" and "teasing," which involved "very little genital contact" as such. In the same passage he remarks, "Sodomy [anal coitus?] is believed to be unnatural and revolting, and informants were unanimous in saying that anyone who would submit to it must be a 'ghost' and not a man." Presumably this was in response to Whiting's query. (Whom and what did he ask? The Sambia, incidentally, who practice fellatio, say the same thing about anal intercourse.) Whiting's statement raises further problems by his odd aside that "this sanction theoretically applied only

---

*Another ethnic attribution? What groups? Says who?

to *the person who played the passive role"* (ibid; emphasis mine). It is well known (e.g., see Sørum, chap. 7) beyond the Sepik that the sexual role of the homosexual insertee is frequently stigmatized in tribal societies, whereas the inserter role is seen as masculine and even honorable, not stigmatized (see Carrier 1980*a*). Here, as with the Iatmul, we may see a symbolic emphasis on the phallic fantasy of anal penetration, as opposed to actual homosexual relations. But this case is too vague and cannot be counted in our sample.

Explicit statements by other ethnographers nevertheless make it clear that homosexual practices are absent in other Sepik societies (e.g., Mead 1935:293 on the Mountain Arapesh and Mundugumor; Tuzin 1980:47 on the Ilahita Arapesh). Likewise it is entirely unreported from the Torricelli Mountains and the West Sepik area, the Upper Sepik, and, more distantly, both south and west, it is absent from the Telefomin area (Fitz John Poole, personal communication).

A HISTORICAL NEXUS?

What can be said of the historical-geographic relationship between Melanesian groups that practice ritualized homosexuality? Although I was initially opposed to speculative diffusionist arguments when I began this study, the data surveyed above suggest prehistoric cultural linkages among (RH) groups which have not yet been explicated and cannot therefore be ignored.

The accumulating evidence indicates that we are not only confronted in these Melanesian cultures with similar cultural and ecological systems; I propose that we are also faced with an ancient ritual complex that diffused through a vast area of lowland and fringe-area Melanesia, perhaps 10,000 years ago or less. Moreover, with the exception of some off-lying island societies of Northeastern Melanesia, all known cases of ritualized homosexuality are identified with non-Austronesian ("Papuan") languages (see table 1.1). These factors in turn are correlated with other regional attributes, the prehistorical and systemic bases of which we may consider.

Ritualized homosexuality is a lowlands phenomenon. The extant data show conclusively that these ritual practices, in one form or

another, are confined to a few off-lying islands of Eastern Melanesia and the New Britain area, to the Ai'i, the lowlands of the
Papuan Gulf, the entire Fly River basin, the Anga, the Great Papuan
Plateau, Southeastern Irian Jaya, and the coastal fringe of Northeastern Irian Jaya. On the entire island of New Guinea, the only
certain Highlands area with (RH) practices is the Anga (e.g., Sambia, Baruya), migrants from the Papuan hinterland. Both the Anga
and the Great Papuan Plateau groups are marginal fringe groups
adjacent to, but not typical of, the Central Highlands cordillera.
The questionable cases, which I shall exclude from this review, are
not exceptions to their geographic distributional pattern, aside
from Akuna, which is too weak to utilize as an ethnographic case.
New Britain, East Bay, New Caledonia, and Malekula should be
seen as an island fringe that rings the northeastern and southeastern circumference of Melanesia. No Highlands examples of
(RH) are otherwise known from Irian Jaya or Papua New Guinea,
an extraordinarily large area with enormous populations well reported for decades.

Taken together, a general pattern emerges in the geographic
distribution of these New Guinea lowland and island areas. Ritualized homosexuality is found in a fringe-area belt along the
Highlands. We can trace this belt from east to west, or vice versa:
it is merely a historical quirk of colonialism that ethnographic
reports emerged initially from eastern-lying groups since the 1860s.
Thus, from the extreme east to west, we can trace two main lines
of this belt. (1) Fiji, the New Hebrides (and probably the Banks
Islands), New Caledonia, East Bay, and then, to the northwest,
parts of New Britain, the Duke-of-Yorks, and finally, leaving aside
the uncertain area of coastal Northern New Guinea (including
Wogeo and the Sepik), Humboldt Bay, the most westerly northern
coastal case. (2) From southeast to southwest, the Ai'i, the Anga
groups, the Fly River and the Morehead district, the Great Papuan
Plateau and Nomad River, and the entire southeastern Irian Jaya
area, including Frederik Hendrik Island, the Jaquai, and the southwestern coast north as far as the Asmat, people of the Casuarina
coast probably being no exception (see map 1).

This vast belt encompasses about 3,000 miles from east to west.
What areas aside from the New Guinea Highlands does it exclude?
(RH) now seems absent from the Solomon Islands, Northern Pap-

ua New Guinea, the Massim area, the Markham River Valley, most of Eastern Papua to the Fly excluding the Ai'i of the Oro district and the Anga, the Telefomin area, and the Bird's Head and adjacent northwest Irian Jaya coastal areas (the Sepik River and adjacent areas, too, although again I would not entirely dismiss the possibility of ritualized homosexuality in these areas). Thus, there are vast parts of Melanesia without (RH). More importantly, the concentration of societies exhibiting this ritual complex are in Southwestern New Guinea and adjacent areas.

If we focus on southwestern coastal New Guinea on both sides of the international border, there is no longer any question that ritualized homosexualty is *universal* there. What this survey has added to the earlier areal arguments on SWNG by Haddon (1936), Van Baal (1963, 1966), and Wirz (1934), is the Ai'i and Anga material. Previously, a line of societies with (RH) could be drawn from the Fly River west. Now that line must be extended farther east, to include the Ai'i south of Orakaiva, the hill-dwelling Anga groups east of the Bulolo River, as well as Anga peoples in the lowlands and highlands ranging west to the headwaters of the Vailala and Purari Rivers. A new boundary can be further extended north to include the Great Papuan Plateau (and probably the Strickland River watershed), and the Lake Murray area all the way west into Irian Jaya. All middle or lowland groups west of the Fly practice ritualized homosexuality, as far north as the Mayo River hills, and as far west (excepting the Mimika) as the coastal Asmat.

For years various New Guinea specialists have argued for one or another kind of historical diffusion in this area (SWNG). Leaving aside the Anga groups for the moment, because they were unstudied until recently, scholars have argued for common origins and diffusion throughout this area. Haddon (1936) and Wirz (1933) both speculated that the Marind-anim, Trans-Fly Keraki, and Kiwai groups were cultural traditions resulting from a single migration/diffusion pattern, from west to east. They saw symbolic reflections of this prehistoric diffusion in myth, legend, and ritual customs (cf. Van Baal 1963). Many writers have also seen striking cultural parallels between SWNG groups (Bateson 1932; Haddon 1920, 1927, 1936; Landtman 1927; Rivers 1904:31; Serpenti 1965:171; Van Baal 1963:206; 1966:597n. and passim; Wagner

1972:19–24; Williams 1936a, 1936c; Wirz 1922). Wirz (1933), supporting his argument with legend and myth, saw the Kiwai as the "focal point" of a southeastern Marind-anim population stream that had prehistorically spread east. At the other end of the Fly River, its headwaters, Haddon (1920:244) saw the Sepik River as a great "cultural causeway" that had allowed diffusion from the Sepik to the Fly: "a convenient route for coastal cultures to reach the interior." This speculative river migration scenario seems plausible: it would enable contact points between the headwaters of the Fly and Sepik, the Great Papuan Plateau, Nomad and Strickland Rivers, and hence, the Morehead district, Lake Murray area, and the Irian Jayan southeastern hinterland and coast.[39]

I have alluded to certain cultural and ecological similarities and to symbolic and behavioral aspects of (RH) among these Papuan groups that link them to the other scattered cases reviewed herein, and I shall summarize these in the next section. But can other evidence be shown to support prehistoric connections between (RH) groups? Yes, though the only other support is linguistic, and here the evidence, while suggestive, is very speculative.

Wurm and his colleagues (1975:935–960) have developed several possible scenarios of Papuan language migrations in Melanesia, following upon Greenberg's (1971) "Indo-Pacific hypothesis" (i.e., interrelatedness between Papuan languages and those of the Andaman Islands and Tasmania). The details of Wurm's linguistic prehistory and postulated ancient migrations are complex and cannot be described here. What matters, for our purposes, is the hypothesis of an original west to east Trans-New Guinea Phylum migration that diffused language elements from insular Southeast Asia into island New Guinea 10,000 years ago or "even much less, with the time element probably greater in the case of the West Papuan and East Papuan Phyla" (Wurm et al. 1975:40).

In Wurm's reconstructed language migration of oldest Papuan elements, we can see a possible diffusionist basis for the regional and distributional relationships between groups that concern us.

The languages of the Vogelkop Peninsula . . . as well as those in the northern part of the non-peninsular main portion of Irian Jaya, contain a common lexical substratum which extends to the south into the eastern part of the Irian Jaya highlands areas. At the same time, a substratum manifesting itself mainly on the structural and typological levels, i.e., in a prevalence of set II pronouns, an overt two-gender system, a tendency to prefixing in the morphology, number marking with nouns, verb stem suppletion and alteration in connection with object and subject marking and the absence of medial verb forms is, in varying degrees, mostly in evidence in the same areas (and reaches further east in the north), as well as in the south-eastern part of Irian Jaya, the adjacent southern parts of Papua New Guinea, and extends its influence, with interruptions, as far east as the Angan Family of the Trans-New Guinea Phylum whose speakers seem to have adopted an East New Guinea Highlands stock type language, though a few of the features mentioned above appear in the Angan Family languages as a substratum element.

It seems tempting to suggest that this far-flung substratum which may have surviving primary manifestations in some members of the West Papuan Phylum . . . may outline the earlier presence in the New Guinea area, of an old language type which entered the area from west of northern Halmahera and the Vogelkop Peninsula and spread from there to the regions of its present occurrence, to be later overrun and reduced to substratum level by subsequent language migrations.

(Wurm et al. 1975:940–941)

Here we see a speculative diffusionist basis of common linguistic origin for the so-called SWNG cultures.

We might speculate that along with some very old non-Austronesian linguistic elements, the migrants carried an ancient "root" ritual complex. Among the aspects of this structural complex was ritualized homosexuality. Perhaps a subsequent type II historical migration influenced and changed the eastern off-lying island world of Melanesia (e.g., New Hebrides), resulting in the interrelated East Papuan Phylum, before 3,000 B.C. (Wurm et al. 1975:941–943). This subsequent Austronesian influence thus resulted in the linguistic differentiation of the Eastern Melanesian group (New Caledonia, New Hebrides, East Bay) from the mainland non-Austronesian SWNG cultures. Yet, in spite of linguistic and probably other changes in their sociocultural systems, the "root" ritual structure of homosexuality among Eastern Melanesian groups remained. From the east, moreover, a major Austronesian migration about 5,000 years ago up the Markham Valley eventually influenced Highland peoples and the adjacent Angan groups of Papua (Wurm et al. 1975:947). Yet, again, we may hypothesize that these historical changes did not sweep away the (RH) practices associated with their ritual cults, at least among the non-Austronesian Angan stock-level language family[40] (see Wurm's language migration maps, ibid.:944–951).

In these speculative waves of language migrations, then, we find tentative support for the idea that a very old ritual complex was introduced by the earliest non-Austronesian speakers. It diffused over a vast area. Subsequent linguistic migrations affected language but not the element of ritual homosexuality. The exact time or geographic routes of these migrations is not my concern. But Wurm's migration scenarios do help explain why all groups evincing ritualized homosexuality are non-Austronesian speakers, excepting the Eastern Melanesian islanders, who apparently sustained later Austronesian influence. (This linguistic argument does not explain why other non-Austronesian or Austronesian groups do not practice ritualized homosexuality, an areal problem discussed in the summary.)

Once this old ritual complex permeated the Melanesian circle, as others have argued (e.g., Haddon 1920; Keesing 1982; Van Baal 1966), the great river systems, Sepik and Fly, may have served as a riverine causeway to adjacent lowland areas. Perhaps these migrants bypassed the Highlands, only touching its fringe areas. Or perhaps they settled early in some Highland areas, only to be pushed into the coastal areas by subsequent, and more numerous populations. We cannot know for certain. (To extrapolate further, perhaps this or a similar ritual complex spread across the Torres Straits: both Róheim[41] and Van Baal [1963] have argued for actual historical diffusion between the Papuan Gulf and Northern Australian cultures. But this speculation is far removed from my argument and need not concern us here.)[42]

One may reject these speculative diffusionist arguments altogether, while still acknowledging the impressive structural and symbolic parallels between Melanesian groups practicing ritual homosexuality. Nonetheless, we find recent precedents for diffusion as a contributing factor in the Austro-Melanesian literature (see Keesing 1982). Meggitt's (1965a) approach to the Australian areal aspects of Walbiri ritual is particularly attractive. He argues that an ancient ritual complex was introduced into Walbiri and then underwent successive regional, social, and ecological transformations in response to local group adaptations. Yet, the "deep" structure of ritual roles and symbols remained. This structure was necessary, but not sufficient in itself, to allow for the expression of the Walbiri ritual complex, which required other sociocultural elements to support its present institutional form and distribution. A comparable argument is made below for Melanesia.

Here, then, is a tentative *ultimate* causal view of the distribution of ritualized homosexuality in Melanesia. Arguments concerning various social structural and cultural underpinnings or concomitants of (RH) in different social units and subregional traditions may be seen as *proximate* transformational causes, discussed next. All these suggestions basically extend the interdisciplinary and scholarly work of others. Even so, I would not care to say more now: this rather shaky diffusionism leaves me, a social anthropologist, cautious and uneasy.

SUMMARY AND ANALYSIS

This survey shows clearly that ritualized homosexuality in Melanesia is more common than was ever thought, not to mention predicted, by contemporary surveys. Nor are its sociocultural forms and ecological distribution shapeless or random. I have argued that these customs belong to an ancient ritual complex manifested primarily in non-Austronesian-speaking groups of the western region of Papua and southeastern region of Irian Jaya and associated fringe areas, and some northeastern Melanesian island societies.

The range of ecological and social traits and institutions associated with (RH) is elaborate and rich. Sexual behavior, as much as or more than other human behaviors, is multivalent (Bateson 1972) in its antecedents and consequences. When one argues correlations, not causes, these factors can be catalogued and listed without concern for evolutionary or developmental sequelae or systemic interactions between environment, psyche, social structure, and culture. But when we choose to explain *systems* such as these, our task is more complex. Then we must seek a hierarchy of constraints (Keesing 1982) that systemically create and maintain the observed outcome: ritualized homosexual behavior.

To deal with systems that produce this outcome is indeed a complex matter. The task involves many variables: ecology; historical relatedness; warfare; population trends; social structure; homogeneity of local kin-based polities (the [1967] Allen hypothesis); cultural definitions of selfhood and personhood, sexuality, marriage, the nature of the sexes and gender development, including beliefs about the body, its orifices, fluids, and boundaries; residence patterns; descent ideologies; sexual morality and restrictiveness; initiation rites; warriorhood; definitions of homosexuality, bisexuality, and heterosexuality; the nature of the homosexual act (is it honorable, shameful, why and for whom?) and associated bonds; peer groups, age-groups; sexual dominance and the social status of women; gerontocracy; ceremonial impersonation, hoaxes, and symbolic communication with spirits; female pollution, semen depletion, and bloodletting; dual organization; secrecy; shame; postpartum taboos and sleeping arrangements; sex-typing; cultural attributes of masculinity and femininity that affect sexual contacts; identity, identification, sex-identity conflict and avoidance behavior, envy, conversion reactions, passivity, aggressivity, misogyny; and on and on. Another book would be required to treat these conceptual issues and associated theories in depth. In lieu of that (and with apologies for an already lengthy introduction), I shall here touch upon only the essential points raised in my survey.

INCIDENCE • The reader may wonder how frequent ritual homosexuality is in Melanesia, given this new distribution. I noted this problem in the preface. For Melanesia, in spite of this comprehensive review, the question is difficult to answer in a meaningful way. Not only is it difficult to convert the literature mess into statistical frequencies but our sample is certainly not random.[43] What ethnographic baseline do we select as our universe of phenomena against which to compare our data? (Highlands versus Lowlands? Austronesian versus non-Austronesian groups?) How do we count our sample? By cultural subregion or by representative social units? (The order of choice will affect tabulation.) For subregions, we could list as many as eight or as few as three— if one accepts the notion of a SWNG fringe area* (see map 1).

---

*These three subareas are: the SWNG area, including Anga groups; Humboldt Bay; and insular island Melanesia, including New Britain and adjacent areas, East Bay, and Eastern Melanesia.

When counting the total social units, the problems (due to Galton's problem) are greater. We may have as few as thirty-two groups,[*] or as many as fifty or so[44] (see table 1.1). Given the available Melanesian data, our survey conservatively results in between 10 to 20 percent of all Melanesian cultures having ritualized homosexuality as defined. Current information does not permit more precision.

ECOLOGY • The societies reported on in this book are, by and large, ecologically marginal populations associated with sago, yams, or taro, intensive hunting, and sparse populations. Shifting subsistence horticulture exists side by side with hunting and gathering in some areas. These peoples have "low intensity" agricultural regimes; mixed agriculture without single staple crops (e.g., sweet potatoes) is the rule (Brookfield and Hart 1971:94–124). Sweet potatoes are secondary crops among many SWNG groups; taro and yams, especially as feast crops, are prominent (cf. Watson 1965). Coconuts and pandanus are economically and symbolically important in most lowland and coastal areas. Hunting is prominent; and head-hunting, although not universal, is symbolically seen as one of its forms in some areas (e.g., Van Baal 1966; Zegwaard 1959; and see Van Baal, chap. 3 below). Moreover, the association between masculine prowess in hunting and exclusive male attachments is marked (Schieffelin 1982; Williams 1936c). By contrast, pig husbandry is of moderate importance (e.g., Marind-anim) or absent (e.g., Kaluli) from these groups. And none are involved in large-scale pig exchanges or ceremonial exchange systems in general (cf. P. Brown 1978; Rubel and Rossman 1978), which distinguishes these societies from those of the Highlands and the Massim area.

As elsewhere in Melanesia, there is a marked sexual division of labor in societies with ritualized homosexuality. Economic activities are identified with gender: hunting is masculine, certain forms of gardening are feminine; warfare is masculine, baby-sitting is feminine. Sex-typing and social status are thus linked, with male activities accorded higher status to the extent that (RH) groups

---

[*] Excluding all questionable cases, i.e.: Manus, Wogeo, the Sepik mainland, Iatmul (and all Sepik groups), Mamberamo River, Akuna, and all questionable adjacent areas of Irian Jaya and Vanuatu.

were called "men-admiring societies" by Layard (1959:108) and "comrad communities" *(genossenschaft)* by Wirz (1922:39–40). Brown and Buchbinder (1976) argue that these politicoeconomic patterns make the sexes complementary, not cooperative, with which I agree. Yet one wonders how far the emotional complementarity extended. Murphy (1959) has argued that sex antagonism—rivalry, ambivalence, envy—is generated in men working in close quarters and being dependent upon women as producers. Clearly, women are vital for the total reproduction of these socioeconomic systems (Donaldson n.d.; Keesing 1982), a fact that these male ideologies generally deny.

These groups, especially those of the SWNG, are demographically tenuous, too. They tend to have small populations numbering from a few hundred (Keraki) to several thousand (Marind-anim). Typically, villages are small, though among the Marind these could run into hundreds of people. Everywhere the man-to-land ratio is low, among the lowest in Melanesia, ranging from 4 or 5 persons per square mile upward to a limit of 40 per square mile (see Brookfield and Hart 1971:90ff., on Marind-anim, Anga, and others). By contrast, Highlands populations are dense, ranging from the Kuma (49 per m²), to Mae Enga (160 per m²), to Chimbu (225 per m²) (see P. Brown 1978:106).

A related demographic factor is sex ratio at birth. Melanesian populations typically show a marked imbalance of males over females at birth (see Malcolm 1970). The data on this factor are uneven. However, Guiart (cited in Allen, chap. 3 below) showed a remarkable imbalance of 231 males over 115 females in his 1950 North Malekula census. Rates such as 120/100 males at birth for the Sambia (Herdt 1981) and 100/71 men over women (Bowers 1965:29) elsewhere are common (cf. Bulmer's 1971 survey). Was this overpopulation of males a factor in contributing to institutionalized homosexuality? It probably was, but how much of a causal role it played is unclear.

Male overpopulation must be seen in context. It is not simply the gross number of males at birth that matters, but how many survive into adulthood, and how women are reproductively controlled through marriage customs. Male deaths through warfare in Melanesia surely also affected the disparity. The role of misogyny, though, with chiefs (Malekula), elders, and war leaders taking several wives, must have exacerbated the shortage of women in these groups. The late onset of menarche among Melanesians probably also contributed to the female "shortage" (Buchbinder 1973:211; Malcolm 1968). It is safe to argue that male overpopulation did *contribute* to the institutionalization of homosexuality, for intuition tells us that a shortage of males would have made such practices less likely. However, correlation is not causation. The Tor of Northeast Irian Jaya had a very high rate of male overpopulation: Oosterwal (1961:38) reports that fully 47 percent of Tor males are bachelors at marriageable age. But adultery still occurs (Oosterwal 1959), and they do not practice (RH), as we have seen. A more detailed regional analysis is needed to clarify this factor.

Low fertility rates may be another contributing factor in these populations. Again, the data are thin. Yet in two areas, Southeastern Irian Jaya and the Great Papuan Plateau, groups practicing ritualized homosexuality were faced with low fertility rates and declining populations at the time of pacification. Van Baal has written of Marind-anim low female fertility, high vaginal irritations, and associated medical complications (due to ritual sexual promiscuity?), and birth-related diseases that precipitated kidnapping and/or purchase of children, which was a "dire necessity for continuity" (1966:31–32, and passim). Kelly (1977) argued that the Etoro declining population was exacerbated by their postcontact epidemics and by the fact that they "taboo heterosexual intercourse for 295 days during the year" (quoted in Kottack 1974:287). These factors, plus the cultural practice of homosexual contacts among young males, certainly threaten the viability of a small population. Yet we must again take care in reading correlation as causation. Other Melanesian groups have sustained low fertility and depopulation (see Rivers 1922), some of whom later thrived. And heterosexual avoidance behavior, expecially in the Highlands, seems marked (Meggitt 1964). Heider (1976), for instance, reports that the Dani of Highlands Irian Jaya have "low sexual energy" and practice extreme sexual abstinence for years at a time; yet the Dani do not practice ritualized homosexuality.

Left unchecked by Western pacification or colonialization, what would the long-term evolution of these marginal populations have been? Perhaps homosexual practices might have contributed to their extinction, but we cannot be certain of this possibility: if one accepts the assumption of ancient migrations and ritual practices, these groups had flourished for generations. But perhaps we look back at them as they were at their zenith, with groups like the Marind-anim having specialized to the point that "could not have lasted much longer" (Ernst 1979:52; Keesing 1976).

In short, (RH) cultures are fringe-area ecological groups whose subsistence and populations were generally tenuous. It seems likely that their peripherality is no accident. In their niches they have little economic competition. One wonders here the extent to which SWNG groups may have been displaced by larger, later migrations of more numerous Highlands peoples, forcing them over generations into fringe areas. This raises the general problem of warfare and warriorhood initiation.

WARFARE • Warfare occurred among all these peoples,* though its forms (e.g., intratribal versus intertribal fighting) and intensity varied from place to place. Why did war occur at all, given their peripherality? The full answer to this problem is complex and far-ranging and remains to be seen.[45] But given the small populations and lack of nearby competitors, a materialist explanation of war makes less sense here than it does for larger Highlands groups, for whom the data do not support it either (Keesing 1982; Sillitoe 1978). Among SWNG groups in particular, several patterns seem to hold true.

First, war was a fact of life that conditioned most cultural domains and social arenas in these societies. Warfare thus influenced the behavioral environment of child development, marriage and the family, gender roles, and sexual behavior (see Langness 1967; Mead 1935; Schwartz 1973).

Second, these groups generally recognized the difference between intratribal and intertribal fighting (Langness 1972). Their community-based warriorhoods did fight each other (though some did not, e.g., Marind-anim), but their real social concern was with intertribal fighting and war raids against enemies. These war raids took the form of head-hunting expeditions among many (Marind-anim, Kimam, Asmat, etc.), but not the Highlands Anga.[46] Indeed,

---

*I shall be speaking primarily here of mainland groups.

the association of heads (body and penis head, coconuts and pandanus) and male substance is symbolically marked in various (RH) groups (see Allen, Van Baal, and Serpenti below). Finally, we know that war raids customarily followed initiation cycles among groups such as the Marind-anim, the Kimam, the Sambia, and perhaps on the Great Papuan Plateau.

Third, (RH) groups tend to use initiation as *the* social mechanism for recruitment to their ritual cults and to the village-based warriorhood corps as well. Survival and social reproduction of communities depend upon the warriorhood, and initiation means introduction to homosexual activity. It also brings with it adult, masculine socialization, through successive ceremonies and related achievements. Thus homosexuality is linked to what are essentially military and age-graded organizations.[47] A number of important manifest and latent social functions stem from these military clubs.

INITIATION • What kind of initiation do (RH) cultures practice? They have initiations, not puberty rites, in Allen's (1967:5) sense: ceremonialized admissions to discreet groups "normally held at set intervals for a number of candidates simultaneously." These are all-male associations, with compulsory membership (but see Schieffelin 1982). Women are, in some places, involved (e.g., Marind-anim). Female initiation is usually confined to menarche or birth ceremonies (see Godelier 1982*a*), and the status and position of women is correspondingly low (cf. Van Baal 1975). Furthermore, initiation usually places boys in men's secret societies from which women and children are formally excluded. Ritual instruments, flutes and bull-roarers, are seen as hostile to women (Gourlay 1975; Herdt 1982*a*; Williams 1936*a*). (RH) ritual and political authority in general is vested in cult elders, compared with Highlands "big man" polities (Allen, in press; cf. Hage 1981).

An important and ignored aspect of initiation in (RH) groups is that it frequently occurs before puberty, often as early as middle to late childhood (e.g., Marind-anim, Sambia, Keraki, etc.). Elsewhere I have argued that this young age is psychologically necessary for the radical resocialization into, and eventual sex-role dramatization expected of, adult men (Herdt 1981, 1982*b*; cf. Mead 1949; Young 1965). A related and still poorly understood aspect is that of ritual secrecy, which has significant psychosocial consequences for gender formation (reviewed in Herdt 1982*a*; Schwimmer 1980). Separation from mother, household and playmates, ordeals and initiation traumas, the liminal stage of seclusion, fasting, and suspension of normal routines and relationships set the stage on which ritual homosexuality is begun.

Long ago Van Gennep suggested a view of erotic acts in initiation that merits renewed attention. In cultures where sex is seen as either impure or as holding magicoreligious danger, as in (RH) groups, Van Gennep (1960:169) suggested that a taboo on coitus would be present. Among such groups, "Coitus is 'powerful': that is why it is sometimes used as a rite of great efficacy. . . . The physical impact of the act—that of penetration—should be borne in mind" (ibid.). Following other initiation ordeals and seclusion, the sexual act becomes a means of effecting ritual transition change in selfhood. "Coitus as a final act in initiation ceremonies I interpret also as a rite of incorporation," which applies equally for heterosexual and homosexual practices (Van Gennep 1960:170–171). The homosexual act incorporates the boy into a new group, the ritual cult, with a new status and role. The boy's insemination coheres with the native view, universal in (RH) cultures, that the key (manifest) goal of homosexual contact is to get sperm inside the boy's body so he can grow.[48] This initiation principle is special. Some Melanesian groups lack initiation rites altogether. But among those who practice initiation, the insemination idea is unique to (RH) groups.*

Yet there are actually three interrelated parties to this homosexual act of incorporation. On the one hand, the boy (and others) may believe that this act will make him grow and strengthen. He is, in this sense, demonstrating his desire to be masculine, to act in accord with ritual ways, to be unfeminine.[49] On the other hand, his counterpart, the postpubescent inseminator, demonstrates his superordinate maleness by the homosexual act of masculinizing the boy (Herdt 1981:205). A third party is the ritual cult itself. The cult in turn is represented at three levels: through its concrete paraphernalia and cult house; through human agents (elders, cult leaders, father, and bachelors); and through spirit beings, who

---

*I exclude here insemination by analogy, i.e., sperm used in foods (see Schwimmer, chap. 6).

may be directly or indirectly personified through masks or dramatic impersonations. The paraphernalia becomes sacred stage, these authorities the audience (women a metaphoric audience for the men) which sanctify the homoerotic act, endowing it with the power of sacred tradition, the supernaturally blessed moral way of life. Thus, the ritual homosexual act serves here as a cultural sign, to self and others, of *submission* to ritual and spiritual authority (see Errington, cited above, and Tuzin 1980 in another context).

The question arises as to the nature of this submission. To what extent are the homosexual relations depicted in (RH) groups "real" or "mythical," in Layard's (1942:474) terms? Our survey is instructive, and it points to a new typology. Type I is represented by *symbolic* homosexual contacts. Actual homosexual penetration may or may not occur; or, as is likely with the Ingiet society on New Britain, it occurs but once only, in first initiation. Farces and hoaxes may be the genre of spirit impersonations. Actual homosexual contacts are not perpetuated thereafter. The person who inseminates the novice may be a spirit being impersonated by an elder. Homosexuality may also be symbolically projected in myth or folktales (see Schwimmer, chap. 6). Type II utilizes actual homosexual intercourse during initiation. It is usually with males who will copulate with the novice afterward. No hoaxes here; the boys' physical growth and the social effects of such for war and the marriage trade are serious business. Homosexual activity may go on in secular life for months or years. In our sample, Type I groups are few. (Does Iatmul belong in this group?) Type II groups are common, and they include all SWNG societies. Some societies, such as Malekula and the Marind-anim, seem to complexly utilize features of both types, with elaborate spirit impersonations and mythology buttressing actual homosexuality (Allen, chap. 2; Van Baal, chap. 3).

My guess is that Type II societies emphasize the actual physical penetration of the boy (in line with Van Gennep's idea). Here, real physical and psychological effects are expected from the male/male sexual act and implanted semen. Changes result, then, in "biological" maturation, which we may "read" analogically as also meaning changes in the boy's experience of self (see M. Strathern 1979) and in concomitant changes in his personhood (Read, chap. 5). In groups such as Kaluli, these actual homosexual contacts may occur late, in adolescence, and may last only a few months. In most SWNG and Eastern Melanesian groups, however, the actual contacts extend from childhood into adulthood on an exclusive and regular basis. (Perhaps, in this sense, they are "profane," not "sacred," the latter more characteristic of Type I groups; cf. Schieffelin 1982.) Again, we should not underrate the power of sexual submission to effect psychosocial changes in the boy's gender identity and role (Herdt 1982*a*; Vanggaard 1972) and societal variations in this power (cf. Allen, chap. 2). Such gender changes involve the boy's incorporation into warriorhood life. He may experience his homosexual contacts with fear, honor, shame, excitement, or all of these; but here, we confront individual thoughts and feelings, not merely cultural rules and ideals, a problem on which there is virtually no data. The initiate is coerced and expected to emulate his seniors, to identify with and probably compete with his peers. This psychosocial process eventuates in his internalization of the warrior role, ritual beliefs, probably misogyny, and behavioral conformity to cult rules and norms. Aggressiveness is inculcated. Again, we should reiterate that some SWNG groups follow initiation rites with a war-raiding party. For the newly initiated older bachelor, this raid is a confirmatory rite demonstrating his prowess, just as his newly achieved role as homosexual inserter to younger boys demonstrates his sexual maturity (Herdt 1981). Initiation rites and warfare thus interact with the inculcation of warrior identity. Homosexuality contributes, that is, as a latent social function in the maintenance of the cult, obedience to authority, and the development of aggressivity and eventual sexual antagonism toward women.

What about the erotics of ritual homosexuality? Let us underline the obvious: without erotic desire, arousal, and consummation, any sexual intercourse is impossible.* The conventional sentiment which I have heard expressed, by laymen and anthropologists, is that "these Melanesians are performing rituals, not erotics." Ethnocentrism aside,[50] it should be clear that these two modes are of one piece—experience—not opposed, in Melanesia. The Marind

---

*Excluding self- or other masturbation of course. The data show that masturbation to arousal is usually unnecessary here.

warrior who copulates with a boy may be aroused and still be conforming to or performing a ritual. The boy, in contrast, may be terrified or thrilled. But erection is necessary for the acts to take place, especially when they go on for a lifetime. The "sexual needs of bachelors" (Hiatt 1977:257) is involved, as are sexual segregation, suppression, and other factors already noted. Likewise, the social attributes of the role of homosexual partners must be taken into account. In most of these groups, the homosexual partners are in asymmetrical, age-graded older/younger relationships; but kinship, marital and ritual status, and other beliefs and rules about the function or purpose and outcome of the inseminating are contingencies. Secrecy, shame, and honor are probably crucial emotional factors (consciously and unconsciously) of sexual excitement here, too. A complex algebraic sum of all these things, as among the ancient Greeks,[51] produces the erotics necessary for ritualized homosexual behavior.

And what is the relation between these homoerotics and adult masculine identity? The essays below only touch upon this issue (see Van Baal, Read, and Schwimmer, this volume; cf. Herdt 1981). The question of sexual motivation, at all levels of awareness (e.g., conscious and unconscious), raise important issues on which we provide little direct data as such; and we are not satisfied to "read" individual motives and experience from customs. Clearly, the male role is problematic in many parts of Melanesia; perhaps this is true for both (RH) and other groups, as elsewhere (D'Andrade 1966). Yet, the involvement of males in homoerotic bonds in (RH) groups implies a kind of sexual and interpersonal fluidity of psychosexual development that may be a fundament of these Melanesian societies, in particular. Power relationships, both in the general sense of managing others and controlling public affairs, and in the delimited sense of dominance over others in everyday life, are germane here. Men in (RH) groups attempt a sexual and social control over all others, a control that is difficult to achieve and sustain, for instance, in the circumstances of domestic life (Rosaldo 1974). The attempt is supported by the nearly universal conscription of boys into warrior life via initiation. All males are thus involved in (RH), and their personal choice is, as we have seen, limited by many factors. The modifier *ritualized* with respect to homosexual behavior addresses this dimension of sexual orientation and identity formation. In spite of universal involvement in homosexual activities, however, no data indicate that these males become habitually motivated to same-sex contact later in life, or that the incidence of aberrant lifelong individual homosexuality, as an identity state, is greater in (RH) groups than elsewhere in the world. Homosexuality is the royal road to heterosexuality (to paraphrase Freud), but it is a temporary one. What remains unclear, however, is the effect of this early and transitional male/male sexual activity on the development or quality of male/female sexual bonds. In some, perhaps many, (RH) groups, men seem to view preinitiated boys as a composite of "feminine" and "masculine" characteristics. Homosexuality is designed, in this regard, to masculinize their selfhood and behavioral comportment in the direction of defined adult masculine roles. Yet, certain feminine characteristics may endure—to be expressed in secret male rites; is this why, perhaps, ritualized homosexuality itself is so often secret in Melanesia? No, (RH) does not make these males into what we Westerners call "homosexuals"; these data instead challenge our own views about what that category means, and what parts of nature and nuture it is made from. Perhaps we should now better look to understand how the fluidity of the human condition allows this Melanesian phenomena and what, in a general sense, bisexuality is all about.

SEXUAL POLARITY • The final set of interrelated conceptual issues may be grouped under the rubric *sexual polarity*. Though Melanesia has long been identified as a culture area with much "sexual antagonism," what does sexual polarity mean in cultures that ritualize homosexuality? Is its form different than in other Melanesian groups (see Herdt and Poole 1982)? I believe it is; and, when we examine the configurations of this theme here, we see how the differences inform, and are informed by, homosexuality. I will argue that sexual polarity takes its most extreme form in (RH) groups.

These are societies in which the gender and social roles of men and women are viewed not only as distinct, separate, and polarized but as hostile in many respects. I have noted this in the economic division of labor and in ritual cultism. To what extent do these differences extend into everyday social action, marriage, and intragroup relationships: not just a house divided, but one at war with itself?

The status of women is low in these cultures. (Social status is here indicated by women's low participation in public affairs; their low access to, or control of, their economic products; their lack of choice in marriage; beliefs about women's polluted bodies; negative images of women registered in idioms, myth, and everyday discourse; and the absence or peripherality of institutions such as initiation for women.) Women are described as being in a low or "degraded state" (William's 1936c term) among the Keraki, the Kiwai, the Marind-anim, the Baruya, the Sambia, the New Hebrides groups, and others, as shown in different ways in the chapters below. Ecological and economic factors are correlated with women's low status. The literature generally indicates that the larger the population, the higher the women's status (e.g., among Chimbu, Hagen, and Enga). Where economic exchange systems and pig husbandry are present, women play a crucial part which seems to provide higher status (Feil 1978; M. Strathern 1972, 1980). But these economic productive features are virtually absent from (RH) groups (cf. Lindenbaum, chap. 9).

These cultures are sexually restrictive. Sexual activity is fraught with rules and taboos, and in adulthood it is thoroughly ritualized through initiation and marriage customs. It is not clear to what extent premarital sexual play is forbidden in children among these groups, but it is strongly condemned among the Sambia and neighboring Anga peoples. Sex is morally charged: adultery and premarital heterosexual activity are generally considered shameful. Certainly rigorous taboos govern sexual contacts between men and women after male initiation occurs. One may argue that a similar situation exists throughout the Highlands, the Eastern Highlands initiatory systems in particular. Yet, (RH) cultures channel years-long male sexual development away from females toward males through homosexuality. *That* restrictiveness is unique to them. (Perhaps RH groups have more "prudes" than "lechers," in Meggitt's [1964] terms.) Sexual restrictiveness raises three related issues: gender differences, sex anxiety, and sexual segregation.

Gender differences are polarized in cultures with ritualized homosexuality. Adult masculinity and femininity are defined as essentially antithetical. The biological origins and cycles of males and females are seen as fundamentally different (Kelly 1977:16). Men's ideology views women as "naturally" competent throughout their developmental cycle (childhood growth, the menarche, childbirth), whereas males need a ritual push, as it were, through initiation (reviewed in Herdt 1981). Homosexual insemination is crucial for male growth and strength. Highlands initiatory systems show similar ideologies of gender differences, but they do not require homosexual contact. What does this difference imply? I think that a pervasive cultural principle separates Highlands from (RH) cultures here, and it has been discussed by Allen (chap. 3) below. (RH) groups focus on milk and semen as critical gender fluids. Eastern Highlands groups especially emphasize blood. Mother's and women's womb and menstrual blood is seen as contaminating and lethal to male development in the Highlands, so bloodletting rites are key initiation activities (see Read, chap. 5). Letting polluted blood is thus a sign of being masculinized (Herdt 1982b) there. By contrast, bloodletting is rare or absent in (RH) groups, except, that is, for Highlands Anga peoples, who undoubtedly imported nosebleeding rites from their Eastern Highlands neighbors. Aside from circum-incision in the New Hebrides, penis cutting is absent from (RH) groups. The differential principle seems to be this: in (RH) groups no distinction is made between male and female blood, and female contamination is not feared (excepting Highlands Anga); but mother's milk and semen are seen as fundamentally different, so gender ideology focuses upon homosexual insemination as a kind of later masculinizing-parturition process.

What accounts for this Highlands/(RH) difference? Population size and integrity are indirectly related (Lindenbaum 1972). The fact that SWNG groups do not generally marry their enemies is surely related (excepting Highlands Anga again). Perhaps these factors are contingent upon an even more important process: the early ritual development of gender necessary for later sex-role dramatization in *adulthood*. Remember that both bloodletting and semen-intake are practices bound to ritual, and ritual makes use of differentiation and contrast by analogy (among other processes). If Highlands' groups pinpoint femaleness in the menstrual act, (RH) groups focus it on breast-feeding; and in male rites, Highlands men emphasize bloodletting, whereas SWNG men emphasize homosexual insemination. Hage (1981) has criticized Dundes (1976) for interpreting these contrary ritual modes as "expressions" of (unconscious) envy, not of analogy. It is unfortunate that Hage sees these two processes as opposed, instead of complementary, as I think they are in this case (see Spiro 1982:168–171). At any rate, as Allen notes below (chap. 2), abundant evidence indicates that men exhibit envy of women's perceived "natural" powers here (cf. Van Baal, chap. 3; Read, chap. 5). Allen also suggests that two contrary images of women symbolically underlie these modes: "menstruating woman/reproductive mother" (Eastern Highlands, Wogeo) versus "wife/nurturant mother" (RH groups).

Does heterosexual anxiety enter in, and if so, to what extent? Sexual anxiety is difficult to measure (Stephens 1962). But it seems pronounced in Highlands groups (Meggitt 1964) and minimal for (RH) groups such as the Etoro (Kelly 1976), the Marind-anim (Van Baal 1966), and others, though I have suggested it is extreme among the fringe-area Sambia (Herdt 1981). Sex anxiety is correlated with the sexual restrictions of postpartum taboos, as Whiting et al. (1958) argue. The secrecy of childbirth, like that of homosexuality, seems related (Schieffelin 1976). Economic cooperation needed between spouses may exacerbate the sex anxiety (Murphy 1959), as does intermarriage with enemy groups, whereby a woman is seen as a potential enemy (e.g., Sambia), though among the Marind-anim such marriages do not occur since the Marind warred against distant enemies. From all these factors, sex anxiety and ambivalence toward women especially, the effects upon the father/child relationship must be significant (e.g., rivalry, jealousy, envy, aloofness, overcompensatory "protest masculinity"; see Whiting and Whiting 1975). Unfortunately, data on this topic in Melanesia are rare (but see Van Baal, chap. 3).

Sexual segregation is marked in (RH) and Highlands groups, and it is associated with the restrictive factors noted above, but here again there is a difference between the two cultural systems. In virtually all (RH) cultures there are men's houses or cult houses where men congregate. In groups such as the Marind-anim, men and women live in separate but close huts. Following initiation, boys usually have to avoid women and children for some period of time—months, years, as the case may be. Yet, in contrast to

Highlands groups, many SWNG societies customarily allow men and women to live together in close proximity. This may mean separate compartments of one long-house (Etoro, Kaluli), or separate male or female spaces in the same sleeping quarters (Keraki, Anga groups). Highlands groups, however, usually have strict sexual segregation in different houses, even in adulthood. In (RH) groups, the result may be a kind of divided (even tense) togetherness. In this regard one may thus characterize the (RH) attitude toward male/female proximity as enigmatic and ambivalent. One may hypothesize that years-long exposure to this ambivalence results in sex-identity conflict later for boys at initiation (cf. Herdt 1982*a*, 1982*b*; Schwimmer, chap. 6; A. Strathern 1970).

Sexual segregation must be counted as a key contributing factor to the institutionalization of homosexuality. When residential separation is added to sexual restrictiveness and socioeconomic polarity, homosexual activity as an acceptable sexual outlet seems likely. Davenport has argued this point:

> It should be noted that throughout Melanesian societies, where institutionalized forms of male bisexuality* are most frequently encountered, there is also a widespread tradition of separating men from women. So pronounced is this nearly everywhere, it can be regarded as a basic principle of social organization. . . . One can entertain the hypothesis that in the strongly gender-segregated communities of Melanesia, when the culture also imposes effective barriers to heterosexual intercourse, there is a likelihood that institutionalized male bisexual practices will result.
>
> *(Davenport 1977:156)*

While I sympathize with this view, a caveat is necessary. It seems a quirk that in the most "strongly gender-segregated" societies in Melanesia, the Eastern Highlands, ritual homosexuality is absent. Gender segregation is therefore a necessary but not sufficient cause of (RH). The other factors noted above must interact synergistically with segregation to produce this special outcome.

A final, and very important, factor remaining is marriage. Marriage in all these groups is customarily arranged. Sister exchange is a common form in (RH) groups. Infant betrothal and bride-service are uncommon but present. But bride-price marriage is

---

*Davenport uses this term in the same way I use ritualized homosexual behavior.

69

rare (e.g., among Marind-anim) and more commonly found in the Highlands. I suspect that sister exchange and moiety exogamy, as among the Marind (Van Baal 1966:122–127), are frequently correlated in (RH) societies; both are present in Irian Jaya, the Trans-Fly area, and Eastern Melanesia. Still, Anga groups such as the Sambia lack exogamous moieties, and intravillage marriage between closely related clans of the same phratry is common. Yet the (RH) inter-linkages between sister-exchange marriage and ritualized homosexuality are impressive. Since bride-wealth marriage is common in Highlands systems, we may see in sister-exchange marriage a structural pattern that distinguishes (RH) from Highlands cultures (cf. Collier and Rosaldo 1981; Lindenbaum, chap. 9).

The pattern that emerges in SWNG is one in which kin groups that intermarry are involved also in homosexual transactions. Women are controlled and traded as pawns by elders in the "marriage trade." Age differences enter in. Given several years' difference between brothers, older sisters, and even older sisters' husbands (as among Australian Aborigines), a woman's younger brother (biological or classificatory brother) is placed in a structurally subordinate position to his elder sister's husband, his brother-in-law (Serpenti, chap. 7). Yet the nature of this subordination is convoluted. Because of sister exchange, both parties are "wife-givers" and "wife-takers." The older man, however, takes his wife *first*, so he is, temporarily, beholden to his younger unmarried brother-in-law. The younger male, though, by virtue of his lower ritual and social status, is socially subordinate to the older man.

Now their kinship relationship enters in. They are not only in a "double" brother-in-law relationship (i.e., wife's brother is sister's husband) in Layard's phrase (1959:104), they can be matrilateral cross-cousins (Keraki), patrilateral cross-cousins (Sambia), or even, in the case of Etoro and Kimam, mother's brother and sister's son (real or classificatory). In (RH) groups that prescribe homosexual relations between these males, we have, in effect, a boy's parents giving his sister to an older male who becomes his brother-in-law and who will (with other members of his kinship group) inseminate the boy. The boy is being ritually "masculinized" into adulthood as his sister is being impregnated by the older man. The most extreme form that homosexual service takes in

(RH) cultures is, among the Jaquai, a rather extraordinary kind of bride-service:* a boy's parents, lacking a daughter to exchange, eventually receive from the older man who inseminated the boy (e.g., Kimam, Kunam) a woman for him to marry, a kind of sentimental gift. Thus, exchange of women and semen circulation go together in these groups (see Herdt, chap. 4).

Lévi-Strauss (1969:307) has suggested that the Nambikwara of the Amazon through polygamy create a "disequilibrium between the number of young men and the number of available girls," making homosexual relations a "provisional substitute" for marriage.[52] His point can be applied to these Melanesian groups, too. In a culture with strictly arranged marriages, male overpopulation, polygamy among older men, and extreme sexual polarity—sexual segregation and heterosexual restrictiveness in particular—ritualized homosexuality is a transitional alternative sexual outlet for males. (Certainly there is no evidence that it is a population control method, as Money and Ehrhardt ([1972:126] or Kottack [1974:287–288] suggest.) Yet it must be clear that this alternative seems to apply only in groups whose history, social structure, and other systemic factors make transitional homosexuality both necessary and sufficient for individual and societal coherence.

Hage (1981) has argued recently that ritual homosexuality in New Guinea is a product of some underlying structure of "sexual symmetry," also expressed in dual organizations, initiation rites, and a "big man complex" that is "rampantly egalitarian." He sees this underlying structure expressed, on the north coast and in the Eastern Highlands, in bloodletting rites, whereas on the south coast its form is (RH). To reiterate, contra Dundes (1976) he argues that it is not envy but this structural "sexual symmetry" that provides a "simpler explanation" of (RH), based on structural-evolutionary principles. Space does not permit a full review of these arguments, but several of his points are germane to my summary. First, the simplest "historical" explanation of homosexual customs is that they are distributed in relation to long-term transformational adjustments to the postulated migration-diffusion outlined above. In this regard, Hage's data are incomplete. Second, neither bloodletting nor semen-ingestion practices follow

---

*Or perhaps it is bride-wealth, if one views semen as a scarce commodity.

71

any simple structural or historical-evolutionary pattern, as I have argued elsewhere (Herdt 1980, 1982*b*). For instance, how would this theory accommodate groups such as the Sambia who practice *both* bloodletting and homosexuality?* Third, Hage's appeal to a probably nonexistent "big man complex" ignores the Western Highlands, where such political figures are most developed but whose societies (e.g., Melpa) lack both bloodletting and homosexuality. Here Hage has it backwards: it is in groups that lack the big man prototype that (RH) is more likely to be present. Fourth, as I noted above, not all groups that practice ritual homosexuality have marriage by exogamous moieties. It seems that such ethnological models will remain inadequate until researchers take the literature of Melanesia as a culture area more seriously.

To what extent can we argue that the ritual complex of homosexuality was caused by male gender ideology, as Layard (1942) argued? This chicken-and-egg problem cannot be answered on the basis of the extant literature, unless, that is, one regards the hypothetical ancient migrations as both a sufficient and necessary cause of (RH), which I do not. Clearly, these cultures exhibit marked sexual polarity; perhaps, and just as importantly, they show extreme ambivalence toward women (Van Baal 1966). These male misogynist ideologies described in this book contain a remarkable view of women, not as dangerous and polluting beings, but as valued and scarce sexual objects to be controlled and envied for their parturition capacities. Perhaps, then, given such ideologies, economic and sexual segregation led to ritual separation (Kaberry 1939), which evolved gradually into ritualized homosexuality.

Ritual homosexuality is a powerful symbolic structure that unites these cultures in a single pattern, in spite of their differences. It is too simple to say that one or another factor caused their customs. But when we combine the whole—the system of presumed migration history, ecology, and sociocultural structures with concomitant effects on personality and sex roles—the synergistic effect makes their form of sexual polarity understandable in time and

---

*No doubt another pseudoevolutionary "transformation" type can be invented to account for such variations.

place. Is not this complex image but one instance of the fact that humanness is complex?

The themes touched upon in this summary are empirically studied in the chapters that follow. And Professor Lindenbaum examines their theoretical underpinnings in her concluding chapter.

The comparative ethnography surveyed here presents such an embarrassment of rich interlinkages and ideas that I must end by expressing my bewilderment at an anthropology that has ignored their theoretical importance for so many decades. Undoubtedly, Western prudery and outmoded research conventions, which excluded sexual behavior from much of anthropology, were responsible. We hope that this book adds momentum to the growing interest in cross-cultural studies on sex and gender in Melanesia and elsewhere.

NOTES

Research funding for this chapter came, in part, from the Department of Anthropology, Stanford University, and I gratefully acknowledge its support. For careful and invaluable assistance in interpreting the ethnology of Irian Jaya I acknowledge with sincere thanks the help of J. Van Baal. I also wish to thank Michael Allen for reviewing this manuscript, especially on Vanuatu, as well as Shirley Lindenbaum, Stephen Murray, Fitz John P. Poole, Robert J. Stoller, and Donald F. Tuzin for their comments. Mark T. Janssen aided me in bibliographic work, and Thomas H. Baker assisted in translation, and I gratefully acknowledge their help. Responsibility for the final product is of course mine.

1. Such general cross-cultural surveys as those of J. Brown (1963), Burton and Whiting (1961), Cohen (1964), Stephens (1962), Whiting et al. (1958), and Young (1965), though they make use of Austro-Melanesian data, do not mention ritualized homosexuality. Allen (1967:96–97, 99) only mentions two island cases and does not review the New Guinea material.
2. See, for examples, Bell 1935–1936:185 and Hallpike 1977:36. Carrier (1980a:101) laments in a recent survey: "Data available on homosexual behavior in most of the world's societies, past or

present, are meagre." They are "complicated by the prejudice of many observers who consider the behavior unnatural, dysfunctional, or associated with mental illness, and by the fact that in many of the societies studied the behavior is stigmatized and thus not usually carried out openly. Under these circumstances, the behavior is not easily talked about. At the turn of the twentieth century such adjectives as disgusting, vile, and detestable were still being used to describe homosexual behavior. . . . In discussing sodomy with some of his New Guinea informants, Williams (1936c), for example, asked them if they 'had ever been subjected to unnatural practice.'" (See below, p. 21.) Eric Schwimmer tells me that F. E. Williams' relates in his unpublished diary how he discovered homosexuality by having been propositioned by a Keraki boy in the forest.

3. Remember that Ellis generously prefaced *The Sexual Life of Savages*, noting that "other students doubtless will be inspired to follow" Malinowski's lead (Ellis 1929:xi). Too bad that never happened.

4. On the Amazon see, for example, C. Hugh-Jones 1979:160–161; S. Hugh-Jones 1979:110; Lévi-Strauss 1969:307; and Murphy 1959.

5. Here is Kaberry (1939:257n.), for example: "Homosexuality amongst the men did exist. The youths of 17 or 18 who were still unmarried would take boys of 10 or 11 as lovers. The women had no hesitation in discussing the matter with me, did not regard it as shameful, gave the names of different boys, and seemed to regard the practice as a temporary substitute for marriage." Cf. also C. Berndt 1965:265.

6. I know of no reports of institutionalized transvestism from Melanesia in which males have lifelong cross-gender dressing and associated homosexual behavior comparable, for instance, to those of the Mohave *alyha* (Devereaux 1937) or the Tahitian *mahu* (Levy 1973); cf. also Whitehead's (1981) recent review of the *berdache*. Melanesian transvestite behavior is, apparently, nonerotic cross-dressing role behavior permitted only in restricted ceremonies (see Bateson 1932:277–278; Elmberg 1965:97, 110, 117; and Tuzin 1980:47n, 227; and other examples reviewed in Schwimmer, chap. 6).

7. Clinically, primary male transsexualism is defined as the conviction of biologically normal males that "from earliest childhood . . . they are really members of the opposite sex" (Stoller 1979:11). Data on this subject are virtually nil in Melanesia; the only report that seems appropriate to this category is still the old one by Seligman (1902), which is not associated directly with ritualized homosexuality. There are, however, folktales (Landtman 1917:293–295) or myths (Herdt 1981:255–294) that may be

hints of collective cultural projections related to transsexual fantasies.

8. There are scattered reports of individual homosexual behavior in acculturated settings such as sexually restricted plantations; see especially Davenport 1965:200–201; and examples in B. Blackwood 1935:128; Hogbin 1951:163–164; Mead 1949:90f.; and Mitchell 1978:160. See also Bulmer's (1971:150n.) comparative note in this context.

9. I used the following procedures in assessing (RH) reports: all reports of any kind available to me (including popular accounts) were read and compared; early allusions were contrasted to later accounts; sources from neighboring groups were compared; and whenever a case seemed questionable, I wrote to the ethnographer who reported, or, if that person was deceased, to another expert who had worked in the same or neighboring areas. I have omitted several early cases of reports by laymen that seemed dubious or were contradicted by subsequent ethnographers. Finally, several Melanesianist scholars have read this chapter, and their critical evaluations of certain sources have also been used in my final interpretations.

10. The only definite report of institutionalized lesbianism comes from Malekula Island in the New Hebrides. Deacon (1934:170–171), the earliest anthropological source, states: "Between women, however, homosexuality is common, many women being generally known as lesbians, or in the native term *nimomogh iap nimomogh* ('woman has intercourse with woman'). It is regarded as a form of play, but, at the same time, it is clearly recognized as a form of sexual desire, and that the women do it because it gives them pleasure. . . . From the Big Nambas [tribal group] alone, it is reported that lesbianism is common. . . ." (See also Godelier 1982a:82.) This puny material is, however, virtually all that has ever been published. (Barker [1975:150] has an unpublished report.) For questionable allusions, see Baumann 1955:228; and Harrison 1937:362, 410. We should be wary of this lack of data on lesbian behavior, though, since most Melanesianist ethnographers have been males who primarily studied males; whether lesbian activity existed elsewhere and was hidden will probably never be known. Cf. below for DuToit's (1975:220) anomalous report of Highlands female "homosexuality play." Inge Riebe mentions that "adolescent girls engage in homosexual relations" among the Western Highlands Kalam (quoted in Keesing 1982:10n.), among whom no (RH) is reported.

11. See Allen (1981) for the changing scene. For popular accounts attesting to the persistence of ritualized homosexuality among the Big Nambas, see Gourguechon 1977:62ff. and Harrison 1937:47–48, 409–411.

12. Haddon (1936:xxviii) reports that such mainland groups as the Tami and Yabim "did not have sodomy" (anal intercourse? his source is not cited) in initiation rites. Cf. also Bamler 1911:496 on the Tami.

13. Parkinson (1907:544) is worth citing at length on the general problem of ethnographic reliability of reports regarding ritual homosexuality: "It requires an acquaintance of many years and an absolute confidence in the interrogator before a native can be induced to divulge these things, not so much because he is ashamed of them, for all the natives do them, and do not think them wrong. . . . These observations are based on the exact, detailed statements of natives, and are confirmed by white missionaries and their colored teachers. . . . The Imperial authorities are now taking steps, at the instigation of the missions, to restrain the abuses. It is questionable whether the ban will have any effect; it is highly probable that what previously took place in public is now done in secret." (Cf. also the translator's note, ibid.:530.)

14. Chowning (1980:15) notes that the Sengseng of Southwest New Britain denied practicing "sodomy" (by which she meant anal intercourse), which also applies to their neighbors, the Kove (Ann Chowning, personal communication).

15. Davenport (1965:200–201) uses a pseudonym to protect the exact location of this group. But they belong in this culture subregion. Like me (Herdt 1981), he feared his informants would be placed at risk by disclosure of this data.

16. See Schieffelin (1976), and Boelaars (1981) quoted below, for examples of identical cultural rules pertaining to homosexual access to a boy.

17. Haddon (1936:xxxii), in his preface to F. E. Williams's *Papuans of the Trans-Fly,* chides the work of the "late Rev. E. Baxter-Riley (1925:201). . . . He does not refer to sodomy; but that proves nothing, as the publishers omitted [i.e., censored] a considerable amount of his manuscript." For discussions of censorship and other facets of ethnographic reports on homosexual behavior in New Guinea societies by the doyen of Highlands studies, see Read 1980*b*:183–188 and below (see chap. 5). Cf. also Carrier 1980*a*; Layard 1959:112; and Mead 1961.

18. Landtman lived with the Kiwai from 1910–1912 (see also Landtman 1954, his last report).

19. See Wirz 1922:39 quoted above.

20. The older men are jurally entitled to have serial intercourse with this woman for the purpose of collecting "fertile" sperm from her vagina after sex in order to anoint the initiates' bodies. This practice is found also among the Marind-anim (Van Baal, chap. 3), the Kimam (Serpenti, chap. 7), and is known from Thurnwald's (1916) study of the Banaro.

21. The structural position of the chief in Malekula (Deacon 1934:261) may be here compared to the Kimam father. See Allen's chapter 3 below.
22. Held (1957:87–88) continues: "Although this [anal intercourse] is not judged to be a direct violation of the manners established by the ancestors, it is considered highly ridiculous, so that it is a serious insult to say of somebody that he is a sodomite (*agho ri-roni*)." Held does not indicate if this derogatory term is applied to both insertee and inserter, but the evidence indicates nonetheless that ritual homosexuality was absent from Waropen, at least by the time of his (1957:156 n. 3) work. Still, as I have noted, there is a danger in reading negative attributions toward the insertee as a castigation of all homosexual behavior (i.e., the inserter role).
23. Here we have a vivid example of the Victorian heritage (e.g., Freud's *Totem and Taboo*) underlying early writings about Melanesia. Notions about prehistoric hominid hordes, patriarchal authority in the family, and the prehistoric preeminence of "matriarchy" over "patriarchy" are explicit in ethnographic pieces such as those of Moszkowski, Atkinson (1903), Layard (1942), Róheim (1926), and Thurnwald (1911). (For Australian studies, see Hiatt 1975.) See Herdt and Poole (1982), who consider these intellectual influences on the concept of "sexual antagonism" in New Guinea studies.
24. As early as 1926 we find Róheim, who was well read in the Melanesian literature, making the following statement: "The Morehead River natives are the neighbors of the Marind (Kaia-Kaia) and frequently suffer their raids. I intend to discuss the close connection between the Marind and the Central Australians in a separate paper" (1926:448 n.4). To my knowledge Róheim never published such a paper.
25. Gebhard (1971:215) flatly states: "Anal coitus is the usual technique employed by male homosexuals [sic] in preliterate societies. . . ." Although he cites no data in support of this claim, it generally holds true for Melanesia. The only certain groups practicing homosexual fellatio are the Etoro, Bedamani, Duke-of-York, and Highland Anga peoples. Anal and oral intercourse seem to be "mutually exclusive" (Read 1980b:185) in Melanesia, which is almost certainly related to cultural beliefs about growth and procreation, though no one has yet investigated this suggestion.
26. Kelly adds: "This is accomplished orally. The boy manipulates the man to the point of ejaculation and consumes the semen." (Cf. Herdt 1981, and chap. 4.)
27. Schieffelin's (1982) paper is significant both in arguing for a more complex set of distinctions than "initiation" or "no initiation," as well as in raising the issue of social constraints upon personal choice in institutional homosexual activities. Yet, interpretive

77

questions remain. Why do Kaluli differ so in both these domains compared with other Plateau groups? One factor may be the nature of Schieffelin's reconstructed material. Homosexual practices and the *bau a* complex were gone by the time he worked, the result of several forces, missionaries in particular. One wonders the extent to which Schieffelin's informants' accounts were idealized and tended to represent (RH) activities as open to more choice than actually existed. I offer this speculation not so much to criticize Schieffelin's fine account as to underline the complexities of interpreting *all* ethnographic reports in this book.

28. Personal communication from a field letter of October 27, 1981, quoted with the author's permission.

29. The Pharisee reports:

> [Government patrol officer:] "They say that if they don't get rid of their mother's blood [through initiation rituals] their skin will never become firm."
> [Simpson:] "And in a fighting society such as theirs a man needs to be a full man. Any pansies in the Kuk [ukuku] garden?"
> [Patrol Officer:] "Never heard of any homosexuality at all among them—though I don't say there isn't. We've been here less than two years, don't forget. There's still a lot we don't know" (Simpson 1953:139). How did the Australian folks back home view this sort of popular tripe?

30. In terms of long-term anthropological research. For fascinating accounts of early travels and medical contacts in these areas, see Farquhar and Gajdusek (1981), on Gajdusek's Anga patrols. Jadran Mimica, a student at the Australian National University, has done anthropological fieldwork nearby, but he has not yet published his findings.

31. Here, as in the other early quotations, we have another example of using vague terms that make ethnographic reports useless. The dictionary defines sodomy as "unnatural sexual relations," though we may speculate that Blackwood meant homosexual anal intercourse. (How else—through what Pidgin words—would one adduce "sodomy": *sutem as?*) One's questions and report must be precise. Again, were one to ask a Sambia or Baruya tribesman (who practice only fellatio) if they engaged in anal intercourse, the honest, and probably indignant, responses would be no.

32. Fischer has not mentioned homosexual activity, though we know he did not see important initiation rites (Fischer 1968:135). As with other cases mentioned above, Fischer should not be misconstrued to mean (RH) is absent. No wonder ethnologists have avoided topics such as sexuality in Melanesia; our literature is such an obstacle course.

33. I shall report elsewhere on these observations.

34. The Sambia, who interact with the South Fore, believe that the latter practice homosexual anal intercourse, but this proves noth-

ing since Sambia fear and hate the South Fore, and also regard anal sex as repulsive. We should remember that many ethnic groups make attributions, usually slurs about other groups, of this sort. However, Graham Scott (personal communication), the linguist, believes that anal coitus may possibly be practiced among the South Fore, and I have it on hearsay from several Fore myself that this is true. But again, these are only stories, and no ethnographer has mentioned (RH) there (e.g., see Lindenbaum 1979).

35. Several years ago a prominent anthropologist colleague who has worked in a Sepik basin tribe told me that he noticed homosexual illicit activities occurring quietly on the periphery of his village. He has never reported this because it is tangential to his research interests. I cannot help but wonder if other instances are not to be found; whether or not they are institutionalized remains open to question.

36. See the quotation below (p. 25) from Godelier, which belongs in this category. Many other examples are to be found in the literature. I would add—though again it is not published anywhere to my knowledge—that heterosexual anal intercourse is said to be acceptable practice in parts of the Sepik.

37. Here is a common example from Mead (1949:106): "When the fear of passivity is also present in the minds of the adults—that is, when homosexuality is recognized in a society, with either approval or disapproval—the fear is exacerbated. The parents begin to pick at the child, to worry about his behavior, to set him trials, or to lament his softness." Elsewhere Mead's equation of "homosexuality" with "passivity" and "inversion" was surprisingly consistent (see Mead 1930, 1935, 1949:73, 93, 107, 376, 378). Cf. Mead (1961), for more sophisticated views.

38. Thurnwald (1916) never mentioned homosexual activity among the Banaro, but see Baumann (1955). Nothing conclusive can be said, other than this; however, the 1916 work describes heterosexual activities in association with the magical use of semen, sister exchange, and the use of sacred flutes and spirit impersonations strikingly similar to that of the Keraki, Kimam (Serpenti, chap. 7, below), Kiwai, and others.

39. In a remarkable early passage we find Haddon (1924:vii) arguing: "Thus there seems to be but little doubt that the Tugeri [Marind-anim], or at all events one element in the population, migrated down the Strickland branch of the Fly and along the Merauke [Mayo River] to the sea."

40. Such a historical scenario implies that various groups who, in their social system, resemble Angan groups, may once have had ritualized homosexuality but abandoned it in prehistoric times, at the period of their Austronesian influence. The Elema of the Papuan coast might be an example. But another example which links

the eastern coast of mainland New Guinea with Malekula and New Hebrides is the Finschhafen ritual cults, which impressed Deacon (1925) in their similarity to Malekula (and cf. Bamler 1911; Haddon 1936:xxviii; Wirz 1933).

41. Róheim's (1926:324–337 and passim) elaborate speculative diffusions—minus the primal horde fantasy (Róheim: "Papuan degenerate survivals")—of archaic Malaya-Polynesian migrations into Indonesia, New Guinea, and hence Australia, may be partially vindicated. A landbridge probably traversed the Torres Straits at that time.

42. The explicit references to ritual homosexuality in Australia noted above should be emphasized again here. Of course, we can do no more than point to parallels between Australian and Melanesian systems, for there are many complex differences between these two culture areas. Nothing more can be said on the subject until a modern ethnology of these areas emerges. Will someone please move us beyond this crude state of affairs?

43. Anthropological studies in Melanesia are so uneven that it is difficult to draw up a complete list of the relevant social units, let alone to compare them on particular cultural patterns. Bulmer (1970:93–96) lists 138 ethnographic studies by writers just for Papua New Guinea, whereas Koch (1974:Map 4) lists 86 studies by professional ethnographers for the whole island of New Guinea. The number would be greater now, perhaps as many as 200 accounts, if one included all reports by all writers. But remember, we are dealing with a total universe of some 700 different cultures and 2,000 different languages in New Guinea and Melanesia. The choice of any of these subsets of the total will be arbitrary in one way or another.

44. Given the range of studies in note 43, we may devise these rough statistics: table 1.1 shows 29 distinct cultures definitely reported. (If we include adjacent groups among the Marind-anim, the Anga, and the Fly, the number would rise to about 48.) If our total baseline is 100 Melanesian societies, we have 29 percent; if 200 is selected, we have 15 percent. I would estimate between 10 and 20 percent as a reasonable estimate of frequency, given what we know.

45. Associated factors included cultural values that encouraged resort to violence and blood revenge as a part of public policy; the lack of redressive mechanisms for peacefully resolving wrongs or for inhibiting de-escalation (Koch 1974); and the range of societal scale, cultural rules, and armaments associated with levels of warfare (reviewed in Sillitoe 1978).

46. The general contrast: lowlands head-hunting (and/or cannibalism) versus Highlands war raids (but not head-hunting) holds for New

Guinea, and, moreover, for Highlands Anga versus Lowlands Anga (east of the Vailala River).

47. *Notes and Queries* (1951:109) had it right years ago: "In some societies with a strong military organization or with age-sets, homosexual practices are usual in certain grades before marriage, and are subject to conventional rules. Such temporary associations may not be regarded as detrimental to subsequent normal heterosexual development."

48. "The worry that boys will not grow up to be men is much more widespread than that girls will not grow up to be women, and in none of these South Sea societies does the latter fear appear at all" (Mead 1949:107). Such beliefs are widespread but not universal in Melanesia (e.g., the Massim). However, I believe that careful study will show systematic Melanesian variations in this belief system, with (RH) groups revealing that most intense form of such ideologies (see P. Brown 1978:155; Herdt 1980).

49. The situation is more complex than this statement suggests, at least among Sambia, but the complexity cannot be examined here. See Dundes' (1976) and Hage's (1981) arguments noted below.

50. It is as ethnocentric to deny eroticism among tribal peoples, i.e., reducing their eroticism to customs and rites, as it is ethnocentric to "read" eroticism into situations where none exists.

51. In spite of the great differences between the ancients and Melanesians, this much they share in common: "Homosexual relationships are not exhaustively divisible, in Greek society or in any other, into those which perform an educational function and those which provoke and relieve genital tension. Most relationships of any kind are complex, and the need for bodily contact and orgasm was one ingredient of the complex of needs met by homosexual eros" (Dover 1978:203).

52. Nambikwara call these homosexual relations "the loving lie"; they go on between adolescent boys who are cross-cousins. "That is to say, in which one partner would normally marry the other's sister and is taking her brother as a provisional substitute" (Lévi-Strauss 1969:307). He argues that the Nambikwara chief's extra wives support his position symbolically: "They are both the reward and instrument of power" (ibid.:307–308).

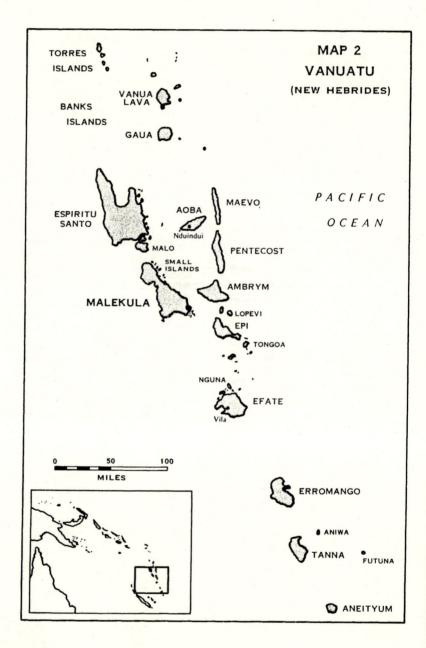

2

Michael R. Allen

Ritualized Homosexuality, Male Power, and Political Organization in North Vanuatu: A Comparative Analysis

The island of Malekula, in north Vanuatu, has for long been recognized as a *locus classicus* for the occurrence of organized male homosexuality. Deacon, who carried out his field researches in 1926, was the first to publish a reasonably detailed account (1934:260–269) of the highly institutionalized variety that occurs among the Big Nambas in the north. But it was Layard, who had worked at a much earlier period (1914–15) on the nearby offshore islands of Vao and Atchin, who subsequently incorporated Deacon's data into an early attempt to appreciate the theoretical significance of the practice (Layard 1942:503–522). Though homosexual behavior as such did not appear to occur in the Small Islands, Layard noted the presence of dramatized representations on the part of ancestral spirits in the context of the boys' compulsory initiation rites. He attempted to provide some explanation for variations such as these but was seriously constrained by the inadequacies of his part-evolutionary and part-diffusionist premises. In a subsequent publication, however, he reexamined not only his own and Deacon's data but also much of the then available material on homosexuality elsewhere in Melanesia (Layard 1959). In the intervening years Layard had been greatly influenced by both Jungian and Freudian psychoanalytic theory, and in his article he produced some interesting evidence in support of the then widely held psychological hypothesis regarding homosexual intercourse as a substitute for incest desire.

Since much of subsequent anthropological thinking, not only about ritualized homosexuality but also about male initiation in general, runs counter to the premises of that brand of psychoanalytic thinking that places great weight on incest repression, oedipal rivalry, and castration anxiety, Layard's views, if correct, would have serious and widespread implications. It is not my intention here to carry out a reassessment of Layard's analysis, however, but rather to reexamine the Malekula and Small Islands data, together with some additional information that I obtained myself in 1970 in Nduindui district, west Ambae (formerly Aoba), an island some forty miles to the northeast of Malekula (see map 3).

My argument can be put simply. In each of these three areas, homosexual behavior is believed to have causal effects of an ontological kind; that is to say, the participants are believed to generate a power that can both physically and spiritually transform themselves, and by extension, others also. This highly generalized belief is associated with a culturally specific form of initiation ritual distinguished by such recurrent features as shark symbolism, the use of elaborate hoaxes, and the importance of the male phallus. Beyond this simple level there are major differences.

Among the Big Nambas, homosexuality is a highly organized form of behavior that occurs in a regular way between senior men and youths who have not yet completed their initiation into manhood. The senior men have the power, physically manifest in their exaggeratedly large penes, to make the juniors grow into mature men, above all into men with similarly strong and effective penes. Though the powerful phallus is undoubtedly believed to be relevant in the context of male domination, especially notable in Big Nambas society, it is also indicative of the capacity of men to contribute to the political welfare of a community dominated by hereditary and polygynous chiefs. In other words, the political function of the power so generated in the context of homosexual relations is the maintenance both of male hegemony and of chiefly preeminence.

In the nearby Small Islands there is, in behavioral terms, no male homosexuality at all. Though male initiation shares many of the features of the Big Nambas rites, including the pairing off of initiators and novices in couples who refer to one another by terms that mean "wife" and "husband" (or more literally, "woman" and "sister's husband"), Layard's (1942:503) informants denied that homosexual connection occurs. Nevertheless, the theme of anal penetration is repeatedly enacted in the context of the numerous hoaxes perpetrated on the novices during their thirty-day seclusion immediately after penile super-incision.[1] But instead of penetration by tutors, the novices are often terrifyingly threatened with such action from ancestral spirits. As Layard, I think, quite correctly argues, these ancestral spirits represent to the Small Islanders "the highest cultural and psychic values that the natives know" (1959:111). The ancestral spirits are the guardians of tribal morality, and it must be inferred that their special power in relation to the novices is, in political terms, the creation and maintenance of a cohesive and solidary group of male agnates. Indeed, the ancestral power is so great that the mere threat of homosexual action is believed sufficient to ensure the transformation of the youths into effective adult members of the village.

In Nduindui the homosexual theme appears yet again in the context of initiatory ritual, but instead of providing an idiom for the expression of either chiefly hegemony or lineage solidarity, it is here associated with the power of big men to attract followers by daring to do that which is normally prohibited. As in the Small Islands, actual homosexual intercourse does not occur, and if it should it would be condemned as abhorrent, in much the same way that incest is also condemned. The Nduindui are fully aware of the homosexual practices of the Big Nambas and regard its occurrence as firm evidence for their view of these people as "uncivilized black savages." The homosexual theme occurs in the context of secret rites in which the participants are divided into initiators and initiands; but unlike both the Big Nambas and Small Islands rites, which constitute compulsory initiations into manhood, the west Aoba counterparts are voluntary affairs periodically organized by big men, and which include both male and female participants. As I shall shortly demonstrate, a recurrent theme of these rites is that the initiates, collectively and individually, are believed to generate powers through the public performance of acts that in everyday life are said to be bad (*hati*), bad either in the sense of invoking the presence of dangerous beings, as with sharks or bush spirits, or as contrary to the conventions of everyday life, for example, in penis or vagina exposure or in dramatic representations of incest and homosexual intercourse. For ordinary men and women in everyday contexts, all of these actions and objects are surrounded with taboos and avoidance patterns: in the context of the rites they evoke powers for the benefit of the participants, above all for those high-ranking men who either themselves perform, or sponsor others to perform, the most outrageous acts.

I shall now support and develop this argument by examining the extant data for these three communities in greater detail.

THE BIG NAMBAS OF NORTH MALEKULA

Deacon only spent a few days in north Malekula, and though he succeeded in collecting a remarkable amount of useful cultural information, his data on social, political, and economic organization are almost nonexistent. We are fortunate, however, in that the French anthropologist Jean Guiart spent some five months among the Big Nambas in late 1950 and early 1951, and published his findings, which included detailed census data (initially in French [1952] and subsequently in abbreviated form in English [1953]).

At the time of Guiart's visit, some 1,137 Big Nambas lived in twenty-five villages scattered over rugged terrain on a high tableland in northwest Malekula. The villages ranged in size from 8 to 98 persons and most contained a number of clustered hamlets. The men of each village were members of a number of named patrilineal clans, the smaller with only some two to four clans, the largest with nineteen (averaging four clans per village). The primary political groups were named localities whose members owed allegiance to the hereditary chief of the dominant clan of that locality. There were eight such chiefs, four of whom Guiart designated as lesser chiefs and four as grand chiefs. The localities dominated by lesser chiefs ranged in scale from one to five villages

TABLE 2.1

BIG NAMBAS SOCIOLOGICAL AND CENSUS DATA BASED ON GUIART
(1952:233–42)[2]

Primary localities (villages or village clusters)	Villages	Clans	Men	Women	Boys	Girls	Total
Nevenbwis	1	8	32	21	24	21	98
Nevinal	1	2	4	3	--	1	8
Ontowalo	1	4	25	19	3	5	52
Mayak	1	4	18	17	3	1	39
Amox	7	24	148	142	105	27	422
Nevinala	2	9	31	33	14	9	87
Maxawe	1	8	17	18	12	9	56
Bwiter	2	8	43	24	15	7	89
Tenmaru and Varas	4	23	46	43	30	18	137
Tenamit	5	11	52	55	25	17	149
	25	101	416	375	231	115	1137

and in population from 8 to 149 persons, those by grand chiefs from three to seven villages and from 137 to 422 persons (see table 2.1).

Guiart especially stressed the flexibility of clans in their residential affiliations and even more so in their chiefly allegiances. As he noted (1953:442),

> . . . clans will be vagabond and change their allegiance from one chieftainship to another, or without relinquishing their relationship to one chief, will move easily from one village to another. The important group of Amox, with its seven villages under one chief, is in great part the result of such a reshuffling.

In other words, in contrast to the great majority of Melanesian societies, where flexibility in clan organization consists in the ease with which individuals can change clan affiliation, here flexibility is rather the ease with which clans can change chiefly affiliation. The difference clearly relates to the crucial political importance

87

TABLE 2.2

Social Structure and Ritualized Homosexuality in North Vanuatu

	Big Nambas	Vao	Nduindui
Descent units	Dispersed patriclans	Localized patriclans	Dispersed cognatic stocks
Local groups	Multiclan villages and village clusters	Clan-villages and double-villages	Multistock villages
Residence	Patrivirilocal	Patrivirilocal	Patrivirilocal
Leadership	Hereditary chiefs	Lineage elders	Big men
Initiatory group	Inclusive male cult	Inclusive male cult	Voluntary association
Homosexual relation	Between initiator and novice	Between clan ancestor and novices	Between initiator and novice in mock form
Penis treatment	Circum-incized and concealed in big wrapper	Superincised and concealed in small wrapper	Reddened with powder and concealed behind apron

of chiefs among the Big Nambas. Power devolves first and foremost on these hereditary officeholders, and it is they who provide the fulcrums about which clans, hamlets, villages, women, and, as we shall see, homosexual boy partners, constellate and form cohesive groups.

Yet another unusual though important feature of Big Nambas society, especially for a society in which the patrilineal principle is otherwise so much stressed, is the prohibition against a man living at close quarters with either his father or his elder brother. The rationale for the prohibition is the severity of the avoidance taboo between a man's wife and these two close patrilateral male relatives. Though propriety can be maintained by hamlet coresidence, provided the houses are divided by a high fence without any opening, most men prefer to set up house in different hamlets. The men themselves, that is to say, father and son and elder brother and younger brother, can and do meet and interact freely in the clan's men's house (*namel*); indeed, male children of any age can wander about and enter this building without hindrance.

I dwell on these restrictions for it seems most likely that they are interrelated with the correspondingly intimate relationship that obtains between paternal grandfather and grandson. According to Guiart, and he speaks with some authority on the matter, it is these two who regularly establish a homosexual relationship. I quote at length from this important passage:

> Much more elaborate and peculiar are the relations between two alternate generations, at least as far as a young boy is concerned, the girl leaving the family too soon for great care to be given her. The boys, in the beginning of their teens, are sent to the paternal grandfather, with whom they live for some years, working for him in the daytime, in his gardens, and at night sleeping with him in the *namel*, the men's club house. This homosexual relation between the two is carried on until the young man is old enough to marry and be given a bark belt to wear; until then he fixes the end of his penis sheath to a narrow plaited pandanus belt . . . The relationship between a young man and his paternal grandmother is almost of the same order. She attends to his sexual education, serves him as a go-between for his intrigues or even sleeps at times with him until he has married or found a younger partner.
>
> *(Guiart 1953:440)*

Deacon, in his account of Big Nambas homosexuality, makes no mention of the grandparental relation, and indeed the implication is that such a possibility would be precluded through the application of incest avoidance and clan exogamy rules that parallel those of marriage.

> In the choice of his *mugh vel* [the term by which a boy lover, as also a circumcision candidate, is known] a man is restricted by certain rules. He need not necessarily select a boy from another clan than his own, but he must be careful that no genealogical relationship can be traced between them. To have intercourse with a boy of one's own clan to whom one is allied by known kinship bonds is to be guilty of incest. Further, sexual relations with the sister's son or with any boy to whom one is related by marriage is similarly condemned. Should a man cohabit with a boy of his own clan who is known to be kin to him, the death penalty is not inflicted on the guilty pair as it would be in the event of such incestuous intercourse between a man and a woman, but both parties concerned must kill and exchange a pig.
>
> *(Deacon 1934:261–262)*

It is unfortunate that Guiart did not comment on this seeming discrepancy between these two sets of data. Nevertheless, I think that some resolution is possible. One possibility would be to interpret Guiart's comments to refer to classificatory and not real grandfathers, an arrangement which, of course, would conflict in no way with Deacon's stipulations. However, the manner in which Guiart wrote inclines me to reject this possibility, as also does the widespread occurrence in north Vanuatu of a sexual bond between a youth and his paternal grandmother. Another, more likely, possibility is that Deacon confused exogamic and incest prohibitions. Though marriage with a woman of one's own clan would violate a rule of clan exogamy, it is likely that among the Big Nambas, as in many other clan-structured societies, sexual intercourse with such a woman would only constitute incest if she fell within certain prohibited kinship categories. Throughout much of north Vanuatu, women referred to as granddaughters, regardless of clan affiliation, are suitable sexual partners, and it would seem that the homosexual tie reported by Guiart is in conformity with this occurrence.

I will shortly elaborate on what I see as the political implications of the Big Nambas alternate-generation homosexual relationship. But first a comment is in order on another and perhaps most important aspect that Layard made central to his analysis. Layard was concerned, as noted earlier, to provide anthropological support for the psychological hypothesis that links homosexuality with repressed incest desire. In his 1959 article he argued that homosexuality in primitive society is commonly found in association with sister-exchange marriage and that indeed the homosexual partners are, prototypically, related as sister's husband and wife's brother. In support of this contention he noted the widespread occurrence, both in Malekula and elsewhere in Melanesia, of the sister's husband term of address used for the senior homosexual partner. The psychoanalytic argument is of course obvious: the junior partner realizes his repressed sexual desire for his sister through a homosexual relationship with a man eligible to be her husband. Layard took particular delight in discovering that Deacon (1934) noted the use of this term of address among the Big Nambas, but because it was used in jest form he failed to pursue the matter. The possibility that Layard may be correct in thus stressing the incest factor is given further support in Guiart's contention that the homosexual couple are related as paternal grandfather and grandson. There are indeed many features of Big Nambas society that might lead one to predict here the presence of a strong Oedipus complex. As Layard (1942:489) noted, "The Big Nambas represent an extreme form of patrilineal culture which they have carried to a pitch exceeding all other New Hebrides tribes in the very low status which they accord to women." It is, in other words, a culture in which a variety of incest prohibitions combine to create a relationship between father and son such that any generalized propensity for oedipal rivalry might well be accentuated.

Let me stress, however, that unlike Layard I do not take the Big Nambas as prototypical for Melanesia as a whole—and even less so for that scarcely tangible entity, "primitive society." As he himself emphasizes, the Big Nambas are indeed an extreme case, and it is precisely this fact that I find so interesting.

We have thus far established that male teenagers enter into regular homosexual relationships with senior initiated men and that such couples, who are most probably related as either real or classificatory paternal grandfathers and grandsons, refer to one another as "wives" and "sisters' husbands," the same terms being used also between guardians and novices during the circum-incision and associated initiatory rituals. Deacon is uncertain whether or not the initial sister's husband (*nilagh sen*) is the same individual who takes the role of initiatory guardian (*dubut*), though this possibility seems most likely. Either way, the dubut claims exclusive sexual rights over the lad:

> He is now the boy's husband and is extremely jealous of any other man securing his *mugh vel* and having intercourse with him. So much is this the case that he will not allow him out of his sight. The *dubut* himself, however, cannot have sexual access to the boy throughout all the thirty days' seclusion which accompanies the circumcision rites. From the time of the operation until the wound is healed, intercourse is forbidden, and the *dubut* only plays the part of a guardian who cares for the novice's physical needs. But when the wound has healed he resumes his marital rights and continues to have relations with the boy until sometime later the latter

91

purchases his bark-belt. The reason, or rather the rationalization which the natives put forward for their homosexual practices is that boy-lover's male organ is caused to grow strong and large by the homosexual acts of his husband. The growth of the penis is supposed to be complete by the time that the bark-belt is assumed.
(Deacon 1934:262)

The youth, who has now become a "man," can take a boy lover for himself.

An important feature of the Big Nambas initiatory complex, as indeed in all other areas where it occurs in north Vanuatu, is the enactment of numerous hoaxes by previously initiated men during the course of the novices' seclusion. But perhaps to a degree unparalleled elsewhere, the Big Nambas hoaxes are so designed as to induce terror in the novices, terror from the imminent threat of painful and possibly even destructive attack by capricious and powerful ghosts. Since the latter are, in most instances, said to be the ghosts of deceased chiefs, it seems reasonable to infer that such hoaxes are intended to convey to the novices something regarding the nature of chiefly power, a power that novices have now in part acquired and which is located in their exposed penis heads. Deacon describes the following hoax as typical of those performed at night:

A man is carefully dressed up in banana leaves and creepers, so that his body is completely covered. His head, especially, is made to appear like a tangled mass of creeper ropes. He is then decked out in all kinds of scarlet flowers such as hibiscus and wild ginger. Thus arrayed he steals at dead of night into the *ghamal* where the novices are lying, and climbs to the top of the lofty centre pole of the house. Here he begins a low weird whistling. The awed novices, crouching on the floor, whisper among themselves and feel their flesh creep. One of the guardians hurries in, tells them hastily that the ghost of a famous fighting chief who was killed in battle is about, and then goes away again. The whistling becomes more and more insistent and seems to come nearer. A light is brought in, and in the dim shadows of the roof the boys discern a fearful figure—unmistakably the ghost. Suddenly it slides down the pole, lands at the bottom, and starts whistling and circling, stamping rapidly and throwing up the dust among the terrified boys. As they shrink and flee from it, it makes as though to clutch and grab them and after a while rushes out of the building and vanishes, again whistling weirdly in the darkness.

(1934:264–265)

I would like to stress the important connections that obtain between homosexual activity, the growth of boys' sexual organ, the belief that a specifically male power resides in the glans penis, and the corresponding necessity both to make evident and to protect that power by the wearing of a huge penis-wrapper. Throughout Malekula, the term *nambas* refers to a penis-wrapper, and the European designation "Big Nambas" is a consequence of the truly enormous version of that garment that these people wear. As Layard (1942:481) has noted, penis-wrappers are exclusively and solely worn in those north Vanuatu areas where either circum-incision or incision is performed during initiation. Furthermore, the largest wrappers are worn by those who practice circum-incision—that is, where the head of the penis is most fully exposed—while the smaller version is associated with the lesser operation of incision. Since fully institutionalized homosexuality is found only in association with circum-incision and the big wrappers, it is evident that these three phenomena are meaningfully associated with one another. In short, the homosexual act not only makes the penis grow to exceptional size but also to be filled with impressive "power," a circumstance that in turn warrants the major operation of circum-incision and the associated wearing of outsize wrappers and impressive bark belts. One might indeed describe much of Big Nambas culture as constituting a highly exaggerated celebration of male power, a feature no doubt itself generated by complex historical and environmental factors of which we are in almost total ignorance. Whatever these factors may have been, I would suggest that they are intimately associated with the parallel development of a most unusual (that is, for Melanesia) system of hereditary chieftainship. In other words, the power generated in the context of institutionalized homosexuality is not just generalized male power, but is specifically that form of male power associated with the persons of chiefs.

The link that I am here proposing between chiefly power and penis power would, of course, be self-evident if it were only chiefs, (or perhaps members of chiefly clans) who entered into homosexual relations, underwent circum-incision, and wore large penis-wrappers. Though the facts, insofar as they can be ascertained, do not conform to this simple pattern, there are nevertheless strong indications of the centrality of chiefs. The published material on the Big Nambas suggests that all males enter into homosexual relations, initially as "wives" and, after acquiring the right to wear a bark belt (which itself succeeds the operation of circum-incision), as "sister's husbands." But the same sources also describe marriage as a generalized phenomenon, with no direct statements indicating that some men miss out. I suggest that it is in fact possible to infer from Guiart's detailed census material (see table 2.1) that the dominant men of the leading clan in each village succeed in establishing a near monopoly over the sexual and other services provided by both the women and the unmarried youths. For example, Vix-ambat, the young grand chief of Amox, a confederacy of seven villages whose members recognize his chiefly status and accept his leadership, is listed as having seven women who "belong" to him, while his father's brother, the old ex-chief Kali, has as many as twenty-seven. The following comment of one of Layard's Small Island informants on the Big Nambas chiefly system, though possibly somewhat exaggerated due to the Small Islanders awe of the Big Nambas, nevertheless provides some indication of the kind of power relations that underlie Guiart's bald figures.

> Each village has a chief, whose title is *Mulon*. The chief has absolute possession over all the men, women and chattels in the village. Every man's pigs belong to the *Mulon*, who can demand them at any time. No man will sell a pig without the *Mulon's* consent. All yams also belong to him, as does every kind of possession. Though the *Mulon* himself has only one wife, yet all women also belong to him, and no woman may be bought or sold (i.e., married) without his consent. He has, however, a right over all women until they are married, but once a woman is married he does not interfere with her. The *Mulon's* word is law. He never eats any flesh except human flesh, and orders the death of any man he may fancy to eat. He never gives his orders direct but always through the medium of officials called *mako*. The office of *Mulon* is hereditary; he is succeeded by his son, who even if a small child, assumes immediately on his father's death absolute command of the whole village, old men and all.
>
> (*Layard 1942:740*)

Guiart's later observations in no way conflicted with those of Layard's informant. He noted that all of a chief's subjects must keep their heads at a lower level than his, and all women, other than his own, must use a special deferential vocabulary in addressing him. The chief's wives, presumably all of those designated as his "women," must never be seen by commoners, and

> To be sure, the frontal roll of their mat headdress is pulled down on the face. If a man was found in the yard where the chief's wives have their houses, he would be strangled on the spot unless he could immediately pay a heavy fine in pigs. A woman who comes and stays in these premises has to stay and cannot be reclaimed by her husband.
>
> *(Guiart 1953:444)*

Whatever inadequacies there are in the accounts of Layard and Guiart, it is quite evident that the Big Nambas chiefs wield very considerable powers and that these are intimately connected with their capacity to control both the productive and reproductive capabilities of women. Unfortunately, there are few comparable data concerning the political and economic dimensions of the relationship between chiefs and their boy-lovers. There are, however, strong indications that chiefs again exercise a comparable monopoly. Deacon, for example, began his account with this observation:

> Among the Big Nambas, as in North Raga, homosexual practices between the men are very highly developed. Every chief has a number of boy-lovers, and it is said that some men are so completely homosexual in their affections, that they seldom have intercourse with their wives, preferring to go with their boys.
>
> *(Deacon 1934:261)*

He then goes on to describe how senior men permit their boy-lovers to have intercourse with other men provided the latter presents the boy with

> . . . some calico, fowl's feathers, or other ornament. This the boy then hands over to his *nilagh sen*. Boys are "sold" in this way only for short periods of time: after a few days they always return to their real "husbands," who have use of them as before.
>
> *(Deacon 1934:261)*

Such an arrangement clearly depicts a market situation wherein some men have a surplus of boy-lovers, while others are obliged

95

to pay for favors in a piecemeal fashion. It would thus seem more than likely that, as with women, only chiefs (or perhaps by extension all male members of chiefly clans) have proprietary rights over the sexual and other services of boys. I should add here that a chief benefits not only sexually but also productively, through the labor provided by his "boys," just as he also gains through the labor of his women. Deacon, for example, noted:

> The bond between *mugh vel* and *nilagh sen* is, however, not only a sexual one. The boy accompanies his "husband" everywhere; works in his garden (it is for this reason that a chief has many boy-lovers), and if one or other of the two should die, the survivor will mourn him deeply.
>
> *(1934:261)*

Guiart's 1950 census figures provide further support for my contention that chiefs exercise a significant monopoly over the homosexual and other services provided by boys. For example, in Amox, the important village cluster dominated by Vixambat and Kali (the two leading chiefs), there were in that year 105 boys as against 27 girls. Since these two men had between them 34 wives, it would seem reasonable to infer that a large proportion of the boys were their grandsons. If Guiart is correct in his assertion that grandsons enter into a homosexual relation with their paternal grandfathers, it must be concluded that these two men exercised a most significant homosexual monopoly. In other words, it is not just undifferentiated male power that is imparted to the novices in the form of semen and is responsible for the production of large circum-incised penes encased in huge and impressive wrappers, but important male chiefly power.

The political significance of the Big Nambas chiefs is especially evident in the way they dominate the local version of the graded society. As in Lambumbu district on the northwest coast, where hereditary principles also greatly modify the otherwise democratic features of the graded society, there are four main ranks recognized among the Big Nambas. Only men of the two highest ranks can eat at sacred fires located in the men's house, an arrangement that clearly places the members of the lowest ranks in a liminal world between that of "true" men and women. Deacon, who unfortunately failed to get much detailed information on the Big Nambas graded society, nevertheless wrote,

> There seems to be some reason for supposing that in the *Nimangki* of the Big Nambas there is a "class distinction" as there is in Lambumbu, and that *Vilvil* and *Meliun* (the two top ranks) are entered only by chiefs and the sons or near relatives of chiefs.
>
> *(1934:372)*

In the Lambumbu district there are also

> groups of people in the community who are never allowed to enter the *Nimangki* at all. They are not permitted to acquire any pigs, or at most a very few, and should their stock rise above the prescribed number, the surplus must be given to the chiefs. Further, while not allowed to obtain wealth for themselves they are expected to help others in its acquisition by working for the "privileged class." These depressed people eat apart from other men at a fire of their own . . . which is not inside the *amel,* the house of the *Nimangki,* but in the village near the women's fire. Just as the privilege of eating at the *naam ruhvaru* (the chiefly fire) is handed down from father to son, so these disabilities are inherited patrilineally. . . . These fires then . . . appear to have been bound up with a stratification of society which is reminiscent of feudal conditions.
>
> *(1934:347)*

A final comment on the actual method of homosexual intercourse practiced by the Big Nambas is in order. Deacon (1934:261), in a footnote, observed that "the act of coition, when intercourse is homosexual, is carried out standing up, not lying down as is usual when cohabiting with a woman." Though the wording is not without some ambiguity, I think it reasonable to infer here that the method referred to is that of anal intercourse. Layard, possibly relying on this statement of Deacon's (or on the basis of his own independent evidence), consistently referred to anal penetration, a method he regarded as universal within homosexual relationships in Melanesia. As we shall shortly see, it is with anal penetration, not by ancestral spirits but by chiefly men, that the Small Island novices are constantly threatened during their thirty-day period of seclusion after penile incision. In Nduindui also, the

97

theme of buttock presentation is prominent during the secret *na nggwatu* rites.

The evidence would indeed be overwhelmingly in favor of anal penetration were it not for Guiart's (1953:440) contrary observations: "I must say that technically the grandfather and his grandson are not homosexuals in the true European sense, of which the natives know. It would be better to say that they masturbate one another." Despite the seeming authority of this statement, I would be inclined to give greater credence to Deacon's evidence. A possible basis for confusion on Guiart's part is that the boy's guardian may be expected, as in the nearby district of Lambumbu, to sleep beside his charge in the men's house during the period of seclusion and to hold "the lad's penis in his fingers, which he warms from time to time at the fire" (Deacon 1934:253). But during this period homosexual intercourse also is strictly prohibited.

VAO

Vao is one of seven small coral islets that lie immediately off the northeast coast of Malekula. The islands, each of which consists of less than half a square mile of land, are purely for residence, the inhabitants maintaining gardens on the nearby mainland. In 1892 the population of Vao was estimated at about 1,000 or more (Doucere 1934:153, cited in Layard 1942:745), but by the time of Layard's fieldwork (in 1914) it had shrunk to 401 (Layard 1942:745). By the 1967 census the population was 816.

Layard (1942:51–172) describes the Vao people as residing in six nucleated villages paired into three sets of double-villages, one double-village on one side of the island, and two double-villages on the other. The male residents of each of these three double-villages are also members of a single unnamed and exogamous partrilineal clan. Of the two villages belonging to a clan, one is said to be the parent village and the other the offspring. Each village is divided into a number of sections, the male members of which constitute agnatic lineages.

The village-sections occupy pallisaded residential units, each centered on a men's house and a cemetery. The men of such groups spend most of their time in the clubhouses, and they cooperate in the performance of mortuary rites and their associated feasts (Layard 1942:63).

The village is the focus of the important grade-taking ceremonies *(maki)*. To it belong the dancing ground and clubhouse used for the performance of the *maki* rites. The village also acts as the initiatory unit.

Each double-village is differentiated from its neighbors as a discrete, locally anchored and exogamous clan. The women of such communities must leave to join their husbands in other double-villages, and the wives must all come in from outside. Speiser (1923:102), who visited Vao in 1910, was so impressed by the structural importance of these double-villages that he described the population as being divided into three large villages. Though Layard (1942:55) fully agreed with the importance attributed to these units by Speiser, he noted that they seem to have declined in importance in favor of the single village during the period following European contact. It may well be that the double-villages were of special importance in warfare and that with pacification they consequently went into decline. It would seem that by the time Layard arrived on Vao, the sole context in which the double-villages were structurally significant was in the regulation of marriage through the rule of clan exogamy. The point to be stressed is that at each of the three important levels of Vao local organization—the village-section, the village, and the double-village—patrilineal descent and local-group exogamy together provide the basis both for male solidarity and the dispersal of women.

Cutting across these otherwise discrete and solidary patrilineal groups is a division of the population into two unnamed kinship groups that consist of alternate generations of coresident male agnates. In village-sections, these lines are known as the "sides of the lodge," and each has its own men's house and cemetery; in villages, by contrast, they are known as "the sides of the stone," and the members act collectively in the two important contexts of grade-taking and initiation.

Let me add a few brief comments on the maki, the Small Islands' version of the ubiquitous north Vanuatu grade-taking institution. Though the ceremonial act is the same throughout the area in which grade-taking occurs—the slaughter of tusked pigs on a ceremonial ground, accompanied by the acquisition of titles and insignia, and succeeded by the eating of sacred food cooked at a taboo oven—each community differs in the selection of individuals, or categories of individuals, who carry out these and other important acts. We have already seen that among the Big Nambas the highest of four ranks are reserved for members of the chiefly clans. Elsewhere in Malekula, and also throughout the matrilineal islands to the east, the focus is again on the individual, but without any formal exclusion of certain sections of the male community. The Small Islands maki differs radically from all of these versions, a fact long ago recognized by Layard.

> One of the chief characteristics . . . that distinguishes the *Maki* in all the Small Islands from any recorded variants of the rite is that, whereas in all other districts of which we have adequate record, advancement in the hierarchy of ranks is achieved by individuals sacrificing purely on their own account, here the whole male community in any given village takes part, each "line" or marriage section consisting of alternate generations in the male line of descent performing the rite in alternating generations.
>
> *(Layard 1942:271)*

In other words, the maki, instead of providing a finely calibrated hierarchy of status positions relevant to a competitive big-man type polity, operates rather as a local group affair in which the two "sides" of an agnatically structured village alternately initiate one another en bloc into two main grades, the low and the high maki. Furthermore, though the stipulated ritual acts are performed throughout north Vanuatu for an identical purpose, the acquisition of ritual powers deemed relevant both for political purposes and for the achievement of a desired state of being after death, in each area the powers vary according to differences in political structure. Among the Big Nambas, the powers are of a kind that reinforce the common belief in the superiority of chiefs, while elsewhere in Malekula and throughout Ambae they give added legitimacy to the authority claims of self-made leaders. In the Small Islands, by contrast, the powers so generated are thought to contribute to the collective needs of the highly nucleated village by establishing links between living and dead clan members.

100

Putting the same point in a slightly different way, one might characterize Small Island political life as constrained within the parameters of a system in which agnatic kinship defines the limits of male cooperation and solidarity. Whereas the highly competitive Nduindui and Malekulan grade-taker increasingly frees himself from the constraints of kinship the further he climbs an elaborate hierarchy of grades, in the Small Islands almost all of the roles and relationships generated in grade-taking ceremonies are strictly defined in kinship terms.

Similar kinship considerations are operative in the context of male initiation. The same village-wide alternate generations of male agnates initiate one another's youths in ceremonies that occur approximately every six to nine years. However, as Layard noted,

> This disparity [in the age of novices], is yet further increased by the fact mentioned above that youths of one "line" only are initiated at once, by which reason the actual time elapsing between the rites for which any given novice is eligible is twice that mentioned, namely anything between twelve and eighteen years. Thus, at the initiation rite in which I myself took part on Atchin the youngest novice was about 4 years old and the eldest about 22!
>
> *(1942:495)*

Each novice has a special tutor "detailed to look after him to tell him what he must do, to tend his wound and share his beatings" (Layard 1942:503). The tutors who would have participated as novices at the previous ceremony, are necessarily no more than six to nine years older than their charges, a marked contrast with the grandfather-grandson relationship among the Big Nambas.

Approximately a year before the main initiatory ceremony is performed, special gardens are established on the mainland, and numerous journeys inland are made to collect materials for the construction of the initiatory house close to the village's main ceremonial ground. On each such occasion, both when the materials are landed on the beach and later when they are transported to the dancing ground, the novices and tutors are beaten with sticks by older initiates. In this context and in many others as well, it would seem that tutor and novice, rather than standing in a relationship of differentiation and opposition, instead identify with

101

each other as supportive fellow sufferers. Throughout, the emphasis seems to be that those who suffer either pain or terror do so for the good of the novices and hence, by extension, for the whole community.

When the materials have been collected, which will take many months, the initiation house is erected: "This takes several days, with long intervals between them. The same beatings and ritual are performed, but on a grander scale, and on each occasion when the work is finished the novices and their tutors feast off puddings made by the novices' mothers" (Layard 1942:505).

When the house (known as *n'ime na mbagho* [house shark]) is complete, all of the six villages of Vao come on separate nights to perform a dance, known as *ro-mbulat* ("the dry banana leaves dance"), on the nearby dancing ground. In view of the terrifying Big Nambas hoax previously described, in which a man wore dry banana leaves as part of his disguise as a chiefly ghost, the following comment of Layard (1942:321) on the Small Islands dance is of considerable interest:

> This word (*ro-mbulat*) means "dry banana leaves," referring to the fact that formerly the dancers clothed in such leaves, which rustle when moved, to represent ghosts. Now, however, for some reason that I do not know, they no longer do so, but instead often carry leafy branches in their hands, holding them over their heads so that the body of dancers resembles a moving forest.

From Layard's detailed description of the dance it is clear that there is no hint of either ghosts or terror; moreover, the illumination for the performance is provided by the novices themselves, who dance in two rows while holding torches.

The main initiatory ritual, that of penile superincision, is performed exactly seven days after the last of the six villages has performed the banana leaves dance. On the morning of the operation, the boys, blindfolded and accompanied by their tutors, are taken to the beach where expert operators cut their foreskins in such a manner that the skin hangs, thus exposing the head of the penis. After the operation the solicitous tutor ritually addresses his ward with the interesting words, "Look down, see, your *ghavigo* ("malay apple") is red" (Layard 1942:508).

For the next thirty days, a period that the Vao people directly link with the thirty-day seclusion of a mother and child after birth, the novices and their tutors remain in the initiation house where numerous hoaxes are carried out, at first of a very severe kind but gradually easing over the period. Many of these hoaxes concern the healing of the wound, whereas others are of a terrifying kind and commonly include the threat of homosexual attack on the novices by ancestral ghosts.

Layard, fully conversant with the Big Nambas homosexual practices, carefully probed for the possibility of a similar relationship between tutors and novices in the Small Islands. After noting that the Vao novices and tutors are referred to by the terms *mov ghal* and *to-mbat*, both clearly related to the terms found in conjunction with a homosexual relationship in the north Malekula rites, he suggested:

> Between these two a special relationship exists, which at first sight would appear to indicate the same homosexual relationship as obtains between novice and tutor among the Big Nambas. Thus, in the ritual terminology of the Vao the tutor is said to be "married" (*e lagi ni*) to the novice, who refers to him sometimes as *teme natuk*, one of the terms used by a wife for her husband. Older initiates not acting as tutors are referred to as "unmarried."
>
> It was, however, repeatedly denied by the Small Islanders that this terminology implied actual homosexual connection between tutor and novice, and being usually lodge-brothers, there is here no possibility of the two belonging to inter-marrying kinship sections such as would appear to be the case by the more specialised terminology in use between men and their boy-lovers among the Big Nambas. Indeed, so far as I could learn, though homosexuality is not unknown in the Small Islands, it is rare, and such relationships as exist almost always consist in a Small Island boy being the passive partner in a temporary union with an adult native from the Malekulan mainland, for which he is rewarded by the present of a money-mat in the same way as men throughout the group make such gifts to their girl-lovers. The Small Islanders attitude towards such relationships are a comic look and they remark "What a waste of time when there are so many women."
>
> On the other hand, as will be seen below, the novices are being constantly threatened with homosexual attacks by ghosts, and in so far as during the hoaxes the tutors and other initiates often take the part of ghosts they may be said to have at least a spiritual connection of this nature.
>
> (*Layard 1942:503–504*)

Though Layard devoted pages to descriptions of hoaxes performed during the thirty-day seclusion, only one included an attack by ghosts, and it is only by inference that such an attack might be understood to be of a homosexual kind. Nevertheless, he reiterated that many of the hoaxes, especially those performed during the first five days, are "based on terrorising the novices and in particular, frightening them with the alleged homosexual appetites of ghosts." In reference to the often repeated hoax that includes the threat of anal penetration by the ghosts, he elaborated in his 1959 paper with the further observation: "To make this all the more realistic, the tutors and other previously initiated make scrabbling noises on the sloping roof of the initiation lodge which the novices are told are made by the ancestral spirits trying to 'get in'" (Layard 1959:111).

Though the seclusion of the novices ends after thirty days, a final rite is held on the 107th day after the operation. An unmarried initiate "climbs up inside the house to the apex of the roof, calling out to all those who have died a violent death (*ta-mat-oamp*) to come and have homosexual intercourse with the new initiates" (Layard 1942:519). Layard makes no comment on this rite, but since it occurs so long after the seclusion of the novices has ceased, I doubt very much if it is intended to terrorize them; indeed, it seems that the rite may well be performed with a view to directly influencing the ancestors.

NDUINDUI[3]

In 1957, as an undergraduate student in anthropology, I made a comparative study of male initiation rites and secret societies in Melanesia (Allen 1967). My interest in such institutions had been in large measure generated through reading the old ethnographies that dealt with the great variety of elaborate male rites found in north Vanuatu. Another ethnographic feature in much of this area, a matrilineal dual organization, also interested me, for, according to the central hypothesis of my thesis, this complex should have a number of consequences for the diacritical features of male ritual. A somewhat ironic fate awaited me a few years later when I went to north Vanuatu to carry out field research for my doctoral dissertation. I selected Nduindui, a district in northwest Ambae, an island which, according to all the old ethnographies, was located in the matrilineal moiety area, had an elaborate version of the public graded society, and could boast of a number of secret societies. Yet I spent many long months searching, largely in vain, for any sign of these fascinating institutions. Part of the trouble was just a matter of radical social change—early conversion to Christianity and cash-cropping, and a direct substitution of the church hierarchy for the graded society (Allen 1968). But if the matrilineal moieties had ever existed in west Ambae, it had been in some remote period long before the arrival of the first Europeans. For many months I thus searched diligently and suspiciously, and it was not until almost a year had passed that I regretfully began to think in terms of cognatic descent and preferential male agnatic affiliation, in other words, the by then fashionable Melanesian structural mishmash: poorly defined descent ideology, somewhat hazy and flexible kin categories, and saddest of all, a prosaic and rather thin ritual corpus; no dramatic male initiation rites, no well-defined sacrificial notions, no male homosexuality, no splendid erect penis-wrappers, and no secret societies.

It was not until I had begun my second period of fieldwork that I discovered that in fact two varieties of secret-society ritual had been practiced, but because the participants had indulged in so many "bad" actions they had been abandoned during the early decades of conversion to Christianity. It was quite clear that despite this early and total abandonment, the rites had once been of considerable importance, as could be simply inferred from the numerous small plots of land scattered throughout west Aoba known as *sarainanggwatu* and *sarainanggwai*. *Sara* means ceremonial dance ground; hence, these were evidently spots on which rites known as *na nggwatu* and *na nggwai* had once been performed. I also discovered that the word *nggwatu*, which literally means "head," is a local variant of *kwat*, the name of an important class of secret society found in the Banks, Mwaevo, and north Raga (Codrington 1891:84–94; Rivers 1914, 1:115; Layard 1942:492–494). Likewise, *na nggwai* is the Nduindui name of a particular class of spirits known generically as *tamate*, which is also the inclusive name for all Banks Island secret societies, the kwat societies included. For a long time I could discover nothing of what had once been performed on these grounds, other than the contemporary judgment that they were both bad (*hati*) and powerful (*huirana*) deeds. Despite the shortage of cultivable land in Nduindui, the great majority of these plots, some as big as football pitches, were covered with large trees and dense growth and were regarded as taboo places. Unwary trespassers were believed to risk illness caused by the still-lingering power of the bad deeds performed many years earlier.

It was not until a fourth brief visit in 1970, some eleven years after my first arrival, that I succeeded in obtaining reasonably detailed accounts from three old men who had attended na nggwatu rites as novices, and two somewhat thinner accounts from men who had done likewise in na nggwai performances. Since these men, all of whom were over sixty years of age, were attempting to recollect events that took place some forty to fifty years earlier, it is evident that I am here indulging in tenuous reconstructive ethnography. I was, nevertheless, impressed with the consistency of the accounts and hence feel reasonably confident regarding the crucial features of the rites. Before proceeding to describe the rites, however, I must first provide a brief overview of relevant features of Nduindui social and political organization.

The Nduindui are a community of about 2,000 people who live in a densely settled area that extends about three miles along the northwest coast and about the same distance inland (to the highest settlements with an altitude of about 1,500 feet). Homesteads are scattered throughout the district, each standing on its own clearing and separated as a rule by thirty or more yards from its nearest neighbors. The district is divided into twenty-two named parishes, each with its own central clearing on which are commonly located a church, store, men's meeting house (*vale*), and ceremonial ground (*sara*). Larger parishes are divided into named sections, usually again distinguished by their men's houses and ceremonial grounds. Section members claim frequently that in the past their sections were fully autonomous parishes, but, either through inadequate leadership or insufficient numbers, they were obliged to join forces with a more powerful neighbor.

There are no named descent groups in Nduindui, though unnamed dispersed cognatic stocks are recognized. The minimal enduring descent unit consists of a coresident core of male stock members, most of whom are related as agnates, together with their families and dependents. These groups are drawn from the cognatic stocks by a process of patrifiliation operating in conjunction with a preference for patrivirilocal residence and patrilineal inheritance. Though most sons choose to remain with their fathers and both dwell on and cultivate land that has passed through a line of male ancestors, they do so as substantially autonomous individuals constrained by considerations of self-interest, rather than as group members acting in conformity with structural prerequisites. As P. Blackwood (1981:53–54) has neatly put it, "The actualisation of the patrilineal principle in the formation and identity of groups is related to the material conditions of life, rather than as an expression of descent group structure."

The cognatic stocks provide extensive and overlapping kinship networks that extend far beyond the boundaries of a single parish. By contrast, the localized descent groups are shallow in depth, small in size and, with very rare exceptions, confined to a single parish-section. There is, indeed, a substantial overlap between parish-section and descent group, just as there is also a high incidence of male agnatic continuity within descent groups.

The contingent and statistical nature of the localized descent group is evident in that it is the parish-section, not the descent group, that is exogamous. Indeed, most parishes, including those with a number of semiautonomous sections, also prefer to avoid intraparish marriages.

The key to understanding Nduindui social structure lies in the system of leadership. Whereas in the Small Islands one could say with some truth that leaders, insofar as they exist at all, emerge in a predictable way as representative members of groups that are themselves predefined in conformity with established structural principles, in Nduindui leaders are by contrast self-made men who emerge in an unpredictable way as the representatives of groups that they have themselves in large measure created. I am, of course, deliberately exaggerating the differences between these two arrangements. No doubt there are "big-man" features of both Small Island and north Malekula leadership, just as Nduindui sons quite often succeed their fathers as leaders of similarly structured groups. The difference in emphasis is, however, quite clear: whereas the Big Nambas leader is the hereditary headman of a particular clan, and the Small Island leader is a high-ranking and senior member

107

of a "dominant family," the Nduindui leader may emerge in competitive contexts from any locality or descent group. Though sons quite often succeed fathers, they do so in ad hoc and contingent manner, rather than in conformity with structural principle.

The Nduindui graded society (*na hungwe*), which ceased to operate throughout the district during the 1920s and 1930s, was a variant of the highly individualistic and competitive version that continues to flourish throughout east Ambae.[4] The *hungwe* consisted of a number of ranked grades, entry into which was gained by the ritual slaughter of pigs, the transfer of payments for insignia and services, and the performance of elaborate dances. Members of the eight main grades were marked off from one another by their exclusive right to certain insignia, titles, and privileges. For the lower grades, the complications were minimal and entrance no heavy drain on the individual's resources. For the higher grades, the requirements became progressively more complex and expensive. Men who attained the highest grades were believed to gain access to supernatural powers, which they could then utilize in their attempts to control the political aspirations of those beneath them.

The movement of individuals through the grades was based primarily on achievement in a competitive entrepreneurial context and was only in relatively minor ways influenced by ascriptive considerations. All men had to begin at the bottom, and there were no formal barriers precluding men of a certain kind from the top grades. Though a high-ranking father or mother's brother might speed a boy through the lower grades, the requirements for entry into higher grades were such that additional and wider support was necessary. Put in slightly different terms, one could say that though kinship status played a significant part in the acquisition of low titles, for the higher titles, the actions of title-takers, sponsors, and donors were only marginally influenced by kinship considerations. The rule whereby a man aspiring to a given grade must find a sponsor of that grade or higher ensured that those near the top of the hierarchy must calculate their chances in political rather than kinship terms. One could therefore describe the Nduindui version of the public graded society as a highly institutionalized context for the selection and legitimation of big men, and for the formation of predominantly personal networks of followers and supporters.

I have described elsewhere (Allen 1981:108–109) two alternative tactics open to men who aimed to achieve the highest grades. On the one hand there were those men, and they were undoubtedly in the majority, who might be described as the conformists. The conformists were those who sought their goal by attempting to persuade their fellows that they best represented in their goals, actions, and values, established precedent and traditional custom. Such men made political capital out of their readiness to play the relevant games according to established norms and conventions—in hungwe contexts, by rising through the grades in an orderly progression and in conformity with an idealized code of conduct known as the "road of the pigs" (*hala na boi*). The nonconformists, by contrast, were men who sought the same goal of social and political preeminence by daring to depart from precedent, some by attempting minor cultural innovations, others by the more daring tactic of rule breaking, and yet others by participation in rites in which awesome powers were generated by the performance of "bad" acts, that is, by participation in na nggwatu or na nggwai rites. I have published elsewhere (Allen 1981:115–126) a detailed description of these rites and will here confine myself to providing an outline of their main features, with particular attention to the occurrence of homosexual themes in the na nggwatu performances.

The two ritual complexes were alike in a number of important ways. Both constituted elaborate sequences of events that extended over many months and involved the participation of large numbers of men, women, and children. They were held whenever a man of substance or, more commonly, two or three such men, decided to sponsor the rites and in large measure provide the substantial wealth required for them in the form of pigs, mats, and garden produce. The rites were said to be his or theirs, and such men gained a great deal of prestige from sponsorship.

Though I could gain no clear idea as to the frequency of either na nggwatu or na nggwai performances, I am reasonably confident that they were both infrequent and irregular, possibly only a few each decade in Nduindui district. Furthermore, though participation, even as a novice, conferred considerable prestige, there was no rule of compulsory attendance. Neither was initiation a necessary prerequisite to either marriage or adult status, as it was among both the Big Nambas and the Small Islanders, nor to high rank in the graded society, as it was in the case of the *tamate liwoa*, the principal secret society in the Banks Islands (Rivers 1914, 2:95).

The participants in both ritual complexes fell into three distinct categories known as *valiu, nggwatua,* and *taviri.* The valiu were the novices, and though there were no restrictions based on age, sex, locality, rank or any other kind of formal criteria, the majority were either boys or young men from the parishes within the sponsors' area of influence. The inclusion of girls among the novices was, so far as I am aware, unique for north Vanuatu and rare for Melanesia as a whole.[5] Unfortunately my informants, all men, were very vague about the girl participants, especially as to how numerous they were.

The term *valiu* (which is clearly related to the Small Island term for novice, *mov ghal* or *mohewal,* and the north Malekula term *mugh vel*), literally means "the other half," with the common implication of some kind of inversion, reflection, or abnormal representation of an everyday phenomenon. The designation of the novices by this term indicates that they were thought of as "the other half" of a pair that included the nggwatua. Since *nggwatua* is clearly related to *nggwatu,* a work that not only refers to the whole ritual complex but specifically to the crucially important exposure of penis heads in the concluding dance, the possibility arises that the valiu, as the "other half," are in some way associated with the vagina, or at least with some kind of counterpart to the penis. I do not regard it as too farfetched to see in these terms some hint of a sexual bond between valiu and nggwatua. The nggwatua, in fact, comprised all those who had been valiu on some previous occasion, and it was they who were responsible for most of the hoaxes performed on the novices. Valiu and nggwatua were not, however, paired off in fixed couples, as was the case in the Small Islands and on Malekula. The third category, the taviri, were those who had participated on some previous occasion as nggwatua. They were entitled to wear special insignia during public graded ceremonies, to eat at a special oven in the men's house, and to receive special ritual treatment at their own mortuary ceremonies.

NA NGGWATU • The main events (as in the Small Islands) began with a long preparatory period during which the novices and tutors made large gardens for the senior sponsoring taviri men, cleared a special ceremonial ground in the bush some distance from habitation, and finally built three large houses, one for the taviri men, another for the male novices and tutors, and the third for the female novices. Informants were uncertain as to who, if anyone, acted as tutors for the female novices. There was also uncertainty as to the location of the women's house; some were of the opinion that all three houses were located at one end of the ceremonial ground, while others stated that the men were at one end and the women at the other.

During this initial preparatory period, the nggwatua arranged a number of hoaxes for the novices, mostly of a mild and somewhat humorous kind, in which they enacted stereotyped inversions of everyday normative behavior. If the novices should succumb to laughter, they were obliged to pay stiff fines to the taviri men. They might, for example, be duped into thinking that the evening's meal of pork was in fact human flesh, a food normally reserved only for those men of very high rank who had dared to sacrifice a human victim in a hungwe ceremony. The aim of these hoaxes seemed to be to make fools of the novices, whereas in the Small Islands and even more so in north Malekula, it was to induce terror, primarily through the threat of dangerous ghostly action.

When the houses were complete, the whole area was taboo to nonparticipants, and during the next month the nggwatua and valiu together constructed a number of large screens known as *ndindi*. These were made of coconut bark stretched across rectangular wooden frames about eight feet tall and painted with vivid representations of the sun and its rays, surrounded with huge shark's teeth. When complete, the sponsors arranged a payment ceremony which was succeeded by various dance dramas.

In the first of these performances the novices, entirely naked, ran from the surrounding bush onto the clearing and then through a corridor of initiators and sponsors armed with sticks which they used with sufficient vigor on the novices' backs and legs to make them cry out. The novices then sat down in the center of the ground while the others withdrew some distance and formed into two companies. Then suddenly one of these companies danced in a fast and aggressive manner back toward the novices. Some dancers, moving in a jerking manner imitating sexual intercourse, were

111

armed with arrows strung in bows aimed at the novices, while others appeared entirely naked with their buttocks directed toward the novices. After the second company did likewise, a number of solo performers might dance up to the novices and either invite sexual intercourse or address them with words such as, "Where is my mother, old friend, I am very thirsty and I want to drink milk from my mother's breast" or, "Good, big penis, penis in the vagina, penis around the fence, around the rubbish man who wants to copulate. Very well, I will give you a hermaphrodite pig." The first statement is curiously suggestive of the Sambia (Herdt 1981:234–235) initiatory practice of fellatio in which the novices should drink their initiators' semen in the "same way" that they once drank their mothers' milk, only here the relationship is reversed, with initiator asking to drink the novices' milk. However, no such action will occur for this reference is just another of the disturbing or amusing "lies" directed at the novices. The second utterance, though somewhat more enigmatic, is clearly an invitation to the novice to engage in copulation with the initiator, since the hermaphrodite pig is the ideal payment a Nduindui man would give a high ranker for the privilege of copulating with one of the latter's wives. The day's events concluded with the whole company participating in a major dance/song complex known as *bile bolo,* "the vagina song." The sponsors and initiators danced in a phalanx with fiercely stamping feet right up to the squatting novices and, after forcing the latter's mouths open, they turned their buttocks toward them and then danced rapidly away.

Later that night all of the novices, both male and female, were gathered together in the female novices' house where they were visited by a group of dancing initiators. The latter danced along the row of male novices with their buttocks turned toward them and then out the other direction. They thus danced the whole night while continuously singing a song believed capable of seducing women. This performance is undoubtedly related to the ancestral homosexual threats enacted in the Small Islands, but here there is no hint of spirits of any kind, and it is seemingly the novices who are invited to take the male role with the initiators presenting themselves in a female manner. I say seemingly, for clearly there is ambivalence in that it is the initiators, not the novices, who sing as though they were the male seducers. The fact that female novices are also said to be present during these performances adds yet further ambiguity. Unfortunately, my informants were very uncertain as to the part played by the female novices.

After this performance the novices remained some days in a naked and unwashed state in their house under the charge of a single taviri man. The male novices were then given their woven aprons (*malo*), while the females were given their grass skirts. Dressed now as junior adults, they left the communal house and proceeded to build their own individual huts around the edge of the ground. They remained in these for a considerable length of time, at least some weeks, during which they manufactured various items they would wear at the grand concluding dance drama, the *hakwa na nggwatu* (literally "dance the head"). During this period the novices and initiators periodically went on the rampage in surrounding villages, stealing pigs and garden produce from non-participants. They also spent much time rehearsing the dance, while the initiators periodically organized various hoaxes designed either to humiliate the novices or to provoke them to laugh and thereby to incur fines.

Toward the end of this period the initiators and sponsors brought out the huge ndindi screens and hung them on a tall fence constructed right across the ceremonial ground so that the men's houses were concealed from public view. They then retired into these buildings, where they secretly constructed the headdresses many of them would wear on the final day. These magnificent structures (called *na nggwatu*) were made to resemble black sharks with white teeth.

Meanwhile, news spread throughout the district and perhaps even farther afield, that the powerful *hakwa na nggwatu*, the dance of the head, would be performed the following day. By early morning, a large audience assembled at the non-taboo, open end of the ceremonial ground. Proceedings began dramatically when the whole company of taviri, nggwatua, and valiu came dancing from out behind the dividing screen, with its brilliant suns and shark's teeth, the taviri wearing their huge shark headdresses and the rest with insignia appropriate to their grade. But a few ambitious nggwatua, perhaps those who aspired to join the ranks of the taviri at the next initiation, performed an act that above all else was regarded as the source of the na nggwatu power—the power that made the ground on which it was performed a taboo place for many subsequent generations. These men appeared entirely naked and, having reached a prominent position in front of the other dancers, held their penes erect, pulled back the foreskins, and let red powder (which had been previously concealed) fall to the ground. They then danced for a short while before the audience exposing their red organs, their *karai nggwatu*. It should be stressed that the term *nggwatu*, used to designate both the whole ritual complex and this final dance, also links the initiators, their shark headdresses, and the exposed penes. Occasionally a female *nggwatua* also danced naked and performed the *karai nggwatua* act, in which she inserted her fingers into her vagina and thereby released previously inserted red powder. Such women, whom I suspect would mostly have been the wives of high-ranking men, thereby earned the right to join the *taviri* at any subsequent initiation. A few informants stated that other participants seeking fame and notoriety would publicly copulate with close kin such as sisters, with whom they must normally practice total avoidance. Again, the sponsors must pay such persons good quality pigs. The payments were in recognition of the awesome power generated by such performances.

At the end of the dance all of the performers retired behind the screen to deposit their headdresses and other regalia in the taviri house. They then ran around the building banging coconut fronds on the ground to scare away the spirits, set fire to the building, and finally ran home to their villages. All male participants, but most especially those who either wore headdresses or made karai nggwatu, were then required to remain for some months in the men's house and avoid any close interaction with their wives and children. Male participants were especially required to refrain from sexual intercourse in order to protect their wives from the power of na nggwatu still associated with their penes. Indeed, some insisted that the power was so great that it would remain in the penis until finally discharged in coitus; hence the requirement that such men should render themselves safe for their wives by first having sexual intercourse with a strange woman from an outside community. It is this same power, the *huirana na nggwatu*, that is believed to remain for many generations on the dance ground where the red dye fell, where the shark headdresses were worn, and where either real or symbolic incestuous intercourse took place.

DISCUSSION • It is, I think, quite evident that *na nggwatu* is the Nduindui version of precisely the same ritual complex that constitutes initiation into manhood in the Small Islands and in north Malekula. That this is so is evident because in all three areas shark symbolism is of central importance, the novices and initiators are referred to by variants of the same words, hoaxes figure prominently throughout the ritual period, spirit beings are believed to be in close proximity to specially built initiatory houses, homosexuality is a recurrent theme, and the key ritual event is the exposure of reddened penes heads, an event that is everywhere believed to generate power. But whereas in the western islands it is the "heads" of all novices that are permanently exposed through the cutting of their foreskins, in Nduindui it is the heads of just a few initiators that are temporarily exposed by the pulling back of their foreskins. Furthermore, whereas the power so generated in the western islands is exclusively male (which among the Big Nambas is most evident in the persons of hereditary chiefs, and in the Small Islands a solidary group of male agnates), in Nduindui not only is the power itself not exclusively associated with men—as seen in the presence of female participants, some of whom themselves generate power by vaginal exposure—but it is particularly associated with the persons of self-made leaders of the big-man variety and their ad hoc collectivity of supporters.

Let me rephrase this most important point in a slightly different way. I have stressed that the dominant theme in the *na nggwatu* rites is the belief that by daring to do what is normally prohibited, by turning conventional morality on its head, and by invoking the presence of potentially troublesome and even dangerous spirit beings, the participants thereby generate a ritual power of great intensity and endurance. What I am now suggesting is that this kind of power is especially appropriate in a polity based on big-manship and factionalism. The idiom of power employed in these rites is analogous to that wherever charisma is an important component of leadership, and as such it differs in important ways from the kind of ritual powers associated with other kinds of polities.

115

Just as the Nduindui big man may, in secular contexts, marry women who fall within the bounds either of incest prohibitions or exogamic rules, or in graded society contexts may skip grades, import or invent new grades, or kill men, shark or bullock instead of pigs, so too may they decide to sponsor either the na nggwatu or na nggwai rites. These rites are, as we have seen, performances that are in many ways predicated on values that are the inverse of those subscribed to in everyday contexts, and hence all of those who dare to participate are believed to be literally imbued with a dangerous power of unusual intensity.

All informants agreed that by far the most powerful act was that known as *karai nggwatu*, the public exposure of reddened penes by naked men and of reddened vaginas by naked women. The full significance of these acts can only be grasped when we realize the great lengths to which the Nduindui went to conceal both male and female genitalia in everyday life. All males over the age of six or seven wore beautifully woven pandanus mats that passed between the legs and looped over a belt in front and behind, while women wore an equally concealing mat skirt. These dress styles contrasted with the entirely naked men and women found in some of the neighboring matrilineal areas, and the equally contrasting male penis sheaths and female fringed petticoats found in the patrilineal islands to the west and south.

Another recurrent theme in the na nggwatu rites was the enactment, either real or mock, of sexual intercourse, in which the male initiators directed their attentions either at the novices, close female kin, or other men's wives. In each instance the sponsors were obliged to pay such men pigs and mats for performing acts deemed both powerful and bad in the sense of prohibited or unthinkable actions in everyday contexts. This was especially so where naked siblings publicly related to one another in a sexual manner. To most Nduindui such rites were truly mind-blowing in their defiance of the normal canons of behavior for, to a degree perhaps unparalleled in the ethnographic literature, these people practiced total avoidance between even remote classificatory siblings of the opposite sex. Much less converse together, they should avoid even seeing one another, and this rule still holds today after almost a hundred years of missionary criticism (see Allen 1964:226–227).

I would interpret the presence of homosexual themes in the *na nggwatu* rites from the same perspective. Whereas in the western islands, ritualized homosexuality is linked to a classic form of compulsory male initiation in which the novices are transformed into men, in Nduindui it is simply yet another inversion of normative behavior performed for the glorification and legitimation of aspiring big men. In the overtly patrilineal western islands, male homosexual behavior does not take the form, as in certain Western contexts, of what might be termed a kind of effeminacy among men, but rather its form is that of highly exaggerated masculinity. Such is obvious in the use of exceptionally large penis-wrappers in those communities in which male homosexuality is also most pronounced. In those communities, the novices are believed both to be weakened by female fluids, above all menstrual blood, and to be strengthened by the injection of semen through homosexual intercourse. In Nduindui, the pattern was entirely different: men wore aprons instead of penis-wrappers, descent was cognatic instead of patrilineal, leaders were big men instead of lineage elders or clan chiefs, and all forms of male homosexual behavior were regarded as dangerously abhorrent rather than as beneficially normative. I could, indeed, find no evidence for the occurrence of any kind of homosexual activity in Nduindui, and hence I interpret its symbolic representation in the na nggwatu rites as an attempt by the participants to generate ritual power by turning conventional morality on its head.

Another notable feature of these rites was the presence of female participants, including novices. One might be tempted to link this feature to the somewhat higher status of Nduindui women compared with that of their sisters on Malekula. That the Nduindui women had such higher status is evident in a number of contexts: they were subject to somewhat less rigorous taboos when menstruating and giving birth to children, they manufactured, owned, and publicly distributed highly valued mats, and they occasionally even killed pigs and took subsidiary grades in the *hungwe*. Unlike in north Malekula and the Small Islands, where men of rank slept and ate permanently in the men's houses, in Nduindui such men only left their families for short periods during and after ritual performances. I would not, however, like to exaggerate the difference too much, for the Nduindui heterosexual relationship was simply a weaker, in some ways a very much weaker, version of the extreme hierarchical dichotomy found in north Malekula. My interpretation of the presence of female participants in these rites is, as with so many other features, by reference to the belief that inversions of the norm generate great powers.

Yet there is another and altogether more complex dimension to male/female relationships and their significance for understanding all three versions of the north Vanuatu initiatory complex. I have thus far stressed that the compulsory Big Nambas and Small Island rites are first and foremost performed with the specific intent of transforming the youths into mature adult men. The use of male semen, the threat of intercourse by male ancestral spirits, and the subsequent wearing of huge penis-wrappers all seem to convey an unequivocal message of male identity—of boys who have now become men with big and powerful phalluses. There is, however, another and, in part, concealed theme of their continuing feminine identity. That men attribute such an identity to the boys prior to initiation is evident because they regard them as being "only women" or "like women" (Layard 1959:110). In other words, the ritual transformation is not just of boys into men, but of "boys who are like women" into men. The question is, what kind of men?

Layard repeatedly stressed that in his opinion a great deal of both Small Island and north Malekulan culture focuses on the key problem of integrating a continuing feminine component into the masculine psyche as a man progresses from boyhood to high maki rank. The initiation rites constitute the first major attempt to deal with this transformation but it also pertains to the symbolism of boar sacrifice in the maki rites (Layard 1955:7–32). In other words, men, and in some ways most especially those of highest rank, continue to identify both with women as persons and with female reproductive functions and capabilities. I quote here from Layard, in the context of a discussion of boar sacrifice in the Small Islands:

> Finally, as yet further sign of the kind of new spirituality that he has acquired, men of the highest grades . . . often assume titles such as Lord Mother or Mother of the Place. They have become spiritually hermaphrodite.
>
> *(1955:24)*

Further evidence comes directly from the context of initiation itself. Again I quote from Layard:

> The concept of the novice's femininity and therefore potential (though psychic) pregnancy is however very evident in that the whole period of initiation lasts nine months—the period of a woman's pregnancy—and the intensive period during which the boy is super-incised (a modified form of circumcision consisting of slitting the foreskin but not removing it, making him bleed like a menstruating woman) and many other trials are undergone lasting precisely a month, which is the period of the menstrual cycle.
>
> *(1959:110)*

(Elsewhere, Layard [1942:179] notes that a mother remains at home for thirty days after childbirth.)

Though the evidence is not, unfortunately, as detailed as one might wish, especially as regards the beliefs and sentiments of the participants themselves, I do not think that I am being unduly speculative in asserting that among the Small Islanders the generative and reproductive power believed to reside in the penis and in semen are themselves directly modeled on the reproductive powers of women. It is most especially in the context of the compulsory male rites of initiation that the novices symbolically identify with women and their 'powers'. As the "wives" of their initiators, they have their penes cut so that the reddened glands are exposed in a manner clearly modeled on female genitalia ("look down, see your *ghavigo* is red"); they are subsequently secluded for the same period required for a woman after childbirth; and they finally emerge as "men," with the secret of their male strength concealed inside their penis-wrappers. These perceived female powers that the men tap through their rites enable them to transform a new generation of boys into strong and effective adult males.

I would like at this point to elaborate on the theme of male-to-female identification for the Melanesian initiation data in general. In my earlier comparative study (Allen 1967:18–27), I noted that the most elaborate rites are significantly correlated with a prolonged and intimate relationship between mother and son. The postpartum sex taboo commonly lasts for two or more years, and boys spend the greater part of their preinitiation years in the company of their mothers and other women. It does not require any profound psychological insight to hypothesize that under such circumstances boys are likely to identify with their mothers as powerful and supportive persons. But these same societies are also those in which armed male aggression is a common occurrence, in which hunting is a highly valued male activity, and in which political unification is predicated on male agnatic solidarity. Hence the boys, nurtured in female company, must nevertheless mature into powerful and effective adult males. It is hard to avoid the conclusion that the highly elaborate initiation rites are intended to facilitate this difficult yet necessary transformation.

Dundes (1976), inspired in part by psychoanalytic theory, especially the envious male hypothesis of Bettelheim (1955; see Allen 1967:15–27 for a detailed assessment of Bettelheim's theory) has recently argued that while the rites undoubtedly make the boys into men, they do so in a seemingly paradoxical way, by feminizing the initiates. Broadly speaking, this process occurs in two alternative ways. In many areas of Papua New Guinea, but most especially in the Sepik and in the Eastern Highlands, boys identify with women by equating penile incision with menstruation, while the senior men identify with mothers by making possible the novices' "rebirth." In (RH) semen-ingesting areas, where initiators and novices are linked through homosexual relationships (parts of Irian Jaya, the Trans-Fly, the Papuan Plateau and the Anga societies, see Herdt's chapter 1, above), novices may identify with the female role by their passive intake of semen.

Hage has recently rejected Dundes's argument on the grounds that the ethnographic facts suggest otherwise:

> The relation between these rites and female physiology is based not on envy or identity but on analogy, that is, a perceived connexion between the onset of menstruation and growth, or on generalisation, that is, between initial and subsequent provisions of semen— if it induces growth in the foetus then it may also be thought to induce growth subsequently at adolescence. They are magical acts which make a man more like a man.
>
> *(Hage 1981:272)*

Hage's argument is impeccable insofar as the growth of the novices is indeed a central concern of the participants. Both penis bleeding and semen ingesting are explicitly believed to be necessary and effective ways of making the boys grow into mature adult males. But, one might ask, why should the men choose to use women as their model for a paradigm of growth? The most obvious answer surely is that the men must perceive the women as having superior growth capabilities. Read (1952:15) has indeed documented that this is precisely what the Gahuku-Gama think. There is, I would contend, a great deal of evidence that this high male evaluation of the growth capability of women is but part of a more broadly based perception of women's power, a power that is manifest not only in their visible and early physical maturity but in their monthly bleeding, reproductivity, and nurturing capabilities. In other words, contrary to Hage, I am firmly of the opinion that a great deal more than simple analogic thinking is at work when boys bleed their penes and refer to this as "mens' menstruation," when senior males orchestrate rites in which novices are reborn, when novices are referred to as the "wives" of their homosexual partners, and when the latter are believed to make their charges grow by offering semen-filled penes in a manner likened to that of mothers offering milk-filled breasts to infants.

The two initiatory syndromes, that is, the bloodletting and the semen ingesting, have the same ontological objective: the transformation, by magical means, of female-associated boys into strongly masculine adult men. But whereas the bloodletting practitioners achieve their goal, at least in the first instance, by getting rid of female components acquired during childhood, which are now seen as impurities, the semen-ingesting practitioners do it rather by the positive tactic of adding extra maleness. Such a difference is suggestive of parallel differences in male/female relations. In the bloodletting syndrome, the power of women with which men especially seem to identify focuses on menstruation and birth, while in the semen syndrome the emphasis is rather on a woman's capacity to receive semen and to give milk. Put in different terms, the female roles that men identify with in the bloodletting areas are those of "menstruating woman" and "reproductive mother," whereas in (RH) areas the roles are rather "wife" (sexual partner) and "nurturant mother."

The Big Nambas, along with Highlands Anga groups (see Herdt, chap. 4), are unique insofar as they seem doubly concerned with masculinizing boys, using both bloodletting and semen ingesting.

121

But if the simple role equations suggested above have any validity, then it must follow that the men of these two communities also extend the range of their female identification over an exceptionally wide range of roles and attributes. Sadly, an almost total absence of information on male/female relations in north Malekula precludes any further analysis.

CONCLUSION

The Big Nambas, the Small Islanders, and the Nduindui are three neighboring communities whose members have been in frequent contact with one another over a very long period. As a result, their contemporary sociocultural systems share numerous features in common. Following Layard, I have argued that one of the most important of such features is a ritual complex of a highly specific kind distinguished by such recurrent themes as shark symbolism, the initiation of novices, the use of elaborate hoaxes, the symbolic importance of penis heads as loci of power, the representation of ghosts or spirits by initiators, and occurrence, either in reality or in symbolic form, of male homosexual behavior. Wherever this ritual complex occurs it is regarded as an efficacious means of generating power, of gaining access to or controlling a force that is believed capable of effecting socially valued ontological changes. It is, however, at this point that similarities cease and differences become apparent. I have argued that the major differences in the three local versions of the ritual complex are significantly correlated with further differences in political structure. Among the Big Nambas, whose hereditary chiefs of patrilineal clans exercise a significant hegemony, it is essentially male chiefly power that is evoked in the context of the rites. In the Small Islands, where leaders are of less consequence and political power is rather a function of male agnatic solidarity, the rites are first and foremost clan affairs in which boys are transformed into mature and effective adult males. Among the Nduindui, where politics are of the big-man variety, the rites are voluntary occasions during which powers of an unconventional kind are evoked for the glorification of aspiring leaders.

In support of this general argument, I examined in some detail the recurrent use of homosexuality as a power theme in the context of the rites. Among the Big Nambas, male power, but most especially male chiefly power, is physically transmitted to the novices in homosexual intercourse; among the Small Islanders, generalized male agnatic power is transmitted to the novices through the threat of homosexual attack by clan ancestral spirits; while among the Nduindui, daring individuals invoke extraordinary big-man type powers by mockingly inviting the novices to engage with them in homosexual intercourse.

A second most important feature of the rites is the belief that ritual power resides in the head of a man's penis. But beyond that simple assertion, major differences again exist. Among the Big Nambas, where such power is, as I have just noted, initially generated in boys through the intake of chiefly semen, the head, after full exposure through the operation of circum-incision, is then concealed in an eye-catching and outsize wrapper. Among the Small Islanders, where there are no homosexual or other procedures for inducing penis growth prior to initiation, the lesser operation of superincision precedes the wearing of a more modest wrapper. Finally, among the Nduindui, the theme of penis power is restricted to the voluntary exposure of penis heads by a few ambitious initiators.

A third distinctive feature of the rites is the enactment of numerous hoaxes by previously initiated men during the course of the novices' seclusion. Though Deacon was uncertain as to the real purpose of the hoaxes among the Big Nambas, apart from their obvious effect in frightening the boys, he nevertheless noted that "the importance of *bagho* (initiation) lies, not in the circumcision itself, but in the series of performances or 'hoaxes' which take place during the thirty days seclusion" (1934:264). Deacon himself viewed most of the north Malekula hoaxes as trials and tests of endurance, though trials of what is not made clear. A brief comparison of the three areas indicates again the important variations that occur in conjunction with political differences.

Throughout north Malekula, the emphasis is on the terrifying representation of supernatural beings who attempt to get into close and threatening contact with the secluded boys. Among the Big Nambas such beings are commonly said to be the ghosts of deceased warrior chiefs killed in battle, but for the Small Islanders they are the altogether more benign spirits of clan ancestors. While the Big Nambas ghosts attempt to terrify the novices through their abnormality and destructive intent, the Small Island ghosts, though no doubt also inducing terror, are believed to act with the good of the novices in mind. In Nduindui yet another theme emerges in which the stress seems to be rather on making fools of the novices for the benefit of the sponsoring big men. By contrast with the western islands, there is little evidence of terror-inducing activity on the part of supernatural beings.

To conclude this chapter, I would like to reexamine the nature of the correlation advanced earlier between ritual performance and political structure. The link between these two elements is provided in the notion of power. The rites are believed by the participants to generate transformative powers which can in turn be used to the political advantage of those who can lay claim to them. Power generated through ritual context is thus directly transferred to the political arena. In linking the two forms of power I am asserting a causal and not just a functional connection. By this I mean that if the two elements should be in a dysfunctional relation, as, for example, when an egalitarian community without prominent leaders purchases and begins to perform a ritual in which chiefly-type powers are evoked, then change of some kind must follow fairly rapidly. If the balance of political forces within such a community are for the maintenance of the status quo, then I would predict a transformation of the ritual powers into a form compatible with the preexisting polity. But it is perfectly possible to imagine the cause and effect relationship put into reverse. If the internal power circumstances of a community should be in a state of flux, it might well be that an imported ritual could be utilized to give legitimacy to the power claims of an emergent group, class, or category. I have no doubt that this reversal has occurred in Vanuatu with great frequency in the turbulent period initiated by European colonization.

It should be evident that the kind of causality that I am postulating here is of that highly restricted kind in which a phenomenon undergoes change, transformation, or modification. It is the kind of causality that is inherent in the notion of historical process rather than of Durkheimian structuralist sociology. I am not, in other words, asserting that political structure generates ritual practice or vice versa. The various component elements of the north

Vanuatu initiatory complex undoubtedly resulted from an extremely ancient and complex history, and it is within the depths of such opaque complexity that the final causes of its ritual lie, and will no doubt continue to lie, deeply buried.

NOTES

1. Though Deacon refers to the Big Nambas operation as *circumcision*, Layard, who describes the full variety of operations found throughout north Vanuatu, coined the term *circum-incision* to refer to the Big Nambas version. After describing the simple operation of incision, in which a single longitudinal slit is made in the foreskin, and also superincision, in which two such slits are made (as in the Small Islands), Layard describes circum-incision in the following manner:

> There are, however, two areas where the operation is carried a stage further, in which the foreskin, after having been longitudinally slit, is then cut around laterally on either side in such a manner that the whole foreskin is removed and thrown away into the water. This is the operation to which Rivers, possibly not knowing how it was performed, applied the term 'true circumcision'. It will be seen from the description, however, that it is very different from the operation of circumcision as practiced by the Jews and so introduced into Europe, and for this reason it is necessary to find a distinctive term. Owing to its close connection with the simpler operation of incision, I therefore propose to coin a new term and refer to this operation in future as circum-incision.
> (Layard 1942:476–477)

   I follow Layard in his usage of all these terms.
2. A striking feature of these figures is the sexual imbalance (647 males and against 490 females). Though the ethnographers do not refer to female infanticide, it would seem as though it must occur with some frequency. Clearly, figures such as these provide, as it were, a demographic basis for widespread male homosexuality.
3. My main fieldwork was carried out from November 1958 to December 1959, September to December 1960, and June 1961 to January 1962. I returned briefly in 1970 and obtained much of the data on the *na nggwatu* and *na nggwai* rites. The main research was jointly financed by the Australian National University and the Colonial Social Science Research Council, and the 1970 visit by Sydney University.
4. For a detailed account of the *hungwe* in east Aoba see Rodman 1973, and for a reconstruction of the Nduindui version see Allen 1964:240–279; 1969:85–110; and 1972:270–282. See also P. Blackwood 1981:42–60 for a comparative analysis of the two versions.

5. The Orokaiva, Koko, and Mundugumor of Papua New Guinea initiated girls as well as boys into certain secrets. The girls, however, were not accepted as full members of the ritual associations and were not permitted to act as initiators (Allen 1967:7). In Malekula, Deacon described in some detail an elaborate and in part secret women's graded ritual association known as *lapas* in Seniang, and *langambas* in Lagalag (Deacon 1934:470–497). It is of considerable interest that Deacon also noted the widespread occurrence of lesbianism in north Malekula. For Lambumbu and Lagalag districts he noted that:

> Between women . . . homosexuality is common, many women being generally known as Lesbians, or in the native term *nimomogh iap nimomogh* ("woman has intercourse with woman"). It is regarded as a form of play, but, at the same time, it is clearly recognised as a definite type of sexual desire, and that the women do it because it gives them pleasure.
>
> (Deacon 1934:170)

He also noted that in these two districts homosexual practices between men were only occasional and sporadic. However, among the Big Nambas, it would seem that lesbianism was again common, but unfortunately he failed to record any further information.

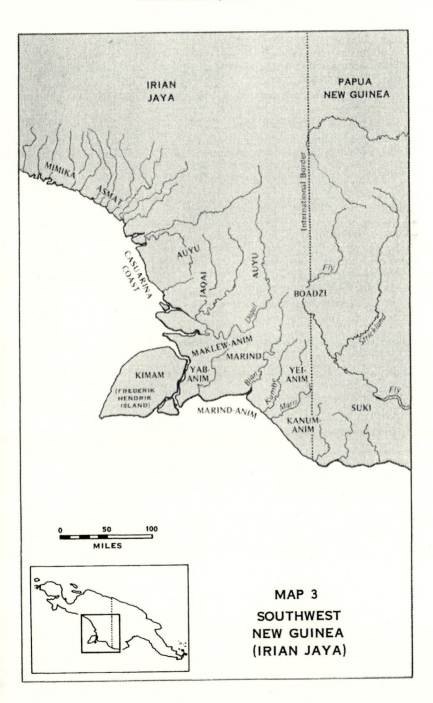

MAP 3
SOUTHWEST
NEW GUINEA
(IRIAN JAYA)

3

J. Van Baal

The Dialectics of Sex in Marind-anim Culture

Marind-anim culture belongs to the past. Today, it is no longer possible to get additional information concerning the sexual habits and erotic feelings of the men and women who participated in the opulent rites of former times. These participants are all dead. Dead, too, are the observers who personally collected information from the participants. The papers they left and the oral information which, at the time, could be acquired from them, have been presented in my book *Dema, Description and Analysis of Marind-anim Culture* (1966). Consequently, the present paper is by necessity confined to a reconsideration of those data that in one way or another bear upon their practice of ritualized homosexuality. Since all these data derive from one and the same source, references have been restricted to cases that, in spite of the book's detailed table of contents and indexes, cannot easily be located by the interested reader wishing to inquire deeper into their proper context.

INTRODUCTION

In 1902, when their daring head-hunting raids into British territory brought the Marind-anim into conflict with the Dutch colonial government, Marind-anim society included some fifty politically independent territorial groups which may conveniently be described as so many subtribes. All these subtribes called themselves Marind-anim: Marind men. In spite of cultural differences and occasional conflicts, they lived in relative peace among themselves. In principle, Marind-anim subtribes never directed their head-hunting raids against other Marind groups, however remote their habitat. They sought their victims among outsiders (*ikom-anim*), people living at a distance of often more than a hundred miles. In this practice, the Marind differed considerably from many other Papuan tribes. The difference is all the more remarkable since the Marind-anim territory was a vast one occupied by many warlike subtribes who were divided into at least three different cult groups and an even greater number of dialect groups. In fact, Marind-anim culture was an expanding culture, spreading from the coast to the interior, and along the coast from east to west. This expansion was particularly evident in the case of the subtribes on the upper Bian River. Their dialect differed so widely from those of the other Marind groups that it can, perhaps, better be considered a separate language. They also had a separate cult which, though reflecting principles similar to those of the coastal Marind, differed markedly from the latter in being less spectacular. And though, in intercommunal traffic, they called their totem clans by the names current among all other Marind subtribes, they used different terms when among themselves.

In this paper I will confine myself to the coastal Marind and those inland communities that participated in either of the two cults, the *mayo* and the *imo*. These had their mythical centers in, respectively, Buti in the eastern coastal area, and Sangasé (Imo in the language of myth) in the central coastal area. Of the two, the imo was inland oriented; most of its adherents were in the interior. On the coast, only Sangasé (with its dependent settlements) and Domandé followed it, together with a not always unimportant number of individuals living in the more western coastal villages

129

where the mayo cult was dominant. As far as the evidence shows, the mayo was the more important of the two cults, both culturally and numerically, with followers in the numerous coastal subtribes as well as in those of the lower Maro and Kumbe Rivers. Both cults had an integrating effect on the diversity of the subtribes following them; yet, there was no hostility between them. The two cultural centers, Buti and Sangasé, were close allies, notwithstanding the distance separating them (Van Baal 1966:95, 667f.). Besides, subtribes cooperated where head-hunting was concerned. A raid, always quite an expedition, used to be a combined action of different, not necessarily adjacent, subtribes.

Each subtribe counts (speaking of them in the ethnographic present) a number of local, patrilineal subclans, belonging to one of the various intercommunal clans that constitute part of either of four patrilineal, exogamous phratries into which the Marind-anim are divided, locally as well as nationally. The four phratries are represented in each of the subtribes. In each of these subtribes the smallest social unit is, apart from the nuclear family, the men's house community. It is a small lineage, counting some four to seven men occupying a common men's house. Adjacent to it are one or two women's houses for their spouses and children. In the immediate vicinity other lineages of the same clan (or phratry) have their houses. Together, they constitute a hamlet. Nearby, though separate, are other hamlets, occupied by members of other phratries. Occasionally, people of one phratry occupy more than one hamlet.

A group of hamlets constitutes a village. Sometimes the village coincides with the territorial group or subtribe, but often the subtribe consists of two or even more villages. Villages tend to follow the same societal pattern as the subtribe as a whole, that of a community in which all the four phratries are represented, each by one or more men's houses. This propensity to integration is probably a result of everyday magic rites. The magic rites aiming at the prosperous growth of various crops are more effective when performed by a member of the relevant totem clan. The crops and principal foods being rather equally divided among the four phratries, that is, as their totems, it is convenient to have them all near at hand. This arrangement provides well for cooperation among the phratries and clans, an important contribution to subtribal unity in a territorial group that does not know any clear form of organized central authority. With the exception of the imo cult, whose leader has authority over the celebration of imo rituals, there are no other authorities beyond the leaders of the numerous men's houses.

In all worldly matters the subtribe is a self-sufficient unit. Subtribe endogamy prevails. Marriage is preferably by sister exchange, a rule more consistently followed in the inland communities than along the coast where, for this purpose, the term *sister* is usually extended in a very wide classificatory sense. The coastal people take the individual preferences of their youngsters fairly seriously, a leniency favoring marital happiness over structural consistency. Consistency has also been sacrificed in another respect. Although ceremonially the phratries two by two constitute opposing moieties, moiety exogamy has disappeared among the coastal Marind. There is one regional exception, namely Sangasé, the ritual center of the imo cult. Here, as in the inland communities, moiety exogamy is still respected, despite the fact that sister exchange seems to be taken less literally than it is in the interior, where the rule is still in full vigor and parents repeatedly have to resort to adoption to acquire an exchange-brother or -sister for their daughter or son. Notwithstanding the slackening of the rule of sister exchange in the coastal communities, one old rule has been maintained: the ban on marriage between cousins, a type of marriage inconsistent with sister exchange.

Polygyny is rare among the Marind. They also prefer marriage partners to be of equal age (Van Baal 1966:128). Although divorce is not exceptional, most marriages are lasting. In spite of various reports on wife-beating and harsh treatment of women generally, the relations between spouses are, on the whole, cordial, at least better than is known among many New Guinea Highlands tribes who, unlike the reputedly "homosexual" Marind, do not indulge in such practices. Instead, these Highlanders practice polygyny. Another difference between the Marind and the Highland Papuans is meaningful. While both have the institution of men's houses, the mountain Papuans are allowed to pass the night in their wives' houses and the Marind may not; and the men's houses of the mountaineers are well separated from those of their women, whereas those of the Marind stand close to the women's houses

131

and, being lightly constructed, are not really isolated from them. Everything occurring in any of the Marind houses can be overheard. The separation of the sexes among the Marind is strict, but ineffective.

All the same, this sexual separation begins at an early age. Past infancy, every boy must sleep in his father's men's house. For the time being, it neither changes his social life nor impinges upon his freedom. This transition happens when the first signs of approaching puberty become apparent. He is then made an *aroi-patur*, literally a black boy. His body is blackened all over, and a mother's brother is appointed to act as his mentor, his *binahor*-father. The meaning of the word *binahor* is uncertain, but it probably refers to the mentor's main function, that of being the boy's pederast who, by "feeding" the boy anally, contributes to his physical growth. The latter is a notion that the Marind-anim share with the surrounding tribes, who also hold the view that a husband should continue having sexual intercourse with his pregnant wife for as long as her condition permits, for the sake of feeding the fetus. It is not improbable that the Marind-anim follow the same custom, but they do not emphasize its necessity. Instead, they stress the desirability of a certain form of sexual promiscuity (discussed in the next section). For the moment, the Marind-anim age-grades demand our attention.

There are three of them, among which the *aroi-patur* grade is the first. In a way, it is only a preliminary grade. It lasts until the boy's hair, kept short when he was a mere child, has grown long enough to plait it into strands to which can be fastened the rushes and leaves that constitute the traditional headdress of the following grade, that of the *wokraved* (pl. *wokrévid*). In principle, the rules incumbent on the wokrévid are the same as those to which the aroi-patur himself has to submit. During the daytime he is not allowed to visit either the village or the beach. He belongs to the interior, to the bush, where the boys have their residence in the *gotad,* a shed within a coconut grove at some distance from the village. They share it with the older boys of the village as well as with the mature men who often visit the place, either to pass their leisure time in gossip or to discuss matters of specifically male interest. Here they also instruct the boys in matters of warfare by relating their own adventures.

At nightfall the boys return to the village. Each of them stays with his mentor (his maternal uncle) in his men's house where he sleeps with him. The boys are under strict supervision. They are not allowed to participate in nocturnal dances and feasts; they must take care not to be seen by women or girls; and, apart from their specific hairdress,[1] cannot boast any other ornament than the black color of their body and face. Since they have few opportunities to take a bath, their bodies are dirty. The one privilege they enjoy is that they may accompany the men on their war raids. After all, they must become warriors and are encouraged accordingly. In all other respects, however, they are severely disciplined and treated as inferiors. The men, referring to the wokrévid's role in homosexual intercourse, mockingly call them "girls."

The boys remain in this age-grade—the *aroi-patur* stage excluded—for about three years. It is as wokrévid that the boys of the eastern section of the Marind pass their first initiation ceremony, unless they have already been initiated when they were still aroi-patur. This first ceremony is their initiation in the *Sosom* ritual, a homosexual ritual which is confined to the eastern section. *Sosom* is the term for bull-roarer, a secret implement in this area. But it is also the name of a giant *dema* (the latter a term that can be translated as, alternately, "ancestor" and "mythical being"). Once every year Sosom leaves his abode at the far eastern border of Marind-anim territory to make a circular tour westward to the Kumbe River and back again to his residence, visiting in turn all the villages on his way. From place to place the men welcome him with bull-roarers (*sosom*) and bamboo flutes.[2] Sosom is pictured as a castrated giant who wears a string of cut-off human heads across his shoulder. The women are warned off well in advance. On a sandy spot near the village, the men draw Sosom's enormous footprints, which, early in the morning, are shown to the women together with a huge pile of excrement produced by the dema, thus giving substance to his surname: *Tepo-anem*, Anus-man.

Toward nightfall the dema really arrives, and the men lead him to an open place in the bush where a big, red phallus has been erected, the phallus of Sosom. The relevant myth states that Sosom is a brother of Uaba, the coconut dema, who is also the father of fire, cassowary, and stork, as well as the ritual representative of the sun. *Sosom* was a brute who, like Uaba, was entrapped in

133

copulation. Unlike Uaba, however, he was not liberated from it. Instead, the girl's mother cut off his penis, and it is this penis that the men venerate by dancing around its image to the sound of bull-roarers and flutes. Meanwhile, the novices (with, presumably, the earlier initiated wokrévid) hold themselves in readiness in the bush for promiscuous sexual intercourse with the men. According to some sources, this is the one and only opportunity for promiscuous homosexual intercourse among the men. Normally, the use of another man's ward is forbidden. One source adds that cases of homosexual jealousy do occur. The evidence, however, is meager; details are not given (cf. Van Baal 1966:479f.), and it would be rash to conclude that the exclusiveness of the mentor's homosexual rights is an established fact.

The next higher age-grade implies an important change. On becoming an *ewati* the boy, by now an adolescent, receives from his mother's brother his first penis-shell, as well as a finely decorated bow and club. The soot is washed from his body which, though it is painted black again, is now covered with a choice of ornaments. His face is painted in brighter colors, and he also receives a new and more elaborate hairdo. Though the gotad remains his residence by day and he must avoid being seen in the village or on the nearby beach before nightfall, he enjoys great freedom in other respects. He participates in the nocturnal dances and feasts, is allowed to meet women and girls in public and to enter into arrangements for his future marriage and, above all, is from now on an acknowledged warrior who fights in the front ranks. Ideally, the ewati-grade might once have been the age for initiation in the mayo ritual, as it still is for the first initiation in the imo. However, I had better refrain from speculation on this point; instead I will focus on the implications of the change upon the young man's sexual life.

Unfortunately, the information available is of a very general nature. At the time most of our data were collected, venereal granulome had spread among the Marind-anim. Shortly after 1920 the colonial government decided to intervene. The gotad and men's houses were swept away, the people were compelled to build new villages with a separate house for each nuclear family, and the celebration of all the great rituals and feasts was forbidden. These measures put an end to the traditional culture. The age-grades disappeared and the old rituals could only be celebrated infrequently in secret and in a rigorously curtailed form. In the eastern section, the mayo rites disappeared completely. The more simple Sosom ritual, however, survived, though in a modified form. Its new form borrowed some features from the mayo, and homosexuality was banned. In 1937 I had occasion to make inquiries about such a secret celebration, and the men swore to me that they no longer indulged in anal intercourse because, in the past, it had resulted in the most awful wounds on the boys' anus and buttocks. At the time, I had my doubts; but subsequent evidence has given reason to accept their words as the truth.

It is obvious that from 1920 onward, the Marind kept silent on the relations between a binahor-father and his ward once the latter had become an ewati. We have to make do with the often vague information of earlier authors. They claim that the relation persisted, but they state also that the boy no longer needed to obey all his mentor's wishes. As a matter of fact, the ewati played an important part in the colorful nocturnal dances. They were the pride of the village, and they knew it. They were renowned for their assertiveness. They also had relations with girls. Though premarital sexual intercourse was frowned upon, at least as far as the girls were concerned, there is ample evidence that it did occur (Van Baal 1966:155). Besides, an ewati used to celebrate his betrothal by exchanging ornaments with his future wife in a ceremony attended by young people only. All the evidence indicates that, in this age-grade, the boy is prepared for heterosexual contacts. It may be that an ewati occasionally indulged in homosexual intercourse with one of the wokrévid in the gotad, but it is out of the question that he would lend himself to playing the passive role in anal intercourse. Such an act is too clearly a function of the state of humiliation characteristic of the preceding age-grade. The fact that, on reaching this grade, the binahor-father hands the boy his first penis-shell indicates that his task of feeding the boy anally has concluded. Another indication is his gift of a club, always a sexual symbol among the Marind. From a relation of authority, it now changes into one of friendship. The gifts presented to the boy testify to this change. Still passing the night in his uncle's men's house, the boy assists in his uncle's garden work and brings the man's wife the spoils of his hunting. The functions of the latter become more important now. As the boy's binahor-mother, she had always prepared his meals. She is also expected to braid the hairstrands to which his hairdo must be fastened. She was busier with it after he became an ewati than before, when he still was a wokraved, for the ewati's role in dances and feasts makes the frequent renewal of his hairdo a necessity.

After some three years all this activity comes to an end. The boy then becomes a *miakim*. It is a passage to full manhood. He returns to the village, to his own (his father's) men's house, the place where he belongs by right of birth. At the rite of passage he is presented as the ideal, licentious male. His new hairdo symbolizes bisexuality. His body and face are painted red all over. His penis is no longer covered by a shell, but defiantly shown: drawn up with the prepuce pinched under the tightly fitting girdle, it suggests an erected penis, the proud image of male virility. It is not merely a sign that he is going to marry soon afterward; it is a reference to the fact that, among the Marind, all fertility derives from the males, from their semen. Fertility is a major social value for them.

MALE VIRILITY AND THE STATUS OF WOMEN

The question arises how the Marind-anim men made true their pretense about male fertility. After all, homosexuality has little to contribute to fertility; and we are puzzled that in their value system homosexuality ranks higher than heterosexuality which, in myth, is time and again associated with castration anxiety and death. Moreover, the Marind male did not stop practicing homosexual activity once he had married. In the course of his married life he could more than once be called upon to be the binahor-father of a sister's son, a vocation that obliged him to act as his nephew's pederast for three to four years. Besides, if he belonged to the eastern section of the Marind, he had to participate once a year in the homosexual promiscuity attending the Sosom ritual. All this need not have prevented a man from paying his wife the sexual attention to which she was entitled, but it is not a good omen for a successful marriage.[3] It even might have adversely affected marital fertility, a possibility that is not so farfetched as it might seem. Marital fecundity was low among the Marind long before they were affected by venereal disease. A medical survey conducted in

1922 produced irrefutable evidence that many women were sterile who had never contracted venereal infection.[4]

The Marind were well aware of the problem. They availed themselves of their head-hunting raids (accompanied by their women) to kidnap as many infants as they could lay their hands on. They adopted them as "natural" blood children who, if possible, were kept ignorant of their foreign origin. They also did all they could to promote the fertility of their own women. Their praise of homosexuality notwithstanding, men married at the fairly early age of about nineteen or twenty years. At marriage, the bride had to pass the first night with her husband's lineage mates, the inmates of his men's house, and usually a number of other clan-mates besides. If there were fewer than ten applicants, she might sexually accommodate them all in one night. If there were more, a second night might be devoted to promiscuous intercourse. Although the ideology was that this was all done for her well-being and future fertility, it might happen that it was more than the bride could stand. According to a relevant report, it might occur that the young woman was so exhausted that she had to make home on her knees. Apparently, the practice was not wholly satisfactory to the participating men either. The same report informs us that, occasionally, a man had to produce the expected semen by resorting to masturbation.

In one way or another, the men, too, had objections to this practice. This is borne out by the curious name sometimes given to this rite of concentrated promiscuity. The official name was *otiv-bombari*, from *bombari* (rite) and *otiv* (many, but also men's house), indicating that its performance was primarily a matter of the local lineage. However, the men often called it *dom bombari*, and *dom* means bad, or objectionable in a moral sense. In *Dema* I have argued that the term reflects the Marind male's objections against heterosexual intercourse. A renewed consideration of the facts raises doubts. A marriage was not the only occasion for otiv-bombari. On the contrary, men indulged in it on a great variety of occasions, and so frequently that it is difficult to accept that Marind males engaged in homosexual acts by preference or inclination. Though the proposed interpretation of the term *dom bombari* finds support in the overt appreciation of homosexuality as more honorable than heterosexuality, it seems probable that it

137

reflects a more complex feeling of discomfort, aroused by, inter alia, the fact that this manner of intercourse in rapid succession did not give the sexual or emotional satisfaction otherwise derived from the act. Otiv-bombari was not mere pleasure; it was, rather, duty.

The rite had to be repeated every time a woman, after having given birth, had been alerted by the return of menstruation that she was ready for a new period of fertility. It had to be performed for a variety of other purposes as well because the mixture of semen and female excretions, flowing after copulation from the woman's genital, was a most powerful medicine. Mixed with food, it was used for curing the sick; with mud, for blackening the teeth and making the color permanent. In purest form the mixture was applied to wounds and to the newly applied scarifications on a girl's body. It was mixed also with festive dishes on ceremonial occasions, and with the various foods presented to the neophytes who, during the mayo initiation, were acquainted with the mythical meaning and background of such foods. The fertility of newly made garden beds had to be promoted by an act of otiv-bombari. And a sorcerer had to call in his assistants to copulate with his wife in order to procure the mixture he needed for brewing his lethal concoctions.[5]

Semen works for good and for evil, but it is never, with the possible exception of the case referred to in note 9, semen procured from homosexual intercourse, and is only rarely acquired by masturbation. On practically all occasions it must be semen that drips from a woman's vulva after intercourse, preferably intercourse of one woman with a variety of males. The exceptions to the rule are as telling as the rule itself. During the *aili*, an imo cult celebration in which women play an important part, the latter receive food prepared by the men which is mixed with sperm produced by masturbation. Another case is that of the young man making love-magic. He mixes his semen with the food he wishes to present to his sweetheart. On all other occasions the use of semen acquired by masturbation is a matter of emergency. For instance, a man who, alone in the dark, fears an encounter with spirits of the dead, will rub his forehead with sperm.

Two conclusions can be safely drawn. The one is that Marind males, stressing their own contributions to fertility, never denied the females' part in it. In spite of their pretended preference for homosexuality, they substantially increased their opportunities for heterosexual intercourse by making the effect of the sexual act dependent upon the cooperation of as many males as feasible. One might even say that, by this multiplication of their efforts, the males unwittingly demonstrated their own weakness rather than the insufficiency of their women. But this is a conclusion they would have denied passionately.

The other conclusion is that Marind women did not suffer from any lack of sexual attention. If they suffered, it was from too much rather than from too little sexual intercourse. Indeed, various authors have attributed their recurrent sterility to the irritating effect of excessive copulation on the female genitalia, causing an inflammation of the cervix uteri. If that be true—and as yet no other explanation for it has been presented—it is just another of the ironies attendant upon Marind-anim sexual customs. The men believed they did all they could to promote their women's fecundity, but the means they applied contributed to female sterility.

Contradictory, too, was the status of women. Such customs as otiv-bombari strongly suggest that, to these seeming "homosexuals," their women were just the objects of their lust and nothing more. The suggestion is substantiated by the custom of wife-lending against payment, a practice noted as early as 1890 by MacGregor* when he contacted a Marind-anim war party. Another custom, which has the same purpose, is that of lending one's wife to an occasional guest from outside.[6] And yet, we noted already that married life is more stable among the Marind than it is in many other Papuan groups; moreover, the relations between spouses are often cordial, while polygyny is decidedly rare. Again, the men marry fairly early. Their partner is always an age-mate, and usually one of their own choice who—and this is even more important—voluntarily agrees to become his wife. Girls are not easily given away without their consent.

There are other contradictory facts besides. One of these is that the women are initiated in the mayo ritual and play a not-unimportant part in the imo rites. These rites are, primarily, fertility rites, and it is quite exceptional that women participate. After all,

---

*Sir William MacGregor was British Papua's first administrator.

139

such rites imply the males' arrogation of their females' productive functions (Van Baal 1981:75–81, and conclusion below).

The Marind-anim even go further than this ritual role for women. The girls have to go through age-grades parallel to those of the boys. They all wear a grade-specific headdress; and, although they stay at home with their mothers, they are, like their brothers, assigned a mother's brother who, together with his wife, take up a special relation with the girl, that of *yarang*-father and -mother. Like the word *binahor*-father, the term is untranslatable, but the parallelism is evident. And, like that of the boys, the promotion of a girl from one grade to the next is a festive occasion to be celebrated. The girl who has reached the age-grade paralleling the ewati is allowed to enjoy as good a time as the boys of that age spent on primping, feasting, and leisure. The one difference between the sexes is that the age-grades of the girls are not combined with any serious ritual function, and so the feasts celebrated for a girl's age-grade promotion are smaller and more often combined with other celebrations, compared with those for the boys. Evidently, these female age-grades are imitations of the male ones.

That they are imitations does not mean they are insignificant. Rather, they intimate that Marind-anim women do not really have a subculture of their own. They have adapted their ways of life to the culture of the males, joining them on their head-hunting raids and assisting their husbands in their duties toward their sisters' sons by playing the role of binahor-mother. They add splendor to the great dramatizations of the various myths, staged by the men, by impersonating minor characters. They act, as it were, like junior members of the gang, less important than the males, less elaborately adorned, and often acting as torchbearers illuminating the beautifully decorated male dancers performing one of the great traditional show dances. They do not merely act as, but are also treated as, junior members of the gang by the males. It sometimes happens that, after such a dance, the men decide that the next night the dance will be repeated by the women, who then don themselves with all the male fineries. And it is significant in this context that in Marind-anim culture, travesty is a theme more associated with females than with males (Van Baal 1966:159f.). It is evident that the contradictions characterizing the sexual habits of the Marind-anim are not simply a matter of their daily life.

They also have an impact on their rites and ceremonies. It is in the field of their religion that we should try to find an explanation of this often puzzling behavior.

THE RITUAL CYCLE AND THE DIALECTICS OF THE SYSTEM OF CLASSIFICATION

The rich profusion of rites and ceremonies celebrated by the Marind has a solid basis in the social order and the division of the society into two closely cooperating moieties, each with its own, well-defined functions in ritual. The two moieties are the Geb-zé and the Sami-rek,[7] which in turn comprise two phratries: for the Geb-zé, there is the eponymous Geb-zé phratry, with the clans of banana and coconut as its main constituents; its other phratry is formed by the clans that have the cassowary, the stork, and the wallaby as their respective main totems, a phratry which, for the sake of convenience, shall be called Aramemb. The two phratries of the Sami-rek are the Mahu-zé, with the dog, the sago, the penis, and the loam as the respective totems of their main clans; and the Bragai-zé, with the crocodile and pig as the totems of their most important clans.

An important point for understanding the ritual (and concomitant social) order is that the main rituals form a cycle: the initiation rites, the head-hunt following them, and the feast for celebrating a successful head-hunt. The leadership of the initiation ritual fell to the Geb-zé moiety, that of the head-hunt and the ensuing feast to the Sami-rek. This division did not mean that the Sami-rek had no function in the initiation cult, however, or that the Geb-zé did not indulge in head-hunting. The contrary is true. The leadership of the one moiety implied the cooperation of the other. They complemented each other even in the location of the celebrations: the place for the initiation rites was always located in the interior (*timan*), a concept associated with the Sami-rek. And among the coastal Marind the big feast for celebrating a successful head-hunt always took place at full moon on the beach, both elements associated with the Geb-zé moiety.

The combination of leadership and cooperation had a deep impact on Marind-anim totemism. It was a multiple totemism, every clan having a variety of totems, the more important ones referring

141

to the clan's position in the overall system of classification, others referring to its position or functions in a ritual supervised by the opposite moiety. Marind-anim totemism was closely connected with every clan's functions in ritual. The Marind-anim claimed that a man and his totem are identical. The navel of a coconut man resembles a coconut, that of a betel nut man a betel nut. Comparisons of this kind suggested differences in essence between the members of different clans. Actually, however, it was only the symbolic functions that differed. The fact that one moiety was associated symbolically with homosexuality and the other with heterosexuality had not the slightest influence on the actual sexual behavior of the members of these moieties. The fact that the sun was associated in particular with the coconut clan and, through the totem fire, with that of the cassowary, did not prevent the Marind of other clans from claiming that the sun belonged to them all. And this was not without reason since, in myth and ritual, the life cycle of mankind is presented as identical with that of the sun. Or the fact that there was a stork clan did not in the least detract from the right of every mature initiate in mayo- or imo-cult contexts to call himself a stork and adorn himself with stork feathers. The various totems referred first and foremost to ritual functions that could be the leading, as well as the auxiliary, ones. In other words, the clans and their respective totems did not derive their place in the system as a whole from the order of nature, but rather from the order of ritual, which connects the order of nature with the promotion of human needs and social solidarity. To clarify this point I shall now turn to the order of nature, that is, to the main features of the Marind-anim habitat as perceived by the Marind themselves.

The order of nature is characterized by pairs of opposites such as: day versus night; male versus female; south(east) and southeast monsoon versus north(west) and northwest monsoon; dry versus wet monsoon; coast versus interior; land versus sea; dry land versus swamp; coconut versus sago palm; harmless animals versus dangerous ones; and so forth. In this system, the opposites of southeast and northwest, and of coast versus interior, are of special importance. They coincide roughly with the cardinal directions. These directions are not however fixed points of orientation, but targets of direction. East and west are associated with the trade winds that blow in a direction parallel with the coast. The southeast monsoon brings dry weather, sunshine, and general well-being; the northwest monsoon brings rainstorms, mosquitoes, and sickness. The southeast monsoon follows the track of the sun which emerges, in the far east, from a hole in the ground to travel westward, where it descends into another hole and travels underground eastward. The path of the sun is also the path of mankind. Born from a well in the far east as the products of *dema* who came underground from the far west, the first humans went westward, following the direction of the sun. The first man to emerge was also the first man to die and the first to go to the abode of the dead beyond the place of sunset.

These symbolic oppositions play a decisive part in the distribution of totems and ritual functions between the moieties and their constituent clans. They can be represented as follows:

Geb-zé	Sami-rek
East, southeast monsoon, and traveling westward	West, northwest monsoon, and traveling eastward
Coast, sandy beach, dry land	The interior, sea, swamps
Coconut	Sago
Peaceful animals, such as stork, cassowary, and wallaby	Dangerous animals, such as shark, crocodile, dog, and pig
Leadership of the initiation cults	Leadership of the war ritual and the great feasts
Homosexuality	Heterosexuality
Male	Female
Sun and moon (full moon)	Night (and dark moon)
Life and the (not always harmless) magic of the medicine man	Death, head-hunting, and lethal sorcery
Associated with places called *Mayo* in myth	Associated with the place called *Imo* in myth

The classification presented here is that of the coastal Marind. Inland, some of the leading orientations are reversed because there the interior is superior to the coast. We cannot enter into those details. All that matters is that the few inconsistencies in the coastal system (such as the confusing place of the magic of medicine men) must be ascribed to the interplay between mayo and imo once the latter (originally an inland cult) appeared on the coast and its adherents entered into close relations with the mayo people of Buti (Van Baal 1966: 665ff., 944ff.). These minor inconsistencies do not detract from the fact that the natural order thus conceived presents a logically consistent framework for the social order.

Yet, as soon as one turns to details, particularly when the relevant myths are taken into consideration, one confronts contradictions of all sorts, contradictions that can be clarified only by the fact that the totemic associations of the clans are defined, primarily, not by the natural order, but rather by the functions of the clans in ritual; and this difference is significant not only in the rituals supervised by their own moiety but also in those of the opposite moiety in which they have secondary functions. It is the ritual functions that count.[8] And even the main functions can be confusing. Thus, the Sami-rek moiety, though associated with the female sex, can include a penis clan, because the penis is here viewed as a penis in copulation with a vulva. I shall return to this point when I discuss the head-hunt and the final feast.

More confusing still are the totemic associations with secondary ritual functions. A relatively simple case is that of Wokabu, the sago dema. He is not only the creator of the sago palm, but also the maker of the first coconut oil associated with small crabs and other animals of the sandy beach. The coconut and the sandy beach are totems of the Geb-zé. The explanation of Wokabu's (and the sago clan's) contradictory associations lies in the fact that their moiety, the Sami-rek, has the leadership of the big feasts. Wokabu is the mythical reveler, the dema associated with festive celebration. Such celebrations are performed on the beach, the crabs make part of the festive dish, and the coconut oil is a major ingredient for the festive decoration of body and hairdo.

More complicated still is the case of Geb, the dema of the sun, the moon, and the sandy beach, who alternately gave his name to the moiety, the phratry, and the specific clan of that name. He is certainly an important dema, and one would expect him to be the mythical leader of the initiation ritual. However, this role falls to Uaba, the coconut dema who, in a certain sense, can be called his son. There is something odd about Geb. The combination of sun and moon in one person is highly surprising, certainly in this part of New Guinea, where sun and moon are always presented as opposites. Yet, the opposition was not lost on the Marind. It is reflected in the dialectics of the relevant myths.

The myth dealing with Geb as the sun pictures him as a red-skinned man living in a hole in the region where the sun descends into the earth. From this hole he kidnaps red-skinned boys whom he devours. A ringworm-infested boy (a moon symbol) discovers his abode. At the instigation of the women, the men attack him and drive him further underground or cut off his head, and then compel him to journey the underground route to the far east where he emerges as the sun.

As the moon, Geb lives at the opposite end of the territory, not far from the place connected with sunrise and the birth of mankind. He lives on the beach. He is a boy whose body is covered with white acorn shell, the effect of his prolonged fishing in the sea. Girls discover him, and the men take hold of him. They clean his body (a painful operation) and then have anal intercourse, after which they rub his wounds with sperm.[9] Then the banana sprouts from his neck, evidently a symbol of the moon, either in its first or last quarter. When they copulate with him a second time, Geb flees and, climbing to the sky, becomes the moon. All this happens in the east on the occasion of a pig feast, which is invariably celebrated when the moon is full. Consequently, Geb must be identified with the full moon. It rises in the east just about sunset.

Pig feasts are under the supervision of the Sami-rek moiety. Putting the two ends of the myth together, the conclusion is evident: Geb is associated with sunset: the first time the sunset is combined with the beginning of the ritual cycle which starts in the west with copulation between sun and earth at new moon (see following two sections), and the second time with a sunset combined with full moon and a feast that is celebrated at the end of the ritual cycle, the feast commemorating a successful head-hunt. The meaning of this tale must be elucidated in the next sections where it will soon become clear that Geb, as the representative of the sun at sunset, could not possibly function as the leader of the initiation ritual who reveals himself as the rising sun.

THE MAYO RITUAL

The ritual cycle begins with the celebration of the mayo ritual.[10] In its initial phase the ritual refers to the copulation of the sun with the earth, in its final part to the birth of the fire (the sun) and of mankind. The relevant myths have in common that they all start with the mayo being celebrated. Not one myth tells of the origin of the mayo. The mayo is simply there, as the origin of all things, the imo ritual included.

One of these myths states that a mayo was celebrated in the far east, and that Uaba (the coconut dema, but also the sun) was among the initiates. He had brought his wife with him in view of the forthcoming otiv-bombari. She was Betel woman, the sister of the crocodile, more commonly called Ualiuamb, the mother of the stork (the bird symbolizing the initiate). The rites had scarcely begun when, fed up with sexual ill-treatment, she ran away from the mayo and went straight to the far west (the region of sunset). Uaba followed her. He saw that she entered a hut. He waited till darkness had fallen and then followed her into the hut. The next morning he was found trapped in copulation from which he was unable to free himself. Some fellow dema had followed him. They now entered upon the scene and placed the copulating pair on a litter. They covered them with a mat (certainly not for decency's sake) and thus carried them back to the east, to the mayo, where they put them down in a hut, all the time covered with a mat.[11] Here they lay until, finally, Aramemb arrived, the dema who is the great busybody of Marind-anim myth and has a hand in all the events decisive upon birth and death. Aramemb came late; he had in vain been searching for Uaba in Imo (near Sangasé, the center of the imo ritual). Back at the mayo, he went straight to the hut and liberated Uaba from his predicament by turning his body right and left until, at last, he wrenched him free. Fire shot out from the woman's vulva (a reference to fire drilling) whereupon she gave birth to the cassowary (fire is an important totem of this clan) and the stork (the symbol of the initiate). Because of this event, Uaba, apart from being a Geb-zé dema, is also the founding father of the Kai-zé, the cassowary clan.

The myth continues with the story of the fire that spread westward all over the country, creating the broad beach as well as the wide savannahs until it was finally quenched by the sea dema, who sent his big waves far inland, thus creating the river valleys. It also tells about the exploits of the cassowary dema, *Dawi,* which will be discussed below. Here, I must confine myself to the main body of the story, a sun myth that narrates how the sun is caught in copulation with the earth (Ualiuamb) and how he, through permanent copulation, impregnates her so that, at his liberation, she gives birth to fire (again the sun), the cassowary, and the stork—the full initiate.

The story has a close replica in the myth of the origin of mankind. It runs as follows: Once upon a time the dema celebrated a feast underground in the far west. (Others say that it all happened at Imo, but this makes no difference because Imo is ideologically identical with sunset.) The feast finished, they went underground to the east. Here, in a well, they emerged at the surface as human beings in fish form, a form reminiscent of the shape of a bull-roarer (Van Baal 1966:209). A stork picked them out from the water, and Aramemb made a fire to give further shape to these formless beings, turning them into real humans who, once completed, went westward to populate the territory. Some variants make mention of a third protagonist, an old woman named Sobra, who later instigated the custom of head-hunting.

The two stories combined reflect the ritual process of the mayo initiation which can be summarized as follows: The rites are performed inside an enclosure surrounding an open space in a coconut grove, situated at some distance inland from the village. The spot is denoted as *timan,* the interior, a term closely associated with the Sami-rek. It expresses the idea that the spot is made available by the Sami-rek, in their function as helpers to the leaders of the ritual, the Geb-zé. Inside the mayo place stands a beautifully carved, wooden effigy. It represents the Old Mayo Woman. Outside, near each of the entrances to the east and west, stands an ugly, colossal straw puppet, the genitals of which are covered with a large triton shell which, on certain occasions, can be replaced by a large detachable penis. We may take it for granted that the puppet represents the male ancestors as well as the neophytes of the two moieties.

On the first day, the novices wait outside the enclosure until an initiate, a man dressed up as the Old Mayo Woman, comes to

147

fetch them, bearing each as a child one by one into the enclosure. Here their hairdo and ornaments are stripped off, their bodies are painted with white loam, the boys receive a triton shell and the girls an unpainted apron to cover their nakedness. Finally, they are blanketed in a wide grass cloak that makes them as utterly shapeless as the first humans in the well. They behave as if sleeping.

For food they only receive loam, mangrove and betel palm roots,[12] all mixed with sperm. The second day the myth of Geb is enacted, and they get the first bananas, again mixed with semen. The third day a coconut myth is dramatized, and then the neophytes receive coconut mixed with semen. Then follows a pause of twenty to thirty days during which nothing happens. It comes to an end when, one day, a bearer of the effigy of the sun appears, connected by a spear with the Old Mayo Woman. Obviously, they are Uaba and Ualiuamb brought back in copulation (the spear is a penis symbol). From then on, ritual action is resumed. One by one all the various myths are enacted, which teach novices the origin of their various customs and foods, the latter invariably larded with sperm when they are handed out for the first time.

It is evident now why Ualiuamb ran away. No food can be safely eaten by the novices unless its mythical origin has been explained previously and the first mouthful of that food has been spiced with sperm. Since the novices must have something nourishing to eat, those first days are necessarily hectic days—hectic also for the women who are protagonists in the various acts of otiv-bombari from which the required semen must be derived. In the myth, however, there is only one woman, Ualiuamb. No wonder that after three days she made off; no wonder either that on her return the ritual process can be resumed. She is now in permanent copulation with Uaba, the leader of the ritual, and the required rites of otiv-bombari can now be performed by other initiates every time there is a need for it.

In the course of the ritual process the novices, learning everything that an initiate should know, reassume human shape. Step by step their disfiguring garments are discarded, their bodies cleaned and their ornaments readjusted, until they are ready to leave the mayo place as new initiates, the miakim among them beautifully adorned with stork feathers, indicating that they have been reborn as storks. Unfortunately, what happens toward the end of the rites has never been described in clear terms. The initiates used to tell outsiders that the Mayo Woman is burned and eaten, but this is too obviously a story for outsiders to give it much credit. For all we know, what is eaten is just a big snake made out of sugarcane and leaves. It lies buried around a phallic scaffolding, apparently a reference to the myth which narrates that, after the ceremonies, the Mayo Mother left the place in the guise of a big python. The supposition that a cannibal meal concludes the celebration has no ground in reality (cf. Van Baal 1966:540f., 571f., 620ff.) Yet, something must occur before the neophytes leave the mayo place. The point is that there is a strong emphasis on a mayo fire which is said to mark the final ceremonies. There can be hardly any doubt that, at the end of the rites, an act of fire-drilling takes place. And it is a fair guess that, on this occasion, the beautiful image of the Old Mayo Woman, which occupies the center of the mayo place, is burned. (Not one of these major pieces of Marind-anim plastic art ever reached a museum.)

The supposition that the Mayo Woman (whether she be called Mayo Mother or Old Mayo Woman) is killed other than in effigy, finds no support in myth. It assures us that she left the mayo place, either as a young woman or in the guise of a big snake. When represented as a snake, she is called the Mayo Mother, who leaves the place with her children, the new initiates. She goes westward, and the children have all sorts of adventures which are of little interest in the present context. More important here is that the snake herself was pregnant, and that she gave birth to a son, the coconut dema Yawi. He is connected with Imo. After his birth he was first stolen by a few girls who chased his snake mother away (she then retired to a swamp in the eastern part of the territory). Later, in turn, Aramemb stole the boy and brought him to Imo. Coming of age, the boy committed adultery with his foster mother, and Aramemb invited the mythical sorcerers to kill him. Once the boy had died, Aramemb regretted his anger and prepared a medicine to bring him back to life. When he was ready to administer it, he found that the boy had already been buried and that, previously, his head had been cut off and buried separately. Aramemb then poured the medicine over the snake, which became cold, cast off its skin, and returned to life. For snakes do not die: they simply shed their skins. If Aramemb had been in time to save Yawi's life, not only Yawi but all mankind would have become immortal. Now something quite different happened. From Yawi's buried head sprouted the first coconut, an event that should not be taken as a just-so story. It has far-reaching symbolic implications. The coconut is the symbol of the human head and of humanity generally. The coconut—the cut-off head—sprouts and brings forth new life. There is a close connection between life and death, and the sprouting of the nut symbolizes how life sprouts from death, an idea that applies both to the imo rites and to head-hunting.

But before turning to the imo rites, let me mention another version of the myth of the adventures of the Old Mayo Woman after the expiration of the mayo rites. In this version, the Mayo Woman (she is no longer referred to as old now, but is depicted as an attractive young woman) travels westward in a canoe. She is with her young son and accompanied by a number of Geb-zé dema, who, seemingly her retinue, take them westward, to Imo, where on a cold and dark night (at new moon, evidently) all go ashore. Here the men of Imo discover mother and son, and take hold of them. After they copulate with the woman, the two are killed and eaten. In the meantime the dema who brought them have returned to the east. But the men of Imo decide that the act shall be repeated. Thus originated the imo ritual, in particular the *bangu* ritual, which is celebrated in preparation for a head-hunt.

THE IMO RITES

The imo rites differ profoundly from those of the mayo. Associated with night and darkness, the imo rites lack any notion of a rebirth of mankind, which is the apotheosis of the mayo rites. A head-hunt, with its vague implications of life sprouting from death, takes its place. Besides, the rites are of relatively short duration, and there is no clear relation between the initiation rites of the imo, and the bangu ritual which precedes a head-hunt. Here, I shall first discuss the initiation rites and then proceed to the bangu and the aili ritual which is combined with it.

The first initiation does not take more than a couple of days. The novices are ewati who, on this occasion, have to meet the Geb-zé leader of the imo. He is presented as an impersonation of Uaba. Details have never been communicated, except that the boys are treated cruelly. They fear that they are going to be beheaded. The various references to head-hunting suggest an allusion to the myth of Yawi, the coconut dema, although no data definitely confirm this suggestion.

The second initiation takes place at a more mature age, when the miakim grade has been reached. It is, in its initial phase, a very trying experience. The novices now must meet the Old Imo Woman, a character personified by a man of the Sami-rek moiety, and a bad character indeed. Unlike the Old Mayo Woman, all motherly care is foreign to her. She is called Bad Woman or Excrement Woman. Instead of carrying the novices into the enclosure of the imo place, she remains in her house inside the enclosure. The neophytes, assembled just outside the enclosure, are literally beaten into it by the men, knocked down, and dragged by their hair to just outside the house of Excrement Woman. Here their faces are smeared with excrement mixed with sperm. They have to lie down until maggots appear in the excrements on their faces. Then, at last, they are brought to a swamp named after the stork (or *Ualiuamb*). Here they are bathed and cleaned. Afterward they return to the enclosure, probably (though our sources are silent on this point) to meet the Old Imo Woman. On a following night, an aili is celebrated, a fertility rite in which the women participate as actors. A second night is devoted to sexual promiscuity in which, in contrast to otiv-bombari, all the women take part.

Obviously, our information is scanty. Yet, there is one point that deserves comment, namely, the role played by excrement in this rite. Excrement is repugnant to the Marind. Dogs and pigs are rudely beaten when they are caught soiling the village grounds. Another typical expression of disgust is that a Marind-anim prisoner hates nothing more than being compelled to empty cesspools as part of the duties assigned to him. I remember a harassed district chief who used to reserve this job for men sentenced to three days of detention (more was impossible) for dereliction of statute labor. He proudly assured me that these men would never fail again in statute labor.

More telling are other attitudes about the body. A Marind-anim male reacts violently to being observed by a woman, even his own wife, while defecating. He gets enraged on the spot and will almost certainly try to beat her, for example, with a stick. A Marind man

151

does not mind appearing in public with his genital uncovered. Sometimes he bears his penis tied up in a way suggesting an erection. But he always covers his buttocks, and more particularly his anus, by a *wib*, a tail of rushes that hangs down from his belt. He is deeply ashamed when these body parts can be seen by others. Obviously, he suffers from what we could call anal shame. It is certainly not farfetched to presume a correlation between anal shame, the repugnance to excrement, and anal homosexual intercourse. The combination points to a highly contradictory experience. We have never been told how a man feels after anal intercourse. That he comes out with a soiled penis is beyond doubt, but we know neither what he does to clean it, nor how he feels about having befouled himself. Yet, it is fairly certain that, whatever the delight enjoyed in the sexual act, its aftermath leaves a nasty taste. And it is significant that the men's detest of excrement is projected not on the boys, the actual source of excremental pollution, but on the representative of the female sex, the Old Imo Woman. She is not merely venerated, she is deeply feared, just as the men fear women generally. And castration anxiety is a recurrent motif in Marind-anim mythology. We shall return to this point later. For the moment it suffices that the fearful supremacy of the female sex makes itself painfully felt in the imo initiation rites.

It does so again in the bangu, the ritual dramatizing the myth of the first Imo Woman. Its celebration must be followed by a head-hunt. The best time for head-hunting being the end of the dry season, the rite must be performed at some time well into the dry season when, as in the relevant myth, the nights are cold. The right time is at new moon. Then the night is dark. For the celebration, an open place in a coconut grove is enclosed. Inside, two huts provide shelter for each of the two leading characters of the rites, Uaba and Ualiuamb (in the myth represented by the Imo Woman and her son). In the center of the place a deep pit is dug. It is surrounded by shields decorated by circles, each with a hole in the center. Toward nightfall the male initiates enter the enclosure. They screw arrowheads into the holes in the shields which, from this moment onward, may not be seen by noninitiates. A fire is kindled by drilling, and the old men sit down to sing the traditional dirge which is, on this occasion, conducted by an old woman who has been permitted to enter the enclosure. All initiates are painted black. They wear a mask in front of their face; the mask represents a spirit of the dead. Outside, other women assemble. On the two opposite sides of the enclosure a lean-to (touching its outer side) is constructed, one for the women of each moiety. Herein they lie down, naked, awaiting the men of the opposite moiety for sexual intercourse. Inside, the old men have alternated the singing of the dirge for that of *gaga,* a song describing the journey of the dema who traveled underground from west to east (Van Baal 1966:508f., 518; see above, on the myth of the origin of mankind).

When gaga singing begins, the men impersonating Uaba and Ualiuamb leave their huts. They are beautifully decorated, their heads crowned by a small imitation canoe, the imo canoe (*imo* is the secret word for canoe). The two actors go to and descend into the pit, and start dancing. They dance for a long time, while the initiates around the pit alternate their singing with a visit to the women. Toward the end of the night a man unobtrusively climbs a coconut palm. Suddenly he hurls down a number of coconuts. The act refers to the founding myth: At the moment when one of the dema dropped coconuts from a tree he had climbed, the men of Imo seized the one-time Mayo Woman and her son to abuse and finally to kill them. On the occasion of a bangu rite, the falling of the nuts is the sign for a sudden uproar. The two dancers hurriedly throw off their paraphernalia and climb from the pit. Other men throw the shields into the pit which is rapidly filled by shoving the earth back into it and trampling it all down. A festive meal, mixed with the semen and vaginal excretions collected by the women in the sheds outside the enclosure, concludes this part of the celebration.

It is evident that the paraphernalia left in the pit by the two dancers before they made off symbolizes Uaba and Ualiuamb, who now start their travel underground to the east. After all, it is the paraphernalia that turned the dancers into the representatives of the two dema. Yet, we could miss a reference to the fact that the two are in permanent copulation. But we need not look far to find it: the reference is in the shields. Since the moment the arrowheads were inserted and the shields tabooed, they were no longer called shields, but *pahui.* This is an intriguing fact because, in daily speech, the *pahui* does not refer to a shield but to the ceremonial club

153

carried by the leader of a head-hunting raid. It is a highly unusual club. A casual observer would call it a ceremonial spear, and a long one at that. It has an elaborately carved fretwork blade extending from just below the point of the "spear" to some two feet below it. At this point a stone disc has been fixed. It has been passed on the shaft of the spear from below, and pushed upward till it stuck just below the fretwork. If, for some reason, the fretwork breaks off, what remains is a disc-headed club, a *kupa*, in Marind-anim language. And this is, indeed, what happens on a head-hunting raid. The pahui is not used to stab a victim; it is beaten on a victim's head or on the ground, just before another man cuts through the victim's throat and neck with a bamboo knife. The fretwork top of the implement then breaks down, and all that is left is a disc-headed club.

The real point of interest is that the disc symbolizes the female genital, the origin of which is ascribed to the pig dema, the leading headhunter of mythology. He shot an arrow at a scrub hen because it spied him while he was defecating. The hen had even laughed at him. But his arrow dipped and landed, end up, in his own excrement, whereupon arrow and excrement changed into a disc-headed club. More important than even the association of the female organ with excrement is the fact that the arrow is a symbol of the male genital. The disc-headed club symbolizes a penis in copulation. So does the pahui; it represents a long and excessively erect penis, piercing a small vulva (Van Baal 1966:273, 730). We do not know what the Marind-anim say (if they say anything at all) when they hit their victim with the implement. Yet, we do know that the Keraki, a Trans-Fly tribe (Williams 1936c) who practiced the same custom, did cry out: "*Tokujenjeni* is copulating with you." (Tokujenjeni is the mythical bull-roarer, and the bull-roarer itself is a phallic symbol; cf. Van Baal 1963). To the Keraki, head-hunting consciously symbolizes an act of copulation, and this is exactly what the Marind-anim symbolism of the pahui suggests: a long penis piercing a vulva. We shall have occasion to return to this point.

For the moment, enough has been said to fathom the significance of the symbolism of the shields which surround the pit. They too are called *pahui*, but they are symbolically inverted pahui: not a long penis piercing a small vulva, but a miniscule penis (an arrow-point) pinched in an immense vulva (the shield). There is, in fact, no more persuasive illustration of the story of the Imo Woman and her son than these shields: a commanding Ualiuamb holding a small and powerless Uaba caught in copulation, permanent intercourse. And thus they are sent on their journey underground, the eastward journey of Uaba and Ualiuamb, as related in the myth of the mayo and, in a deviant form, in the myth of the origin of mankind (see above).

One problem, however, still stands out: during the bangu ritual the men, by their masks, impersonate the spirits of the dead. Why? Are the dead the substitutes of the dema? The dead do not play an important role among the Marind, and we have insufficient reason to suppose that the imo poses an exception. If we take these masks for just what they are, symbols of death, it suddenly becomes clear why the mayo-Marind participants are afraid of the imo whom they associate with night, death, the dark moon, and head-hunting. Did not the death of Yawi teach us that life sprouts from death? And is not Yawi, the son of the Old Mayo Woman, identical with Uaba, a coconut dema like himself? It is certainly not without significance that the burial of the two dema, Uaba and Ualiuamb, follows immediately after the throwing down of a number of coconuts. Life comes from death, and the burial of the two dema is a life-giving ritual because it signifies an act of copulation.

A life-giving ritual is also the aili, performed one or two days after the bangu ceremony. The men go to the bush where they drill fire, and afterwards prepare a dish mixed with sperm acquired by masturbating. They carry the fire and the dish to the imo enclosure where the women are in waiting. Before they left their homes, the women extinguished their hearth fires. On arrival the men first give fire to a Kai-zé woman (the Kai-zé or cassowary clan is also the fire clan) who distributes it among her fellow women. The men then sit down around their own fire and sing gaga, the song relating the eastward journey of the dema underground. The women line up and one by one receive food that the men have prepared for them.

Then dancing begins. The women circle the fire. Behind them, the men form a second circle. The dance itself consists of an endless series of frantic jumps with both feet off the ground. At midnight the dancing stops. Two stout bamboos, deposited outside the en-

155

closure, are brought in. The women of one phratry, dividing into two parties, take them between their legs. The bamboos are called *imo*. (We noted already that *imo* is a secret word for canoe.) Now dancing is resumed. The women dance with the bamboo between their legs. The leaders of the dancing women, one in front and one at the rear, see to it that the bamboos vibrate through all sorts of erratic movements. Dancing goes on till some women, exhausted, fall down. The other women follow suit. They drop down as if dead and have to be brought to by some older men. It is said that they have been struck by the imo and that, by now, the imo calls them to a new life. After this, the women of the next phratry dance with the bamboo, and so on, until all the women have had a turn and it is up to the men to follow their example. They go on till daybreak. Then the bamboos are burned. The sound of the bamboos bursting in the fire is hailed as a sign that sickness and danger are chased away. A hearty meal concludes this part of the celebration. Then all go off to sleep.

After some minor ceremonies during the following days, a big hunt is organized. It results in a large, festive dish that is consumed and followed by a night of sexual promiscuity. Often, on the night before, a sham fight between men and women is staged. The finale comprises a procession that carries all sickness and pollution to a river west of the place of celebration.

Aili are celebrated on various occasions: linking up with the bangu and with the second initiation ceremony, as well as in case of epidemic disease and for the promotion of the fertility of certain plants and crops. In the context of this paper, two related aspects are of interest. The first is concerned with the role of the women in ritual. It is not limited to their copulating with the dead during the bangu; in the aili, dancing with the bamboo, it is the women who board the imo canoe and play the part of the Imo Woman. The other is that, in spite of so much benevolence with regard to female participation in ritual, the antagonism between the sexes persists and finds direct expression in a sham fight.

Sham fights between the sexes are also reported from the fertility rites (*arih*) performed by the eastern Marind. And it is worth noting that on this occasion the men pelt the women with excrement!

THE HEAD-HUNT AND THE FINAL FEAST

A head-hunt follows both the performance of a mayo initiation or an imo bangu, two rituals in which the mythical woman reigns supreme and the supervising moiety, the Geb-zé, is associated with the male sex. With the head-hunt these positions are reversed. Now the supervising moiety (the Sami-rek) is associated with the female sex, whereas, in the pahui, the symbolism of man is presented as supreme. Yet, this supremacy of the male sex is but partly confirmed by myth. It ascribes the origin of head-hunting to the instigations of Sobra, the old woman whose name is repeatedly invoked in the *ayasé,* the song that accompanies the dancing on the eve of a head-hunt.[13] Sobra is also a mother figure: she assisted at the birth of mankind. And, significantly, she is a spirit of the dead as well! Her husband is Nazr, the savage pig dema and the mythical leader of the head-hunt. He is called Déhévai, Killing Father. He and his wife form a remarkable counterpart to the pair constituted by the Old Mayo (Imo) Mother and her consort. In a way, Sobra is a primeval mother herself (Van Baal 1966:551, 662, 951). And though her share in the origin of head-hunting suits the fact that its leadership is entrusted to the moiety associated with the female sex, to present the male as superior does not fit in too well with the ceremonial practice.

Equally contradictory is the myth that reveals the proper nature of the pahui: it had been mayo in *Yavar-makan* (Ancestor Land) somewhere in the east. A number of dema departed by canoe to Senayo on the Maro River, there to celebrate a big feast. Not a word is said about head-hunting, but the route followed by the canoe (it is called the *Diwa* canoe) led straight through traditional head-hunting territory. Besides, the presence of dema Sok (*sok* is the bamboo knife used to cut a victim's throat) in the canoe leaves little room for doubt with regard to their actual purpose. After all, a head-hunt must follow a mayo celebration. Diwa, from whom the canoe takes its name, did not board the canoe but traveled by land. He was a man with an extraordinarily long penis which he had to carry across his shoulder. He took more or less the same route by land. Somewhere upstream Senayo, an old woman, kindly ferried him across the river in her canoe. She had her daughter

157

with her. During the passage, Diwa molested the girl with his long penis. The mother, enraged, cut it off and it dropped overboard. Meanwhile they had reached the opposite bank, and Diwa, shrieking with pain, continued on foot to Senayo where, shortly afterward, the Diwa canoe arrived. A great celebration followed.

On the face of it, the tale is sordid and utterly pointless. Yet, it must have a meaning: the story begins with a mayo celebration! Besides, Diwa is an important personage. The main officiant at a pig feast, the man who, beautifully decorated, dances all the night through and, at dawn, kills the pigs, is called Diwazib, Son of Diwa. Since a big feast is always a pig feast also, it is evident that Diwa had to proceed on his way to Senayo. He had to be there, but not for the pig feast alone. In fact, the myth is but seemingly a dirty story. A long penis, carried over the shoulder, is an exact description of what a pahui represents. This implies that Diwa's molesting the girl is not merely an act of copulation but one of head-hunting as well. What could Diwa's castration mean other than that the pahui is crushed in the ceremonial act? Of course, it may refer to the fact that the penis hangs down after the act. But that view has exactly the same purport; namely, that ultimately the female is triumphant, a view well substantiated by the fact that the big feast to which Diwa proceeds is, in essence, a feast of the rebirth of the whole universe.

Is this interpretation of Diwa's story mere speculation? Certainly not; it has a solid ground in mythology. To demonstrate this, it is necessary to turn to the clubs used by the Marind-anim headhunters. There are two kinds of them, the *kupa* and the *wagané*, the former with a disc-shaped stone at its outer end, the latter with an egg-shaped one. The kupa is a female symbol, invented by the pig dema Nazr, the husband of Sobra and the leading headhunter of mythology. *Wagané* is also a dirty word for penis, more especially an erect penis. The penis of Sosom, venerated in the eponymous ritual, is a wagané. What makes it interesting in this context is that a number of pahui have been found with an egg-headed stone instead of a disc-headed one. They are properly wagané. Apparently, these are the pahui carried by Geb-zé war parties. They lack the significance of the Sami-rek kupa, which is the symbol of their leadership of the ritual. Rather, they are the form under which the Geb-zé cooperate in the ritual supervised by the opposite moiety.

A good instance of this symbolism is presented in the myth of *Dawi*, the cassowary dema who, after the mayo that resulted in the birth of fire, cassowary, and stork, tried to dampen the fire by beating the ground with his wagané. The story is utterly contradictory. Dawi ran eastward to extinguish the fire, whereas the wind blew from the east and the fire spread to the west. There could not be a fire there that had to be extinguished! Beating the ground with a wagané (which presumably is a pahui) refers to a head-hunt. This is what resulted: the story tells us that, by beating the ground, Dawi separated an island from the mainland. Blown by the wind, the island, Habee, drifted westward. It finally halted somewhere in front of the western section of the coast. Here an iguana (the very image of a crocodile[14]) holds it in its teeth. Now, the island Habee itself closely resembles a human head. Moreover, it is overgrown with coconuts. The story is, to all intents and purposes, the symbolic story of a head-hunt, but one that is not, however, followed by an opulent feast. Rather, all sorts of complications (cf. Van Baal 1966: *voce* Habee) follow, which have no interest in the present context other than as confirmation that a truly successful head-hunt demands the leadership of the Sami-rek and not of a Geb-zé dema such as Dawi.

Of great significance are these symbolic associations: that Dawi used a wagané as a pahui, that Dawi is a Kai-zé (cassowary) dema, and that Sosom is also a Kai-zé dema whose part in ritual must be played by a Kai-zé man (ibid.:268, 479). Moreover, Sosom's penis is also a wagané, and he is said to wear a string of cut-off heads hanging from his shoulder. In other words, Sosom is a head-hunter who may be identified with his clan-mate, Dawi. After all, Sosom is the brother of Uaba, who fathered the fire and the cassowary (*kai*). If, for once, we read the symbolism of Sosom as pertaining to Dawi, we are confronted with a close parallelism between Dawi alias Sosom, and Diwa. They shared the same fate: both were castrated by an old woman who was the mother of the girl they molested. And not only this: there is also the wordplay inherent in their names. *Dawi* is a metathesis of *Diwa*. But the Marind did not even leave the correspondence at this. Diwa has

Yugil as a second name, and Dawi has a classificatory son, the ancestor of a big Kai-zé subclan, whose name is *Yagil*. And it is certainly not by chance that *Yugil* is the feminine form of *Yagil;* the Sami-rek are associated with the female sex.

The opposition of Dawi alias Yagil versus Diwa alias Yugil gives persuasive evidence that the Marind were well aware of the symbolic meaning of Diwa's penis and castration and cannot have had the slightest difficulty with such misleading details of the story as Diwa's continuing his way "shrieking for pain." They will have interpreted it as his song of triumph. Noteworthy also is the hidden nexus between head-hunting and homosexuality presented by the analysis of the story of Dawi (Sosom), a remarkable counterpart to the overt relation between heterosexuality and head-hunting as embodied in the person of Diwa.

The final feast which concludes the ritual cycle differs markedly from the conflict-laden rites and ceremonies described thus far. It is a real feast, which is a relief. It is not simply an opulent meal, larded with a profusion of pork. It is far more. Guests and hosts compete in the performance of magnificent dances which, even to a European public, are a feast for the eyes. They culminate in the performance of a *dema-wir,* an impersonation of the totems and dema, and a dramatization of their adventures. Here the dema appear in their pristine glory, each of them accompanied by his *dema-nakari,* the "young sisters" of the dema who impersonate minor aspects of his behavior and totems. These roles are played by the women and girls of the relevant clan or subclan. The final feast is always an intervillage celebration. The actors are people of either the host- or a guest village. Consequently, there is always an outside public audience, so the women of the performing village need not, as so often, stand aside merely to applaud the performers: there are plenty of guests to do this. They can have a share in the performance and thus add to the glory of the show. Of course, the part these women play is essentially minor, but this does not detract from the fact that they (as "junior members of the gang") participate and contribute to the luster of the display.

It is a display concerning the essence of the universe, concerning the dema who created and molded it, and concerning the totems that populate that universe and make for its fullness. In short, it is a symbolic rebirth: the effect of the ritual exertions of the men. Yet as a rebirth, it is also a triumph of the goddess who covertly commands the ritual process. This goddess is a mother figure, and it is significant that, in the ideology of the head-hunt, she is a spirit of the dead married to a Killing Father. After all, it is death that generates life.

CONCLUSION: THE DIALECTICS OF SEX

The facts presented above give ample evidence that the Marind-anim were not as devoted to homosexuality as suggested by their praise of anal intercourse and its honorable place in their value system. Once conditions changed, they had no difficulties giving up a practice that, in its aftermath, must have been repugnant to them. Besides, they eagerly multiplied the opportunities to indulge in heterosexual intercourse. We are forced to admit that, to the men, homosexual intercourse was not a privilege but a duty. Its recognition as a duty explains the elevated place of homosexuality in their value system and all the good that was said of it. Still, it does not explain the practice. To that end we must turn to their sexual relations with females. These relations were frequent, very frequent even; but they were loaded with conflict.

An indubitable symptom of conflict is the role played by castration anxiety in myth. The Geb-zé dema Sosom is a notorious case. His brother Uaba scarcely escapes a similar fate. He is, for months on end, held entrapped in heterosexual copulation. Another castrate among the dema of this moiety (but only a minor one) is Koneim-anem. In the moiety associated with the female sex, the castrates are more numerous. Apart from the case of Diwa who, like Sosom, had his penis cut off by an older woman, there is that of Opeko-anem, a crocodile dema. He was tied head down to a pole in the river by his own *nakari* ("younger sisters") who covered his genitals with a woman's apron to prevent him from further copulating. Another is that of Awassra, whose excessively long penis was cut off, again, by an old woman. In another version he lost his wagané (club) to a number of girls but later managed to get it back. Apparently, danger lies in the old women. In other stories the motif reappears in a thickly veiled guise, that of a falling

161

tree or pole (Van Baal 1966:321f., 377). Finally, there is the *Märchen*[15] of the man who had a nightmare and dreamed that his girdle shell was stolen (ibid.:318).

Evidently, Marind men feared the women. They admired and resented them. Their resentment is expressed in the association of the female genital with excrement in the myth of the origin of the kupa. In sham fights between men and women, the latter may be pelted with excrement. The antagonism between the sexes and the ambiguity of the men's feelings reaches its apex in the big cults. It is Woman who stands central and occupies the most honorable place. Yet, she is also Excrement Woman, and she is overpowered by the fire at the end of the rites. She must be conquered, and yet she lives on. Actually, the women are a mystery to the men. This is unwittingly borne out by the word *kuma*. *Kuma* means secret, the kernel of something. *Kuma meen* (*meen* = speech) is the formula used in magic. It contains all that is essential. But the term *kuma* is also used metaphorically to denote the female genital.

The ambiguity of relations between the sexes is typical also in daily life. There are men's houses and women's houses which keep the sexes strictly separated. Yet, the separation is not effective; they can always hear one another. The separation is a perfect excuse to exclude women from many things that are for men only, and yet women are allowed a number of ritual functions that, in other societies of this type, are refused them. They are treated by the men as junior members of the gang, with a mixture of rudeness and kindness that easily complements stable relations such as can be noticed in their marital life. But all this fails to explain the resentment and hostility against women projected by the men into the images of their gods.[16] In ritual we note an excess of sex antagonism which has no parallel in daily life. Why should this be?

The rites themselves give the answer. They are fertility rites, rites by which the men try to increase the fertility of their women, and to promote fertility in general. These rites are necessary because they claim that all fertility stems from semen and the exertions of the men. It is a remarkable pretense. It reveals that the men are envious of the women and claim a greater share in the realization of fertility than is allotted to them by nature. The phenomenon is far from exceptional. In a way, it is even "natural." In *Man's Quest for Partnership*, I have argued at some length that the male's role in ancient and primitive society is functionally inadequate (see 1981:67–82). A man's contributions to the daily board of the family rarely exceed one third of the nutritional value of the food that is needed. All the rest is provided by the women who, moreover, produce children and provide daily care to all the members of the family, their husbands included. In comparison to the women, the men are mere loafers who dispose of lots of leisure time. Actually, they have little else to do. Even the protection they provide their women and children is a mere pretext: it is a protection against the unruliness of their own sex. The men need something to live for, such as the women have in their children.

The Marind males symbolically solved this perceived inadequacy by stressing the significance of the sperm that they alone could produce. They claimed that it was an indispensable medicine for everything, and of a high nutritional value besides. To legitimize this claim, they indulged in otiv-bombari on the one hand, and homosexuality on the other. The boys did not disappoint them. They grew well as before, and were disciplined besides. But the women created another problem. Not that they did not cooperate. They willingly did. But their fecundity did not increase. The men had resorted to means that unwittingly damaged the women's fertility rather than increased it. The men doubled their efforts, both in excessive copulation and in the opulence of their rites. It made them more dependent on their women who willingly cooperated; but the desired effect was meager, to say the least. An immense anger must have filled the men's hearts, an anger not directed against their own women (who did all they could), but over generations against the hidden powers behind the visible world, the powers that commanded fertility. These powers required the utmost sexual exertions of the men but rewarded them sparingly. Onto these powers, the primeval mothers of mythology, the men have projected all their resentment, fears, and hopes; it was they who threatened the men with castration.

So what remained to the men was their anger. It exploded in head-hunting. They knew head-hunting was cruel, and yet they delighted in it. They did not indulge in it for self-defense or revenge. They lived in peace with their nearest neighbors. The indulgence and relative self-restraint characteristic of the relations between the sexes were also observed in their traffic with related subtribes and neighboring peoples. Their sole motives for head-hunting were that it fostered the fertility of the coconuts (apparently a reference to the belief that life stems from death) and it provided names for their children. The latter was the motive more commonly advanced. Every child got a name borrowed from a head that his father (or another relative) had taken or had assisted in taking. Such names were memorials of the older men's prowess. In these names they lived on as true men, aggressive males who dared to take a risk.

The Marind-anim male is a kind and highly sociable man, but aggressiveness lies at the bottom of his heart. It can be overheard in the sonorous songs accompanying their great, olden-time dances. I attended one on the last day of August 1937. Two solemn circles of men sang and danced in opposite directions. They were surrounded by a wider circle of torch-bearing women lighting the colorful shapes of their males so that everyone could admire their magnificent attire and dignified demeanor. It was beauty itself. Yet, well after midnight, the psalm-like sonorous singing took on an undertone of threat which, gradually, became stronger and stronger until, around about four o'clock in the morning, I became aware of a savage aggressiveness about to be unleashed from the hearts of these otherwise kind and jovial men. Half an hour later I intervened.

I acted on my own, utterly subjective interpretation, and for a time I wondered whether my intervention had been justified. I was reassured when, many years later, I found that well before me Wirz had been similarly impressed by exactly the same, seemingly innocent, dance (Van Baal 1966:755). Their true and valued object lay somewhere else: the close association between head-hunting and copulation expressed in the ritual act of crushing the pahui. A nexus between head-hunting and sexual intercourse is, to all intents and purposes, utterly irrational. If it has a meaning—and, of course, it has one—it is the expression of the men's deep dissatisfaction with the effect of their sexual role, the subconscious awareness of their failure in the fertility process, on which their lives depended for meaning. Trying to achieve the unachievable, anger filled their hearts, and this anger drove them to acts of violence which could not solve an inner, unsolvable problem.

POSTSCRIPT

In the article presented here, I have tried (without entirely succeeding on this point) to avoid comparisons with other New Guinea tribes in order to let the Marind-anim case speak for itself. However, after submitting the text of this chapter to the editor, I had the opportunity to analyze (and edit) the late Verschueren's posthumous description of Yéi-nan culture. The Yéi-nan or Yéi-anim are neighbors of the Marind, linguistically closely related to the Trans-Fly tribes described by F. E. Williams in his *Papuans of the Trans-Fly* (1936c). To my surprise (I had been given reason to expect otherwise) I found among the Yéi-nan an even more stringent correlation between sex antagonism, ritualized homosexuality, and head-hunting than among the Marind (cf. Van Baal 1982). It convincingly corroborates the theoretical views presented here on this point.

NOTES

1. Each age-grade, male as well as female, has its own, grade-specific forms of hairdo. Information on the symbolic meaning of these various types of hairdress is restricted to that worn by the new *miakim*, which is said to be "a symbolic representation of the male and female genitals" (Van Baal 1966:157).
2. They are not proper flutes. For a description, see ibid.:476.
3. Unfortunately, we have no information concerning the consequences of a binahor-father's duties upon the sexual practice of his own married life.
4. This explanation of female infertility was presented by the medical specialist, Dr. Cnopius, who in 1920 conducted a survey of the incidence and effects of venereal granulome among the Marind. Actually, it was a hypothesis rather than an explanation based on a laboratory supported diagnosis. At the time the means for laboratory research were limited and those available could hardly be of any use in a primitive outpost such as Merauke was at that time.
5. It has been suggested that the collective fertilization of a woman by her husband's men's house community might be an effort at producing a magical means of expressing a collective agnatic identity. However, no facts have become known that can give support to this hypothesis.

6. In parentheses: an irrefutable indication that the Marind males were not so single-mindedly homosexual in orientation as they pretended to be.

7. *Geb-zé:* descendents of *Geb; Sami-rek:* belonging to *Sami.* The term *Sami-rek* can also be used for the *Mahu-zé* phratry. Similarly, *Geb-zé* is not only used for the moiety and phratry of that name, but also for the banana clan, the *Geb-zé* proper.

8. It is impossible to interpret these differences in function as differences in ideology. The Geb-zé are as ardent headhunters as the Sami-rek, and the latter indulge as often in homosexual acts as the former. What counts is the leadership or assistantship in the relevant rituals.

9. Sperm acquired from an act of anal homosexual intercourse? The myth gives no details on this point, and it is of no use to enter into speculations of a dubious nature.

10. Up to a point the same can be said of the imo rites. However, they do not make such a perfect cycle as those of the mayo.

11. The copulating pair under the mat symbolizes the sun in the underworld.

12. Apparently, the loam refers to the muddy well from which the first humans originated, the betel palm roots to the name of the Mayo Mother, Betelwoman.

13. Since the mayo initiation took place at intervals of four and probably more years, the Mayo Marind also organized head-hunting expeditions which were not preceded by the initiation ritual. In those instances ritual preparation for the expedition was confined to a series of nocturnal dances under the singing of *ayasé.*

14. The mythical crocodile had its house at the bottom of the sea, and it was full of prepared heads (Van Baal 1966:369).

15. When the book *Dema* had already appeared in print, my late friend Verschueren pointed out to me that the Marind make a terminological difference between a myth and a *Märchen,* and that the present story should be classified as a *Märchen* (folktale).

16. Dr. Herdt kindly reminded me of the essay by D. F. Tuzin, "Ritual Violence among the Ilahita Arapesh" (1982). I may add that this is only one of the many reasons I have to thank Dr. Herdt for his support and stimulating remarks. I feel happy that the last word of this lengthy text can be one of sincere gratitude.

4

Gilbert H. Herdt

Semen Transactions in Sambia Culture

INTRODUCTION

The theme of this study, semen transactions, may appear esoteric, not to mention vulgar: certainly the question of who gives and receives sperm is not one that much concerns Westerners today. Indeed, human fluids in general seem obvious and trivial, even embarrassingly natural, or unnatural, as the case may be. Seldom do we wonder how and why they are produced, or where and when they are consumed or discarded, or by whom. The perspective in certain Melanesian societies, however, is contrary to our view, for semen, like other body fluids, is of considerable interest (and is neither obvious nor trifling but is vulgar) in the sense that semen as a scarce resource is among the everyday concerns of common folk. If we recognize and study these concerns in their own right and in their own symbolic environment, we are led to examine how and why they inform the structure and meaning of sexuality in general and institutionalized homosexual practices in particular. I want to analyze why, that is, peoples such as the Sambia of the Eastern Highlands have fetishized semen, transforming it from an object into a subject, a living "commodity," with a personality and vital signs of its own.[1]

The more one thinks about this symbolic transformation, the more remarkable it seems. A simple bodily fluid, endowed with much significance, has become a sort of director of people—predicating their perceptions and interactions, molding their selves, marriages, families, and clans—thereby making them all objects valued against itself. In Western culture we have perhaps made money and sex into predicate subjects of this sort. In Melanesia, it seems, there are a few such subjects: pigs and shell valuables, women, spirits, blood, and semen. Access to or power over these things makes individuals and groups valued and powerful.

We have long known that some Melanesian cultures use the body (e.g., of humans, animals, spiritual beings) as a conceptual model of and for social action, speech, and thought (e.g., Leenhardt 1979; Malinowski 1929; Mead 1935; Newman 1964). Typically, though, the significance of these symbolic models has been obscured in anthropological preoccupations with individualism, group solidarity, and exchanges of wealth ("norms of reciprocity," i.e., "linear sequences basically concerned with discrete acts of giving and receiving" [Weiner 1980:71; see also M. Strathern 1979]). The meaningfulness of these cultural commodities, including how they are transformed from things into predicates of relationships between persons, as elements in cultural systems, is what concerns me.

If we take accord of the full value Sambia invest in fluids such as semen and breast milk, then we can trace the systemic contours of the circulation of these valuable fluids in their culture. In this view, semen as a cultural idea and semen transactions may be understood as a special language, a kind of symbolic discourse for signifying the value and identities of persons, groups, and social and religious entities. Such a symbolic discourse may be trained on many objects (see Herdt 1982b; Weiner n.d.). But because of its centrality, semen as a commodity valuates and conditions basic Sambian cultural institutions—personhood, marriage, clanhood— as well as key social relationships in the family, village, and ritual cults, between men and women, humans and spirits.

Analytically, the value of semen may be understood at several conceptual levels that synergistically interact. For the Sambia we may ask: How do individuals valuate other persons, groups, or relationships (e.g., sexual, familial, kinship) as semen donors or recipients? Or we may ask: How do semen transactions underlying social relationships define who is related as kin or affines as well as what the nature of those social bonds is? Sambia men practice both homosexual and heterosexual activities. And since sexual intercourse may be defined by Sambia either as work or play, we may ask: Is it the mode of semen exchange or the type of sexual intercourse that registers the difference between, say, sex as work or sex as play? If semen is a scarce resource—a means of social reproduction of babies and hence, heirs, gardeners, and hunters, and females for marriage exchange for production, and warriors for group protection—who or what regulates this commodity in Sambia culture?

I will examine these perspectives in the following study of Sambia ritualized homosexual practices. My interest lies mainly in demonstrating the symbolic relationship between *ideas* about semen and all forms of sexual *transactions* in Sambia society. Thus, this account is primarily cultural and sociological in orientation; I am not concerned here with describing erotic acts or individual constructions of semen beliefs in gender identity or psychosocial functioning, phenomena I have touched upon elsewhere (Herdt 1980, 1981; Stoller and Herdt 1982).

SAMBIA CULTURE

Sambia are a fringe-area Highlands people. They inhabit isolated ranges of the southern part of the Eastern Highlands near the Papuan border. Their high forest territory is vast, while the population (around 2,300) is small. Population density averages between 5 and 10 people per square mile throughout their territory. Historically, they migrated from the Papuan hinterland around Menyama during the last two centuries. Myth and legend relate that they fled after a great war. They share in cognate cultural traditions with other Anga tribes in the area, such as the Baruya (Godelier 1982a), with whom they also warred and traded. But Sambia have also been influenced by Eastern Highlands groups,

169

especially the Fore (Lindenbaum 1979). So their society and culture embodies and reflects long-continued influences and transformations of imported patterns from both Papua and the Highlands.

Social organization and economy revolve around small sedentary hamlets built atop high mountain ridges for defense. Gardening and hunting are the main economic pursuits. Sweet potatoes and taro are the chief staples. Women do most garden work. Men do all hunting, primarily for possum, cassowary, birds, and eels. Pigs are few and are of little ceremonial importance. Descent is ideally organized on the basis of patriliny. Postmarital residence is patrivirilocal, so males grow up in their father's hamlet, inherit his land, and reside there. Marriage is by infant betrothal or sister exchange; bride-wealth was introduced only in the mid-1970s. Some men, especially senior leaders, have several wives. All marriage is arranged by elders, women being traded between exogamous clans, either within or between neighboring hamlets, though interhamlet marriage is the norm. Hamlets may have two or more constituent clans, which tend to be internally organized as an extended family. Inside hamlets, nuclear (or polygamous) families live together in small separate huts; but there is also one or two men's houses wherein all initiated, unmarried males live. The hamlet tends to function as a corporate group in matters of warfare, subsistence activities, marriage, ritual, and dispute settlements.

Sambia society is comprised of six different population clusters of hamlets in adjacent but separate river valleys. These population clusters are divided, in turn, into subgroups (phratries) believed related by ancestry, ritual, and common geographic origin. Each phratry has between two and six hamlets, situated on ridges often within sight of one another. These local hamlet groups, known as confederacies,* intermarry and engage in joint ritual initiations every three or four years. But they sometimes fight among themselves. Warfare has indeed been rife throughout the entire Highlands Anga area, taking two forms: intertribal war raids to kill and loot; and intratribal bow fights designed to bluster and get revenge for perceived wrongs. In other words, within the Sambia

---

*Confederacies here marks the same social unit as "parish" and "subtribe" in other New Guineast typologies.

Valley, my fieldwork site, hamlets have intermarried, initiated, and fought—sociopolitical dynamics of the behavioral environment that are crucial for understanding social and sexual life.

Relationships between the sexes are highly polarized. One sees expressions of this polarization in virtually every social domain. A strict division of labor and ritual taboos forbid men and women from doing each other's tasks in hunting and gardening. Women are responsible for food preparation and child care. Authority rests in the hands of elders and war leaders. Men are in charge of public affairs, though women have interpersonal influence to some extent in domestic affairs. The hamlet itself is divided into male and female spaces and paths tabooed to the opposite sex after initiation. Men's rhetoric disparages older married women as oversexed or lecherous and younger women as prudish or shy. Men fear being contaminated and sapped of their strength (*jerungdu*) by marriageable women.

Furthermore, male/female sexual relationships are generally antagonistic, and many marital histories reveal arguments, fights, jealousies, sorcery fears, some wifebeating, and even suicide attempts. Wives (much more than female kin) are stigmatized as inferior, as polluting and depleting to men, because of their menstrual and vaginal fluids. Sexual intercourse is supposed to be spaced to avoid depletion and premature aging or death. (Couples may have sex every three to five days, or as infrequently as once every two or three weeks, depending upon their ages, length of marriage, personalities, etc.) Prolonged postpartum taboos prohibit couples from engaging in coitus for up to two and a half years following the birth of a child. These generalizations indicate trends: Sambia heterosexual relationships are often extremely polarized compared even with other Highlands groups (Langness 1967; reviewed in Herdt and Poole 1982).

How do Sambia understand the nature and functioning of the sexes? Male is the socially preferred and valued sex. Female is perceived as inferior in every way, except reproductively. Infants are assigned either to the male or female sex, and sex-typing of behaviors and gender traits is rigid from childhood onward. Females, however, are believed to mature "naturally," without external aids, for their bodies contain a menstrual blood organ (*tingu*)

171

which hastens physical and mental development, puberty, and eventually menarche, the key sign a woman is ready for marriage and procreation. (Menarche occurs late in New Guinea and is now between ages sixteen and nineteen for Sambia.) At menarche a woman is initiated in secret ceremonies in the menstrual hut forbidden to all males (cf. Godelier 1982a:74ff.). Males, by contrast, do not "naturally" mature as fast or as competently. Womb blood and maternal care not only hold them back but endanger their health. Males cannot attain puberty or other secondary sex-traits (e.g., facial hair, mature penis) without semen. And their bodies, their semen organs (*keriku-keriku*), do not internally produce semen, Sambia believe. Therefore they require inseminations and magical ritual treatments of various kinds over many years to "catch up" with females and become strong, manly men (for details, see Herdt 1980, 1981, 1982a, 1982b).

Male development and masculinization after childhood are the responsibility of the men's secret cult and its initiation system. This cult is organized and perpetuated by the confederacy of hamlets. Boys are initiated at seven to ten years of age, when they are separated from their mothers, natal households, and younger siblings. Thereafter, they must avoid all females for many years while living in the men's house. Avoidance taboos are rigidly enforced with shaming, beatings, and ultimately death (the last used to keep boys from revealing ritual secrets). Males undergo six initiations in all over the next ten or fifteen years. First initiation (*moku*) graduates are called *choowinuku*; second-stage initiation (*imbutu*) occurs between ages eleven and thirteen; and third-stage initiation (*ipmangwi*), bachelorhood puberty rites, is for youths fourteen to sixteen years of age. These initiations are all done in sequence on large groups of boys who become age-mates. They are from neighboring hamlets, thus making them members of a regional cohort. Initiates also become members of a warriorhood, which has local units responsible for defending their own hamlets. Fourth-stage initiation (*nuposha*) may occur anytime afterward. It is a public marriage ceremony, associated with secret male rites and sexual teachings for individual youths, to whom a woman has been assigned for their marriage. Fifth-stage initiation (*taiketnyi*) occurs when a man's wife has her menarche. The bride then has her secret initiation in the menstrual hut. Afterward, the couple can engage in coitus. The final, sixth-stage initiation (*moondangu*), is held when a man's wife bears her first child. She then undergoes a final women's secret ceremony too. Two children bring full adult manhood (*aatmwunu*) and personhood for both sexes.

The men's secret cult is ideally organized as a social hierarchical system according to ritual rank. Initiates are lumped into ritual categories: *kuwatni'u* is a category term for first- and second-stage prepubescent initiates (who may also be referred to as *choowinuku* or *imbutnuku*, ritual-grade titles); *ipmangwi* (or *moongenyu*, "new bamboo") bachelors are third-stage initiates of higher adolescent status. Pubescent bachelors dominate prepubescent initiates; older youths and young married men dominate them; and elders are seen as politically and spiritually superordinate over everyone (Herdt 1982*b*). War leaders and shamans lead in fights and healing ceremonies, respectively. There is nothing unique about this kind of ritual system, for many similar forms can be found in Eastern Highlands (e.g., Read 1952), Papuan Gulf (e.g., Williams 1936*a*), and Telefomin (e.g., Barth 1975) societies. What is special, and what links Sambia and their Anga neighbors with Papuan lowland systems (e.g., Keraki, Kiwai Island, Marind-anim), is the widescale institutionalization of homosexual activities.

Sambia practice secret homosexual fellatio, which is taught and instituted in first-stage initiation. Boys learn to ingest semen from older youths through oral sexual contacts. First- and second-stage initiates may only serve as fellators; they are forbidden to reverse erotic roles with older partners. Third-stage pubescent bachelors and older youths thus act as fellateds, inseminating prepubescent boys. All males pass through both erotic stages, being first fellators, then fellateds: there are no exceptions since all Sambia males are initiated and pressured to engage in homosexual fellatio.

The symbolism of the first homosexual teachings in initiation is elaborate and rich; the meaning of fellatio is related to secret bamboo flutes, and ritual equations are made between flutes, penis, and mother's breast, and between semen and breast milk (see Herdt 1982*a*, for a detailed analysis). Boys must drink semen to grow big and strong. At third-stage initiation, bachelors may experience personal difficulty in making the erotic switch in roles. Thereafter, they may continue having oral sex with boys until they father children. Essentially, youths pass from an exclusively homosexual

173

behavioral period to a briefer bisexual period, during which they may have both homosexual and heterosexual contacts in secret, and finally to exclusive heterosexual relationships. Social and sexual failures in masculine personhood may be defined as the failure to achieve these transitions (Herdt 1980).

SUBJECT AND OBJECTS • For the Sambia, who ritualize obligatory homosexual practices on a broad scale, it may be said that two forms of sexual behavior characterize their culture and developmental experience. For males, first sexual contacts are secret, transitional, male/male oral sexual behaviors; for adult males and females, the parallel form is initial male/female oral (i.e., the woman is fellator) sex in marriage. Later, heterosexual genital contacts occur. To my knowledge, no other form of sexual behavior occurs, including masturbation to orgasm. The rules and norms surrounding these two sexual modes are, in certain respects, both similar and different; I shall describe them below. But in both cases, semen acquisition is an imperative organizing principle of people's social interactions and sexual behavior. Its magical power does things to people, changing and rearranging them, as if it were a generator. They, however, can do little to affect this semen principle: it does not reflect on them, but merely passes through them as an electrical current through a wire, winding its way into bodies as generator coils for temporary storage. Because it is instrumental to growth, reproduction, and regeneration, sperm (and its substitutes) is needed to spark and mature human life. Humans are its objects.

This view may seem upside-down to us, yet it is essential as a rational outcome of the Sambia point of view. By thus beginning with its novelty, we may hope to achieve a better understanding of the relative relationship between heterosexuality and homosexuality, subjects about which we Westerners assume so much. I will first examine cultural ideas about semen, and then study how these ideas influence sociological types of semen transactions, between males and males, and males and females. Taken together, these ideas and social transactions form a system of objects of the predicate semen. Though these two perspectives are conceptually distinct, their complementarity suggests how normative goals affect individual social action and the developmental cycle of the group. When we view all of the valuations based on this predicate, we are led to a systemic view of the structuring (but not the experience) of sexual interactions and eroticism in Sambia culture. It is essential to stress that semen predicates two different sorts of relationships: *direct sexual transactions* between semen donors and recipients, either on the individual or group level (in the latter sense, I am speaking normatively); and *indirect semen transactions* that affect changes in a third party via the semen recipient, who is believed to serve as a transformer of sperm (e.g., father to mother to baby). The concept "transformer" compares with Meigs's (1976) use of "transmitter," in which she argues that a person's body may store or deliver fluids (e.g., blood or semen) or essences to someone else. "Transformer" differs because of another dimension needed, transformation, that is, *changing* semen into something else, as medieval alchemists were thought to change lead into gold. I will later disentangle these levels of description and analysis.

CULTURAL IDEAS OF SEMEN VALUE

Sambia have five main cultural categories of semen valuation. These include erotic play, procreation, growth, strength, and spirituality, all of which are connected with sexual behavior. The metaphoric and analogical uses in rhetoric and imagination of these categories can be found in other domains, too (see Herdt 1981). Here, though, I shall explore their social significance for insemination.[2] The study of these categories will involve us in understanding how persons (and in some ways, nonhuman entities) are represented as potential semen donors or recipients, transformers, or transmitters of semen value, in Sambia culture. This section is concerned with the cultural level of these concepts.[3]

There are two analytic senses in which I shall use the term *value*. First, the anthropological sense of conventional valuations in a culture: attributed or assumed meanings shared and assigned to persons, institutions, and substances. Thus we can speak of the cultural regard for semen and the social esteem with which it thus endows persons and relationships. (There is also a libidinal value, present in conscious and unconscious thought, which will not concern us.[4]) Second, there is the Marxist sense of the value of a commodity, such as gold, which "when impressed upon products, obtains fixity only by reason of their acting and reacting upon

175

each other as quantities of value" (Marx 1977:248).[5] Hence, we can analyze semen as a scarce resource that can be consumed and produced, "conserved," "invested," or otherwise "spent." Persons and relationships may be valuated (as a means to an end) in regard to their status as donors or recipients of the commodity semen.

In Sambia sexuality, there are several tacit assumptions underlying the relation between semen and the categories examined below, and I begin with them. (1) Semen is the most precious human fluid. Because it is believed vital for procreation and growth and is in short supply, sperm is more precious than mother's milk, its closest cultural equivalent. But precious does not necessarily mean powerful: menstrual blood is the logical antithesis of semen, it is dangerous and, in some rituals, is equally as efficacious as semen (Herdt 1982b; cf. Faithorn 1975). (2) Sambia are by character prudish people (may I refer to them as "prudish lechers"? cf. Meggitt 1964). Semen, other fluids, and sexuality are sensitive subjects: the data and viewpoints described below took years to assimilate, even though the presentation makes my analysis seem easy. (3) Sexual pleasure is seen by Sambia only in relation to another person; that is, there is no equivalent to the Western narcissistic category "sex" (used in relation to masturbation, pornography, etc. as an indefinite noun, e.g., "sex is . . . good, bad, fun, boring," etc.). Sex, in the Sambia sense, is only spoken of as: duvuno (pushing or penetrating into) a boy's mouth or a woman's vagina; or as the slackening of one's erect penis (lit., laakelu mulu, "penis fight") via "his bamboo orifice" (metaphor for boy's mouth) or "her thing down below" (euphemism for vagina). Again, the verb duvuno is not used for masturbation and only rarely for wet dreams in which the dream images concern copulating with persons (e.g., interpreted as spirits).[6] (4) When men refer to erotic desire (e.g., "I swallow my saliva [thinking about sex] with him/her") they tend to refer to their sexual outlets as if their alters' orifice (mouth or vagina) were fetishized objects like a commodity (i.e., they use "food" as a metaphor for their sexual needs). (5) All sexual intercourse may be defined as either work (wumdu) or play (chemonyi) or both. For example: it is wumdu to produce a baby by copulating with a woman many times; but it is chemonyi to promiscuously copulate with a boy once or twice knowing he will not procreate. Insemination is also an action that mediates (e.g., like ritual, *pweiyu*) between work and play, sacred and profane. Let us examine each category in turn.

EROTIC PLAY • When Sambia use *chemonyi* (play) as an adjective in relation to sexual intercourse, they normatively refer to sexual release as erotic pleasure.* Semen is expended and orgasm (*imbimboogu*) achieved. I begin with this category not because it is most crucial—Sambia themselves would rank procreation first (Herdt 1981)—but because it is essential for understanding semen valuations, and also because anthropologists often ignore erotic motivation as a native category.

The most general cultural attributes of erotic play may be sketched as follows. First, the factor of the sex of one's partner: erotic play symbolically typifies male/male sexual contacts more than male/female contacts. Male/male sexual contacts are culturally defined as behaviorally promiscuous. Male/female contacts, normative only in marriage, are viewed (unless adulterous) as steady transactions aimed toward procreation. Erotic play is of course an aspect of all male/female contacts, but it is not their most important one. *Exclusive* sexual access to a person seems inversely related to erotic play: a man's wife, as his sexual property, as Sambia see it, is less exciting than a boy or woman taken at first (i.e., as a virgin), or only once, on the sly. Age is a contributing factor here: sexual partners are perceived as having more "heat" and being more exciting the younger they are. A second factor is reciprocity: the more asymmetrical the sexual partners (youth/boy), the more erotic play seems to culturally define their contact. (By contrast, I have argued elsewhere that the husband/wife dyad is the most symmetrical relationship in Sambia culture; see Herdt 1982b.) Third, sexual constancy, that is, greater frequency of sexual contacts, generally transforms sexual contacts from erotic play

---

*There is no marked category for erotic play as such: it is signified in ideology and social intercourse by *chemonyi*, "orgasm," and several conditions of sexual excitement (e.g., erection). The term *sexual* has a wide range of connotations in English; *erotic*, however, refers specifically to that which stimulates sexual desire and psychophysiological arousal, so I prefer *erotic* in this usage. I shall not attempt to describe sexual excitement here, but see Stoller and Herdt (n.d.).

into something else. Husband/wife contacts are the most constant in Sambia sexual life.

Erotic play may be defined also according to the social purpose of insemination. Erotic pleasure is attached to male/male and male/female sexual contacts, and to both oral and vaginal intercourse.* But only heterosexual genital contacts result in procreation; all other sexual contacts fulfill other quasi-reproductive functions (e.g., growth of spouse) or are for erotic play. Since homosexual fellatio cannot eventuate in reproduction (consummation of marriage), it becomes a demonstration of a fellated's psychosocial maturity, that is, of his power to masculinize a boy. But this valuation is of significance for *donors*, whereas boy-recipients highly value semen for "growth." What donors value also is the fellator's mouth as a sexual outlet: the social purpose is sexual release.

Erotic play may be defined, lastly, according to the flow of a scarce commodity. Semen is viewed as a very scarce resource by Sambia, for, in the reproductive process, it is believed instrumental from conception to adulthood. It takes many inseminations to procreate: large expenditures of time, energy, semen. From this viewpoint, all male/female contacts may be construed as benefiting procreation (see below). Homoerotic play unevenly fits this paradigm. It is, after all, play, not work: procreative work is defined as producing babies. So how do they benefit the donor? Essentially, homoerotic play is culturally defined as an unequal exchange of commodities: recipients acquire semen, donors get sexual services. This exchange is unequal because (as Sambia see it) a man's sperm is being depleted, but he gets only erotic pleasure in return ("which is insubstantial"). Homoerotic activity thus creates a dilemma for bachelors, which is perhaps why some engage in it less frequently as they approach marriage. Homoerotic play is, however, less depleting than heterosexual intercourse (work) which is, in part, why bachelors usually do not replenish the semen "lost" during their early homosexual activities.

---

*All sexual contacts are symbolically defined against the norm of penetration and ejaculation into an insertee's mouth (initiate or woman) or vagina, insemination resulting from (the belief that) the full seminal emission is ingested/absorbed by the recipient's body (mouth or vagina is entrance).

PROCREATION • Procreation is defined as genital-to-genital heterosexual contacts that lead to the birth of offspring. Sambia regard vaginal intercourse as primarily focused on the production of babies. Oral insemination prepares a wife's body for making babies by "strengthening" her, as well as by precipitating her menarche (if she has not already attained it). Fellatio also prepares her for lactation by semen being transformed into breast milk. Oral sexual contacts are not believed to make babies in anyone; only vaginal intercourse does that. All heterosexual genital intercourse contributes directly to procreation in one's own marriage, and *all* sexual contacts may be viewed as contributing directly to the recipients' procreative competence (wife or boy-fellator) or reproduction (wife).*

Procreation is jurally defined as resulting from genital-to-genital sexual contacts between formally married husband and wife. Since heterosexual contact is not morally or jurally allowed outside of marriage, privilege of sexual access to a woman's body is restricted by marriage; exclusive sexual rights belong to her husband. Likewise, exclusive access to a husband's body and semen, after birth of their first child, is his wife's right (which view is a key argument women use to resist polygyny). Traditionally, only infant betrothal and bride-service marriage (which was rare) required the transfer of goods or services to the donors bestowing a wife. Infant betrothal, though, required meat and small food prestations only, whereas bride-service required more wealth, in addition to the bridegroom's years'-long work for his prospective affines. Sister exchange requires no exchanges other than that of the women. Since infant betrothal is preferred, and sister exchange marriages far outnumber those of bride-service, marriage transactions are not much related to bride-wealth in its usual anthropological sense (cf. Collier and Rosaldo 1981). The "wealth" exchanged (e.g., meat prestations) is largely produced through the labors of hunting by the wife-receivers.

Genital-to-genital intercourse creates a fetus by successively injecting semen into a woman's womb. After initial oral sexual con-

---

*Oral heterosexual contacts indirectly help procreation; see below under section on "growth."

tacts, a woman's body is viewed as ready to procreate. One instance of vaginal intercourse does not a fetus make: Sambia have no notion of conception in our Western scientific sense. The womb is the container and transformer of semen. It changes the sperm into fetal tissue: primarily bone and skin, but also muscle and internal organs. The semen coagulates inside the birth sac; this "biological" process is central to fetal development, and its imagery is important in social thought (Herdt 1981:167–172ff.). Womb and umbilical blood also become circulatory blood in the fetus; they do not produce any other parts of the child, which result only from semen. Social ideology thus defines procreation as productive work (not erotic play) in two senses: it is hard work to feed enough semen into a woman's womb to create a fetus; and it is hard work for the woman's body to change this sperm into a fetus, sapping her own blood, and carrying the child in her body for so long.

Blood and semen also differentially contribute to the sex of the offspring and his or her gender differentiation. First, both parents can magically influence the fetus's sex by ingesting various plants. They do this both because Sambia ideally prefer a boy as the firstborn and because they want to make the infant more attractive. Second, it takes more semen to create a girl than a boy. Two other beliefs explain why, and they pertain to the procreative/economic productive capacities of males versus females (i.e., in social reproduction). The most important is that females do more hard work (i.e., garden work) all the time; therefore, the female fetus "pulls" more semen from the mother to make itself. (A magical elaboration of this idea is that since females think about garden work constantly, their fetal thought anticipates and drains more "semen strength" in preparation.) The other belief is that a female fetus has a *tingu* (menstrual-blood organ), which makes the mother's vagina "hot," and therefore drains off more semen from the father during sexual contacts that create the fetus. During womb life, the sexes receive blood in differential amounts too. Essentially, girls have some of their mother's menstrual blood transmitted to their own menstrual-blood organs *in utero*. Later, during postnatal growth, this blood stimulates girls' psychobiological feminization (sexual and gender differentiation). Boys, by contrast, have no blood transmitted to their inactive tingus. Nor do they receive any of their father's semen for use in their own semen organs: father's semen in both sexes merely creates fetal tissue. (Mystical aspects of these fetal processes are described below.)

Marriage is fully consummated after the birth of a child. Procreation results in final but distinct initiation ceremonies for the husband-father and wife-mother alike. The new father and his clan bestow a meat prestation on the wife's cognatic kin, especially patrilateral female kin, and her ritual sponsor, in public village ceremonies. Because procreation defines full adulthood for men and women, childless adults are not perceived as full persons. Nonetheless, all childlessness in a marriage is attributed to barrenness in the woman or contraceptive sorcery by other men (usually thought to be envious fellow villagers who wanted the woman for themselves). Sambia men dogmatically deny the possibility of sterility in a husband (see also Read 1951); indeed, such is never discussed in social discourse, and the only category for sterility is "barren woman" (*kwoliku*). Childlessness is thus an acceptable reason for taking a second wife, but not for divorce. Once a marriage is consummated, it is contracted for life and cannot be broken: a woman is rarely taken back by the donor group; when warfare occurs, a woman's ties with her natal group (i.e., enemies) are severed; divorce is thus extremely rare and usually instigated by a husband over his wife's perceived adultery; their children become jural members of the father's clan; and so only death breaks the marital bond.

GROWTH • Sambia believe that biological growth in humans results from ingestion of semen and several equivalent substances (mother's milk, pandanus nuts). Sexual intercourse for growth is described as: *pinu pungooglumonjapi* ("pushing" to "grow" he/she, where *pinu* is an alternate verbal form of *duvuno*). This idiomatic form may be applied to both male/male and male/female sexual contacts.

The value of semen for human growth comes in successive stages which differ according to the mode of semen transmission and one's sex. Initial growth for every fetus occurs through semen accumulations in the mother's womb. Postnatal growth in babies results mainly from breast-feeding. A woman's body is again treated as a biological transformer of semen in this regard: a man's inseminations (especially oral) amass in and are transformed by his wife's breasts into mother's milk (*nu-tokeno,* breast food). Mother's milk is vital for the baby's growth. After breast-weaning, growth in early childhood is aided by eating pandanus nuts, which are seasonal but are treated as nearly equal nourishment to that of mother's milk. (The productive source of this nut food is one's father's trees and his "hard work" in tending and scaling them to procure the nuts.) Meat fed to children also contributes smaller increments to growth. Following weaning, though, girls continue to grow without further aids, whereas boys falter, staying weak and puny.

Male growth after weaning comes mostly from homosexual inseminations following initiation. This semen-nourishment form is male *monjapi'u,* * which men liken to breast-feeding (Herdt 1981:234–236). Oral sexual contacts feed semen into a boy's body, distributing sperm to his maturing skin, bones, skull, and producing changes toward masculinization (i.e., eventuating in biological puberty). The bulk of externally ingested semen goes to the boy's semen organ, where it accumulates as a "pool." This pool is drawn on after puberty for two purposes: it produces pubescent secondary sex-traits, especially musculature, hairiness on the body, and the development of a mature penis; and it provides semen for later sexual contacts. (The first sign of surplus semen in the body comes from seminal emissions in wet dreams.)

Girls require and are permitted no inseminations until marriage. Men believe that postmarital oral sexual contacts in cases of marriage before menarche provide a young wife's body with semen to stimulate the final "growth" changes necessary for childbearing. They also argue, as noted above, that women need semen to create breast milk. (Some women dispute these views and argue that a woman's body "naturally" creates breast milk; however, other women disagree with them on this matter.)

In sum, semen creates biological growth directly in initiates and wives through sexual contact, primarily fellatio, whereas it creates growth indirectly in fetus and newborn through being transformed by a woman's body into fetal tissue and milk. For the spouses, then, growth and procreation are concepts that refer to different

---

*Shortened by men from *pinu pungooglumonjapi.*

aspects of the same sexual contacts. For the offspring, as third-party semen recipient, postnatal growth is vital after birth, and long postpartum taboos prohibit marital sexual intercourse for fear the infant will be harmed (be stunted or ugly, an outcome that would shame the parents, especially the father, who would be viewed as lacking sexual restraint). In homoerotic activity, men offer boys the normative goal that semen "grows" them. But from the donor's standpoint, although initiates' growth does provide vicarious (because of homosexual promiscuity) long-term confirmation of the fellated's manhood, a fellator's growth is not of direct importance to a bachelor's personhood. Rather, homoerotic play takes precedence as the fellated's motive; the boy's growth is a latent social function of the bachelor's behavior (and is, I think, largely a rationalization on the men's part).

STRENGTH • Strength (jerungdu) is a key concept in Sambia culture; we shall here examine only its implications for semen transmission and thereby human maturation.

Strength is absolutely derived from semen and its symbolic equivalents, mother's milk and pandanus nuts. But more than those latter substances, semen masculinizes a person's body; there is no substitute for it. Unlike procreation or growth valuations, strength can be obtained directly only through semen. In Sambia thought, there is a general tendency to play down strength and stress growth as characteristic of the breast-feeding relationship. Suckling milk definitely grows a baby, but it is much less associated with strengthening it. Sperm in the womb forms the skeletal fetus; nursing helps create the baby's teeth, the hardening of its skin and skull. But milk is more for growth. The "strong" results of milk, Sambia believe, are transformations of semen: mother ingests sperm, which her breasts convert into milk. The "strong" part of milk is also more crucial for male infants, but it alone will not masculinize them. Thus, in analytic terms, strength is not intrinsically produced but is rather derived from the mother/infant relationship, itself a product of marriage. In male Sambia terms, however, strength is a transactional product that makes use of the father's secret sexual acquisition of semen from other men, which he feeds to his wife, whose body, in turn, has a "natural" capacity to store the fluid and turn it into breast food that strengthens and matures the infant.

As with growth, a father can indirectly add small amounts of strength over the years following weaning by providing meat and pandanus nuts to children. Cassowary meat, too, which may be eaten only by males, has fat (*moo-nugu*) that sometimes is treated as a second-rate semen equivalent (Herdt 1981:110). (Other kinds of fat, e.g., from pigs or eels, are never likened to semen.) But these are small increments.

If one follows the semen cycle, we see a chain of links in which men strengthen persons: husband strengthens wife through initial fellatio; father strengthens baby through mother's milk; bachelor strengthens initiate through fellatio. Symbolically, homosexual fellatio provides the key ritualized strengthening of boys' postpartum bodies. As I have emphasized elsewhere (Herdt 1981, 1982*a*), fellatio insemination is chiefly seen as growing a boy, the perceived outcome of which is strength. Culturally, the act of feeding/inseminating is equivalent to the verbal category *monjapi'u,* male nursing, the social/perceptual outcome of which is the state of being *jerungdu,* as seen in both its physical and psychosocial manifestations: large size, attractiveness, valor, forceful speech, sexual potency, and many social achievements, including progeny.

There is another secret source of strength that is important in male thought and which concerns the nonhuman sources for the replenishment of semen expended in sexual intercourse. Analytically, this semen valuation might be treated as separate from the "strength" concept because of its ontogenetic status in the male life cycle (adults give semen away and then must replace it to stay strong). But Sambia do not think of the matter in this way, for this replenishment is seen simply as a further extension of strength-building. Yet, since this replenishment practice is learned later in ritual life, and comes from trees, not men, we shall here examine it as an auxiliary replacement process.

In semen transactions, one person's loss is someone else's gain: semen, which embodies strength, depletes the donor, whose strength therefore diminishes. Fear of semen depletion is an important theme in male ritual discourse and ideology. (It is registered, too, in individual gender aberrations; Herdt 1980.) Concern with too frequent semen loss is an inhibitor of initial homosexual contacts, bachelors being cautioned to go easy. (Here, again, fellateds and fellators are at odds.) Yet bachelors' fears are not great; and the early use of ritual mechanisms for semen replenishment in fellateds is played down. Among married men, the situation is quite different. A key pragmatic focus of fifth- and sixth-stage initiation ceremonies is teaching about secret ingestion of white milk-sap from trees, which is believed to replace semen "lost" to women. (Pandanus nuts are another semen replacement, though of lesser importance because they not always available.) This milk-sap comes from a variety of wild forest trees and vines, and the sap is referred to as *iaamoonaalyu,* "tree mother's milk."

Trees are, in general, regarded as if they and their products were primarily of the female sex, e.g., as with pandanus trees. And myth also genderizes them this way (Herdt 1981). Thus, there seems little doubt that the imagery and symbolization of the adult man's semen replenishment is not, then, symbolic insemination, but rather that of symbolic breast-feeding. This interpretation is confirmed by their drinking of sap from long aerial roots of pandanus nut trees: the trees are ritually referred to as "females," and the roots are likened to "women's breasts." We see, therefore, that semen comes initially from homosexual fellatio, which can later be replaced by milk-sap (and, to a lesser extent, by pandanus nuts and cassowary fat); and semen, in turn, is transformed into breast milk and fetal tissue by women. At rock bottom, male ideology seems to postulate that these forest trees create *new* semen.

SPIRITUALITY • The final category of semen valuations I shall refer to as spirituality, though it is not a marked category in Sambia culture or language. Spirituality is, in our terms, an animistic composite of both natural and supernatural elements. These elements include most noticeably spirit familiars (*numelyu*) of various sorts, believed to be *transmitted* (not transformed) through semen for males (and through blood for females). The reproduction of spiritual elements in persons and groups is entirely a social outcome of sexual intercourse over which individuals have little control.

Before describing familiars, two other matters deserve mention. The first is the concept of soul (*koogu*), a spiritual aspect of personhood that is related to sexuality and parenting. There is no clearly formulated theory of the soul's origin in individual development. Some men attribute it only to the father's sperm. Others say it is a combination of semen and material in the mother's

185

womb (they do not specify which parts of semen and/or blood). Though the womb is important, some people attribute the birth of a child's soul not to fetal life but to postnatal socialization. Men normatively relate the father's sperm to the child's soul in both sexes, especially in boys. This ambiguity is no doubt an expression of all persons' normative blood ties to mother and matrilateral kin. Yet, since the soul survives death and becomes a ghost, forest spirit (big men), or hamlet spirit (prominent women) haunting its clan's territory, its patrilineal origin and afterlife influence seem clear in sociopolitical organization. The skull and bones of the deceased also become powerful weapons in sorcery and are most efficacious when used by biological kinsmen, sons especially. In both cases—souls and bones—spiritual essences of semen are thought to survive death. The other concept is "thought" or *koontu*, which I gloss as personhood. "Thought" is the totality of one's experience, beliefs, and knowledge. Personhood is mainly a product of social training; its relation to body substance and biological inheritance is less certain. Socialization is its chief source, however, and this means that both mother and father influence personhood. (The ritual negation of maternal influences on boys' personhood is addressed by the process I have called "accountability"; Herdt n.d.)

Without question the most significant semen valuation for spirituality is the child's inheritance of spirit familiars. Transmission of familiars is ideologically clear and sex-linked. Boys inherit only their father's familiars via his semen. Girls inherit their mother's familiars through her blood. (Mother's milk, a semen derivative, is ignored in this domain.) Genealogical inheritance of clan familiars (i.e., totems) among males seems to derive from the semen that creates a son's body tissue. Later, males acquire other familiars attracted to them through ritual ceremonies: the nature of this attraction again implies that father's semen is instrumental. Shamanic familiars, transmitted through semen from father to son in the mother's womb, is a clear case of necessary patrilineal inheritance required for legitimate performance of the shamanic role (Herdt 1977). Other familiars, both personal and clan-related, ensure longevity, spiritual protection, or strength. Male ideology generally denies women such blessings from their natal clan familiars. Men may have their familiars "stolen" unwittingly by male children, which leads to sickness or premature death. Homosexual inseminations do not transmit familiars to semen recipients (cf. Schieffelin 1976, 1977). Finally, men's ingestion of milk sap from trees is consistent with the perpetuation of their clan familiars (though this idea is not fully conscious in Sambia thought). We shall return to these points below.

SEMEN "VALUE" IN SOCIAL TRANSACTIONS

Who may and should have sexual intercourse with what categories of persons in Sambia society? What are the principles of these social transactions? In this section I examine social action in relation to the cultural ideas of semen valuation already described. The sociology of semen transactions involves two viewpoints. First, there are *direct* semen transactions between persons resulting from sexual intercourse. Second, there are *indirect* semen transactions with a third party believed to occur by the transformation of sperm into something else by a second party; whether the source of semen is human or nonhuman (i.e., trees), however, the semen transformers are always humans. A subcategory of indirect inseminations may be seen as *delayed exchanges* between social groups, semen being returned to donor groups via former recipients in the subsequent generation. I will study each of these types in turn.

DIRECT SEMEN TRANSACTIONS • All sexual contacts are restricted by exogamous taboos and social norms. Sexual contacts are permissible only between unrelated people; that is, those related through common cognatic links, especially agnates, are forbidden sexual partners. Marriage should be arranged between different clans, preferably of different villages. Statistically, though, up to 50 percent of all marriages are contracted within certain hamlets; FZD marriage is normatively permitted in delayed-exchange marriage contracts; and MBD marriage, though frowned upon, occurs rarely when no alternate wife can be found (Herdt 1981). Homosexual contacts are likewise prohibited between all clansmen, matrilateral kin, age-mates, and with ritual sponsors. (Homosexual infractions occur, however, as between matrilateral cross-cousins, or distant kin not normally encountered, though these are unusual.) Male initiates' ritual sponsors are called "moth-

187

er's brother," a social title, since only some sponsors are actual or classificatory mother's brother. Nonetheless a boy's sponsor becomes, in effect, a pseudokinsman who combines both maternal and paternal attributes, making it very wrong for any sexual contact to occur between them. In general, all sexual contacts are highly regulated and tend to occur with people of other hamlets (who are potential or real enemies), so sexual contacts distinguish kin from nonkin, and friendly from hostile persons.

In direct sexual transactions, all the above cultural ideas of semen value come into play, but the domain of erotic play is especially important. Erotic play is a social motive and goal that applies mainly to adult men. Their motive for erotic play is sexual release, that is, orgasm. Boy-fellators never have orgasms in homoerotic play. And men deny, in general, that women experience orgasm, though they believe women are lascivious and that some enjoy sexual play.

Men's enjoyment of erotic play changes through the life cycle. Some older boy-fellators do experience vicarious erotic pleasure from homosexual fellatio, as indicated by their reports (near puberty) of their own erections while fellating a bachelor, or by certain feelings or body sensations during fellation. Bachelors (fellateds) engage in homoerotic play to (in local idiom) "straighten their penises," that is, to reduce sexual tension/frustration, or to "feel *ilaiyu*" (here meaning pleasure) from orgasm. Men get erotic pleasure from copulating with their wives, first through fellatio, and then in genital-to-genital intercourse, which most men favor over fellatio. To reiterate: male/female oral sexual contacts, like those with boys, are regarded more as erotic play.

Male social ideology defines both homoerotic and heteroerotic play as transactions in which the older male is *always* the inseminator. No role reversals are ever situationally permitted. The older male is viewed as the socially active party who should control the behavior interchanges that lead to the insemination. A man's control over sexual contacts is established by the social norms regulating the behavioral conditions of sexual intercourse. Men are physically bigger than boys and most women. During intercourse the man either stands over his fellator (who kneels) or lays on top of his wife (in the "missionary" position), methods that allow a man instant freedom to withdraw from body contact at will. Men are also usually years older than their insertees, either boys or women (even though men curiously regard younger wives as of like age and maturity; see Herdt 1981:177, 181). Again, these interactions are defined as asymmetrical: women and boys get semen, men get erotic pleasure. Most men are (consciously) un-interested in the erotic arousal of either boys or women, so direct sexual transactions emphasize the sexual excitement of the inserter.

In spite of the men's view, the concept erotic play admits of some social reciprocity between all sexual partners. Men grudg-ingly recognize that women have erotic interests; for instance, sexually experienced wives are rhetorically described as lascivious harlots consumed by insatiable erotic appetites (Herdt 1981:187). Perhaps this dogma is the men's response to knowing that women favor certain men over others as mates. Men also know that boys joke about fellatio among themselves and that initiates favor some bachelors over others in regard to the amount and taste of their semen.[7] Bachelors likewise favor certain boys over others: those who are more attractive to them are either more or less sexually aggressive and/or willing to perform fellatio. These reciprocal as-pects thus underscore the frame of play, and they are not found in notions of sex for procreation, growth, strength, or spirituality, all of which are merely passive outcomes of insemination as a one-way street.

Since semen is highly valued as a means to valuable social ends—personal strength, marriage, offspring, personhood—it should be conserved and wisely spent. Men assume that women and boys *desire their semen* for those social ends; no other motive is searched for in understanding why insertees engage in sexual intercourse. (*We* know the situation is more complex: for instance, boys must at first be coerced into fellatio; but men also "know" this.) The seeming personal conflict on men's part, at least in homosexual contacts, is that *they get only sexual release in return for their sperm.* They recognize this in idioms that depict the penis as having a mind of its own: for example, "that no good man down there [penis] gets up and we follow its nose [euphemism for glans penis]." Meaning: men inseminate from sexual impulse, almost against their own will. Here, then, we may see a perceived conflict between private impulses and rational norms.

This psychosocial conflict is felt in two other ways. First, women

189

are more prized as sexual outlets than are boys. Women are *owned*: this ownership is itself a contributing dynamic to the sexual excitement of Sambia men. Male/female relationships are, in general, filled with more power than are male/male contacts, for heterosexuality is more highly regulated. Sexually, women are also more powerful, for they can contaminate as well as deplete; and women deplete semen more than do boys. Moreover, sexual impulses leading to adultery are a tremendous social problem in Sambia society (see below). Second, when orgasm occurs it is treated as being beyond conscious control. Wet dreams are the best example.[8] For women, breast-feeding may also apply: some women report that they experience *imbimboogu,* which they liken to orgasm, when feeding, although it is not clear yet what this social labelling of their experience means (see Stoller and Herdt, n.d.). All these points support the conclusion that individual sexual impulses are stronger than the social need for semen constraint in heterosexual versus homosexual contacts. They also suggest that Sambia men are later motivated more toward heterosexual relationships.

What seems to underlie this conflict is the fact that sex for erotic play is the only sexual mode that produces no social advantage to the semen donor. Because all ejaculation is potentially debilitating, and semen is a male's most valuable resource, all sexual contacts are viewed as a "careful metering of semen" (Gell 1975:252). Seen this way, erotic play represents what Gell (1975) refers to as a "nemesis of reproductivity": it makes no personal sense in the scheme of things, even though it is personally pleasurable. All other categories of direct sexual transactions may be defined as work, not play, for this reason: like other forms of work (e.g., gardening), sex for procreation, growth, and so forth produces social products. One's semen is spent to reproduce heirs and perpetuate one's clan. With this view in mind I will now contrast other cultural ideas pertaining to heterosexual and homosexual contacts.

The idea of procreation applies only to male/female sexual contacts. In native theory all heterosexual contacts, oral or vaginal, contribute to a woman's reproductive competence. In practice, however, only early marital contacts are treated this way: oral sex is infrequent after a woman bears children. My impression is that both men and women in later years prefer genital-to-genital contact (and I think most women always prefer vaginal sex). Though homosexual transactions are not procreative (but cf. individual boys' fears of becoming pregnant [Herdt 1981] and similar beliefs about male pregnancy elsewhere [Meigs 1976; Williams 1936c]), semen in boys does assist in their overall attainment of reproductive competence as adults.

The concepts of growth and strength are applied to both homosexual and heterosexual transactions. In theory, boy-fellators as semen recipients "use" sexual contact first to grow and then to get strong. Until third-stage initiation this norm holds; youths are thereafter accorded biological maturity and may no longer serve as insertees. (By definition, a Sambia man who sought semen from another male would be terribly stigmatized as unmanly; and to do so with a boy—pederastic fellatio—would be morally unconscionable; Herdt 1980.) Growth and strength apply differentially to women as semen recipients. Essentially, all heterosexual fellatio grows and strengthens a woman until she is a mother. Later oral sex does not grow a woman, for she is viewed as biologically mature. It does replenish her strength, however; a sort of perpetual fountain-of-youth men must give up after bachelorhood. Indeed, men complain that women are healthier and outlive them because of this constant source of orally ingested strength. (In this sense, a wife is like a boy-fellator.) Vaginal sex is generally believed to contribute neither growth nor strength to a woman: instead, indirectly, a man's sperm grows and strengthens fetus and infant.

Finally, the concept of spirituality applies unequally to direct sexual transactions. No transmission of spirit familiars occurs between males and females. None is imparted to one's wife: she is simply *one* source of the transmission of soul and familiars to one's offspring. Again, men believe that only sons inherit father's familiars (either indirectly, through sperm via mother, or directly, through cult ceremonies that call forth one's father's familiars after his death). A daughter's familiars come only from her mother; but her soul is linked (the notion is vague) to her father and his clan territory, though not irrevocably.[9] Moreover, there is absolutely no sense that a boy-fellator acquires his familiars from any bachelor-fellated; but the idea is neither here nor there, since Sambia never seem to consider the possibility.[10] Analytically, though, we should underline that their folk model of spiritual transmission keeps familiars discreetly in clans and firmly embedded in the

191

genitor's procreative role. Here we see a firm separation between spirituality and sexuality, on the levels both of ideology and social action. The division between spiritual and material reproduction in marriage is especially notable (cf. Tuzin 1982).

There is one other notion, which we may define as spiritual, that involves direct homosexual transactions. *Kwolaalyuwaku:* * a multivalent concept referring to masculine decorations and ritual paraphernalia (as a category term) which is also a ritual secret pseudonym for semen. (It is also close to *kweiaalyu-waku,* which literally means "sun's white grease," an alternate for cassowary fat [*kaiouwugu moo-nugu*]). The semantic referent of the semen aspect is esoteric, yet clearly signifies a collective semen pool. This pool is perceived as the semen contained in the bodies of all men living within neighboring hamlets: it therefore reflects the ritual cult and the confederacy. The idea is that boys have access to this pool, which they can tap into through homosexual insemination, strengthening themselves. Symbolically, then, *kwolaalyuwaku* is a metaphor for the men's collective cult.

But on the individual level, the concept is bidirectional. For a long time I was skeptical of men's statements that it *strengthened themselves* to inseminate many boys. How could this be? Men argue that just as a boy draws strength from numerous men, who deposit their semen in his reserve for future use, so men are kept strong by having their sperm safely contained in many boys, who are likened to a sort of magical string of semen depositories for one's substance, spread throughout society. Should a man or any of his semen recipients get sick, other recipients remain strong and healthy. And since recipients harbor parts of one's sperm (strength) inside them, so, too, one is kept healthy (in sympathetic-contagious magical thought). A woman lacks this protection: she is not a cult initiate, and her semen comes from only one man, her husband. Nor is a man likewise protected by inseminating women or creating children: the concept is not extended beyond homosexual contacts. Thus, semen not only bestows but maintains strength, the only concrete evidence known to me that explains why homosexual

---

* *Kwol,* marks male; *aalyu,* water; *waku,* a type of strong betel nut and a cover term for certain decorations. Sometimes the term is shortened to the secret name, *Kweiwaku,* which men use explicitly to refer to "the semen of all men."

insemination is less depleting than that of heterosexuality. In this ritual sense, homosexual practices are placed within a spiritual framework and are opposed to heterosexuality and marriage.

All the above sexual contacts concern normatively appropriate semen transactions between donors and recipients. *Illicit* heterosexual semen transactions (adultery) reveal the social boundary of ideas about exclusive jural claims over a man's semen. All adultery is severely condemned; a man may use violence against a wife suspected of it. Therefore, it is hidden until discovered, when the spouses fight. If a husband is accused of adultery, or of wanting to take a second wife, the fight is called *kweikoonmulu,* literally "semen fight." Semen fights entail dreadful cursing and brawls. This adultery can be seen as "stealing another woman's semen," though it involves much more, of course. Accusations of a wife's adultery (which is rarer, for Sambia treat adulterous women harshly) also concern semen in two ways: fears that a husband's penis has been contaminated by intercourse with his wife's vagina after sex with another man (thought to bring him sickness); and questions about the wife's lover's semen contributions to a future child. In sum, adultery reveals that marriage bestows the right of exclusive spousal control over semen and insemination exchange as scarce resources.

What are the social effects of these direct sexual transactions on group relationships? Let me examine the most general latent and manifest functions of sexual contacts in the same generation. First, semen flow mirrors marriage transactions between groups. Semen may only be normatively transacted between persons of groups who can intermarry, that is, homosexual contact is forbidden with matrilineal kin and clansmen. The same clan that donates a wife thus has clansmen who are appropriate homosexual partners (cf. Kelly 1976). Affines of the same generation (e.g., brothers-in-law) are especially appropriate homosexual contacts. The paradigm of this affinal homoerotic bond would be a young man who marries a younger woman and who can inseminate her younger initiate brother, either consanguineal or classificatory WiB (cf. Serpenti, chap. 7, and Sørum, chap. 8, this volume). This man manifestly inseminates his wife to grow and strengthen her, and to procreate, and may (along with his fellow clansmen) inseminate her younger brother for erotic play, the effect of which is to grow and strengthen the boy. These sexual transactions would define a man and his clan as semen donors, while his wife and brother-in-law would be recipients. Yet ego's clan is also a wife recipient from his younger homosexual partner's donor clan. This set of social transactions is common in Sambia life.

Second, marital/sexual bonds tend to create closer political ties between unrelated groups. Sambia engage in marriage and homosexual contacts only with propinquitous groups in the same confederacy. One does not receive or give semen to true, intertribal enemies. Affinal ties, in particular, create closer political affiliations for mutual defense between and within hamlets. Affinal ties also establish marriage contractual obligations and sentimental bonds that persist in the next generation, influencing alignments among hamlets.

Third, semen metaphorically defines political power: inseminators are more powerful than recipients in virtually every sense. All male persons eventually serve as both direct semen donors and as recipients. All females are always direct recipients, or indirect donors, to their offspring whereas males constitute a category of both direct givers and takers. And their sexual status, of course, flip-flops during the male life cycle. Symbolically, I think, Sambia define the administration of semen as a masculine act, whereas the taking in of semen is a feminine act. One of the manifest functions of the secrecy of homosexual fellatio is to hide from women the shame men feel at having earlier performed in this feminine way (Herdt 1981:chap. 8). A latent function of homosexual secrecy is to rationalize and disguise men's use of boys as a sexual outlet. By the same token, the ritual secret of homosexual growth and strength unites all males as a category against all females. This social link, which also mystifies the nature of male/female relationships, politically reinforces male power and thereby perpetuates the men's ritual cult (Herdt 1982b).

INDIRECT SEMEN TRANSACTIONS • This mode of social transaction is based on the symbolic principle that sperm is transmitted to someone whose body transforms it into something else useful to a third party. The paradigm is the nuclear family triad: father ⟶ mother ⟶ child. The alternative form of indirect insemination views men as replenishing their semen from tree sap, which their bodies turn into semen: tree ——► man ——► semen recipient. Having already described direct sexual contacts, these semen transformations can be easily outlined.

We have seen that sexual intercourse between spouses involves all cultural ideas of semen value except spirituality. Now when we examine the effects of her husband's semen on the prospective infant, the woman's role as transformer is clarified at two developmental points. First, as we have seen, her orally ingested sperm is specifically transformed into breast milk. This milk is stored for the infant's nourishment after birth. Subsequent semen from vaginal intercourse is stored and transformed in the woman, converted by her womb into fetal tissue, as we saw. Both the intrauterine formation of the child, as well as its postnatal breast-feeding, are indirect products of the father's sperm.

In this type of indirect transaction, there is a subtle interplay of cultural beliefs being applied. Erotic play occurs between the spouses, leading to procreation; but the concept is not extended to the transformative outcome, since the father never has sexual intercourse with his offspring. Indeed the paradigm of sex as work suggests that woman, as wife/mother, is *the means of production* man needs to effect children's adult reproductive competence. Semen is indispensable for reproduction, yet so is a woman's body (breasts and womb). Moreover, no matter how much the men's ideology attempts to claim procreation as solely their production, a wife is vital for social reproduction: she not only gives birth but nourishes and cares for heirs, transforming semen into strength. She also transmits her husband's spirit familiars to sons, and her own to daughters. Both parents contribute to the child's personhood or thought; but men believe only they produce its soul. Following weaning, a girl is believed to mature on her own, but a boy needs more semen for growth and strength. Thus, a boy indirectly taps the semen pool of his father through homosexual contacts with other men who substitute, in his father's place, as ritual semen donors, motivated out of erotic play. The sexual cycle is completed when this son becomes an inseminator, and his sister is traded for his wife, sister and brother having reached sexual maturity.

The other form of indirect transaction consists in men ingesting the white tree saps. It may seem odd, here, to juxtapose this secret ritual practice with reproduction. But Sambia male ideology treats tree-sap ingestion as a part of the whole adult cycle of reproduction; and, in my experience, men directly associate tree-sap drinking as normal and regular links in a chain of psychosexual activities that are as much a part of everyday life as their own sexuality. Drinking tree sap is not actually taught until a man's last initiation, when he is a new father. Thereafter, men regularly ingest it at various times, but always in abundance after sexual intercourse with their wives. Men are thus preserving their biological maleness (semen) and restoring their strength. Neither erotic play, growth, nor procreation as cultural ideas are applied to contacts with trees. Drinking tree sap simply regenerates semen and preserves health against depletion. So this ritual practice may be considered a defensive tactic—and the more so because it is secret—yet it is also more than that.

Drinking tree sap also has a latent creative function: the creation of *new* semen that flows into the societal pool of sperm. Sambia men do *not* view it this way: to them, drinking tree sap merely replaces what they have personally lost. But, besides that, they see their society as a "closed system," its resources limited, for a variety of reasons I shall not here detail; suffice it to say that their religion is animistic and their ethos dominated by warrior values that recognize adulthood as a personal achievement which is, nevertheless, carefully structured through a strict ritual system of norms and customs that regulate people, marriage, sexuality, and semen. This view is predicated on a cyclical model of time (cf. Leach 1961). Seasonal movements, ceremonies, and customary transactions repeat in regular cycles. They do not recognize that their population is now expanding or that the concomitant stress on their resources (means of production) may be increasing; nonetheless, men believe that they expend sperm and that they get more from trees. Let us now consider the implications of this view for their use of the concept spirituality.

The trees from which men acquire sap are on clan territory. The land itself is one's main material inheritance from previous generations; it is held in agnatic corporate estate, though men own specific tracts of it from which they exploit resources (game, pandanus nuts, milk-sap trees). Land is coveted and defended against other groups; it is central to a clan's residential and territorial organization. It is guarded also by clan spirits. Ritual practices, too, are a social heritage, customs valued in themselves and for group identity, having been handed down from previous generations. It seems obvious, therefore, that the social ideology of trees provisioning new semen through the bodies of clansmen is a latent function of the regeneration of patrilineality.

Patrifiliation thus provides land and trees, ritual practices, and the social personae needed to transform tree sap into sperm. Tree sap without an adult male body is just tree sap. The male body—the product of a long process of procreation with outside women and homosexual insemination from outside men, of magical ritual treatment making it fertile and procreatively potent—is the instrument that regenerates society. Tree sap maintains maleness and masculine personhood. It regenerates one's clan, its patriline and hamlet-based warriorhood, and thus the community itself. These social identities are conceptually placed, in time and space, through concentric social networks based on a magical notion of successive degrees of purest patrilineal substance. Hence, male ideology claims that father, son, and clansmen are of one semen substance, one common origin place, one residential location—all elements of genealogical ancestry that fan out to embrace a pool of spirit familiars, ancestral spirits, and the semen underlying all. Whether the trees are seen as beginning or finishing this process is beside the point: Sambia have a cyclic view of their system that makes tree sap pivotal in a greater chain of being. What is the nature of semen value in this whole system? This problem forms the last part of my chapter.

DELAYED EXCHANGE • The final category of indirect semen transactions concerns exchanges across generations between groups. This subject is very complex indeed, so I shall merely sketch contours of the system of intergroup relationships. What do groups give and receive? And do their exchanges of semen balance out across time?

The key principle of delayed exchange is that groups who exchange women also exchange semen through homosexual contacts. Group A takes a woman from group B. They become affines. Their initiated males of different cohort at different life cycle stages engage in homosexual intercourse both ways (giving and receiving semen). Children of groups A and B become matrilateral kin in the following generation. In delayed exchange (infant betrothal or bride-service) marriage, group A later returns a woman to group B. In direct exchange (sister exchange) they will not. Marriage between generation 2 of these groups is frowned upon, except in the case of delayed exchange infant betrothal to father's sister's daughter (FZD), that is, a daughter of group A goes back to group B. Yet actual FZD marriage (addressed as "sister" by her MBSo) is also disliked; more commonly FZD is traded for another woman from a different group. Homosexual contacts between generation 2 are also forbidden. In effect, generation 2 shares ties of blood and semen: boys of group A were formed from the blood of a woman of group B, and their body tissue came from their father, some of whose own semen may have come from males of group B. These boys (of group A), must turn to a third, unrelated group, in order to take both a wife and semen.

What do groups A and B exchange? Group A gets a woman as garden producer and maker of babies. She reproduces heirs to perpetuate group A. Group B gets food gifts and a promise of a return woman (possibly her daughter) in the next generation. Boys of group A get semen from bachelors of group B, and vice versa. Homosexual insemination ensures masculinization and adult reproductive competence. Boys of groups A and B may receive ritual sponsors from each other's group (in purest form, MB). This man is the boy's guardian and teacher in sexual matters (remember they are forbidden to have sex). So each group provides boys of the other group with nuturance and sexual tutorship. In generation 1, a man may copulate with both his wife and her younger brother. The man gets a wife and another homoerotic transitional sexual outlet. His wife and her younger brother both receive semen: growth, strength. And the younger brother (or, if not himself, his sons or clansmen) will eventually receive a return wife, the brother-in-law's daughter, which the latter's sperm created and nourished.

What does intermarriage do to social relationships? First, marriage transforms groups from unrelated enemies to less hostile affines. Where homosexual contacts occur with groups who are politically hostile, and between which warfare and masculine competition are common, marriage places affines in a set of productive relationships where none existed before. Second, they exchange women as resources. It is in the wife-giver's best interests to ensure that the marriage is productive in every way, so that they receive a woman in return. Marital sex for procreation is productive social work; it outweighs erotic play in homosexual contacts and results in social sanctions against adultery and barrenness. Third, women and semen thus become circulating commodities. Unrelated groups exchange semen, on both sides, with the wife-donors getting a wife out of the bargain. The initiated boys of both groups require semen to complete their personhood, while the men need wives as sexual outlets and procreators to step out of the adolescent stage of homosexuality into the adult stage of marriage and family. Semen, therefore, although a crucial commodity, is secondary to women as a commodity: without wives men cannot attain full personhood. Even though semen is needed to attain manhood, and though it provides a village with the new warrior recruits it requires to protect and expand itself, this warriorhood goes for naught unless women are available for the group's economic and biological reproduction.

Finally, the value of semen as instigator of social reproduction at both the individual and group levels pits males against one another in symmetrical competition. This competition takes two forms, intragroup and intergroup transactions (Forge 1972). The one is intrahamlet individualized competition for homosexually procured semen in order "to grow" and have first pick of wives needed for reproduction later. Here, boys as age-mates try to outperform one another in a contest to achieve maturity first. (In fact, older brothers encourage their youngers toward this end.) The other competition is between hamlets, and, in a wider sense, between a confederacy of intramarrying hamlets vis-à-vis the other confederacies of Sambia society. Men aspire to make their confederacy outdo others in war and overall productivity. Hamlets also act together to find women for their bachelors so as to produce more children—potential warriors and females for the marriage trade—compared with other groups. A social race is on: its outcome is social reproduction. Social conflicts within hamlets do erupt over men competing with one another for wives and resources. Conflicts over women with peers in other hamlets also occur, sometimes precipitating warfare. But intrahamlet competition is overshadowed by the normative stress on achieving social maturity in concert with the best interests of one's own village group. Ultimately, social survival requires competing neighbors too, for they provide women and semen, and are the best defense—strength in numbers—against attack from true enemies elsewhere.

CONCLUSION

In this chapter I have explored Sambia semen valuations from several different points of view: what seemed at first esoteric, vulgar, and trivial seems now complex and symbolically significant in understanding native concepts of sexual contacts and the structure of social relations and modes of production in Sambia culture. Ritualized homosexuality belongs to this symbolic field and cannot be understood, either subjectively or objectively, except in relation to the meaningfulness of this field seen over time.

Melanesianists have typically ignored ritualized homosexuality, especially in the construction of comparative models of social organization and culture. Even heterosexual activities have, in general, been scarcely studied as such; and the meaning of the temporal and symbolic structuring of heterosexuality has not been accorded much analytic value beyond the vague category "sexual antagonism," which has been implicitly used to support whatever explanatory model an author advanced (Herdt and Poole 1982). But what matters more, for my purposes, is that the fluids of sexual and reproductive acts—semen, blood, and milk—have been narrowly studied as entities and artifacts in exchange, or as parts of the growth process in reference only to individual development or societal functioning: they have not been seen as symbolic objects and commodities, expressed through concepts and social transactions, whereby the natives reproduce the identities of persons, social roles, clans, and intergroup relationships across generations.

Past analyses of semen and blood as culturally constructed concepts in New Guinea belief systems, for instance, reveal this structural-functional emphasis. These fluids have long been seen as important in native notions of sexual temperament and gender (e.g., Mead 1935). The great interest in procreation beliefs evinced in the 1920s, first raised by Malinowski (1913) among Aborigines, and then in Trobriand descent ideology (Malinowski 1929, 1954), illustrates this interest. Writers questioned whether natives were ignorant of procreation, and what this ignorance of conception meant (Ashley-Montague 1937; Róheim 1945; and see Bettelheim 1955; Leach 1966; Spiro 1968). We see now that denial of semen valuation in kinship and procreation belongs to a broader cultural ideology of social regeneration and reproduction (Weiner 1978, 1980). In Highlands studies, from Read's (1951, 1954) work onward, ethnographers have noted consistent concerns about the role of blood and semen in notions of the body, sex, and gender. Accounts of the norms of sexual contacts, dogmas about conception, sterility, and reproductive competence, and ideas about exchange of menstrual blood and semen between people as patrilineal kin and affines, all illustrate how ethnographers functionally related body fluids to sociosexual relationships and the positioning of persons in networks of social groups (e.g., see R. Berndt 1965; Glasse and Meggitt 1969; Langness 1967; Meggitt 1964; Newman 1964; Reay 1959; A. Strathern 1972; M. Strathern 1972; Wagner 1967). Preoccupation with the exchange of sexual fluids between groups has, in particular, addressed Western concerns with "discrete acts of giving and receiving" (Weiner 1980:71; cf. for example, A. Strathern 1969a, 1972). More recent theorists have gone beyond exchange constructs, or structural models that view body treatment as "reflections" of society's divisions and boundaries (Douglas 1966), to conceptualize semen, blood, and other entities as the culturally valued materials out of which gender and reproductivity are symbolically constructed and perpetuated (Gell 1975; Herdt 1981; Lindenbaum 1972; Lipuma 1981; Meigs 1976; Panoff 1968; Poole 1981, 1982; M. Strathern 1978, 1980; Weiner 1980).

With the Sambia, and other societies reported upon in this book, we are dealing with peoples whose cultural systems use sexual relationships and fluids as objects and commodities to recreate social order in successive generations, for these are among the scarcest and most vital resources in this process. Weiner has stated this view succinctly.

As these resources circulate through time, i.e., as they are embedded in others, they produce value in others because they embody a shared code that speaks directly to the processes through which identities such as clan, ancestors, kinship, or kingship, actively are

201

> transmitted through generations. Transmission, however, is not ha-
> bitual, nor is it automatic. The work of reproduction is enacted
> with a counter awareness of the force of decay, rotting, and death.
> A cultural system is grounded in the very paradox of things running
> out. . . . The regenerating/degenerating paradox found in nature is
> no less understood as the very same paradox underlying the at-
> tachment of individuals to each other through time.
>
> *(Weiner n.d.:7–8)*

Semen and other fluids are not just things that *are:* they have a
value beyond themselves for extending one's personhood—that is,
existence—beyond the present. No doubt many experiences of
these material things (e.g., fluids, sex, and others' bodies) entail
this transcendent attitude. Sambia spiritual concepts speak to this
issue directly,[11] just as the conflict between sex as work or sex as
play addresses it indirectly. "Religion is an art of making sense
out of experience, and like any other art, say, poetry, it must be
taken symbolically, not literally," Firth (1981:596) recently said.
His view is certainly germane to the ritual treatment of semen.

The social fact of semen for Sambia is that it is a scarce resource
that circulates through time. Its material and phenomenological
attributes make it usable as a commodity that can be consumed,
stored, and given away. Its perceived use-value derives from the
fact that (1) sperm can be "contained" indefinitely in bodies, and
(2) then be seemingly passed, from person to person, without
changing its essence or efficacy; (3) it represents an investment of
labor (food, care, procreation of children), acquired through direct
individual sexual transaction or indirect transformation (sperm
into milk), that can be given or received; (4) in being transmitted
semen extends its transformative value to make the recipient more
reproductively and socially competent; (5) these recipients, in turn,
will produce more wealth and future individuals who will fill productive roles and fill out social groups; and (6) by so doing, semen
transactions recreate the social links between the living and the
dead, the worldly and the spiritual realms, between ego and others,
and between the divisions of society.

Semen extends its value as commodity through four types of
transformations that underlie related modes of "biological" reproduction among Sambia. First, semen through oral sex strengthens and finishes the growth of wives. Second, it acts through wives'

bodies to create fetuses, and becomes milk to feed babies after birth. Third, semen is "fed" through fellatio, ritually disguised as "male breast-feeding," to strengthen and grow homosexual partners. Last, sperm is produced in men by drinking certain tree saps, symbolically considered the "breast milk" of these trees, thus regenerating them and making more sperm available. In this last mode of production men, as biological transformers of tree sap into sperm, are recipients, not donors, but the semen cycle remains unchanged: men turn back to society as the dominant donors. Thus, semen as a commodity regulates and generates marriage and the family, clans and village units, and makes possible the ritual cult, which requires, in particular, secret homosexual intercourse.

In Sambia social reality, individuals are born and die, but semen flows through them (along with blood) to recreate society. Individuals pass on. Growth, as an aspect of these individuals, dies with them. But strength persists: in the form of bones and skin tissue in offspring; in spirit familiars; in ghosts and spirits; and in the deceased's bones, which after death may be used for sorcery. Erotic play passes on too, is useless, except insofar as it has effected growth, strength, and procreation. Sex as work is far more productive, if less exciting: family and heirs result. In this model, a woman's body as sexual-procreative property belongs to her husband, as much as his semen belongs only to her. Her blood, after marriage, belongs to his clan, through his offspring, which must be "paid for" in birth ceremonies. Both fluids are necessary for procreation, but it is semen that men "own" and control best. The "natural" fact that semen can be drunk (passed on) like any drinkable fluid sustains the view that it is a circulating, valuable, unchanging resource, which must be, nonetheless, internally transformed in certain ways by certain persons to achieve the desired ends.

The most powerful social fact of homosexual contacts is that they may only occur between potential enemies who may become affines (generation 1) and then kin (generation 2). Semen transactions not only define who is related and in what salient ways but homosexual contacts predicate the partners' relationship as prospective affines in their generation, which makes their children matrilateral kin in their own. Structurally, social ties based on blood and semen should not be mixed via sexual relationships:

semen relates nonkin, who in turn, through women as links, have descendants sharing semen and blood. (A male ego may receive semen from his brother-in-law, whose children, that is, the ego's sister's children, possess her husband's semen and her blood.) Ties of semen, and blood (via women traded), flow in the same direction. The seeming exception is marriage to actual (not classificatory) FZD, a marriage Sambia frown upon. Such marriages are acceptable only when the FZD cannot be traded for a woman from another group. In these rare marriages, however, spouses share no blood, though they may indirectly share semen via their fathers' homosexual contacts with each others' groups. Thus, the cultural principle not to mix blood and semen is contravened, and people resist such marriages. In general, this cultural linkage (blood and semen) makes heterosexual relationships more socially important and multiplex than homosexual contacts. Both men and women, their bodies and fluids, are needed to achieve biological and social reproduction in this model (cf. Lévi-Strauss 1949; see Pettit 1977:70–72).

This view does not explain ritualized homosexuality among Sambia; it merely elucidates the phenomenon in broader terms. For to seek causes, not just of the sociocultural system of values, but of individual acts of homosexual behavior, we should have to examine its individual subjectivity and developmental context, according them an analytic role I have here ignored. Yet, Sambia do shed light on other, similar systems of social reproduction in Melanesia.

These systems should be seen as a continuum in relation to the value of semen. At one extreme, semen is regarded as rare and precious, so that it must be conserved and regulated, but not *replenished*. Here, we might see situated groups such as the Enga, Kuma, and Gahuku-Gama (Meggitt 1964; Read 1951, chap. 5, this volume). Sexual antagonism seems associated with the low social status of women here. At the other extreme would be societies in which semen is just another fluid, not regulated or conserved, so that it plays little or no role in descent ideology, such as among the matrilineal Trobriands (Malinowski 1929). Here, sex antagonism is weak and women's social status is high. A third type of system could be seen as one that highly values semen that comes from homosexual contacts first, flowing then into heterosexual contacts, as among Kaluli and Marind-anim (Van Baal 1966, chap. 3, this volume; Schieffelin 1982). Sambia, who also use semen replenishment techniques, would represent the extreme end of this valuation of semen. Among these groups, sex antagonism and women's social status is either ambiguous or, as among Sambia, high and low, respectively. The exact arrangement of such a typology is hinted at by Lindenbaum (chap. 9).

What of the nature of the value accorded semen as a commodity in such Melanesian systems? Here, the gender researcher thinks immediately of the multiple facets of fetishism. We must distinguish between what Freud (1962) called erotic fetishization (a person or thing, e.g., shoe, breast, semen, creates sexual excitement as a representation of an unconscious object), and what Marx called fetishism in commodities. I have elsewhere considered erotic fetishization in relation to ritual flutes and Sambia homosexuality (Herdt 1982a). Though much remains to be said, I shall not pursue that discussion here. Yet it is clear that *because* the semen of most males *looks* the same, one can sustain the cultural illusion (Freud 1961) that the same substance is being circulated through time and space. Of semen as fetishized commodity, however, more can be said.

The value of semen does not merely derive from its economic "exchange value." Its significance stems from being necessary to socially and biologically reproduce the cultural identities described above. But because of its portable properties, and its relationship to sexuality, semen comes to take on the characteristics of a commodity in both male/male and male/female sexual contacts. What is the nature of this commodity? Godelier's (1978:155) comment on fetishism and magic is illuminating:

The "exchange value" of a commodity is the value relationship established in exchanging the commodity for other commodities. This relationship does not create the "value" of the commodity because the value is born with the productive process of the commodity and not in the process of its circulation between producers. Circulation does not create value. The value *exists* before the commodity is circulated. Once commodities circulate or are exchanged, they enter into value relationships which may or may not correspond to their value. They may be sold, for example, for a price exceeding their value.

Semen may be "sold," to extend Godelier's metaphor, for homosexual access to a boy and marriage to his sister (Serpenti 1965:164ff.). But that mystified value of semen existed before the marriage exchange took place. For Sambia, again, it is the symbolic place of semen in the overall productive process of social relationships that compels actors to assign it use-value as a scarce resource. The point is that their cultural ideology bestows multivalent value on semen: the value is not intrinsic simply because sperm circulates or can be exchanged.

But we should not overlook the mystifying and rationalizing effects of this ideology for the politics of the men's secret cult. (We have, after all, been dealing with *male* ideology.) By positioning semen as a valued resource, men are placed firmly in control of *their part* of the means of sociobiological reproduction. And what is their part? It is the crucial role semen plays in every cultural domain described above; indeed, its biological role is unique in the generation of growth and strength in initiates (via homosexual contacts). Yet in regard to infants, growth and strength and procreation can occur only through the mother. Attitudes toward spiritual aspects of personhood reflect a tenuous hold, at best, on exclusive claims to patrifilial allegiance. Semen as commodity may thus exploit the rhetorical, paramount role of men in society. But the value relationships of semen are so caught up in the complementary requirement for women's procreative powers that the regeneration of social identities is conditional: affines and enemies live in close proximity with divided loyalties. Women's social status, interpersonally, not normatively, is probably higher and more consequential than men's rhetoric allows. Absolute control of sexual intercourse, through restriction of sexual access to women, female avoidance taboos for initiates, and obligatory homosexual activities, helps ensure the stability of the men's part in the social-reproductive process. The metering of sperm, so crucial for social development, keeps boys and women "in their place." Thus it is no mystery why Sambia severely sanction adultery, why childhood sexual experimentation is forbidden, or why men keep tree milk-sap drinking secret. If semen were free, easy, or readily at hand, its value would deflate. The traffic in women and, perhaps, the sexual activity with boys, would be undermined.

But only perhaps. This political economy perspective throws open the question of how semen valuations operate through time.

Children become initiates and then men: at each life cycle stage they gain and lose certain social trappings of power and responsibility as their capital (e.g., semen) changes. Insemination in a boy is, in a sense, a gift to him, his reward for erotic play. Inseminating a wife is different: the value is on the "hard work" of making this investment pay off. Next to semen, a man's sisters are his most important capital in the marriage business (Van Baal 1970). Here, direct and delayed semen transactions become complex indeed.

> Until he has given in return, the receiver is *"obliged,"* expected to show his gratitude toward his benefactor, or, at least, to have regard for him, to refrain from using against him all the weapons he otherwise might, to pull his punches, lest he be accused of ingratitude and stand condemned by "what people say," which is what gives his actions their social meaning.
>
> *(Bourdieu 1977:6)*

Yes, the semen given in a homosexual act may not, after all, be free: it can be purchased at the expense of the boy's sister. If so, the two males are bound to refrain from direct conflict (e.g., see Allen 1967; Meggitt 1964). If not, the recipient is at least obliged to remember where some of his strength came from. At any rate, these two parties (semen donors and recipients), or their children, can become affines and then kin in time.

Understanding Sambia ritualized homosexuality depends upon this diachronic view. The inter*actors* live in the same small world: they are not going anywhere. Resources that flow out of one's group are destined to find their way back, if not in this generation, then in the next. Cyclical models of time have this reciprocal expectation built into them. Semen transactions, in homosexual and heterosexual contacts, imply this circularity; hence our use of *ritualized* as an adjective. It is not just the sex of one's partner, the social motives or outcomes, or the commodity value of semen that informs homosexual acts: the *time* of ritualization counts, too, in their social meaning.

> Everything takes place as if the ritualization of interactions had the paradoxical effect of giving time its full social efficacy, never more potent than when nothing *but* time is going on. "Time," we say, "is on his side"; time can also work against one. In other words, time derives its efficacy from the state of the structure of relations within which it comes into play. . . . When the unfolding of action

207

is heavily ritualized, as in the dialectic of offence and vengeance, there is still room for strategies which consist of playing on time, or rather the *tempo,* of the action, by delaying revenge so as to prolong the threat of revenge. To restore to practice its practical truth, we must therefore reintroduce time into the theoretical representation of a practice which, being temporally structured, is intrinsically defined by its *tempo.*

(Bourdieu 1977:7–8)

The practice of homosexual behavior is embedded in a cyclical tradition of semen transactions that made one's mother and father, and will define one's own future relationships with boys and women. Identities follow from this semen flow. The tempo of such an ancient practice is to be found not only in this day's contacts or that's, but in the last generation and the next. The system sets rigid constraints, but individuals and groups follow strategies around broad time posts to maximize the value of themselves and their resources. Time does not forget who gave and who received semen.

NOTES

1. Research among Sambia (1974–1976, 1979, 1981) has been supported by the following institutions, and I gratefully acknowledge their assistance: the Australian-American Education Foundation; the Australian National University, Research School of Pacific Studies; the National Institute of Mental Health; the Department of Psychiatry, Neuropsychiatric Institute, UCLA; the Department of Anthropology, Stanford University; the Stanford Center for the Study of Youth Development, Stanford University; and the Wenner-Gren Foundation for Anthropological Research. For their very helpful comments on this chapter, I wish to thank Michael Allen, Jan Van Baal, Nancy Lutkehaus, Fitz John Poole, Eric Schwimmer, Marilyn Strathern, and Donald Tuzin.

2. These cultural categories cross-cut various symbolic domains and social arenas, such as taboos (*kumaaku*), ritual (*pweiyu*), food sharing, myth, etc. One certainly could abstract from action and rhetoric the normative and metaphoric operations of these categories (cf. Wagner 1967, 1972). As I indicate below, sexual interaction is a conscious, although not always marked, frame for acting and speaking among Sambia, but I cannot here provide a complete description of all its manifestations.

3. See Herdt 1981 for conceptual models. This essay considers mainly the male viewpoint, and it is not meant to be a complete cultural analysis, by any means.

4. Sambia tend to treat and think of semen as an energy force in individuals and society which may be compared, by direct analogy, to Freud's concept of libido. The analogy is apt in several ways: this energy force circulates through others (e.g., as subjects) who may be taken in (e.g., as objects) via semen or its equivalents (mother's milk); and it can be dammed up or released—the imagery of the hydraulic model is apt (cf. Heider 1979:78–79, who thinks otherwise). We could also distinguish, following Federn (1952), between subject-libido (energy available to self qua subject) and object-libido (energy available for investment in objects). Technically, I think, semen as a symbol among Sambia is used narcissistically (object-libido invested in ego is narcissistic libido) in self/other interactions.

5. My use of the terms *commodity* and *fetishization* are not meant to indicate a homology with Marx's usage, which was tied, of course, to the specific analysis of capitalist production, characterized by the production of commodities that emerge in a market economy. By analogy, though, these terms are useful for my analysis. Marx broadly argued that the results of human activity transform resources into items of use-value, which are assigned an exchange value by society (see my conclusion below); the worker's time is overshadowed by the supreme importance attached to the commodity, a process through which the capitalist extracts surplus labor as profit. The Sambia, however, acknowledge semen to be a result of social relationships of production (e.g., as in marriage bonds), and they tend also to stress the importance of semen as a fluid that can transform resources into more useful reproductive items or characteristics (e.g., babies, warrior strength). Nonetheless, the way in which men fetishize semen as a circulating commodity has a mystifying effect upon these social relationships of production: they deny women's essential part in the reproductive process and claim final biological development in boys is achieved only through insemination. This mystification of the total reproductive process thus enables men to extract from others the resources needed to sustain and expand themselves and their clans, and to control the related scarce resources in relation to women. Finally, I do not mean to imply by use of these terms that other Melanesian groups, or even all (RH) societies, use semen as a key resource in the same way as Sambia, or that they fetishize it as a commodity in their systems of circulation in order to reproduce social entities. Elements or fluids such as semen and blood clearly have variable significance in Melanesian societies; our separable analyses of them must, in a certain sense, renegotiate their meaning in each cultural system.

6. For instance, Sambia do not use *duvuno* in reference to masturbation, their term for which means "peeling away the glans from

penis." Genital rubbing, in the limited sense (not necessarily erotic) of stimulation of the genitals, occurs; I have seen children do it, boys sometimes do it to bachelors (to produce erections for fellatio), and men sometimes report doing it to themselves in preparation for coitus with their wives. But what they *mean* is self-stimulation without ejaculation. This conceptual distinction is important and should not be misunderstood. Spilling one's own seed not only makes no sense to Sambia, it does not seem erotically exciting for them. Their fantasy life and erotic scripting have no place for it, an argument I will pursue elsewhere.

7. Sambia have invented an art we could call *semenology:* they are fascinated with the forms, textures, and tastes of semen, which they discuss frequently, like wine tasters. Among boys, a fellated's penis size is not accorded much importance, whereas his seminal fluid, amount of flow, etc., is. (Privately and unconsciously, though, penis size is sometimes important.) Among women, the situation seems the reverse: a man's penis size (and sexual prowess) is important—women prefer men with big penises—whereas semenology is less significant, or so say men.

8. Sexual behavior in the imagery of dreams is viewed as erotic play: wet dreams are pleasurable but wasteful erotic play with spirits, who may wish to harm the dreamer. Breast-feeding, even though women say they experience *imbimboogu,* is not ever conceived of as erotic play by women, as far as I know, though breast-feeding is apparently a common image and form of scripting for *men's* erotic daydreams (vis-à-vis fellatio performed upon them).

9. However, there is ambiguity here, since a woman who lives in another hamlet (her husband's) long enough, becomes after death a ghost or hamlet spirit who may haunt there, rather than returning to her natal hamlet or clan territory. Even so, the souls of females are not a subject in which men place much interest.

10. Cf. the Great Papuan Plateau societies, especially Kaluli (Schieffelin 1976:127f.; 1982), which have institutionalized such beliefs about homosexual insemination (see also Kelly 1976; Sørum 1982). On the individual level, Sambia boys evince fantasies and beliefs that make it clear that psychological introjection and projective identification are a part of their homoerotic experience, including, for instance, notions that incorporating a fellated's semen may bestow his personality traits.

11. One is tempted here to note similarities between Sambia male ideology and certain Hindu ideas, the latter of which couple semen retention with male spiritual prowess (see, for example, Eliade 1976).

5

Kenneth E. Read

The *Nama* Cult Recalled

"Fantasy is revealing: it is a method of cognition; everything that is imagined is true; nothing is true if it is not imagined."
Eugène Ionesco, *"La démystification par l'humeur noir," L'Avant Scène (1959).*

When Gilbert Herdt asked me to contribute to this volume,[1] I wondered what I could add to my published work on the Gahuku-Gama (Read 1951, 1952, 1954, 1955, 1959, 1980*a*). The data on which those materials are based were collected thirty years ago. Using Herdt's (1981) phrase, the Gahuku-Gama I have described are a people "frozen in time." Until 1981, I had not been back to them since the end of 1952. Some of my Gahuku friends are dead now; but there are a few old people (and some younger ones) who knew me and are still among us. The contacts I have had with them have been limited, however—no more than a few personal messages that have had nothing to do with my original research. Therefore, any lacunae in my data on the Gahuku *nama* cult and male/female polarities

211

still exist. But anthropology does not stand still. Some of the interests I had thirty years ago were not at the forefront of the discipline then; and those who have made them a focus for inquiry nowadays not only have vastly augmented bodies of material to draw on but also possess a far greater degree of theoretical sophistication with which to marshal and interpret them.

On reviewing my old work in the light of more recently published articles and books, however, I realized that there were a few things I might add. I did not originally omit this material for any reasons of propriety or for any discretionary safeguards required to protect the rights of human subjects, but simply because of the exigencies of space—although my publishers did question me on the suitability of including *one* reference to homoerotic exhibitionism (masturbation) in the culminating stage of Gahuku-Gama initiation in *The High Valley* (Read 1980a). That book was first published as a trade book (1965), and a sensitive editor suggested that the single reference might not be proper reading matter for some younger members of the audience they hoped to attract. Extended passages in the same work depicted *homosocially* patterned behavior that is in relatively stark contrast to some of our own mores (leading two distinguished anthropologists, who visited me for one or two days while I was in the field, to speculate, in a derogatory manner, that there "must be a good deal of homosexuality here"),[2] but this material was not explicitly sexual and apparently passed unnoticed.

I must point out that as far as I know, ritualized homosexual behavior was not included in the Gahuku-Gama cycle of initiation rites considered necessary to transform a biological male into a "man." Yet Gahuku ideologies of femininity and masculinity are so similar to others reported in this book that they may be included in a spectrum of male/female polarities that extends far beyond the Highlands of New Guinea.

The possibility that the secret male cults of the Gahuku-Gama included some homosexual behaviors cannot be entirely dismissed. My statement (Read 1955) that homosexual behaviors did not exist is open to skepticism, although it receives support from those who followed me chronologically and who did their research in groups that are geographically close to the Gahuku; but as Melanesianists know, geographical proximity does not assure uniformity in the details of custom and does *not* preclude striking differences. I did not observe any homosexual behaviors among Gahuku, and I have no verbal information that they existed. I inquired, of course; but when people denied it, I did not press the matter. Gahuku knew quite well what I meant when I asked them about anal intercourse between males. They laughed, considering it a curious custom practiced by "some people over there" (other tribal groups) and, in the same breath, said that some of their youths had been propositioned to *pus-pus* (fuck) by American servicemen when there had been a small "rest center" not far from Goroka during the final year of World War II. The possibility of homosexual practices and interest did not outrage them: they would not judge. But as I have tried to show (Read 1955), they did not have the same generalized and abstracted notions of what *all* men are or should be as those associated with the Western conceptions of human nature. Their morality was contextual and, in a sense, they were far more thoroughgoing and *empirical* relativists than those who represented that school of thought in Western social science.

So what did it matter, what did it signify, that some other people (those "over there") may have practiced ritualized or other forms of homosexuality? Nothing, really. Gahuku had no conception of a universalized *person* that is, or should be, shared cross-culturally by *all* members of the species man. Indeed, the Gahuku "apperceptive style or mode of thought" (Schweder and Bourne 1980) that I described in 1955 is very similar to Dumont's (1980) observations on India and Geertz's (1973) characterization of the Balinese. For example, Geertz (quoted by Schweder and Bourne 1982) remarks that,

> the Western conception of the person as a bounded, unique, more or less integrated motivational and cognitive universe, a dynamic center of awareness, emotion, judgment, and action organized into a distinctive whole and *set contrastively both against other such wholes and against a social and natural background* [emphasis mine] is, however incorrigible it may seem to us, a rather peculiar idea in the context of the world's cultures.

What this means in the context of the essays in this book is that Gahuku did not perceive homosexual behaviors among other peo-

213

ple as necessarily unnatural, wrong, or immoral; for human nature did not provide an inviolate standard for *cross-cultural* judgment.

The opposed Western view has both bedeviled and inhibited anthropological studies of homosexual behavior.[3] For centuries Westerners have regarded homosexual practices as foremost among behaviors that are contrary to nature. At its publication, the first Kinsey report (1948) on male sexual behavior in the United States produced shock waves throughout the society, since it rent the veils surrounding the "vice without a name" and demonstrated that "unnatural" sexual experiences were, after all, rather commonplace among men. A lot of men knew this already, not only those who were homosexual but also many who lived heterosexual lives but who had participated in homosexual activities in their youth. These activities, however, (including male-to-male exhibitionism, masturbation contests, and so on), were more or less a male secret. They became indicative of normatively unnatural sexual identifications only if they persisted; and the knowledge of the shared experiences was neither referred to nor overtly recognized between friends and acquaintances at later stages of life.

In Western cultures this fairly widespread male experience is suppressed, primarily because it is labeled as a pathological aberration (an illness, a sin, or a crime). Herdt's Sambia (Herdt 1981,1982*a*) also suppress their ritualized male homosexual practices, but *not* for the same reasons. Indeed, there is absolutely no way, in the context of Sambia ideology, that they could be called unnatural, for within that context they are, rather, a natural imperative, a charge given to older men to ensure the growth, development, and masculinization (Herdt 1981:205) of the younger members of their gender for whom they are responsible. Attitudes toward and the evaluation of male homosexual behaviors vary cross-culturally; but it is primarily the Western view (and Western inhibitions) that have colored the anthropological record, not only in those instances where homosexual practices have been mentioned but probably, too, in many in which one is led to believe (or to assume because of the absence of any references to them) that nothing of the kind exists.

Twenty years ago, the late Margaret Mead (1961) cautioned us to be skeptical of reports that deny the existence of homosexual behavior in a given culture or that dismiss it as limited and insignificant. If the behavior is not conspicuous (institutionalized to some extent), the ethnographer may not have observed it, may have been reluctant to inquire about it, or, if he did, may have been reticent about publishing his data as well as predisposed to cast the information in the mold of his own culturally negative response to it. To this I would add that even in cultures where the practices are institutionalized (but are secret), the Western investigator may be kept in ignorance of them, his subjects knowing full well the ideological aversions of his culture and its punitive sanctions.

Until recently (though still largely true), most anthropologists have been males nurtured in Western cultural traditions, which include the notion that sex is a peculiarly private activity. Cross-culturally, sex is usually private; yet Western reticence is probably partly responsible for the paucity of sexual data in the anthropological record extending over three-quarters of a century (cf. Davenport 1977:121–122). Almost certainly, Western ideology and a male bias have contributed to placing homosexual behaviors into the recesses of the anthropological closet. Why, one is encouraged to ask, did Evans-Pritchard delay so long (almost thirty years) in reporting institutionalized male homosexuality among the Zande (Evans-Pritchard 1970)? He may have decided (but I am skeptical of this) that the information was not important and had little bearing on his principal interests; but the belated appearance of the data raises doubts about what we assumed we "knew" about Zande ideology, male relationships, and political structures.

Because of Western aversions to homosexual practices and the assumption that they are relatively rare cross-culturally, some investigators may have accepted at face value their informants' denials, the negative responses absolving them of having to inquire further into a subject that was not only morally tainted but with which they were also personally uncomfortable (as most Western men are uncomfortable with homosexuality). Twentieth-century anthropology, though committed to the idea of cultural relativism, could find no justification for homosexual behavior. It was far easier, for example, to excuse infanticide (a custom also abhorrent

215

by Western standards) since it could be shown to have a "rational" basis in some demographic situations: it "produced" something. But homosexual behavior did not "produce" anything and was, therefore, merely an affront to nature. This is not true symbolically, even in societies where it is ideologically suppressed and punitively sanctioned; and where it is institutionalized (though remaining secret), we can be sure (as these chapters show) that it has important ramifications.

It is a moot point whether the sensitivity of Western anthropologists has inhibited their studies of human sexuality in general (cf. Davenport 1977), but there is no denying the paucity of anthropological data on homosexual behavior (cf. Fitzgerald 1977). Though it is usually a minority behavior, it is far more widely distributed around the world (in countries large and small) than anything that can be gleaned from the Human Relations Area Files. Almost any reasonably knowledgeable person knows this and (if they took the time) could verify it by referring to various international "gay guides," which list, for example, some 130 countries and territories (virtually all of the United Nations organization) in which it occurs and, it must be noted, not only in special locations and facilities provided for tourists. Since anthropologists have done research in many of these same places (and have reported nothing), it is possible that they have been misled, have been more or less blind, have been morally queasy, or for other reasons have refrained from reporting what they knew.

None of these reasons can be dismissed out of hand. As I have said, Western evaluations of homosexual practices are often an adequate justification for the members of some tribal societies to conceal and deny them; and in the process of image-building, many third- and fourth-world countries have not only made them illegal but have also placed them on a list of subjects proscribed for research. Responding to these international sensitivities, because anthropologists need the support of many foreign governments, the Executive Board of the American Anthropological Association resolved in 1975 "not to endorse anthropological research on homosexuality across national borders." Though I believe the resolution was subsequently rejected, following protests from some of the membership, the blanket ban, which did not take into consideration the possibility of some positive responses from host governments, is indicative of the persistence of Western attitudes toward homosexual behavior as a "sensitive" subject which, though it is probably as prevalent as witchcraft, is morally distasteful and unnatural, that is, less than "human."

Thomas Fitzgerald (1977) is correct in saying that the anthropological record on homosexuality is obtuse and that "most anthropologists mentioned the phenomenon, if at all, only in passing or hid such descriptions in the most obscure corners of their ethnographies." Codes of ethics designed to protect the rights and privacy of human subjects may have caused some investigators to refrain from reporting information in their possession, but such codes can be observed in ways that fall far short of total inhibition. Moreover, they have only been adopted in recent years.

One other consequence of the discipline's uneasiness with homosexual behavior is the generally woeful imprecision and resulting confusion in the use of terms by those who have referred to it. The recent controversy concerning the Omani *xanith* is partly a debate over terms, as Carrier's (1980*b*) contribution suggests. It is not, of course, that anthropology is the sole offender, for the disciplines of psychology, psychiatry, and sociology are rife with inconsistencies and contradictions in the use and definition of terms; but some consistency is beginning to emerge in these fields, largely as a consequence of research concerned with gender identity. Anthropology continues to use some key terms in popular (vernacular) ways that have been shown to obscure the complexities of homosexual behavior in our own culture and that may well bend it beyond recognition in other cultures. Though Herdt's *Guardians Of The Flutes* (1981) is a study of ritualized homosexual behavior (required of all initiated males) among the New Guinea Sambia, Sambia have no concept of "a homosexual," contrary to what Westerners might be disposed to assume from the data. Such is also true apparently of Schieffelin's (1976) Kaluli, Kelly's (1976) Etoro, and Williams's (1936*c*) Keraki, to mention only a few reports from Melanesia. Much closer to home, Carrier's (1977, 1980*a*), and Murray's (n.d.) forthcoming set of studies indicate fairly clearly that homosexual behavior by dictionary definition (that is, sexual acts between persons of the same sex) may not have the cultural implications that we customarily ascribe to it. The spectrum of sexuality in which it appears is far wider than anything subsumed by the heterosexual "unimodel" derived from our own cultural attitudes.[4]

I have admitted elsewhere (Read 1980*b*) that some of the attitudes of my own culture and the circumstances of my rearing in it may have contributed to my reluctance and discomfort with inquiring too deeply into Gahuku sexual customs; and I also resented, on behalf of "my people," the facile readiness of my two visiting mentors to make pejorative judgments based on some everyday, customary, and polite behaviors between men (which I also followed as a matter of course when I lived there, and with which, incidentally, I was entirely comfortable). Perhaps I was sexually naive, but I don't think this is a peculiarly personal failing: sexuality was not among the most prominent (or legitimate) concerns of the anthropology to which I was exposed during my apprenticeship. If the Gahuku-Gama as I have described them are "frozen in time," then I, too, the person who observed, questioned, and described them, resembled the glaciated bones of a woolly mammoth.

But this fact must also be remembered: by the time I arrived among them, Gahuku had already moved out of their own "glaciated" past. It was early in colonial change, it is true; but domestic arrangements were already changing, and many young men and boys foresaw far different futures than the culturally limited prospect of being warriors. The rites associated with the nama cult that I observed were quite probably the last of their kind that anyone, including younger Gahuku, has been privileged to see; and it is not beyond the realm of possibility that I know more about them (even though my knowledge is limited) than later generations of their own youths. But I did not observe the full cycle of rituals involved in "making a man." First-stage initiation, for boys around six to eight years old, should have occurred, for example, at the same time as the graphic events I witnessed (Read 1980*a*), but it was not included. Nor did I observe the final rite announcing that a group of male age-mates were sufficiently mature to cohabit sexually with the women to whom they had been betrothed, a rite that implies a great deal about Gahuku male and female polarities since it required each young man to "wound" his bride in her right thigh with a small three-pronged arrow called "anger."

The nama cult was not fully operative during those years of 1950 to 1952. The men's houses were no longer a feature of many villages in the Asaro Valley, though they were conspicuous in most of the villages I passed through when (in 1950) I accompanied the assistant district officer for the Eastern Highlands (the late Dudley Young-Whitforde) on a "first contact" patrol into the areas south of Mount Michael. This journey (walking all the way) occupied about three weeks; and because we usually only stayed overnight at inhabited sites (and were often not allowed to sleep inside the settlements), I had little opportunity to question the people I met.[5] But I noticed some gross similarities with certain aspects of Gahuku life that eventually led me (after extending my observations into the Western Highlands) to suggest that male/female polarities constituted a highly important axis in Highlands cultures (Read 1954). This was no more than an intuitive leap, one that was not warranted by any systematic investigations outside the Gahuku-Gama; but it has proved fruitful, since it has engaged the attention of many fieldworkers from 1954 until the present (see Brown and Buchbinder 1976).

That 1950 patrol of areas south of Mount Michael was also the first occasion on which I heard the haunting, questing cries, of the nama flutes. On many days when we were inside the forests, Gahuku men who accompanied us made flutes from stands of bamboo and played them, in a company of men only, in the dense silences of alien country. I had no idea of their significance then, thinking they might be only toys used to temper the boredom and the hazards of our progress; but I noticed a quickening of excitement when they were played. Not knowing a word of Gahuku at that time, I could not understand what they said to one another; but their voices were infused with a quality I recalled many months later on hearing the flutes played, and comprehending their reactions in the Gahuku ceremonial context. The sounds, though they had other implications as well (Read 1952), were clearly erotically stimulating (Read 1980a:117).

Along with other elements of the nama cult, even the flutes had been publicly denied by burning them in the presence of women in some settlements close to the Lutheran Mission on the north side of the Asaro River. Possibly because Gahuku had no identifiable deities, their religious beliefs must have seemed puzzling, elusive, and amorphous to people reared in a different and doctrinaire tradition of certainties. The task of conversion was a little like wading into a spongy morass, and the missionaries seem to have concentrated on the flutes as the only available concrete manifestation of pagan ignorance and error, requiring converted populations to make this public gesture of apostasy as a sign, using a currently popular phrase, of their rebirth and enlightenment.

The Gahuku (that is, the men) with whom I lived, and others even farther from the Lutheran orbit, knew of these mission-inspired autos-da-fé and were not only critical of those who had allowed them to take place but also fearful of their consequences for themselves and their secret knowledge—a "knowledge" that women were, indeed (and contrary to anything that could be assumed from their social status), biologically more "complete" than men at birth.

This notion is the very core of the Gahuku male cult and, I venture to say, is more widely distributed in Melanesia, though it is expressed differently in different local idioms and in local ritual variations, the manifest functions of which are to produce full (biologically complete) Men from males.

My statement that there was no homosexual behavior among Gahuku must, perforce, stand as I wrote it, recognizing, however, that I cannot pronounce it without any shadow of doubt. But if it is accepted, it does not exclude the Gahuku from a place within the focus of this book. Herdt (1981:15) has kindly credited me with capturing "a stupendous dilemma present within the difference between male dogma and secret ritual behavior." I believe that he and others have correctly identified a dilemma (which I, too, may have perceived) that is far more widespread in traditional Melanesian cultures and that many other investigators (no fault to them) have largely overlooked in pursuit of other ends. Male cults have been known from Melanesia for a long time, and I think they share a common, basic, and underlying theme. To put it as simply and colloquially as possible, it is this: "Girls *will* be women" but "boys *will not* necessarily be men." One may indeed say that "male" and "female" are opposed to each other as "nurture" to "nature," and thus the cultural necessity for promoting masculinity, of finishing through ritual an "unfinished" and possibly ambiguous biological entity.

We know of cultures in Melanesia in which the nurturing of the biologically incomplete male includes ritualized insemination either by anal intercourse or fellatio (but apparently not both). It is tempting to regard such practices as a logical extension (though perhaps extreme from some points of view) of these basic notions of femininity and masculinity. Certainly, one would have to agree that ritualized fellatio among the Sambia has a logical place within the context of their biological and physiological ideologies concerning the birthright endowments of males and females. Herdt's (1981) study is, as far as I know, the only full-scale and thoroughly detailed account we have from Melanesia that places ritualized homosexual behaviors within this broader ideational context. But we may surmise from Herdt's review (chap. 1, this volume) that it is also true of other cultures in Melanesia from which ritualized homosexual behaviors have been reported.

In Melanesia there is, I believe, a broad spectrum of ideologically connected "man-making" rites (some of which include ritualized homosexual behaviors). The connecting link is that men are a cultural artifact and women (in a far more fundamental sense) are simply what they were born to be. This contrast provides the tension and the dilemma in these highly masculine, male-dominated and -oriented societies; for men's image of themselves (as I said so long ago for the Gahuku) is built on unstable sands and therefore requires the excessive props of ritual, secrecy, and, in a sense, duplicity to maintain it. Hogbin (1970:103), speaking only of the island of Wogeo, remarked that their initiation rites were different from those reported for Africa: "The purpose of the rites here [Wogeo] is to make certain the boy will grow into a man, and the elders direct all their endeavors to this end." Herdt (1981:320) has also drawn attention to the fact that what we customarily refer to as initiation rites are sequential and developmental in many parts of Melanesia, beginning (as they did among Gahuku) long before puberty and continuing thereafter. "It is hard to make a man," Gahuku often said to me; "it's a big work"; and I gathered it was not a "big work" to make a woman, indeed, no work at all: they had a natural advantage over men.

This is the theme I wish to address for a short while; for even in the absence of ritualized homosexual behavior, it places the Gahuku-Gama within the ideological spectrum in which such practices occur.

MEN AND WOMEN

Herdt (1981:15) has quoted two passages from my early work that are important for understanding some of the functions of the secret male nama cult. I reproduce them again:

> Men like to see themselves as superior both physically and intellectually [to women]. . . . But in actuality men, for their own security, are continually compelled to reaffirm their supremacy in ritual.
>
> *(Read 1951:162)*

> In the final analysis, the idea which men hold of themselves is based primarily on what men do rather than what they have at birth. They recognize, indeed, that in physiological endowment men are inferior to women, and characteristically, they have recourse to elaborate artificial means to redress the contradiction and demonstrate its opposite.
>
> *(Read 1952:14)*

It is true that these observations tend to become lost in my Durkheimian analysis of the nama cult. Though I repeated them in later reports, I do not think I was academically equipped to carry through with them, not equipped to know the questions that must be asked, nor equipped by the positivistic traditions of my training in anthropology to know how to deal with a personal conviction that Herdt (1981:63) states in this way: "The mystery of the world is the relationship between the visible and the invisible, of cultural disguises and subjectivity."

This was not a point of view likely to be appreciated by those belonging to and representing the dominant school of British structural-functionalism during my apprentice years in the mid-forties and early fifties of the century. Malinowski had died. Radcliffe-Brown and his followers were ascendant. Most of them, following in the positivistic sociological footsteps of the master, had little interest in what they considered to be peripheral and speculative areas of inquiry and offered no encouragement and little guidance for investigating anything beyond their relatively narrow segment of concern.

It was apparent, however, that "cultural disguises" were involved in the nama cult of the Gahuku, and I do not use these words to refer only to the secrecy surrounding (and therefore "disguising") the male rituals. I mean that the palpable, public, and almost everyday expressions of male superiority disguised, in a sense, the knowledge shared by men that they were biologically inferior to women. Maleness compared with femaleness, was fragile, not at all certain, and had to be husbanded, promoted, induced, and helped along through ritual. This is what I meant when I originally wrote, "In the final analysis, the idea men hold of themselves is based primarily on what men do rather than what they have at birth."

In the everyday public domain, the ascendence and dominance of men over women was obvious and indisputable. Domestic living arrangements traditionally separated the sexes and suggested it was worthwhile looking into ideologies of female pollution;[6] but it was also clear that this physical separation (after a certain age for males) was carried over into other major areas of social life. Women had no official, public voice, in secular or sacred matters. They were not excluded from the gatherings (Read 1959) called to air and decide *some* internal public issues, but they were present only as spectators who were not permitted to express their opinions. This subordinate place (sometimes enforced by physical means) characterized the status of women in public life. It does not mean that they had absolutely no influence and could not in certain circumstances (for example, in matters of divorce or the termination of arranged betrothals) behave in ways that compelled men to actions they wanted them to take; and when they were old and long past childbearing age, they were given some special marks of respect even in the context of the nama cult, old women being allowed to stand *outside* the village houses (not hiding inside them) when men paraded with the flutes in the street, though they had to close their eyes as the procession passed to the men's house. Their important role in the husbandry of pigs was also recognized. Theoretically, a man could dispose of his pigs as he wished (that is, apply them to any one or other of a number of culturally recognized ends); but I noticed that men usually consulted their wives before committing themselves; and when they did not do so, they sometimes encountered protest and more than usually strained relationships. The wives of men who had made noteworthy contributions of pigs to the *idza nama* festivals were also accorded a kind of reflected glory, being allowed to wear some characteristically male decorations and to accompany the men's dances of welcome and assertions of pride.[7]

From the standpoint of the objective outsider, it seems obvious that the subsistence tasks assigned to men and women were complementary, but this is not the equitable way in which men perceived them.[8] Women's work or women's sphere (excepting their childbearing capacity) did not begin to match the importance of what men did and were expected to do. The Gahuku-Gama were a warrior society; in 1950 this past was still so close to them that although there was no longer any need to do so, most adult men carried their bows and arrows when they walked the tracks to the gardens or went visiting. Old enmities persisted. The honoring of blood spilled by friends and allies was an important obligation recognized at the distribution of pigs in the idza nama festival, and a great deal of the formal oratory at intergroup gatherings centered on fighting.[9]

The ideal qualities of maleness were subsumed by the concept of *strength* (Read 1955). This concept did not imply mere physical vigor. It meant demonstrated excellence in all the activities in which men were dominant; and, characterologically, it also meant forcefulness, aggressiveness, pride in one's self and one's masculinity, and, in the extreme, a refusal to recognize others as your equal. Men did not attach a great deal of either private or public importance to the things women did, except when their behavior seemed to be challenging. They recognized that women possessed some knowledge that was closed to them, but as a rule they tended to dismiss it in a cavalier fashion. In short, masculinity was *the* focus, the lynch pin of cultural pride, the supreme cultural achievement.

Ritual centered on men. They were obviously dominant in everything concerned with the nama cult (which, in turn, occupied the dominant place in ritual), but there were also few collective rituals that focused on the persons of women. Possibly, women could be ascribed a central place in first menstruation and first pregnancy rites, but even in these it was the significance of the events for men that was ideologically emphasized.[10] Men not only managed all the ritualized aspects of life but most of them also concerned men, on whose welfare (using the word in its broadest sense) the welfare of society itself depended.

Other investigators (Langness 1974; Herdt 1981), in reviewing my 1952 paper, have noticed that the religion described there was a "peculiar" kind of Durkheimian religion in that society worshiped only males. I see no reason to dispute this. Insofar as the activities associated with the nama cult dominated ritual life, and insofar as they were concerned principally with masculinity and male achievements, it could be said that they served to express, reaffirm, and promote male solidarity and thus to support the structure of relationships on which the constitution of society could be said to rest. Societies are composed of men and women, but we know full well that this does not mean that the sexes are accorded equal importance. The major values of Gahuku-Gama culture were weighted on the side of men. Whatever a group achieved was primarily of their doing and making, and therefore they were responsible for the general welfare. Women had a reflected glory only, a shine they achieved only through their subordinate and dependent relationship to the ideal public image of the grand and noble sex; and this is not so unfamiliar that it should be startling or even controversial.

I will, therefore, let my previous analysis of the nama cult stand without correction; but as others have pointed out, the Durkheimian viewpoint ignores, or at least neglects, a great deal that is significant. I do not possess data that approach the richness of almost all of those who did their research in decades closer to us, and I have suggested some reasons why this is so (not only personal inadequacies and sensitivities but also the relatively limited or restricted range of theoretical interests and approaches that characterized the society of anthropologists in which I was enculturated). Yet something may be added.

ELEMENTS IN THE ANTIPATHIES BETWEEN MEN AND WOMEN

Why, in the clearly male-dominated society of the Gahuku-Gama, should it have been a particularly "hard work" to "make a man"? Though the question is rhetorical, it is one the Gahuku recognized and one to which they would have provided an acceptable answer

225

in the context of their ideology. Summarizing and also extrapolating from the data, it boils down to this: all of a female's basic potentials were given by sex at birth, and this was by no means the situation for those who were born male. Both males and females had certain biological potentialities at birth, but the fruition or fulfillment of the potentialities required very different courses of action. Indeed the development of immature girls into adult women required almost no assistance, being a natural (inevitable) process as contrasted with a cultural process.

At first glance, this seems familiar. After all, we tend to give more attention to turning boys into cultural men than we do to making cultural women out of girls, encouraging (not to say forcing) the former into activities characterized as manly and masculine. Both, of course, are enculturated to accept the roles our culture (like all cultures) assigns by sex; yet I think our attitudes suggest that ensuring that males become masculine requires more encouragement (and is therefore more doubtful) than its opposite.

This was clearly one of the functions of the nama cult. Let me quote from Herdt (1981:204–205):

> The ritualized simulation of manhood is the job of collective initiation, and that is precisely how men see it. Male initiation is a rigidly structured form of inculcating manliness step by step. It begins when boys are seven to ten years old and, in the ensuing ten to fifteen years, effects the transition from childhood to adulthood.

Herdt uses the concept of *masculinization* to aid his description and analysis of the Sambia data, and the dictionary glossing of the term is appropriate, since semen to the Sambia is analogous to a biochemical androgen. Semen, taken through ingestion, is necessary to modify a boy's body (thus making him a complete man) as well as imparting to women, through the ingestion of smaller quantities, the "strength to bear and suckle children" (Herdt 1981:205, n. 1). This latter point does not apply to the Gahuku-Gama, but everything else in the passage quoted above can be transposed to them without alteration. Thus, it is possible to use the term *masculinization* in a less specific sense than Herdt to characterize the cultural intent and direction of the rituals associated with the nama cult. The extended series of rites (punctuating about fifteen years of a boy's life) were concerned with making and promoting stages in male maturation, but this was by no means all that was involved. Biological gender was assigned at birth: one child was male because he had a penis; another was female because she had a vagina. But a child born with a penis (and therefore biologically male) had to be induced to acquire a constellation of secondary sex-traits in order to become not only male but also masculine. This was the crux of the rites of incorporation included in the nama cult.

I have said elsewhere (Read 1955) that the Gahuku-Gama seemed preoccupied with the physical attributes of the person, and in the same context, I noted that the physical growth and development of children was a major concern and a focus for ritual treatment and recognition. One such ritual included both boys and girls (ages about eight). The ceremony, with its bestowal of gifts, was an obligatory recognition by a male parent (and his kinsmen) of the residual rights of interests of his wife's kinsmen in her offspring, interests that did not end until their death; but its visible focus was to note and admire the physical development of the youngsters. Following this, however, there were no further rites concerned with female maturation until first menstruation, whereas concern for the maturation of boys increased as they were drawn further and further into the orbit of the nama cult, a concern that continued for years beyond puberty.

It may be simple observation, but I think the Gahuku-Gama noted that the signs of sexual maturation are more obvious (visible) in females than in males and seemed to constitute an inevitable sequence from the gradual development of female breasts to the dramatic event of menstruation: women appeared to be more basically endowed than males to complete and fulfill their biological destiny without assistance.[11]

I have no doubt that this is how men saw things and that they also fastened upon menstruation as a critical watershed in the disparate development. They did not hesitate (without any prompting) to liken the nosebleeding rites of the nama cult to menstruation, explaining that both were necessary to complete the processes of maturation and also acknowledging that men had to simulate (ritually induce) an event that occurred naturally in women. But more than this was involved in ritualized nosebleeding and vomiting for men (Read 1952, 1980a).

Boys were introduced to nosebleeding and cane swallowing in the next-to-last ritual concerned with making a man (around the age of thirteen to seventeen); and while the former may clearly be viewed as simulated menstruation, both were also purification rites, necessary not only to promote the physical growth and well-being of males but also to effect their masculinization.

Transposing once more from Herdt (1981:205), "men believe the maintenance of (biological) maleness is arduous, its resulting masculinity tenuous." To accomplish both ends, men had to be purified or cleansed of their prenatal and postnatal contacts with women. This was foreshadowed as early as about ages six to eight, when, during the dramatic initiation rites of teenagers in the great idza nama, they were ritually separated from their mothers and other women and "washed" in a stream by adult men. This rite was physically separated from the events involving the older youths. The children were not allowed to see the nama flutes or any of the other events occurring in another section of the stream; and after their ritual bathing, they were returned to the custodial care of mothers and older sisters. But most of them went through the experience one more time before their final initiation.

The long period of prepubertal (that is, prior to residence in the men's house) contact with women was detrimental to the development of biological maleness and masculinity. Nosebleeding and cane swallowing were the most dramatic examples of the care men had to take to ensure that their welfare (in the very broadest sense) was not affected adversely by their inevitable contacts with women; and it must be remembered that they were not once-in-a-lifetime occurrences. Following the compulsory introduction to them, both became self-administered rituals that men were expected to perform to preserve the integrity of their maleness and masculinity, a bonding duty that increased following the assumption of sexual relationships with their wives. Even in 1950–1952, a probable majority of adult married men wore canes looped around their waists as a customary and relatively inconspicuous item of everyday apparel. I was told that women did not know their significance; they were part of the secret lore of men. And I was also told that men always used them before undertaking a hazardous masculine activity such as warfare. But they were also used more frequently, especially by "strong men" (Read 1959), who had a heightened sense of their own masculinity and a sometimes overweening attachment to the extremes of behavior in which this important quality was expressed. But men who were less "strong" but by no means "weak" (ibid.) also bled their noses and swallowed the canes from time to time. Both were necessary to maintain their manly vitality.[12]

Manly vitality was sapped by a male child's association with women, including not only the period from birth until he was weaned (about two to three years old) but also during gestation. Men knew nothing about the actual procedures women followed in childbirth. Special circumstances enabled me to witness birth on several occasions. Men knew this. Indeed, it was always they who requested my attendance; but they never once asked me a single question about the event I had witnessed and which they had never seen. I have no data that suggest that Gahuku-Gama men had any of the fears or suspicions of Sambia men concerning what women might do with a newborn child (Herdt 1981:206–208); but they believed women did not want to bear children (because of the pain and danger to them) and knew ways to prevent conception as well as to induce abortions. If a new bride, following the assumption of sexual relations with her husband, seemed to be visiting her mother and female relatives too frequently, older men characteristically warned the young husband that she was learning from them ways to prevent him from achieving his masculine right to fatherhood. In the same context, it was never suggested or, apparently, even thought possible that a man might be to blame if a couple were childless (Read 1951). This unfortunate state could be attributed only to female perversity, to their general inclination to challenge the interests and the social welfare of men (cf. Lindenbaum, chap. 9).

But such assumed or suspected social challenges were grounded in more basic physiological differences and opposition between maleness and femaleness. In the womb, a fetus developed in and was nourished by a coif of female blood and came into the world covered by it (so much, at least, men knew or suspected). Semen, too, was necessary to make a child, but the "manufacture" of a fetus required cumulative amounts of semen (apparently from the same male), and semen loss could adversely affect manly vitality.[13] Thus, the very act of procreation was potentially hazardous for manliness.

It was, however, the assignment of sex at birth that determined the general direction of the respective paths the newborn would take toward maturity. The mother's blood and milk, as well as the infant's dependence on females, could affect a boy's progress to manhood. These prenatal and postnatal influences thus had to be "washed" away or expelled by purification rites, followed by an increasing social separation of boys from women and their incorporation into the society of men who were responsible for masculinizing them. The oppositions between male and female were, at their root, the expression of antipathetic "biological" principles, the future implications of which were established in the womb.

What was at stake after the birth of a male child was not only his growth (assuming he survived) but ultimately his manhood (vide masculinity). Gahuku did not disentangle these concepts, for the first was a necessary, and problematic, ingredient of the second. Not so for female children. I do not think Gahuku saw much need to "feminize" girls, apart from introducing them (at a much earlier age than boys) to the round of tasks they would be expected to perform in adult life; and, as noted above, minimal ritual attention was given to their maturation. Clearly, they outstripped boys in this respect. Youths were betrothed to girls (about their own age or a few years younger) during the idza nama. Thereafter they were required to avoid each other for some four years. These betrothals were almost notorious for their instability (Read 1980a:154–155); and in explaining why they did not endure men always said that the girl "outgrew" her intended spouse. Indeed, with the exception of its reference to the oral insemination of males, the statement by Herdt's (1981:1) Sambia informant, Tali, is a precise echo of the remarks of many Gahuku men: "A boy must be initiated and (orally) inseminated, otherwise the girl betrothed to him will outgrow him and run away to another man." Such was the invariable explanation adult Gahuku males offered to explain the tenuous character of first betrothals: girls outgrew boys.

At least two things are involved here. One is that women became sexually mature earlier than men.[14] Both attained puberty (it must be assumed) at about the same rate of growth; but a boy was not ready for his male role in reproduction for many years thereafter, whereas a girl did not have to wait. This contrast is another facet to the antipathies between men and women. Gahuku men found sex pleasurable, and judging from men's attitudes and remarks, so did women; but males had to forgo such gratification until their elders decided that the development of some secondary male characteristics made such relationships safe or, more precisely, relatively safe for them. Women were not disposed to wait. In a sense, they were seen as more "naturally" sexual creatures. They were also, from the male point of view, characterized as sexually demanding and even irresponsible. Young men accused of making a girl pregnant always insisted that she had initiated the encounter, and this was also the invariable defense of a married man accused of adultery with another man's wife. In neither case were men's accounts necessarily true, of course; married men often confided that they had initiated an extramarital sexual liaison (and a few boastfully drew attention to the scars on their upper right thighs that were indelible reminders of their "conviction" for infringing the sexual rights of husbands over wives).[15] But the men's defense was at least publicly appropriate and more or less acceptable, given the indoctrination that males had to exercise self-discipline in sexual activity (for the sake of their manhood and masculinity), whereas there were no such inherent inhibitory restrictions placed upon the expression of female sexuality.

Gahuku-Gama boys, youths, and young men were confronted with this dilemma during their incorporation into the nama cult. All of its activities glorified maleness and the superiority of masculinity; yet neither manhood nor masculinity were certain, and their production required a great deal of surveillance, harsh criticism, and self-discipline. Since intimate contacts with women were harmful for the development of manhood and the maintenance of masculinity, it was necessary to effect both social and psychological distancing between the sexes. The former was effected by gradual but regimented stages, beginning with the first "washing" of male children (above) and ending with their reception into the men's house, at which point the traditional domestic separation was established. The psychological separation (and I must say that I know virtually nothing theoretically about this process) included instruction that males should resist the "precocious" sexuality of women until they were sufficiently mature to reduce the risk to the achievement of masculine strength. Paradoxically, however, instruction in the masculine ideal taught that a sign of a male's maturity and strength was his ability to draw women to him sexually.

Both sides of the coin were present in the institutionalized courting parties initiated by girls (Read 1980a:155–157). From the male perspective, it is difficult to avoid concluding that such activities fitted one aspect of the public image of women—as "sirens" enticing initiated youths and young men into hazardous situations (ibid.:191–192). At the same time, however, older men encouraged and expected youths to participate and often questioned, with a good deal of acerbity, the masculinity of young men who, following the termination of a first betrothal, had not been able to induce a girl to "run away with them" (ibid.:156). Young men were entangled in more than a double bind. Among other things, they were taught that the promotion and preservation of their masculinity (and therefore the preservation of male superiority) required not only social separation from women but also harsh kinds of self-discipline (nosebleeding and cane swallowing; cf. Herdt 1982b) and a self-denial in gratifying sexual drives that was not as strictly imposed on women (at least until their marriage).[16] The "catch-22" was that males, as members of the grand sex, *should* be desirable sexual objects, and this, apparently, was by no means certain. Youths who went to the girl's courting parties entered a situation charged with this ambiguous excitement, and they always went armed with magical substances (revealed to them by men following their reception into the men's house) that were supposed to make girls desire them. The frequent breaking of first betrothals (almost always by girls) and the subsequent long, tedious, and frustrating attempts by youths to induce a girl to run away caused a great deal of anxiety to young men; for, contrary to the precautions instilled in them and the ideal of masculinity presented to them, a male was not fully masculine without a woman, and women could (and apparently did) withhold from men, or threaten to prevent them from achieving, their full masculinity.

In far many more ways than one, it is possible to say that women were perceived as the "enemies" of men, but enemies who were as necessary to the ideal of masculine strength as the traditional enmities between adjoining tribal groups. In many of my previous remarks on this subject, Melanesianists will see a direct link to Bateson's (1958) characterization of Iatmul masculine pride, which resisted the notion that anyone was your equal. For the Gahuku-Gama, true strength (i.e., adult masculinity) required individuals and groups to assert their ascendancy over others. Equality was antithetical to the grand ideal of masculinity (Read 1959) and masculine pride, and the constantly recurring (and tedious) chronicles of intertribal warfare epitomized one aspect of the dominating ethos; for unbridled warfare (*rova*), as distinct from feuding (*hina*), required no precipitating event (though often some were cited). Warfare did not lead to conquest (in the sense of extending boundaries or imposing sovereignty over others), though one of its aims was to destroy the villages of enemy groups and force their inhabitants to seek temporary sanctuary elsewhere.[17] But in the course of time, the defeated (who always intended to return) were commonly invited back to serve once more as a foil for testing and demonstrating the ultimate expression of strength and masculinity.[18]

As the contest of strength seesawed back and forth between enemy groups (and also in the context of ceremonial exchanges between friendly groups in the idza nama ceremony), so it also teetered on the fulcrum of ideologies of sexual oppositions. Other fieldworkers have taken up the theme of "sexual antagonism" that I suggested could be an important dimension in the Highlands cultures of New Guinea. By and large, they have confirmed its pervasiveness, with some local modifications here and there and with some differences of opinion concerning how to account for it, that is, how to connect sexual antagonism in some causal way to other dominant features of the traditional cultures (cf. Langness 1967; reviewed in Herdt and Poole 1982). All of these explanations and analyses have merit; but few of them, excepting only Herdt (1981) and Poole (1982), have reported at length on the idioms that express the ambivalence and oppositions between maleness and femaleness or have given much attention to how they are related to subjective experiences. Unfortunately, my data do not allow me to contribute much to these intrinsic elements of the debate; but since ritualized homosexual behavior in Melanesia apparently occurs in very similar ideological contexts, I wish to emphasize again that male/female polarities among the Gahuku-Gama enormously transcended the commonplace cultural assignment of social and economic roles by sex.

Notions concerning the polluting characteristics of femaleness are themselves rather commonplace cross-cultural data; but for Gahuku they were the ideological watershed on which the opposition divided, though Gahuku did not carry them as far as other Melanesian groups.[19] They were clearly an important underpinning in the social distancing of traditional domestic living arrangements, but they were also expressed in other, less conspicuous forms of social (and presumably psychological) distancing. For example, it was a grave trespassing on the personal boundaries of a man for a woman to step across his legs, to walk too closely behind him while he was seated, or to touch his hair or his nose. As I suggested above, the Gahuku paid far more attention than we do to the physical attributes of personhood. I tried elsewhere (Read 1955) to show that "the part stood for the whole," and, in this light, it is easier to appreciate the affronts to male personhood occasioned by any of the above behaviors on the part of women.

The nose is probably particularly significant in this context. Once more, I am struck by similarities between Gahuku ideas about the nose and Herdt's (1981) far more detailed examination of Sambia "nose idioms." Gahuku conceptions of male beauty, manliness, and strength focused on the nose (not, however, to the exclusion of some shades of skin color). The most admired form was the rather "arrogant," long and aquiline shape,[20] but every form represented something about potential traits of character and thereby provided, we might say, *one* diagnostic for behavior in adult males and, in the young, some prognosis for their future affirmative demonstration of ideals of masculine strength. The male nose was symbolically linked to masculine personhood, though it was not unique in this respect; for all the bodily excretions also contained or expressed the person of an individual: feces, urine, semen, and even the loss of blood or the cutting of hair. The "loss" of any of these, even in natural elimination, was a loss sustained by the individual, and for men, the loss of semen was the most damaging of all. Thus, female trespassing on any of the physical attributes of the male person carried the implication of a potential threat; and the male nose, having a phallic association with male-ness and masculinity, was a particularly sensitive subject of concern.

I do not have (since I was not equipped to obtain it) any psy-chological data to support my statements that male hostility toward women was a basic element in relationships between the sexes; but in addition to anything I have noted so far, such hostility seemed obvious enough in some of the abuses to which women were subjected: for example, sticks thrust into a vagina as a pun-ishment for adultery;[21] public whippings with canes if women presumed to speak from the sidelines at gatherings (see above); and stomping on them in the heat of marital disagreements. I should make it perfectly clear, however, that such dehumanizing treatment did not preclude the development of apparently re-warding and enduring affective relationships between individual men and women within the confining boundaries of sex.[22] In any society, individual relationships are not cut to the same precise and invariant pattern or from precisely the same piece of cloth; and those who had recourse to these extreme measures (excepting perhaps, the public whipping) represented extreme charactero-logical examples of the phallic ideal of masculine strength.

Yet women were presented as a potential threat to masculinity and possibly even to life, for the most virulent recognized form of sorcery required some of the intended victim's semen, and women were assumed to be the sorcerer's agent for obtaining it, not en-tirely excluding a man's own wife (at least until she had proved her identification with his interests and those of his patrilineal group by bearing him a child).

For obvious reasons, I know virtually nothing about a woman's subjective experiences of being female or of her sense of self or personhood in relationship to males, though I doubt that the latter, at least, conformed entirely to male ideas of what it ought to be; for men were quick to see or suspect challenges from women, who were opposed to them in the fundamental biological sense and could use also their biological endowments to jeopardize male interests and even to question some of the ideal components of masculinity. This sense is the rhetorical form in which women might be said to be the enemies of men—the very enemies, or possible enemies, and inhibitors of the development of masculinity.

235

No wonder, then, that Gahuku men were misogynists in many ways. Yet their misogyny was not "all of one piece" either; for women could not be simply excluded and given no attention. On the contrary, they were a constant source of trouble and a focus for male anxiety and peer competition.

The male ideal often foundered, like all ideals, on the practical exigencies of living; but it was no less important because of this.

THE NAMA CULT AND MASCULINIZATION

Like all rituals of incorporation, the rites of the nama cult were intended to produce, seal, and maintain a social and psychological bond, in this case to produce a community of men whose common interests were set apart from and, ideally, above the community of women. To accomplish this, it was necessary to inculcate in each generation of males a subjective awareness and experience of what it meant to be male: to secure their adherence to a shared sense of maleness, the almost ineluctable bond that transcended most other personal bonds. This also required, as the other side of the coin, measures to ensure that women were reminded of their subordinate position through the customary treatment reported above and the ritual wounding of brides prior to the assumption of sexual relationships with their husbands. Yet it also seems clear that from the male perspective the community of women, their common interests and shared sense of a female self, was a more "natural" social and psychological entity. This fundamental difference constituted the unstable sands beneath the edifice of male superiority; and the ritual communication of it, the subjective recognition and sharing of it, and the measures to support it firmly were the bonding interests of the cult.

The ritual processes involved physically violent and psychologically traumatic assaults on boys who had to be made into men. This began with the first "washing" of six-to-eight year olds. At this time (and in the larger context of the idza nama) they were plucked from the company of their mothers and sisters (who were daubed with the yellow and white clays of mourning) and carried to a stream on the shoulders of men dressed in the paint and decorations of warriors. Older men, recalling the experience for me, said they had been frightened by the noise and the general atmosphere of menace. Though the flutes were not disclosed to them, their shrilling cut through the tumult of shouts and warrior chants, and the little boys probably remembered that they were supposed to be the voracious cries of carnivorous birds that devoured their elder brothers. This was the official explanation given to women and boys, who had to hide within the walled security of their houses whenever the flutes approached the villages. Torn away from women, with whom they had their closest, most intimate, and most exclusive associations, the children were suddenly pulled inside the periphery of a separate and menacing world.

I do not think they were subjected to harsh physical treatment at this time or to much didactic ritual teaching. Gahuku believed that a male child's "ears had to be opened" gradually before he could absorb (presumably internalize) much formal instruction concerning his masculine identity; and, as far as I know, the most crucial ritual teaching was administered later in a massive dose. Nosebleeding (in addition to being a simulated menstruation) was the critical event in this process. It was necessary to "clear" the heads of youths who were on the threshold of manhood, that is, to eliminate the stultifying effects of their prenatal and postnatal association with women (not excluding the "bad talk" of women) and to produce the acuteness of thought and vision that distinguished the ideal man from the slower and more "thick-headed" sex. The washing rites, as well as others associated with physical development, were referred to by a phrase that can be translated as "his nose they cut," which seems to imply a foreshadowing and gradual preparation for the major ritual purification and teaching.

The "washing" of boys was usually performed once more before they were forcibly introduced to the innermost secrets of the nama cult. In the intervening years (when their status was indicated by distinctive, long-tailed headdresses), they would have been resident in the men's house. This was not, however, the case for ten- to thirteen-year-old boys in the village where I lived. Susuroka, the village, was a new settlement (only a few years old when I arrived there), and it did not have a men's house until Makis, my Gahuku friend, took advantage of my presence to build a reasonable substitute near my own dwelling. But as far as I was able to observe, the novices had few duties, nothing approaching the demands made upon even younger girls. They sat with the men (but at a short distance from them) at feasts and gatherings and were frequently ordered peremptorily to fetch water or sugarcane for male visitors, requests to which they responded with a rather characteristic surliness and lack of grace. This behavior often provoked an outburst of brief but sharp threats from adult men, but I never saw a man make any move to implement the warnings. The novices were not present on any occasion when the flutes were played and, as far as I know, they knew nothing of what was in store for them just a few years ahead.

I have published an account of the occasion when the novices were forcibly introduced to the secret practices of the nama cult (Read 1980a:111–140). Though it was written from the perspective of a participant-observer, my sense of shock was only an echo of the initiates' experience. A sympathetic thread joined me to the frightened and violated youths, for on three occasions, between ages ten and eighteen, I had been forced to participate in "rites of incorporation" into masculine associations in my own culture, the last occurring in my freshman year as a resident of an upper-class Church of England college at my university, when the collective rite for members of my class included being immersed in and struggling through a foul-smelling bathtub filled with a concoction based upon sump oil, and crawling naked down a cloister with a cake of soap between my legs. This "civilized" rite may say something about the insecurities beneath the hypermasculine (and also somewhat misogynist) Australian ideal of male bonding; but apart from this, I remembered it with empathy when I observed and Gahuku youths recalled for me their fears on facing their own violent tests.

The Gahuku rites must be called violent under any reasonable glossing of the word, and they were harbingers of more to come. Following the stream-side introduction to nosebleeding and cane swallowing, and the subsequent furious confrontation with protesting women (Read 1980a:135–137), the initiates were confined in specially constructed men's houses, where they remained for several weeks. Many events were being arranged at this time, including their first betrothals and the final arrangements for the distribution of pigs on the concluding day of the idza nama. In their confinement, the initiates were excluded from all these undertakings, but this was also the most intensive period of ritual instruction.

The initiates did not leave the men's houses by day, being allowed out only at night and under escort to urinate and defecate. They consumed only cold food and were forbidden to drink water, sugarcane providing their only liquid nourishment. They were also subjected to constant criticism. Adult men openly vented their usually contained resentment of the youths' slow and ungracious responses to the few demands imposed on them. Their previous behavior and physical development were found to be wanting in almost all respects, and these harsh personal judgments were often reinforced with physical abuse.

The principal rites performed on initiates in the men's house were again concerned with purification and manly development, that is, with ridding them of the deleterious effects of their past associations with women and with encouraging and producing secondary masculine characteristics. Their bodies were rubbed with "expunging" materials to "tighten" or "stretch" the skin and also to make it shine; and particular attention was devoted to promoting the growth of chest and facial hair. On their ritual reintroduction to the village, all the initiates wore artificial beards (cf. Read 1980*a*:photograph). This was obviously a simulation of a critical indication of progress toward sexual maturation and responsibility. The initiates were now betrothed (the Gahuku word was the same as *married*) but they were forbidden any contact with their wives until older men decided that they were ready to assume sexual relations with them, and their decision was based largely on their observations of the growth of facial hair.

Summarizing the teaching received by initiates during their confinement, it is possible to say that it included (1) that their manhood and masculinity was a product of the concern of other men but that its maintenance thereafter was their own principal responsibility; (2) that women threatened the achievement of manhood, not only because of basic physiological antinomies but also because women were disposed to protest their position and to take advantage of men; (3) that a truly masculine man should place the preservation of masculine qualities above all other personal inclinations; (4) that masculinity itself (the end product of all the rites)

239

was fragile; and (5) that the ineluctable male bond was to promote, preserve, and demonstrate it.

The flutes were clearly a central symbol in this ideological complex. Initiates were brought face-to-face with them for the first time during their confinement. I did not observe this confrontation with the innermost symbol of the male cult, but I do not think it had any of the overt implications for the indoctrination of homosexual behavior that Herdt (1981:279ff.) describes for Sambia boys, who were introduced to the flutes at a much earlier age than their Gahuku-Gama counterparts. Though the ideologies of the two people connect at many points, there are also some basic differences, and ritualized insemination is, as far as I know, the most striking. The Gahuku-Gama appeared to trust and accept me and to confide in me. Unlike the lowland Ngarawapum, with whom I lived in 1944–1945, they did not make transparent efforts to prevent me from seeing or learning about matters they considered controversial (because their previous experience had taught them that they were looked on with disfavor by members of the European "tribe" to which they had assigned me). This prior reluctance to proffer trust disposed me to tread carefully in areas that *I* assumed might be sensitive to Gahuku, a caution that was sometimes ludicrously shattered when men taxed me because I had not brought my notebooks and camera to their closed, ritual gatherings. I also had close personal relationships with some initiates and novices; and I found nothing either in their words or behavior that pointed to the existence of overt homosexual behaviors. Yet I do not eliminate the existence of homoerotic elements within the ideal bonding of males. Such elements, falling short of practice, are often covert ingredients in relationships between members of groups and associations characterized by ideals of close and exclusive male bonding, including some that are regarded as being particularly "masculine" in our own culture (Dundes 1978).

The nama flutes of the Gahuku-Gama stood for many things. They were linked to kinship groups and to the continuity of such groups over time through their essential core of males. They stood for the characteristics and quality of the bond between male agemates (the pairs of flutes were referred to by this term) which, ideally at least, was the only relationship having no implications of superiority and subordination.[23] They were linked to affiliations and alliances (including marriage) between male-based groups and symbolized the cultural ascendance and authority of men, being, as Herdt (1981:283) says of the Sambia flutes, "a political weapon" employed to teach, frighten, and keep women and boys in their place. But they also stood for something else as well: for the very concept of masculinity, for the arduous road that had to be traveled to achieve it, and for the shared experiential bond between those whose maleness imposed the journey on them.

The Gahuku-Gama flutes did not have much significance as material objects (Read 1952, 1980). They were not passed down from generation to generation within the descent groups with which they were identified. They were made anew at the beginning of each ritual cycle, and at its conclusion they were simply broken and thrown away. Unlike the Sambia flutes, however, they were, on some occasions during the ritual cycle, anointed with pig's grease and their mouthpieces stuffed with cooked pork while they rested in pairs on beds of leaves (cf. Berndt 1965); thus it may be possible to ascribe a fetishistic quality to them. But the tunes that were played on them embodied far more in social and personal understandings than anything that could be attributed to them as material objects.

I still believe, as I said in earlier papers, that the tunes also stood for an immanent (unnamed) supernatural power upon which everything in nature and society depended, which upheld and sustained things as they *are* and *ought* to be, and upon whose operation all achievements and all elements of the "good life" depended. This power and "the good life" were associated particularly with men. The cycle of rituals and other activities included in the idza nama festival included not only the initiation (and masculinization) of boys and youths but also the recognition and celebration of all the other basic institutional arenas of living for which men were responsible. The nama flutes also appeared in one other ritual context, called "our ancestor" (*asijo teho*).[24] I did not observe this rite since it was, apparently, performed only once in about a generation; but in a village only an easy walk from where I lived there was a relatively new structure associated with it (a fenced enclosure containing a "table" made of saplings and hung with the jawbones of pigs), and there were a couple of sites closer to Susuroka that were said to be places where similar struc-

241

tures had stood. There was in Susuroka no sign of their former existence, but very occasionally an illness was attributed to the patient having walked unknowingly over an abandoned site that was still charged with supernatural power. As far as I know, the rite called *asijo teho* was intended to ensure for the clan group performing it the assistance of the immanent power ultimately responsible for success and ascendency in all arenas of life important to Gahuku-Gama. But the point is this: the inclusion of the nama flutes in this important ritual of renewal and security suggests that men were both the guardians and, ideally, the embodiment of the creative and life-sustaining forces. My data on this point are not conclusive, though I have little doubt that these forces were linked to male potency in the broadest sense of the word, that is, not simply to the male role in reproduction (and remember that a man was never assumed to be infertile) but also to the official dogma that the masculine principle was ascendant in nature as well as in social life.

The historical cross-cultural record suggests that male homoeroticism and ritualized male homosexual behaviors are often associated with sharply differentiated and distancing gender roles and the superordinance of ideals of masculine bonding, though it is obvious that male homosexual behaviors are not linked to them in a causal way. The close ideological, psychological, and social bonding of males among Gahuku-Gama included homoerotic elements, particularly in ritual contexts. A tremendous excitement infused the companies of men playing and parading with the nama, the supreme symbol of their masculine bonding; and when the flutes were laid aside and the men were together in the seclusion of their house, their overwrought comments to one another had unmistakable erotic implications (Read 1980a:116–117). The ritual masturbation in the culminating phase of initiation (ibid.:129) possibly has a place in the context of this excitement (cf. Herdt 1982a). It occurred amid a great swirl of activity, and I quickly forgot about it as more dramatic and violent events unfolded. When I recalled it later and inquired about it, I got the impression that it had no didactic significance. Sexual activity among Gahuku-Gama was private and their behavior modest (excepting, from a Western viewpoint, their customary forms of greeting), and thus this single instance of public exhibitionism is extraordinary.[25]

I do not have a ready explanation for it. First, Gahuku verbal commentaries (that is, the lack of them) were no help, and, second, I do not control the psychological literature on eroticism that might allow me to place it in a more general context of behavior (and the anthropological literature on eroticism is almost no use at all, being virtually nonexistent). But I see no reason to question Herdt's (1981:321–322) conclusion that in addition to their other consequences and intentions, Gahuku-Gama initiations were concerned with the "manufacture of a certain phallic sense of maleness and masculine cultural identity." The cultural primacy of male bonding and the official dogma of masculine superiority and potency (despite the doubts that it concealed) fostered a phallic sense of "being" that included (homo)erotic elements. Others possessing a greater degree of contemporary knowledge and methodological sophistication could undoubtedly address the subject with less reliance upon intuition; yet there is little reason to question the phallic symbolism of many ingredients of male ritual behavior and ceremonial self-presentation: the adornments of erect possom tails on the heads of dancers,[26] the pendulous wands of feathers attached to dance frames, and the stridently assertive character of the dance and the art of oratory. Though it probably has no legitimate place in ethnographic reporting (because it is only impressionistic), the atmosphere (let me even say the *smell*, in a figurative sense) on all but the most ordinary occasions when the sexes divided was dominantly masculine and man-to-man (and *smell* may not be such a farfetched figure of speech at that, for it also subsumes the atmosphere of the associations of the locker room in our own culture and, according to some observers, their covert homoeroticism and exhibitionism).

The exhibition of masturbation in the stream during the culminating phase of incorporation into the male cult (and I doubt that it was noticed by the frightened, traumatized youths facing far more violent ordeals), seems to me to be like a spontaneous expression of all the underlying phallic characteristics of male bonding, an almost blatant assertion (prompted by the sexual excitement of the larger activity) of the end product of the entire initiation cycle: namely, to produce, secure, and maintain the ideal sexual potency and social and cultural ascendancy of masculine males as compared with women.

CONCLUSION

One of the developmental purposes of the secret rites of the Ga-huku-Gama nama cult was to prescribe and provide subjective experiences that would lead eventually to the individual assumption of a masculine identity, a context within which males could move with reasonable assurance as to their entitlements and sense of selfhood (though it is also clear that there were some men whose personalities and interests positioned them on one or other of the extreme poles of the ideal characterological continuum). This process is precisely what the Durkheimian sociological approach neglects, since it reifies the end product at the expense of the process that is "going on," and because its other-worldly or normatively timeless character ignores matters of subjective nuance and problems of societal change, both of which seem particularly significant for transformations within the belief systems of many tribal societies of island New Guinea.

Once again, Herdt (1981:322) provides me with a fitting conclusion to this essay. "The problem" (he says of Sambia and other male initiations in New Guinea),

> is not one of males being masculine or feminine, but rather of the creation of an intense, phallic masculinity defending one against any possibility of ever turning quiet or soft. . . . To build that strident subjectivity and the gender behavior it commands must be reckoned as [Gahuku] masculine society's greatest imperative.

That is, it is to cement the building blocks of an ediface that included ceaseless warfare (with all its attendant dangers) and the ritual ascendancy of men in all matters concerning collective welfare and the dogmas of their superiority and opposition to women. Such values required the "strong man" (*amuzave*) not the "soft" or "weak man" (*hoipave*), though there were some of these also among the people I knew. The latter could not be said to be "gender anomalies" in the sense that is popularly attributed to men and women having homosexual preferences in our own society. The men, of course, were not effeminate in any way at all; and sometimes the making over of Gahuku males into ideal masculine men appeared to succeed too well, for those who epitomized the sought-after qualities were often touchy, overweening, intransigent, and a constant source of trouble (Read 1955).

NOTES

1. I am particularly grateful to Gilbert H. Herdt for his suggestions and criticism in the preparation of this essay.
2. One of these was the late S. F. Nadel; the other is still living and therefore is not identified.
3. This subject is given a more extended treatment in appendix 1 to my book *Other Voices* (Read 1980*b*).
4. Cf. Read 1980*b*:188–189.
5. The principal difficulty was one of language and interpreters. In many of the villages we were literally the first white people any-one had seen and absolutely none of their inhabitants knew any Neo-Melanesian Pidgin. Moreover, we passed through at least six different linguistic groups. Though the observations contained in my journal of the "expedition" are sketchy, they might have some historical value, since other fieldworkers have been located in some of the groups in far more recent years. One outstanding impression remains with me: the evidence of warfare and the tight defenses of many villages. In Papua New Guinea, anthropologists have seldom been members of "first contact" patrols into un-mapped areas or have been associated at such an early stage with the processes of extending central (colonial) control. Perhaps this experience deserves a more extended note in some other place.
6. The absence of these separate living arrangements among other Melanesian people does not, of course, imply the absence of no-tions concerning the polluting characteristics of women, notions that are in fact almost a panhuman ideological and behavioral phenomenon.
7. Among Gahuku-Gama, dancing occurred only on infrequent cere-monial occasions, and then it was only men who danced: the mass of women simply watched (and, presumably, admired) the aggres-sive warrior spectacle (cf. Schwimmer, chap. 6). Even the women who were allowed to "dress as men" (which is merely a figure of speech that subsumes some of the decorations they were permitted to wear) twirled on the periphery of the massed men in an exceed-ingly subordinate and limited choreography, which does not imply that the choreography of male dances was any more inventive. It wasn't; it was a back-and-forth, attack and counterattack affair, which expressed the limited themes of competition (the struggle for ascendancy) and the strident bravura appearance of the noble male as the "man of action."
8. In traditional New Guinea societies, the division of economic tasks was sharply compartmentalized by sex, with the result that it has been characterized as complementary rather than cooperative (Brown and Buchbinder 1976:4).
9. In collecting genealogical information, for example, there was con-stant reference to people (almost always men) as "killed by the

Uheto," "killed by the Notohana," and so on, although Gahuku-Gama had almost no interest in remembering relatives further back than grandfather.

10. After her first period a girl was ceremonially reintroduced to her group wearing an adult woman's style of dress. The group's spokesman, holding her hand, turned her in the direction of the cardinal points of the compass and announced: "Men of all places, come and marry our daughter." At first pregnancy, a woman with a small boy (armed with a toy bow and arrow) positioned between her legs was encased in a cocoon of bark wrappings. When these were removed, and the last one fell away, the small boy leaped out and menaced the assembled men.

11. That is, in all respects except conceiving children.

12. Most men acknowledged that the forced introduction of boys to cane swallowing was dangerous and on occasion led to death (from peritonitis?). Perhaps it was a thankful circumstance that it followed nosebleeding, when the initiates were too tired and traumatized to offer any resistance.

13. I say "apparently from the same man" because denials of paternity were generally accepted if an accused man stated he had "slept" with the woman only once. But see Herdt (chap. 4) on Sambia suspicions.

14. Cross-cultural studies have also shown that girls tend to acquire speech and motor coordination abilities earlier than boys (reviewed in Herdt 1981). Presumably, these were among the visible facts persuading Gahuku-Gama that "girls outgrew boys."

15. A man accused and convicted of adultery with another man's wife could be required to expose his right thigh to be shot by the husband with the "anger" arrow. Penalties imposed on the offending woman were much harsher.

16. Gahuku-Gama did not condone premarital sex either for girls or youths, but the courting parties tended to encourage such attempts. The erotic play in these situations was not supposed to lead to coitus, but youths (and some older married men) hoped to prevail. At marriage, however, sexual rights over a woman were transferred exclusively to her husband.

17. This fighting was different from the type of warfare shown in the film *Dead Birds,* for example, which resembles Gahuku-Gama feuding (*hina*) rather than warfare (*rova*). The evidence of burned settlements during my 1950 journey through areas to the south of Mount Michael suggests that the type of warfare described above was common throughout the Eastern Highlands.

18. The Ozahadzuha clan (of the Nagamidzuha) among whom I lived had been "dispossessed" by the Gehamo and had subsequently been "invited" back by them. Relationships between the two groups remained strained during my sojourn.

19. Gahuku-Gama women were not traditionally secluded in isolated menstrual huts during their periods, nor were they required to travel to the gardens along special paths.
20. One of the unexpected dividends of living with Gahuku-Gama was that my own aquiline nose was often excessively admired!
21. I should emphasize that this particular punishment was not usual; only the "strongest" and most intransigent men seemed to exact it. But, by the same token, Gahuku also said that a husband could kill his wife for adultery.
22. Adult men showed far greater affection for young girls than for boys, and there was a strong affective and social bond between "brothers" and "sisters." The tensions focused mainly on wives or women who were potential sexual partners; but there were also a few outstanding examples of close affective bonds between husband and wife (cf. M. Strathern 1972; Lindenbaum, chap. 9).
23. The ideal notwithstanding, there was a good deal of competition between age-mates (see Read 1980a:141–171).
24. *Asijo* is a kin term denoting "grandparent" (or more remote relative) and "grandchild." This rite was also referred to as *ozaha neta: ozaha* ("elder" or "old person") and *neta* ("thing" or "object").
25. Gahuku-Gama men denied the practice of private, let alone any form of group, masturbation. See also Herdt 1981:165, n. 10.
26. Gahuku-Gama live in deforested grasslands containing very little in the way of small game, and they do not burn off the grasses, as the lowland Ngarawapum of the Markham Valley did, for annual drives to collect small game. Hunting was an exceedingly minor activity, principally a pastime for youths. Possum tails and fur were, however, valued male decorations and were obtained mainly from people living in the surrounding (but distant) forested mountain ranges to the north.

6

Eric Schwimmer

Male Couples in
New Guinea

OROKAIVA DANCERS

Traditionally, Melanesians dance in couples, but men dance with male, and women with female, partners. They perform in troupes made up almost entirely of a file of couples. In Oro Province, such double columns are made up of men, but female couples dance at the troupe's periphery. Dance leaders also form couples. These appear in front in some dance movements, yet they are likely to move to the back, to the center, or to split apart and move to one side of the column, changing their position constantly.

Partners in a dancing couple change their relation to each other from movement to movement: side by side, face to face, pirouette, and so on. As the men dance, they beat their drums, normally held at waist level; however, there is one favorite face-to-face movement during which one partner dances with his drum held low, while the other holds it over his head. Both then dance a full turn. When they face each other again, they exchange positions, the low drum now being held high and vice versa. The couple thus expresses a multitude of formal internal relations.

There are other movements where adjacent couples face each other and express similar aesthetic relations. Or again, one couple pirouettes forward and the other backward, so that their rank order in the column changes though a movement to the back is followed by an opposite movement to the front again. Leaders are distinguished from the others by having an extra dimension of freedom, both spatially, since they have no fixed position in the column, and choreographically, as they vie with one another by inventing complex variations of the steps executed by the *corps de ballet*.

During a typical night's dancing of many hours, some six to eight dances are performed, distinguished by different drum beats. For each beat, there are many songs. Dance movements are determined by the beat. The most common beats, in Sivepe village, where I learned to dance, were the following:[1]

1. *Gururu* (quick, soft, continuous beat): beginning of any performance.

2. *Baruka* ("name of a fish that dances this way when caught in a net"): always follows directly after *gururu*.

3. *Bororia* ("step imitates how a wallaby hops when it sees a man"): common beat, used inter alia for imitating a wallaby.

4. *Kevojo* ("a hornbill dances like that as it eats").

5. *Gagara: kevojo* alternating with *baruka*.

6. *Titiro* ("pendulum movement of heavy dancing of man brandishing spear").

7. *Foroka* ("Tufi word; image of snow coming down").

8. *Orokoro* ("name of man from Tufi; all in Tufi language").

9. *Ohoho*: marks the end of a performance.

Dancers abandon the double column and mass together. A moment of great joy and excitement.

With the exception of the excited finale, the couples are never changed or dissolved and continue to dance, drum, and sing together. Though the composition of the dance group is fairly variable from one performance to another, depending on who is in the village at the time, dancers rarely change partners. People tend to choose their dance partners early in life and stay with them forever. Men not participating in a practice would explain that they were not joining in because their partner was unable to come. Or, again, another man had stopped dancing altogether after his partner died.

There are no kinship criteria for the choice of partners. Some are brothers, cousins, cross-cousins, or distant relatives from the same village. One man always danced with his father. Others had a partner from a different (though nearby) village. The partner is a person to whom one feels attuned, with a dance style close to one's own, an agreeable and attractive companion.

A typical dancing troupe performs several times a year: at Christmas, at Easter, in the feasting season from Easter to August, as well as on other important occasions. During the feasting period, dancing performances and practices absorb most of a community's time and energy. Off-season performances tend to be preceded by several weeks of practice, five hours per evening or more, and on most evenings. Dancing couples therefore spend much time together.

The present discussion of Orokaiva dancing and feasting shall remain strictly confined to transactions between the dancing couple. Let me note, however, that Orokaiva feasts and dances are believed to bring about a multitude of magicoreligious blessings, from the growth and well-being of the firstborn sons and of taro, to the removal of sorcery spells placed over gardens and hunting grounds, to ensuring a strong sun and good rainfall and thus the invigoration of the whole community. The quality of drumming and dancing is perceived to have a direct effect on the success of feasts and their purposes, for a faultless performance is viewed as the work of ancestral spirits who have entered the dancers. Magic is used to protect dancers against aesthetic errors. Dance costumes are also representations of ancestors. Though no masks are worn, body decorations (including paint, headdress, shell, bone, and plant ornaments, mouth-held pigs' jaws, etc.) are thought to make the human wearers unrecognizable. They may not be addressed by their real name when so decorated, for their being is then fused with the ancestor's being. Their identity as particular members of the community is suspended.

Spirit impersonation invests dancers with awesome and overwhelming power and seductiveness. Impersonation is the form in which the forces of ancestral nature become visible to man. This form is composed of couples, thus expressing the widespread New Guinean view that the universe is made up of dualities, and that whatever is complete has two sides. Between these two sides there must, however, be perfect interdependence. To embody a spirit, a man must have a partner with whom he is perfectly attuned.

The songs, still composed every year, are often concerned with visions of dead relatives. Though most drumbeats are traditional, new ones do appear even though their newness (as exemplified above by the two beats borrowed from Tufi) usually means combining a variant that has a long, active life with another beat. Feather, shell, and bone decorations are arranged in new combinations for every occasion; and much time is spent on these arrangements. What they communicate is hard to verbalize, but colors, designs, feathers, and the history of decorative valuables are all carefully weighed. They are meant to convey the perfect impersonation of an invisible model, present in the mind of the decorator and attuned to his personality as the performer.

The dances also communicate sensually, homosensually as well as heterosensually. I use the term *homosensual* to refer to aesthetic awareness of the body of a person of the same sex. Homosensuality, not homosexuality, is the bodily interdependence of the same-sex couple of dancers molded over years of intimate experience with each other.[2] It is through the close awareness of one's partner that each is able to realize his own godlike identity. Each makes the other into a god.

Women enter this scene in two ways. First, those who move on the periphery of the column, often young married women, use different steps, different movements—and they may hold a flower, simulate holding a flower, or impersonate a flower—communicating to the male troupe an ambience of feminine seductiveness. Their performance, as much as that of the men, seeks identification

251

with the spirit world: it has the same magicoreligious motivations. This magical identification is consistent with the status of Orokaiva women as fully initiated and fully socially involved, like the men, in the realm of the spiritually unseen.

The male troupe is surrounded by spectators, including younger, mostly unmarried women, who are overwhelmed by the spectacle, not only as a religious but also as an erotic experience. It happens that some are overcome as they look at particular dancers whose power strikes them. It seems as though something has literally struck them. For instance, a girl in the audience jumps back, stumbles, almost falls, screams out in wonder, and then runs off into the dark. A particular dancer knows that as she did so, she was looking at him. The man may be a stranger, or he may have been absent from the village for a while, or the girl may have seen a familiar figure in a new way.

The girl's act is astoundingly public—everyone sees it—but it is also private, for no one can be certain at which dancer it is aimed. At the same time, her act indicates that the sexual energy of the dance, homosensual in its genesis, is heterosensual (and sometimes erotic) in its outcome. This sexual energy adheres to Orokaiva male couples more generally for, outside the village, Orokaiva young men often travel as couples—cross-cousins, fictive cross-cousins, or just friends—and one of their favorite activities is chasing girls.

A COMPARATIVE VIEW OF OROKAIVA
GENDER SYMBOLISM

SOCIETIES AND CULTURAL FEATURES CHOSEN FOR COMPARISON • The present study is comparative; Orokaiva observations are but its starting point. The male couple of dancing partners is found throughout island New Guinea, usually in relation to initiatory experiences. The two processes uppermost in these initiations and in the forms and functions of dancing are: (1) the promotion of miraculous physical growth (in Williams's [1928:122] sense); and (2) the expulsion of excessive feminine traits from male novices. The chief means used to pursue these ends are physical and theatrical.

The role of same-sex couples in these initiation processes is often underestimated on the assumption that either the individual or the group is necessarily the key religious "subject" (agent). Even Burridge (1979:89f.), though a New Guinea specialist, gives no thought to the role of couples. He argues rightly that in New Guinea only a chief, a prophet, or a sorcerer acts as an individual religious agent, but then hastily concludes that the principal religious agent must then be the group.

Yet couples are ubiquitous in New Guinea religious life: for dancing, for playing sacred flutes, or for representing spirits in some context or other. A couple may represent two moieties or some other aspect of dual organization; or it may be formed by two equals or by a senior and a junior. The religious importance of the couple lies in both parties representing spirits, masked or in masklike attire: each knows himself to be a man, but when he looks at his partner he can see a spirit. In their religious aspect, such couples provide the ordinary man with a spiritual counterpart (just as the sorcerer has his counterpart in spirits of the other world), but one represented by his palpably human partner.

The couple is thus the medium through which the ordinary man receives and transmits messages from the spirit world. In that sense it is the couple, not the individual or group, that is the minimal unit of religious experience.[3] As such, the dancing couple resembles, both in function and form, the couple that elsewhere in Melanesia is involved in ritual homosexual activities. The functional convergence between their two forms does not lie in any aim to promote individual growth, strength, or maturation, but rather in the underlying model of male gender identity that is communicated by the dancing couple in some societies and by the (RH) couple in others. Homomorphism between the dancing couple and the (RH) couple lies in the complex system of symbolic transactions between partners. While devoid of overt sexual content, dancing expresses sensual relations of symbolic supremacy, submission, and balance, not only in male gender identity but also in the essential nature of male bonding.[4]

Taking as the problem the establishment and transmission of male gender identity, one may compare various societal modes involving or not involving (RH). Specifically, I shall compare modes of dealing with these issues in the following three types of societies:
(1) Ai'i, Duke-of-York Islands, Etoro, Kaluli, Keraki, Kimam, Marind-anim, Baruya, and Sambia;
(2) Iatmul, Kiwai, and Wogeo;

(3) Arapesh, Baktaman, Elema, Gahuku-Gama, Gnau, Lakalai, Nalum, Orokaiva, Purari, and the Upper Mamberamo.

In this selective list, ritualized homosexual behavior has been confirmed for societies listed in (1), plausibly inferred for societies listed in (2), and convincingly found to be absent for societies listed in (3). Yet all twenty-two societies have an initiation system for adolescents—for both sexes or for males only—involving concepts of miraculous ritual rebirth and miraculous growth. Of the nine societies practicing (RH), eight were shown by Herdt (chap. 1) to practice it in the context of inseminating growth rituals. The ninth society, discussed in detail below, is the case of the Ai'i, where (RH) was certainly practiced only before marriage, but not directly in the context of either initiation or growth rites. Even though the Ai'i facts are imperfectly known, this case serves to discourage ad hoc theories claiming any particular function as the sole purpose motivating ritualized homosexuality in Melanesia.

A COMPARATIVE MODEL OF GENDER IDENTITY • While this chapter analyzes the symbolic behavior of male couples on island New Guinea, most of the known material on the subject concerns Papua and involves comparison between highly diverse patterns in a multitude of small-scale societies. Anthropology has three basic methods for conducting such comparisons, each of which has an uncontested field of utility. One is to establish social laws based on concomitant variations of sociocultural phenomena, including ecology, technology, and demography. This method is valuable, indeed indispensable, if we wish to explain why New Guinea (and Melanesia) as a whole frequently manifests practices, such as ritualized homosexuality, that are rarely practiced elsewhere as a general and obligatory part of socialization. We then need to establish the explanatory significance of certain objective regional factors such as the ecologically determined smallness of groups, endemic warfare, the lack of an economic and technological base for stable alliance systems, or the reliance on enemy groups to provide wives.

A second method is to establish paths for the diffusion of cultural traits or complexes. This method is valuable in explaining, in the manner pioneered by Kroeber and continued by Herdt, why (RH) is distributed as it is within the Melanesian area. When applied to the analysis of symbolic behavior, the concept of diffusion tends, however, to become excessively diffuse. Should we still speak of diffusion when traits are transformed in unpredictable ways? Can (RH) be related historically to the practice of the Gnau, for instance, who promote male growth by the transfer of penile blood rather than of semen (Lewis 1980)?

The third, and most flexible, method is the structuralist one, which would analyze the symbolic systems of all New Guinea as forming a combinatory set made up of a large but finite system of elements yielding a different combination in each society studied. On such a supposition, it would not be necessary to explain why a society adopted one combination of elements rather than another (for this configuration is assumed to result from historical fortuities). In practice, such studies are usually limited to a modest selection of structural elements. Thus, my study deals only with male couples. The assumption is that the symbolic behavior of a particular culture may appear incomprehensible unless different modalities of that behavior are studied in different cultures of the region and compared.[5]

Such a method blends structural, psychoanalytic, and functional perspectives. Thus the structuralist study of the male couple in New Guinea inevitably introduces the figure of a promiscuous and/ or castrating mother-figure in ritual discourse and collective representations. To explain this figure, I use a method proposed by Lévi-Strauss (*L'efficacité symbolique,* 1958), wherein a shamanistic cure effected purely by the presentation of symbolic material to the native patient is compared with Western psychotherapy, inasmuch as "repressions" hitherto unconscious are dissolved by the presentation of symbols. The actions of the male dancing couple constitute a sort of "text" that might, in a similar manner, be objectively curative for persons whose gender conflicts consist of what psychiatrists call the *close-binding intimate (CBI) mother syndrome.*

We have no clinical way of establishing the prevalence of such a syndrome in Orokaiva or other New Guinean societies. We may, however, legitimately observe that the normative conditions of childrearing in the region (which may well be explainable in good part by ecological, political, and demographic factors) correspond to the normative conditions that lead to the CBI syndrome. One

255

might therefore envisage a functional explanation of the actions of male couples as being to control and counteract this syndrome. By the same token, it would be hazardous to explain New Guinean folk theories of childrearing by such a psychoanalytic teleology. It is therefore better to make a more limited claim and describe the relationship between the indigenous and psychoanalytic curative methods as one of parallelism or resemblance (as Lévi-Strauss does himself; ibid.) or, better still, one of analogy, as De Coster did in his excellent little book on analogy in the social sciences (1978).[6]

In taking gender identity as the starting point, it may seem that I am taking a Western scientific perspective. Even this perspective, however, is purely analogical, inasmuch as psychoanalytic studies such as Stoller's[7] concern clinically studied individuals, whereas the anthropologist normally deals with the phenomena of public symbols,[8] such as are found in ritual and in forms of discourse shorn of their idiosyncratic elements by careful ethnographic reduction. It is only in this latter sense that one can say that mothers in cultures that institutionalize homosexuality are overpowering or overprotective; or that fathers are inadequate (see Freud 1962). By the methods ethnographers usually employ, one cannot speak of these mothers and fathers individually; but we may study whether social conditions in a particular society encourage such behavior and the extent to which it may be treated as normative and expected in the ritual discourse and collective representations of that group.

To illustrate: sleeping arrangements in certain groups may result in what psychoanalysts call "sexual overstimulation" implicit in extremely close intimacy (cf. e.g., Whiting et al. 1958). At the same time, these cultures may have strict incest rules resulting in mothers sexually inhibiting their sons. Where relations between men and women tend to be distant, mistrustful, and somewhat cold, and where strongly held beliefs define heterosexual intercourse as debilitating and dangerous to general well-being, the mother may tend to communicate to her son a negative image of heterosexuality. Such attitudes may likely discourage psychologically comfortable masculine attitudes and behavior patterns in the son. Finally, if preadolescent boys in such groups are removed to a bachelor's or man's house, not only for initiation but for generalized male companionship, this tends to be justified in local discourse as protection against "polluting" feminine influence (cf. Meggitt 1964). Fathers may be hampered in countering such influences. Since in many societies men sleep separately from their wives, sons may easily prevail in competition for mothers' favors. Fathers may be "inadequate," then, on account of cultural rules that keep them at a distance (Herdt 1982b; Whiting and Whiting 1975).

In Western societies, such familial characteristics are associated with CBI mothers (Bieber et al. 1962; Stoller 1975, chap. 12) and with the gender development of many (but not all) Western males practicing exclusive homosexual behavior. Yet what is defined as deviation in one culture may be normative in another. Inasmuch as it is part of a very different cultural system, the socialization of a New Guinean-type "CBI mother" will have a very different effect from that of her Western counterpart. For again, those New Guinea systems that most typify this CBI syndrome tend also to practice the most rigorous male initiations.

One question I shall ask is how such rituals and their related discourse encourage the development of male gender identity, a sense of maleness, in Stoller's sense. Such an inquiry would be wholly vitiated if one relied on Stoller's or any other Western theory for the analysis of Melanesian ritual and discourse. This analysis will thus rigorously confine itself to concepts drawn from within Melanesian cultures themselves. What will be said about gender identity has the status of an analogy. The only significance of this analogy is that it may help in reflecting upon Western attitudes toward homosexuality. For the remaining symbolic features, I shall use the structural comparative method.

APPLICATION OF THE METHOD TO THE OROKAIVA • As a first demonstration of the method proposed here, I shall apply it to the Orokaiva ethnography. Let me therefore first summarize the main features of their initiation system insofar as it concerns us here.

Growth Ritual: The growth rite takes the form of preinitiation seclusion in a dark hut where water is forbidden but where food is rich and plentiful. Separation from father and mother is essential. Coconut, applied internally and externally, is the main "growth" agent. It is applied to the skin just as sperm or pork fat is applied

257

in other New Guinea cultures (cf. Serpenti, chap. 7), for the sake of promoting growth.

Seeing the Spirits: Initiation is principally the experience of being shown the flutes, the bull-roarer, and especially the clan spirits—that is, men disguised as ancestors. It is only after initiation that novices understand that dancing is an impersonation of the spirits. The relatives from whom the secluded novices had been hidden will later marvel at how much the initiates have "grown." After initiation, the male or female novice has learned about the invisible world, and dancing couples are always conscious of this ritual knowledge.

Can the above features be explained by reference to gender identity conflicts that may be set up by Orokaiva cultural rules? My data suggest that such conflicts, though milder than in (RH) cultures, are nonetheless present here in similar forms.

In contrast to (RH) cultures, one finds among the Orokaiva little evidence of overclose intimacy between mother and son. The father lives and sleeps in the same house, taking a very close interest in his son's development. Mothers normally do nothing to block this, nor are her relations with her husband notably mistrustful. Orokaiva lack cultural representations that would make heterosexual intercourse seem debilitating or dangerous to male health or that would have the general effect of inhibiting heterosexuality. Intercourse during pregnancy is considered beneficial to the baby, and it is not forbidden, as among the nearby Ai'i. When one asks why people grow weak with age, the answer may refer to the accumulated effect of sorcery attacks and rarely to sexual activity as such. In Orokaiva mythology, there is indeed little reference to dominant female ogres who had to be overcome for men to set up the classical good way of life.

Yet, none of the above themes, prevalent in (RH) cultures, are wholly lacking among the Orokaiva. Not only was preinitiation seclusion rigorously enforced (cf. Williams 1930) but Orokaiva mythology also depicts sexual intercourse as fatal in certain unpropitious circumstances. Thus death came into the world through the fault of a man who copulated with his wife when hunting. Again, there was a female ogre known as the coconut girl, who had spiked breasts by which her lovers all died during intercourse. But the former story explains why intercourse is taboo on a hunt;

the myth of the coconut girl serves only to explain why coconuts are presented to affines at mortuary ceremonies (cf. Schwimmer 1973, 1974, 1981d, 1982a).

As far as Orokaiva men are concerned, we have, therefore, prima facie evidence that they must follow rules drawn from the familiar Melanesian feminine-pollution repertoire. There are many examples of such among Orokaiva: neither a manslayer nor a secluded initiate are allowed intercourse; nor is a menstruating woman. And a man should never be placed behaviorally or metaphorically below or behind female genitals.

These rules are supported by a general classification, prevalent in Melanesia, of objects categorized as either masculine or feminine. This classification tends to follow the principle that male things are hot and dry and feminine things are cold and wet. There are contexts of conditions when a man must reduce the feminine component in a situation. Thus, for instance, wetness and coldness must be kept away from secluded novices, who are thought to suffer from a surfeit of feminine components. This rule applies equally to girl novices.

Two kinds of remedies generally pertain to such conditions: a reduction of feminine components and an increase of the masculine ones. This can be done in two ritual codes: physical and theatrical. The present discussion will show that these remedies and codes are less radical among Orokaiva than in other New Guinea cultures, though they take similar forms.

All the above-listed cultures under consideration use a physical code for expelling excessive femininity and for promoting miraculous growth. For the former goal, there are such devices as penis bleeding (Wogeo, see Hogbin 1970; Arapesh, see Tuzin 1980), transfer of penile blood (Gnau, see Lewis 1980), nosebleeding (Gahuku-Gama, see Herdt 1982b; Read 1952), tongue bleeding (Wogeo), and cane swallowing (Sambia, Gahuku-Gama, see Herdt 1981; Read 1952:12). For promoting growth, the use of sperm appears to be confined to (RH) cultures, though other cultures substitute symbolic semen such as pork fat (Baktaman, Nalum, see Barth 1975).

The chief product associated with miraculous physical growth among Orokaiva is the coconut, which is marked as a male fruit. Men will carry pairs of coconuts, tied together so as to resemble a phallus (the stalks represent the penis and the nuts the testicles). Oil from these coconuts, extracted by the women, is copiously applied to novices' bodies. I have elsewhere shown that Orokaiva see this substance as a vegetable equivalent of sperm (Schwimmer 1974).

Among Orokaiva, as elsewhere in New Guinea, the chief product associated with the expulsion of cold, wet, feminine elements and the generation of heat and dryness is the betel nut. Its essential physical property lies not in any of its three ingredients but in the fact that areca nuts, when mixed with lime and betel pepper, turn red in the mouth. This redness is regarded as heat in its purest form. Since areca is classed as feminine, heat is considered to develop only in the mixture. It is given also by women to men when they intend to have sex. Sorcerers, considered professional experts in the creation of heat, are claimed to be notably efficient at producing a very red mixture in their mouths, and even to be detectable by the way they chew. The betel nut is included with other magical substances as sources of heat and for expelling cold and feminine impurities. In chewing betel nuts, it is hence very important to spit out the residue.

I have already mentioned the theatrical codes in Orokaiva purification ritual: spirit impersonation, playing of flutes and bullroarers (for men), and spirit impersonation and the playing of transvestite roles during the emergence of spirits at initiation. It may be concluded that, as far as male gender identity conflicts are concerned, their manifestations and the processes used to counteract them are comparatively mild, even though spirit impersonation itself is very frightening, as we shall see. Orokaiva physical and psychological ritual ordeals lack the severity seen elsewhere in Melanesia.

With regard to Orokaiva female gender identity, I know of no inquiry in New Guinean studies aimed at discovering whether females have difficulty in identifying firmly with their mothers' gender roles. The inquiries into gender identity in the present volume appear limited to males. I will show below that the Orokaiva give an important role to female transvestites in initiation. This theme raises several issues: Can female transvestism in general be linked to female gender identity conflicts? Do Orokaiva have cultural patterns that, from the viewpoint of psychoanalysis, make them especially prone to such conflicts? Finally: Is transvestism an isolated Orokaiva phenomenon or is it in fact widespread but ignored by unconscious scholarly censorship, in the same way that (RH) has been in the past?

These are crucial issues for the argument since my chief concern will be to show that the deep structure of the male couple is triangular, with women constituting the third apex. In Orokaiva initiation, this triangle is made up of the male couple impersonating spirits, and the woman impersonating human enemies. Paradoxically, therefore, our understanding of the male couple depends on our prior understanding of the female transvestite.

We lack adequate data on Orokaiva female gender identity conflicts. Moreover, even though there is a vast feminist literature in the West, little clinical psychiatric material is available on female gender identity. At first glance, Orokaiva women seem to the Western observer to be masculine in some respects. It is normal for them to fight; they even have a specifically feminine weapon, the quarterstaff, present in most houses. They use it to fight other women, their husbands, their husband's father, anyone. They strongly encourage their men in warfare. Yet, in other ways they are fully absorbed in feminine values, styles, and codes, and control many socioeconomic fields with proud self-sufficiency.

Much attention is still given by Orokaiva to women's initiation, which never ceased, even after initiation for men was discontinued in the colonial period. Not only do women have puberty seclusion and a generalized initiation, but other special cults for women have also sprung up, each with their own songs, dances, and paraphernalia. These are women's performances, while men play the bull-roarers and flutes.

A tentative hypothesis might be that there is an imperfect fit between women's femininity and their notable ability to challenge and compete with males. Since they live in a notionally patrilineal, strongly virilocal society with a marked sexual division of labor and are excluded from formal leadership roles, women's inferior social status is clear on some levels. At the same time, their informal power is considerable. They readily use their right of participation in public discussions and collaborate effectively in many warlike pursuits. Women must often feel that the capacity to play male roles is largely within their grasp. I suspect that this notion has become to them a sort of collective fantasy, a ludic cultural resource. Feminine transvestism appears, above all this, like a fascinating game, which copes with a comparatively mild, yet real internal societal contradiction.

TRANSVESTISM

Though no survey of transvestism in New Guinea has been made, there is reason to doubt its supposed rarity. At least eight of the twenty-two societies mentioned here have transvestism: Orokaiva, Elema (Williams 1940a:278); Lakalai (Goodenough 1971:287); Iatmul (Bateson 1958); Duke-of-York Islands (Parkinson 1907); Marind-anim (Van Baal 1966); Upper Mamberamo River (Oosterwal 1967:188); Wogeo (Hogbin 1970:59f.); and Baruya (Godelier 1982a:78–80). I shall consider here only the cases that bear directly on my hypothesis and general theme.

Judging by Hogbin's data, I believe that in the arena of competition, the position of women among Wogeo resembles that among Orokaiva. He states that sexual groups are in "balanced opposition," in the sense of being mutually dependent and of nearly equal status, "with men having only a slight edge" (1970:98). This pattern coincides with extreme Wogeo theories of sexual pollution. Indeed, there is no generalized reason why the level of women's social status should always be negatively correlated with the strength of pollution beliefs. Why could not the latter be grounded instead in status competition?

Furthermore, Wogeo men are notably competitive with women regarding the ability to "give birth." Like many other New Guinea groups, the Wogeo initiate novices by having them "swallowed" and "reborn" to a new life. The introduction to this process is "to separate them from their mothers to make them grow" (Hogbin 1970:106). Wogeo, however, go one step further and are almost unique in explaining their practice of penis bleeding (performed to ward off female pollution) as a kind of male menstruation (which is found also among the Arapesh and Gnau). Finally, Wogeo use a female transvestite (when possible someone with histrionic talent) to impersonate a pregnant sea monster wading to the shore and giving birth to twins or quadruplets in the men's clubhouse.

Transvestism thus becomes yet another device of Wogeo males to vie with women in the matter of reproduction.

Transvestism among Iatmul was the subject of Bateson's masterly analysis, and he stressed its strongly competitive motivation. He shows that only certain classes of relatives of the person being ceremonially congratulated take part in transvestism. They are of the classes whose relation to the celebrant may be expected to be most ambivalent. Bateson (1958:209) comments: "While in matters of economics the boy is grouped with his father, his feats are regarded as the achievements of his mother's clan." Hence, "The *naven* behavior of the *wau* [MB] is an act which symbolically lays claim to the *laua*'s [ZS] achievement."

Naven distinguishes sharply between two kinds of ambivalence, namely, that expressed by ludicrous transvestites in rags, and that expressed by transvestites in warlike finery. The prototype of the former is the MB, while the prototype of the latter is the FZ. The former type of transvestism, expressing self-abasement, therefore belongs to the rightful claimants upon the ZS's achievement, while the latter type, expressing proud hostility, belongs to those to whom that claim is addressed. This dichotomy is thus not that of opposed sexes, but rather of opposed agnates and uterines; while the inmarrying spouse tends to be classified with the consanguine one.

OROKAIVA INITIATION • The chief dichotomy here is between men and women. Williams's (1930) description, supplemented by data from Chinnery and Beaver (1915), covers most of the points that concern us. Participants come not only from the feasting village but from several surrounding villages as well. The performance is enhanced by participants, many of whom are not familiar to the novices. Initiation does not overtly express conflict between men and women, but two related problems emerge: the novice's overattachment to his/her mother, which is challenged by the performing spirits and enemies; and women's ambiguous status, due to their being both novices' mothers and representatives of potentially hostile clans and villages.

The initiatory performance, occurring at the end of the novices' seclusion, introduces them to the spirits (*embahi*). They are normally sponsored by the MB, who will be among the embahi at the ritual, which takes place under moonlight. In the opening phase, novices are in the village, surrounded by nonparticipants. The embahi move stealthily from the bush, in the usual formation of dancing couples, and then halt at the edge of the village by a scaffolding that has been erected for pig sacrifices, where they utter a crescendo of yells and shrieks. The novices emerge: the embahi chase them. They are, according to Chinnery and Beaver (1915), "followed by the women, waving spears and all uttering cries and yells and rubbing and youngsters' arms, legs and bodies. They now make a wild rush towards the scaffolding, throwing the lads on it." Even in this account, the women's act seems peculiar, for spears are definitely not a female weapon. My own information is that these women used to dress up as men, with full decorations and warlike finery. Andre Iteanu, who participated in Orokaiva initiation in 1981,[9] states that such is still the custom today. Novices are beset by female transvestites, women normally from other villages who are meant to represent enemies.

Novices, then, have three categories of assailants to deal with: (1) the embahi, who frighten them most and whom they never saw before; (2) the enemies, females in male warriors' disguise, with male weapons whose harassment is homoerotic in appearance but heteroerotic in fact; and (3) the mob who drags the fleeing novices back to the scaffolding, to give the spear-carrying libidinous warriors another chance at them. In the final phase, the embahi resume the principal role, mainly by making feint attacks on the novices, using clubs. There is no doubt that the terror in this scene is compounded by the various categories of assailants.

The spirits' presence signifies here that they wish to appropriate the novices and incorporate them, thus separating them irrevocably from their mothers' world. The third group, the mob of nonparticipants who help in harassing the novices, though purely residual, is symbolically important in that their act leaves the novices absolutely without allies. The novices' only recourse is therefore to accept the embahi, who in the end incorporate them into their dance group and thus ensure their protection.

To understand the women's act, one needs only to recall an elementary crutch for reading initiatory language. Initiation reveals the reality underlying sensory appearance, a reality that is always ambiguous. Thus, the embahi are an underlying reality of Orokaiva life revealed during initiation; but initiates learn also that the embahi are really men in disguise. Similarly, human enemies are an underlying reality, yet initiates learn that these are really women. Conversely, it is implied that women are the true enemies.

This representation is not quite what Meggitt (1964) and others have implied by demonstrating that some Highlands groups "marry their enemies." Statistics show that most Orokaiva marriages are within the security circle, and that marriages arranged with enemy villages are a small minority (Schwimmer 1969). By the same token, the ritual representation of marriages (from the pledging and paying of bride-wealth to the giving of a woman in return) symbolically depicts the two sides as enemies, and the marriage as a truce in their hostilities (Schwimmer 1981a). Here, ritual does not concern the appearance of social relations, but their deeper reality. Initiation expresses that deeper reality by representing women as enemies rather than as mothers or wives. The women's act symbolically bars the novices' way back to the womb and maternal security.

MALE THEATRICAL TRANSVESTISM: AIKA • Let us now compare this female transvestism with male transvestism in the same culture. This transvestism is limited, in ritual, to theatrical performances that may be seen throughout the Orokaiva-Binandere language area. No women ever appear onstage, but there are female roles acted by male transvestites. I observed some of these plays at Orokaiva feasts, though the actors were guest performers from distant villages. I was able to study the plays only among the Aika, a tribe whose language and culture much resembles that of the Plains Orokaiva, except that the former's performative drama is far more developed. Aika live in the swamps on the western boundary of Orokaiva territory.

I was unable to see performances in their sacred setting since there were no feasts at the time, but some plays were staged for my benefit. I was told frankly that a few minor modifications had been made to deprive the performances of magical efficacy and magical danger. These modifications indicate where the truly sacred parts in these performances lie. Because a brief description

265

of these data is already published (Schwimmer 1979*b*), I shall confine myself here to their implications for gender identity and transvestism.

All the dangerous elements of the dramas lay in theatrical transactions between males in the original script. No changes were made in the text, the music, or the drumming. But the clowning parts, which were especially sacred and represented ancestors, were acted by children (who gave a technically excellent performance). Since the actors were uninitiated, nothing th·y said could anger the spirits. The male couple that would normally lead the dancing was also too sacred to be shown. Here, the traditional concept was that this male couple represented a man and a woman, though in sacred performances the woman's part was always acted by a man. This transvestism was enacted for the reason mentioned above, namely, that in these cultures sacred communication is possibly only by the mediation of same-sex couples. In the performances I saw, a very charming young woman was substituted for the male transvestite. People explained to me that this would make the performers *magically innocuous.* (The stage director, Philip Ngongore of Poho village, was a talented artist whose troupe was widely regarded as the most professional and brilliant in Oro Province. His small modifications enabled him to communicate his art to foreigners without magical danger and with its aesthetic value intact.)

What concerns us here is that Aika practice both the male transvestism sketched above and the same female transvestism already described for Orokaiva. I have shown that female transvestism in initiation presents onstage a woman representing a human male (enemy). Male transvestism in drama presents a human male impersonating a female spirit (ancestor). In the performances I saw, the impersonated male and female ancestors express in one way or another the sacred complementarity of man and woman. This message of mystic interdependence does not directly contradict the other image of woman, whereby she appears as enemy: the two viewpoints are complementary in these cultures. This message of the interdependence of the sexes (frequent in myth as well as drama) is, however, conveyed by male rather than female transvestites.

THE COMPARATIVE STUDY OF TRANSVESTISM • Transvestism, among Orokaiva and elsewhere, is a device resorted to
in diverse contexts. No psychiatrist or anthropologist has ever
found a model to explain all its manifestations, nor do we claim
such a model can be constructed. Initiatory transvestism in New
Guinea is, however, a special form that remains basically similar
in a variety of cultural systems.

Thus many New Guinean cultures use male transvestites if female characters are portrayed in sacred dramas. In addition to
those described from the Orokaiva-Binandere area, examples can
be found in the pregnant Wogeo *lewa* deity described by Hogbin
(1970, chap. 3), and in the buffoonery in Elema mask performances (Williams 1940*a*). Transvestism by male hunters on the
Upper Mamberamo River, as reported by Oosterwal (1967), falls
in the same category, for hunting may be perceived as a kind of
sacred drama. Most cases of New Guinean male transvestism I
encountered in my sample are of this type.

Female transvestism is a dominant theme of initiation ceremonies for, it seems, a masculinized woman is a common male fantasy,
especially among adolescents. It occurs in four cultures from my
sample: Orokaiva initiation, Baruya female rites, the naven ceremony of the Iatmul, and mortuary ceremonies of the Lalakai. The
feminized-acting man of naven appears to be a pseudohomosexual
inversion of the masculinized-acting woman. The assault by female
transvestites in these cultures is pseudohomosexual in appearance,
but heterosexual in reality. The assault of the Iatmul maternal
uncle is heterosexual in appearance, but may have been homosexual in reality (see Herdt, chap. 1).

In the Duke-of-York Islands, as well as among the Iatmul, we
find feminized-acting males who portray the insertee in a simulation of homosexual intercourse. In the Duke-of-York Islands, the
transvestite is the senior partner (usually the inserter) whose disguise signifies that he is represented as an insertee. The Iatmul
have an act of ritual copulation in which the *wau*, with a symbolic
clitoris in his anus, portrays woman while his wife plays the role
of male and of inserter, intercourse being anal (Bateson 1958:20).

In this respect again, Iatmul and Orokaiva resemble each other.
For, like the wau, the Orokaiva female transvestite has two alter-

nate strategies: either she makes an assault that is homosexual in appearance or she offers herself anally, as in the tale of Suvahe, not presented here. Yet the fundamental implication is the same in both cases: the novice is being drawn away from his attachment to mother. Among the Iatmul, it is possible but unlikely that a homosexual partner is meant to take her place, but both the Orokaiva and Iatmul initiatory experience has the effect of changing the novices' perception of women.[10] The perception it teaches is that the masculinized-acting woman, anal-erotic, is essentially an enemy warrior. (To be sure, the mother herself is rigorously kept out of these proceedings.) As such, the Orokaiva system is as complex as that of the Iatmul. Homoerotic symbolism is not *absent* from Orokaiva ritual, but the homoerotic act is talked of as a meaningless activity of bachelors, a very different matter. This ideology conveys that in males, masculine gender identity should be dominant, while the feminine component (inevitably present) should be kept subordinate. The fact that men find one another sensually attractive makes the institution of male dancing couples compelling. Still, homosexual intercourse is disvalued.

What has this analysis of transvestism contributed to our understanding of the Orokaiva male couple in particular and to (RH) in general? My argument has been that the male couple is a triangle, the apex of which is the female. It resembles (RH) in function but differs from it in form: where it differs is that the functions it serves among Orokaiva by integrated male/female ceremonies are served among Iatmul and Wogeo, for example, by separate ceremonies for members of one sex only, while in other cultures ceremonies dealing with female gender roles are absent.

Where males and females participate in common collective ceremonies, ambivalent feelings are not suppressed. In Orokaiva ritual, for instance, females are put onstage in roles manifesting masculinized, promiscuous, or castrating symbolic connotations. The present discussion of transvestism has shown that such roles offer women agreeable opportunities for expressing gender tendencies usually hidden. They are therapeutic for the reasons already spelled out by Bateson (1958). These roles simultaneously correspond to profound fantasies in Orokaiva male adolescents. The role contains information required for the development of masculine gender identity. This information completes what may be learned from the experience of being in a male dancing couple. It is for this reason that I suggest that the total information available to those experiencing Orokaiva rites corresponds to a triangular model including a masculinized-acting woman as well as the male couple.

Two questions now arise in this comparative perspective. The first is whether (RH) in Melanesia must always have the function of promoting physical growth, strength, and maturation. Can we find instances where (unlike among Orokaiva) homosexual activity is given ritual value but not in connection with promoting growth? If such a case can be found, it would run counter to the hypothesis of an (RH) culture complex where form and function are diffused together. It would, instead, support the hypothesis of cultural transmission resulting in a combinatory set whereby each culture establishes its own internal connections between form and function independently. It is with this question in mind that I shall now discuss the case of the Ai'i.

The second question, reserved for the final section of this chapter, is why females are kept off the ritual stage of most (RH) cultures, and why they are devalued to the point of being given no overt place in the sacred and unseen world portrayed in Melanesian initiation ritual.[11] Are they really absent, or does structural analysis reveal, in those cultures, the same triangle of male couple and female apex that we find among Orokaiva? If so, why is the apex suppressed in cultures such as Kaluli, Etoro, and Sambia?

RITUAL HOMOSEXUALITY AMONG THE AI'I • Nearly all Oro Province tribes belong to one or two very different cultural complexes. The Orokaiva-Binandere, whom I have been describing, live in the plains and on the foothills; inhabiting the mountains north of the Owen Stanley Range are speakers of the Koiarian language group (Dutton 1969), whose cultures resemble in many respects those of the western-lying Sogeri (Williams 1976:123–160), the Tauade (Hallpike 1977), and even the Anga (Godelier 1982a) or Etoro (Kelly 1977). The barrier between these two cultural complexes is great in matters of language, social organization, and ideology, even though detailed comparisons reveal many resemblances and borrowings in material culture, myth, and ritual.

According to Barker's reconstruction, a classic Ai'i village usually accommodates two clan groups, each with one longhouse for men, one for women, and one for pigs. There are also unmarrieds' clubhouses, one for bachelor boys, one for girls. Men and women have no common residence. Boys stay with their mothers until, it seems, the end of the latency period. Separation from mother thus occurs much later than among the Sambia and some other Highlands groups, but no earlier than among the Orokaiva. Yet for the Ai'i it is more radical, for boys move from a wholly female to a wholly male environment. They sleep thereafter in the bachelors' house but spend much time in the men's cult house.

Relations between men and women are distant. Barker reports a prepartum and postpartum taboo on sexual intercourse of about three-and-a-half years' duration for every birth. Ai'i believe that sexual relations debilitate and endanger both men and women. Illness is said to result from initial sexual intercourse, and it remains a risk in subsequent relations. Not only is the man so threatened (as is believed in many New Guinea cultures); semen is thought also to have the power of killing the woman. Sore throats and coughs are explained by reference to sexual pollution. The available psychological data indicate the likelihood of overclose intimacy between mother and son, and of women being dependent more on sons than husbands. One may expect mothers in such a society to impart a negative and repressive view of heterosexuality to their sons. The model for Ai'i masculine and chiefly behavior, stated in the myth of the chief deity Wasia, represents femininity in the form of a snake, Wasia's wife. Her children by Wasia are likewise snakes, probably a kind of boa constrictor (Barker 1975; Schwimmer 1981d).

Though our data on initiation are limited,[12] certain general patterns are clear. Boys' first initiatory act is the eating of a red yam (iro bara), supposed to encourage their growth. This is one of many Ai'i rituals using red vegetable matter (e.g., red-skinned bananas, red leaves, red sugarcane, red areca pods) to promote the interconnected qualities of dryness, heat, and growth. The second initiatory ritual, normally in preadolescence, is the dressing and tending of a long hair tail, grown by boys and in principle also by girls, to make their bodies grow big. Their initiator, normally a mother's brother, attends to this ritual. The third rite, which is performed just before preinitiation seclusion begins, is

270

the piercing of the nasal septum. During seclusion, there are no food prohibitions, but there is a strict rule of sexual abstinence, extended to those who visit novices at night (and who should not sleep with their spouses). If this rule is violated, the initiate's "nose will get sore."

With regard to homosexuality, it is best to quote Barker:

> The land holding–land using group is often formed by a unit based on co-residence in the single boys' house, formerly the initiatory group. Between males at least this unit is bonded with an institutionalized homosexual relationship. The homosexual is known as *ina'e*, loosely: "one who makes poison." It is probably a derivative of *ina'a*, which is usually given the connotations "young person, uninitiated, irresponsible" and "maker of poison" or homosexual. A homosexual relationship with a brother or cousin is deemed suitable for the uninitiated and unmarried boys and men and for spinsters.
>
> *(1975: 215-222)*

This passage needs to be interpreted with caution, but it is clear that the initiatory group would in the main be made up of age-mates standing in a classificatory relationship of brothers or cross-cousins. It is less clear how land could become vested in such a group, but Barker states that land rights may be obtained by co-residence from various categories of consanguines and even affines. He also states that such transfers of rights require a kind of mystical male bonding. Landholding rights are symbolized by a bird-of-paradise of a certain variety, which lives on the land and is identified with a particular person. The bond between the bird-of-paradise (*rabijo*) and the person is usually transferred to that person's sons, but the person may also choose to include in this bond other men with whom he had become closely identified. Homosexual relations between coresident age-mates thus were evidently thought to lead to sharing the same bird-of-paradise, with the implication of bonds of common landholding.

There is no information that the homosexual act is actually mythologized as such, or that Ai'i relate it directly to the promotion of growth. Homosexuality is assigned a different manifest function which may be at least as critical for Ai'i, namely, same-sex bonding. Such bonding is in principle limited to bachelors. Barker gives no

271

examples or rules suggesting that once a man is married he would be bonded to another rabijo.

In spite of its ritual value in establishing land rights, (RH) enjoys only modest status among the Ai'i, falling somewhere between its status among the Orokaiva (who wholly disvalue it) and the Kaluli or Etoro, who idealize it.

As for the position of women, Barker judges it to be rather low. Yet, comparing his report with what is known of other New Guinea Highlands groups, it is clear that Ai'i women are protected from sexual pollution, they are allotted land of their own, and they are allowed lesbian bonds.

With regard to same-sex bonding, the Ai'i have a problem that arises much less among the Orokaiva, whose social universe is wider. Since the latter system is described in detail elsewhere (Schwimmer 1973, 1975, 1982a), let me underline only that the Orokaiva bachelor, who is extremely mobile and enjoys a large, varied, and solid friendship network, seems mainly preoccupied with finding more friends (male and female) farther abroad without losing the ones he has nearby. His Ai'i counterpart, however, seems considerably more restricted, operating within a much more limited security circle, and he is discouraged from aggressively pursuing girls. He is lacking in most of the dimensions of the Orokaiva *simbo-otavo* system.[13] These factors, added to the identity conflicts that might arise out of childrearing patterns, place a greater burden on the Ai'i initiation group, which must furnish companionship, land resources, models for masculine identification, as well as objects of sexual desire.

It follows from this discussion that (RH) among the Ai'i does support the formation of masculine gender identity, but Ai'i do not invoke the ideological fiction that it promotes "miraculous" physical growth. They are interested in this latter goal as well, but its promotion takes different forms, summarized above, which are all rather similar to practices found in New Guinea Highlands populations. The Ai'i evidence makes one wonder whether (RH) resulted from the diffusion of both the forms and functions of a culture complex. These data are perfectly consistent, however, with my earlier hypothesis of a combinatory set.

Let us now turn to the second question raised in the preceding section of this essay: Can the Ai'i system be understood as part of a triad consisting of a same-sex couple and a kind of CBI mother in one of her various guises? Such a woman does not appear in the rituals described either overtly or in recognizable symbolic form. Nor are there Ai'i myths depicting such mother or female figures. Indeed, the only known Ai'i creature resembling such women is Simo, the snake-wife of the high god Wasia. Let us therefore look more closely at this creature.

Simo is a bald snake whose children by Wasia are also snakes. She has a small pond that goes wherever she goes. Wherever she is, Wasia comes and feeds her and her brood twice a day. Barker notes that her offspring are called "Wasia's pigs," but that while pigs are fed only once a day, humans are fed twice. They are, then, intermediate between pigs and men. Now there are, as noted, three longhouse structures in an Ai'i village, the one in front for men, the one at the back for pigs, and the one in between for women. Women are then, spatially speaking, intermediate between pigs and men; and Wasia's snakes are placed, by feeding, in an analogous position.

Another version of a man who fed snakes was collected by Susan Rogers (1975) at Sirorata (a boundary village of basically Orokaiva culture, but with much Koiarian influence and fairly close to the Ai'i border). Here the snake-feeder suffered from an affliction that sealed all his body apertures. Cultural analysis shows that this affliction is treated by Orokaiva as an excess of the element of humidity and a lack of the element of dryness or heat. The image of domesticated snakes evokes excessive humidity in its most horrifying form.[14] The same classification schema probably applies also to the Ai'i, for Wasia is above all else the god of dryness, a desiccated type able to withstand famine since he needs very little food. It would seem, then, that his wife Simo represents a sort of cosmic counterpart, a principle of humidity.

For the Ai'i as for the Orokaiva, man in his natural state is a mixture of the principles of dryness and wetness. By contrast, the female is much wetter than the male. Hence, ritual efforts are made to dry her out, especially at critical times such as menstruation and pregnancy. A very studied and systematic dryness is, however, required from any man aspiring to leadership status.

Following this line of thought, (RH) among bachelors might perhaps be regarded as part of such a process of metaphysical

273

desiccation. Such a hypothesis, however, is supported only by the most general indications. Wasia, god of dryness and famine, is the model of a man who carries a minimum of flesh and moisture, who makes a minimum of body movements, and who therefore is able to survive the famine months common to the Ai'i. The cultivated plant food resources of this people suffice for only about half the year, forcing them to rely for the rest on precarious hunting and collecting. Moreover, the rainfall is very high (700 cm per year), ensuring a surfeit of wetness at most times. These patterns help explain the symbolic significance given to dryness and wetness as elements in this culture.[15]

While no direct evidence links (RH) with protection against the wet, there are clear indications that it protects against femininity which symbolizes wetness, and against the constricting and murderous potentiality of the feminine principle as symbolized by Simo. In this sense, my structural analysis tentatively suggests that Simo may represent the apex of the triangle completed by the male couple. We thus see that even in a culture where no miraculous growth is credited to (RH), ideologies and practices accord with Layard's (1942) perspicacious perception of its essential qualities: an extreme reverence for the penis and a belief in the extreme holiness of maleness. Ai'i men, like those of other (RH) groups, tend to perceive women as the locus of trauma, frustration, and hostility.

A culture that builds its dominant ideology, including the gender identity inculcated in its men, on a homosexual restitution of an Oedipus complex (Stoller 1975) is bound (by logical coherence) to reduce the ideological importance of women. Indeed, there is no generalized reason why the level of women's social status should always be negatively correlated with the strength of pollution beliefs. Why could not the latter be grounded instead in status competition? Conversely, of course, it does not follow that societies devaluing women practice (RH). Relations between men and women among Ai'i are, if anything, better than those among Baktaman (Barth 1975) or Mae Enga or Kuma (Meggitt 1964), where (RH) is absent. Irrespective of whether (RH) is present or absent, there are strong similarities in man/woman relations in all these Highlands cultures, from east to west. And perhaps Hylkema's

(1974) ethnography of the Nalum has gone furthest in making intelligible, by sympathetic penetration into the thought patterns of men and women, how such systems are experienced on both sides of the sex barrier.

THE MALE COUPLE AND ITS IDEA OF WOMAN

The purpose of this section is to track down the variant forms of the triangle made up of the male couple and the female fantasy, for which the CBI mother is the prototype. What forms does this fantasy take in New Guinea societies where the male couples practice (RH)? The question is of interest because in secret male cults in New Guinea, the women who are excluded turn out to be the cults' real subject (Schwimmer 1980, 1981c). Initiation is a second birth; but in these cults it is a birth provided by a man to a boy. It is birth into a community comprising not only the living (the community entered at the time of the first birth) but also the dead (who became "visible" only at initiation). The secret of this birth is the procedure by which the initiated are enabled to enter that enlarged community.

(RH) is one of these key secret procedures. An adequate description of (RH) must consider all the relations within the triangle: (1) the modalities of relationships between the male cult members; and (2) the modalities of relationships between each of the male cult members and women. Let us therefore look at these aspects in turn.

Bonding to the invisible world in separation from mother always involves bonding with other males. First, this bonding may be either between age-mates who undergo initiation together and remain intimates thereafter (Ai'i, East Bay); or it may be between seniors and juniors, the former transmitting knowledge about ritual practice and spirits to the latter. In most societies where ritual homosexuality occurs, bonding is between senior and junior, though there are exceptions (see Davenport 1977; Serpenti, chap. 7). Perhaps we could, on this basis, set up a distinction between socially oriented homosexual bonding as among Ai'i, and reproductively oriented bonding where the transmission of semen signifies both individual and cultural reproduction. Socially oriented bonding

275

would be between coevals, reproductive bonding between seniors and juniors. In some societies partnerships are constant; in others they are promiscuous.

Second, we may distinguish between bonding in groups and bonding in couples. In most (RH) cultures, there is (a) a purely ceremonial pattern, restricted to the period of the bull-roarer or flute ceremonies (as among Keraki and Marind-anim) or to the hunting lodges (as among Etoro and Kaluli), a sort of homosexual saturnalia for all ages, during which novices are in principle available to all men of the opposite moiety; and (b) an everyday pattern following the ceremonies, when the (RH) relationship is confined to the couple whose senior partner is chosen for the junior by his guardians. In most societies of the sample, sexuality is but one aspect of a many-sided relationship between these partners. I will also discuss groups such as the Sambia who practice promiscuous homosexual activity.

Among the Marind-anim, for instance, the novice's *binahor* was his initiator, not only sexually but in all phases of ritual treatment. He was also a foster father who, together with his wife, provided for the boy's daily nourishment, while the foster son helped his binahor in the garden (Van Baal, chap. 3). In the Kimam system, the age difference is only significant between members of successive initiation groups, but the homosexual relationship seems almost as diffuse as among Marind-anim. Serpenti (1965, chap. 7) has shown the extraordinary complexity of the exchange relations between the differential social groups of the novice and his mentor.

Among the Keraki, the senior (RH) partner is typically a cross-cousin of the preceding age-grade, but his overall role is more limited. Keraki have two initiating functionaries (*tabulamant*, Williams 1936c:188), the elder of whom is a consanguine one generation senior to the novice, who is in charge of the ceremonies. The junior tabulamant, who is "privileged to sodomize the boy," has no other ritual responsibilities. He initiates the novice into homosexual intercourse during a specific phase of the bull-roarer cult ceremonies. He continues thereafter to have sexual claim on his novice, who is supposed never to refuse him.

Sambia, Baruya, Etoro, and Kaluli novices take their homosexual partners from socially distant groups. The range of potential male bonds available to those groups is therefore enlarged by (RH). The Etoro, whose *preferential* marriage partners are taken from as close as the exogamy rules allow, prefer to take their (RH) partners from further afield—in fact, from outside the security circle, at the outer limits of their social universe. The Etoro also preferentially marry a particular type of distant patrilateral cross-cousin but prefer (RH) partners who are unrelated (Kelly 1976). Sambia (and Baruya) preferentially marry outside their hamlet and prefer (RH) partners "drawn from hamlets of potential enemies" (Herdt 1981:238).

Here we find a variant of a frequent New Guinea pattern of maintaining two types of alliance networks, one that serves to bind together a person's security circle, the other (by somewhat different procedures) to maintain political, military, and commercial bonds outside it. Both Orokaiva and Ai'i, for instance, have a two-sided marriage system with different rules for each network (Schwimmer 1981*a*). Sambia, Baruya, and Etoro appear to use marriage to solidify the security circle but rely on (RH) to attend to the more distant alliances.

Though the senior partner in an (RH) couple tends to be married or to have a fiancée, the junior one is always forbidden heterosexual activity. The male couple often resides away from the village, or the promiscuous homosexual contacts occur outside of it, the junior's movements being restricted so as to avoid heterosexual encounters that would harm his growth or reestablish his mother's influence. The rules of secrecy prevent the novice from passing on significant messages to females. Masculine gender identity is established in the novice by teaching him of a separate world order from which women are excluded, even though it contains functions that would be feminine in the profane world. Among such functions are: acting as a homosexual insertee, and representing notions about pregnancy or giving birth. The Managalese and Omie of Oro Province, among many others, represent the womb by a trench dug in the ground and covered over, in which novices lie embryolike and from which they emerge in a simulation of birth.[16] This "sacred womb" is like a phallus; and it is contrived by men. In the same vein, Sambia and Etoro practice homosexual fellatio which is designed to carry the ritual message of breast-feeding via

277

initiatory code. The novice is taught to behave toward the penis of the fellated as though it were a mother's breast (cf. Sørum, chap. 8).

Let us now turn to the modalities of relationships between the males and the female. The notable characteristic of (RH) cultures is the elimination of women in the symbolic representation of normally feminine functions, including not only the generative function but also the sexual function and, among Baruya, Sambia, and Etoro, the nurturing function. My concern here will be with patterns of folk explanation of such symbolic transfers.

Such patterns may be found in offstage ritual talk within the groups in question. Herdt (1981, chap. 5) documented such talk among the Sambia, devoting an entire chapter to the "phantom cassowary," the Sambia's familiar male fantasy of the masculinized female. Cassowary and woman are equated in this discourse (ibid.:187). Fathers do not wish to entrust the development of their sons' masculinity to their wives. So Sambia men say: "Your mother curses you" (ibid.:225). They adopt magical measures to safeguard their health against the supposed dangers of heterosexual coitus (ibid.:248) but see little danger in homosexual activity.

Since reports of offstage ideological discourse are rare for most of these cultures, we need to rely heavily on the corpus of recorded myths. In the mythology of Marind-anim, Kimam, Keraki, Kaluli, Etoro, and Sambia, two themes about the nature of women appear to predominate. One of these is the theme of the incestuous (and wanton) woman, and the other concerns the castrating woman.

Both themes are found among the Marind-anim. The incestuous mother who, according to Wirz, occurs in the founding myths of all secret Marind cults (especially the mayo cult) is called Old Woman of the Mayo (Wirz 1922–1925, 2:62–64). After escaping from a mayo ceremony where a woman had been killed, the Old Mayo Woman flees in a canoe with her son to a new refuge. There also a mayo ceremony is in progress. A spy who spots the couple reports to his village that a boy has arrived with a girl. The two are captured, sexually used, killed, and then eaten. The men then said: "Such a feast should be repeated every year" (reviewed in Van Baal, chap. 3).

Wirz (1922–1925, 2:62–64) makes an interesting comment on the term *Old Woman:* "The Marind habitually use such expressions and turns of phrase to designate an object they for some reason do not wish to call by its right name. Thus they will say 'Old Woman' when they mean 'girl' even in everyday life." Perhaps the Marind-anim did not resort to such deceptive speech only to mystify their intentions, for the *mayo* rite itself was ambiguous. On the one hand, they liked to capture girls for mayo ceremonies wherein they stimulated heterosexual activity, for sperm production, and hence for the well-being of the novices. On the other hand, their violence was aimed, in psychological terms, at the Old Woman figure, identifiable as a kind of CBI mother complete with dependent overaged son, and who was herself presumably guilty of incest and thus an object of vengeance.

We meet the castrating mother in one of the myths cited to explain the homosexually oriented Marind Sosom cult. Here Sosom, fornicating with a woman, was unable to extricate his penis. The woman's mother finally separated the couple by cutting off the man's penis with a knife. After this, Sosom was unable, with the part of his penis remaining to him, to perform other than homosexual anal intercourse (Wirz 1922–1925, 3:38–39). Interestingly enough, exactly the same myth (of a penis caught within a vagina) is told by the Orokaiva, but here the mother uses no knife. She separates the couple by putting them underneath her own bed. They emerge from the ordeal very emaciated, but with their genitals intact.

Marind-anim and Orokaiva share the symbolic code of this myth but not the precise message. The fact that the Orokaiva also have a similar form of myth is more easily explained if we suppose that it is simply part of a general stock from which many New Guinean myths are composed. There is indeed no reason why vagina dentata stories should have an outcome in homosexual activity. We may still grant, however, that at the present stage of Melanesian studies, the hypothesis of an ancient ritual complex is fruitful in stimulating research.

Still, the "charter" for (RH) among the Marind-anim is this collective image of a castrating mother. One might feel inclined to blame family life: spouses who reside separately, eat separately, work separately; boys introduced to the men's house between the ages of four and five. Bonds within the same-sex age groups are far stronger, according to Wirz, than familial bonds. Yet the neighboring Kimam have a very similar ideology, and they spend their childhood in conjugal family dwellings. Kimam have ritual practices similar to those of the mayo and sosom cults. Kimam express the potential dangers inherent in all sexual intercourse through a myth whose heroine is very much like the bionic woman of the well-known American television series.[17] She is described as a "widow" (a sexy word to the New Guineans) whose mourning cape is part of her body. She tempts men so she can cut off their penes with her vagina dentata.

At this point a problem arises. In some (RH) cultures, such as the Etoro and Kaluli, there is little direct reference to women of the CBI type (whether promiscuous or vagina dentata). In these cases the fantasy is not absent but transposed, I would suggest, to the witchcraft syndrome. These peoples systematically equate the effect of sexual intercourse with the effect of witchcraft. Like Sambia, both groups believe man has a limited stock of vitality which is depleted by semen outflow but augmented by semen inflow (Herdt, chap. 4). Kaluli and Etoro also believe that witches who attack this stock of life force are the cause of all deaths. Witches are most often males who accumulate malignant power, as one might say, in their penes. This predisposes them to doing harm, but they become actively destructive only when motivated by malice toward particular persons.

Even though the witches are in fact normally males, they are often symbolically equated with women. Thus, both cultures idealize the life of bachelors in hunting lodges, far away from women and from witches, which is beneficial to male vitality as evidenced by success in hunting and in enhanced personal beauty. It is only after marriage that witchcraft becomes critical for males. Male affines are in fact the kin category to which witchcraft in both cultures is most commonly ascribed. The two cultures differ, however, in their prescription for the proper response to witchcraft. Kaluli, whose ideology favors marriage with very distant kin or nonkin, respond to witchcraft by elaborate and somewhat grim rituals of revenge. Etoro, whose ideology favors marriage with much closer kin, appear to take a fatalistic view of the faults of the universe and of attacks by witches; they try to suffer them with equanimity (see Sørum, chap. 8).

In mythology, however, these witches are represented either as always or principally as female. According to the Etoro (Kelly 1976:49), the originators of witchcraft were three children: a brother and sister who copulated and produced a baby (*contra naturam*). These three all became witches after they were killed, but the girl-mother was the principal figure in this scenario. Structuralists may here see a transformation of the Marind myth of the Old Woman of Mayo (discussed above), for in both cases the origin of killing was explained as a spontaneous reaction to incest: incest brought death into the world. We should note that the Etoro story does not refer to the killing of witches; it merely accepts their existence fatalistically.

The Kaluli myth of the origin of witchcraft, published by Schieffelin (1976:154–155), likewise connects it with brother/sister incest,[18] but with a different twist:

> Newelaesu was living on Wilip, and Dosaeli with his sister Towa was living nearby. Dosaeli had a wife but Newelaesu had none. Newelaesu asked Dosaeli for Towa to be his wife, but Towa was unwilling and Dosaeli refused. Newelaesu killed a cuscus and put its heart up on a pole. "Everyone gather," he called out, "this is the heart of a witch I have killed." So some angrily demanded wealth compensation and others going to Newelaesu's side helped him to pay it.

Schieffelin explains that Newelaesu is a typical trickster figure, who created not witches (who had originated earlier) but "how they first came to be killed." This story seems like a transformation of the simpler, possibly prior, Etoro myth. The guilty party here is undoubtedly the brother/sister couple whose refusal to separate is interpreted as incestuous. According to the Kaluli, it is not the killing of witches that destroys them but the setting of their hearts up on a stake, thus *revealing* (by the yellow appearance of the heart) the witchcraft in the person killed.[19] Without suggesting that in these cultures witchcraft and the feminine principle are equated, it seems clear that the only sure way to avoid the former is to avoid the latter, and thus to stay in a hunting lodge which is free of witchcraft.

It is unfortunate that so much of my evidence has been mytho-

281

logical, for it is not the purpose of this chapter to compare my-
thologies. I have tried to reconstruct the image of women available
to the minds of male couples in (RH) cultures. Myths interest us
because of what they teach male couples to think. From this viewpoint, two other widespread themes must be briefly reviewed. One
is the tradition, almost ubiquitous, that the cult house was originally built or controlled by women and that men subsequently
seized it. Hence, there always is a feminine spirit in the cult house,
who is revered as its original mother. The other theme is that of
a triangle involving a high god, his wife, and his male lover (a
novice initiated by the high god). In these tales the novice and the
wife have intercourse and are caught in the act. In spite of his
strong love for the novice, the high god kills him because he too
cannot accept the triangle.

There is a highly ritualistic flavor to this series of negative female
representations in the (RH)-associated discourse in these cultures.
As mythology, this discourse may not be worth detailed study; I
hope to have shown that the myths all have the same simple ar-
mature. The pragmatics of the discourse may be of more interest,
however, since it seems unlikely that all the men in question continued steadfastly to reduce woman to the oedipal fantasies cited
above. It is more likely that such discourse constitutes a somewhat
hackneyed and no doubt unjust reduction of what is said when
(RH) is practiced—a sort of ideological justification of homosexual
activity. For, in spite of the mythopoetic power of these cult house
teachings and the profound truths they enunciate, I was sometimes
reminded of the ruminations on women I used to hear in New
Zealand pubs where women were excluded. Though lacking nothing in frankness, these conversations excluded vast areas of experience about women by a sort of unconscious censorship which
marked a very strong sexual barrier.

Do all (RH) cultures fit this mold? Let me briefly discuss one
that is more subtle: the Kiwai Islanders as described by Landtman
(1927). The Kiwai live on the boundary between the (RH) Marind-
anim groups and the eastern-lying Gulf Province cultures which
lack (RH).[20] With regard to homosexual relationships, their practices are not completely clear. Herdt (chap. 1) rightly notes signs
that strongly support the presence of (RH), but one is left to
wonder whether (RH) was pervasive or covered only part of Kiwai

territory. In Landtman's data, semen transactions are reported (usually a sign of the presence of RH) but they differ notably, both in form and function, from the classical type reported for Keraki or Sambia.

The greatest ceremony of the Kiwai is Horiomu, a masked performance somewhat reminiscent of the *hevehe* performance of the Gulf Province Elema. Among the Kiwai (but not the Elema), an elderly couple (the feast-giver and his wife) have open ritual sexual intercourse just before the emergence of the masks, the resulting sexual secretion being smeared on marine grass planted around the cult shrine. It is believed that this old couple will die shortly afterward. Since the object of the feast is the increase of *dugong*, and because the marine grass in question is one on which dugong feed, the semen "transaction" conveys to the younger men a very particular potency, namely the capacity to catch more dugong. In terms of Williams's (1928) classification of magic, one could say that this secretion (the mixture of semen and vaginal fluid) is not a "magical specific" (i.e., a secret ingredient ensuring efficacy) but rather a "magical catalyst," a medium of general magical efficacy to which something must be added to bring about a desired result. This contrast may seem a small technical point, but it is worth noting that, on the boundary of the Marind-anim cultures, semen—still an essential and potent constituent for prosperity—has been allotted a less central ritual function.

The rest of the Kiwai symbolism is similarly a mixture of (RH) and non-(RH) traits: boy novices are carried to a stream by *female relatives* . . . to take away the *smell of woman*. They are then given medicines to enable them to *attract women*. On the novice's return, the mother (a woman, not a transvestite male as among the Iatmul) lies down on the threshold of the house. He walks over her. The MB seizes him. He is harassed by masked spirits and carried "to make him grow quick."[21]

Kiwai have their equivalent of the mayo ceremony. Called *moguru*, it is a ceremony in which novices are fed a medicine containing *vulva secretion* and *sperm*. Sexual instruction is given here to boys and girls together. The girls (but not, in Landtman's account, explicitly the boys) perform sexual acts to generate these secretions in adults. Both sexes are thus initiated into sexual life at some point during this ceremony. Irrespective of the presence or absence of (RH) in precontact Mawata, the growth-promoting medium is never stated to be sperm but always a mixture of sperm and vulva secretions. The same substance is, in effect, applied externally and internally to male novices during Marind-anim and Kimam ceremonies, but the literature always refers to this as sperm and indicates it was applied only to boys. One wonders whether the female component of this substance was treated as neutral. Certainly the Sambia, Kaluli, and Etoro used only semen for these ritual treatments.

This intermediate position of Kiwai appears most clearly in the *mimia,* or fire ceremony. The goddess honored in this important rite is another kind of bionic woman but with a difference. Known as Mimia-Abere, she tempted many men. She seduced Badabada in a boat, dropped her nose-stick in the water, made him dive for it, and then tried to kill him with the paddle when he came up. Still alive, he chased her, but she escaped by causing a certain grass (*mimia*) to grow so densely about her that no one could find her. She is usually pictured in the company of adopted girl attendants with whom she catches crabs. She is the mother of the northwest wind (wet monsoon). She killed all the people on her island except the adopted girls. When she threw down her grass skirt, a banana tree grew there. Her girls were subsequently transformed into ant hills. The headless body of one of the girls became a drum. Once, when Abere was having intercourse in a boat, the rocking caused waves in the sea. Afterward, the man washed his penis in the sea, which has ever since been muddy near Kiwai. Abere and her girls shared a lover called Mesede, who shot the crocodile that killed Abere's son. Abere and the girls rolled Mesede's hair tresses with mud; then they all had intercourse secretly in the men's cult house. Names for Abere's girls are used for effigies carved on posts of the cult house and, by extension, for the posts themselves.

Landtman has recorded a song describing the building of Abere's house and her journey (1927:428–431). In this song she is identified with the deity who created the cult house, the customs surrounding it, and the rules for constructing it.[22] Abere and her companions dance in the cult house, but afterward they pull it down. They take it away on a raft which falls apart at sea. Abere and some of her people nonetheless reach Kiwai, bringing the sago plant (as husband for the girls), bananas, yams, taro, and the like to the Kiwai people.

There are two sides to Abere: she is creator and benefactor. At the same time she and her girls resemble the Gandei women in the Sambia tale recorded by Herdt (1981:appendix E), who likewise killed all the men and took a giant tree as a husband. As ambivalent as the Greek goddess Cybele, she is a unique figure found on the boundary between (RH) and non-(RH) cultures who reunites two opposing views of the place of women in society. The suggestion that there are in fact two such opposing conceptions in New Guinea is not new; it has been systematically demonstrated recently by Marilyn Strathern (1981). By the same token, many cases can be found that are intermediate between the Melpa or Baktaman and the Trobriand Islanders as described by Weiner (1976). In the preceding discussion I have described such intermediate cases, which are marked by strong competition between the sexes and a multiplicity of competitive strategies, of which (RH) is one. Kiwai are situated at the boundary between two different competitive strategies. They are intermediate between a culture area (situated to the west and north) in which the CBI mother figure remains the dominant image of woman, with all the wantonness and castration fantasies such a view entails, and another area wherein that image is more positive, where woman is revered for what she has created, where she is more easily accorded a respected place in the community, and where she is protected, along with men, against sexual pollution. It is in this second area that, for example, the Orokaiva and the Elema are found; also included here are large parts of the Sepik.[23] This area is by no means free of sexual competition, nor of sexism, but such is mitigated by strong bonds between brother and sister and by the destruction, rather than the cultivation, of the negative mother prototype.

CONCLUSION

The discussion has so far remained on the periphery of the major hypotheses put forward by Herdt in chapter 4. Herdt wishes to demonstrate "the symbolic relationship between ideas about semen and the various forms of sexual transactions in Sambia society." To this end he advances what seems to me a brilliant hypothesis: "Sexual contacts may be defined according to the acquisition of a scarce commodity." The best way to conclude this long essay is by commenting on this hypothesis, which I sustain, though in a slightly qualified form.

First let me say that the creation of a self-identity is basically the reproduction within oneself of earlier models that are being absorbed (with transformations) through the mediation of other persons or cultural products. This process of reproduction may be symbolized in many ways, the transmission of semen being only one. Even though one may like to describe such reproduction metaphorically as a "transaction," one must distinguish between transactions by which the social self is reproduced from generation to generation, and transactions in which external products of the self (pigs, ornaments, and the like) are traded between exchange partners as a means of establishing and maintaining a network of associations.

The distinction suggested here is made several times in my own writings but more recently also by Andrew Strathern (1979), Marilyn Strathern (1981), Annette Weiner (1979, 1980) and Daniel de Coppet (1981). I refer to it as a distinction between metonymic and metaphoric gifts, but Weiner and de Coppet prefer to distinguish between "reciprocity" and "reproduction." The latter terminology is especially useful since the "reproduction" to which these authors refer always involves the transmission of spirit essence from an ancestor to a living man (in whom the spirit is being "reproduced"). Now it seems clear that ritualized homosexuality involves precisely that sort of transmission, the senior partner mediating between the ancestor and the novice. For spirit essence originating in an ancestor, and immanent in semen, is transmitted to a junior through a semen transaction. This principle underlies "miraculous" physical growth in the novice. It is a principle that depends, as Layard (1942) recognized, on an extreme reverence accorded the penis and a belief in the extreme holiness of the male.

The suggestion made here is that the notion of a "semen transaction" in that sense depends on a certain conception of women. For it is no accident that in the Sambia calculus, the semen *expenditure* in sleeping with a woman is much higher than that from sleeping with a man. Why is the effort so much greater? Perhaps it is the burden of sexual competition that makes it so hard. If (RH) can be reduced to any social laws, to any correlations, it may be linked to the degree to which women are a threat or a danger, not just to men but to the functioning of the community as a whole. For Orokaiva, I have shown that the perceived threat is comparatively mild. Hauser-Schaeublin's (1977) excellent ethnography of the Iatmul gives the impression that there the competitive threat perceived by males may be more severe.[24] Van Baal's (1966) assessment of women's position in Irian Jaya where (RH) is especially prevalent suggests that there again (RH) may have been a reaction to the fear of female dominance. The evidence is less explicit for Sambia, Etoro, or Kaluli, but it points in the same direction. In contrast, we find little (RH) in those New Guinean societies, prevalent in the Highlands, in which women's position is notably weak (Meggitt 1964; A. Strathern 1969).

All (RH) societies discussed by Herdt (chap. 1) have marriage systems where partners are preferentially taken from a category of fairly close relatives. If Strathern's and Meggitt's empirical generalizations hold, these are societies wherein women hold a relatively strong position. At the same time, these women still owe loyalty to social groups different from those of their husbands. They are likely to promote their brothers' political and military interests (Allen 1967). Groups are small enough to be highly vulnerable internally. Thus, male ritual secrecy and (RH) are male warriors' responses to such perceived threats. These responses tend to be rationalized by the cultivation of fantasies about the masculinized female and by doctrines about the extreme holiness of the penis.

My conclusions differ in two minor ways from Herdt's perspectives in the introduction to this volume. First, I have not taken account of the diffusionist theories proposed there. This is not because I doubt the correctness of the migration paths traced by Herdt, but because my own studies in Oro Province show a bewildering variety of migration paths in all directions, so that I begin to suspect that culture elements from anywhere in New Guinea may easily be diffused to any other part of New Guinea. Second, I doubt whether (RH) societies are necessarily those where women's status is lowest. My own analysis has certainly confirmed and emphasized Herdt's contention that (RH) is the product of warrior societies welding together a fighting force by various ritual procedures, where initiatory status and, in certain cases, homosexuality, become part of the male gender identity of the warrior. My analysis of (RH), however, links this form to patterns of sexual competition rather than to sexual dominance. I believe that only further research will provide answers to these complex problems.

These minor differences should not obscure that our separate analyses, pursued from different vantage points, agree on essentials. The crucial point, supported by all contributors to this volume, is that these cultures are sexually restrictive. It is perhaps because of this polarity that Melanesia has proved such a rich source of information on sexual symbolism, based on the most varied fantasies (whether they were acted on or merely imagined is a secondary question). If we tend so often to turn to New Guinea to extend our insight into *the nature of sex,* this is precisely because sex is often problematic to New Guineans. Their reflections, their insights, even more than their practice, have led Westerners to inquire and to search for understanding.

NOTES

1. Unfortunately, no adequate choreographic analysis of these dances and beats is yet available. A description of Aika beats is given in Williams (1930:222–223). In contrast to Aika, singing accompanies all Orokaiva beats except *pururu.*
2. The term *homosensual* is definitely not used here to suggest that the phenomenon it characterizes resembles the habitualized same-sex intercourse of homosexuality, but rather to emphasize that no sense can be made of *homosexuality* unless it is seen as a relation between two persons of the same sex emitting body signs to each other. I am suggesting that there is homology between body signs in homosexuality and body signs between dancers of the same sex. It is this sign-emitting, sensual, communicational aspect rather than the erotic aspect of homosexuality that is being considered in this article, in line with a general semiotic perspective in anthropology.
3. Though the individual remains the minimal unit of religious experience in a subjective, psychological sense, the practice is for each member of a couple to gain religious experience by using the other as mediator. Hence the couple is the minimal social unit.
4. Again, this homomorphism emphatically does not suggest a physical relation between dancing and homosexuality, but refers to

signs emitted in body language. It is a homomorphism between formal patterns of movement of the dance and formal patterns of social relationships arising in ritual homosexuality and expressed in physical acts.

5. This is not the place for a general discussion of the structural comparative method, but see Lévi-Strauss (1958, 1962, 1973) and Schwimmer (1981a, 1981b).

6. De Coster (1978) argues that analogy is a useful tool in the social sciences inasmuch as it may establish important parallels between levels of conceptualization that cannot be correlated by statistics or other empirical means. He develops his argument on the basis of examples taken from Weber, Panovsky, and Lévi-Strauss; and De Coster does not deny that such "analogies" have a subjective aspect, inasmuch as they always require an investigator to point them out. Yet, even if the theological "meaning" of cathedrals, for instance, can be read only because Panovsky *asked the question,* he was still rigorously objective in the way he derived the answer. Semiotic anthropology requires the same license and the same constraint. (On this epistemological principle, see Schwimmer 1982b.)

7. Stoller's (1968, 1975) view, though based mostly on his analysis of cases of transsexualism, has a wide cross-cultural application, as Herdt (1981) already recognized. We are indebted to Stoller for the important distinction he made between "sex" and "gender," for this not only elucidates his own clinical materials but also certain New Guinea childrearing practices.

8. For the useful term *public symbols,* I am indebted to Firth's (1973) distinction between public and private.

9. Andre Iteanu, personal communication. He has not, however, observed the use of spears or other manifestations of female transvestism.

10. Dr. Brigitta Hauser-Schaeublin, whose restudy of the Iatmul (1977) is based on close observation, suggests that Iatmul do not have today, nor had in the past, (RH) in any explicit form, even though they employ a wealth of symbolism alluding to homosexual practices (personal communication, 14 December 1982).

11. Though women play a ritual role among Marind-anim, Kimam, Keraki, and others, their role seems limited to aiding in the procurement of semen through intercourse. A good example of ideological suppression of the feminine theme among (RH) groups is found in Godelier's (1982a:111–113) analysis of a sun/moon origin myth among Baruya. The exoteric version gives sun/moon as husband/wife figures, but in the version told to initiates, these figures become elder brother/younger brother (the ritual term for wife is *younger brother*). For an insightful discussion of the suppression of the feminine theme in (RH) and other Papua New Guinea cultures, see Hauser-Schaeublin (1977–1978).

289

12. At the time Barker made his study, initiation had been discontinued for almost twenty years. Though he obtained useful data, these do not include the transaction between men and spirits that usually forms part of initiation. The main ceremony is omitted.

13. For an analysis of the Orokaiva friendship system, see Schwimmer 1975. The three chief concepts are those of brother (*apa/eambo* or *namei*), cross-cousin (*simbo*), and *otavo* (partner). Dancing partners are *otavo*, though these may sometimes also be kinsmen of the *apa/eambo* or *simbo* categories. *Otavo* relations as such are competitive, for partners vie with each other in trade, prowess in war, hospitality, and expressiveness in dance. Outside their particular shared activity, *otavo* need have no obligation to one another.

14. This analysis of Wasia, based on a comparison of Orokaiva, Sirorata and Ai'i material, is fully developed in Schwimmer 1981*a*.

15. The dry/wet opposition is fully presented in ideological and mythic material from Ai'i and Orokaiva, in Barker 1975 and in Schwimmer 1981*a*. Space precludes the detailed presentation of this material here.

16. My inquiry into secrecy (Schwimmer 1980, 1981*b*) employed a model showing relations between the secret-holder, the secret-sharer, and the party excluded from the secret. This last party tends to be the object of secret discourse between the others. Discourse between the secret-holder and the excluded partner is included in the model.

17. The bionic woman is part of a set of contemporary television characters of American origin. The set as a whole is of anthropological interest because they impersonate superhuman powers that Augé (1982) would classify as pagan. They are not bound by laws of nature and can be unambiguously classified as divine or diabolic, for some protect the innocent and punish only the guilty, whereas the others afflict the innocent. The most famous of these figures is Superman. The bionic woman belongs in the divine category. Her distinctive characteristic is that she has all the features of the conventional American female sex symbol (except for her superhuman strength and independence of the laws of nature). Her beauty attracts and unbalances the evil characters she is supposed to punish afterward. The general message she appears to convey is that it is dangerous to give in to the erotic attraction one might feel toward the bionic woman (i.e., the generalized American female sex symbol). Perhaps she is, in another sense, the mythological expression of the women's liberation movement.

18. We treat brother/sister incest cases as equivalent to CBI mothers, in that New Guineans say females of all ages have this power to weaken a man and to threaten his masculine identity.

19. There is less emphasis on revenge in Etoro and Sambia representations of the CBI mother. This may be related to the fellatio/breast-

feeding theme in these cultures. It may also be that the choice of distant (RH) partners (more distant than for the preferential category of marriage partners among Etoro) makes them more suitable—because they are nonkin—to act as initiatory mothers.

20. Interesting resemblances in kinship, residence, religion, ritual, and other aspects of culture may be traced between Elema (Williams 1940a, 1976), Purari (Williams 1924), Kiwai, and other tribes on the Gulf coast. These apply especially to ceremonial institutions that are closely related.

21. We refer here to the Mawata practice observed by Landtman (1927), not the practice at Masingle where Beardmore (1890) noted homosexuality. At the same time, Landtman's account ends at a point where we would have expected some sequel, some further ritual acts and additional attention to the growth process.

22. Williams alluded to such a deity several times in his works about the Elema and the Purari, without ever obtaining specific data such as given by Landtman.

23. The near equality and strong rivalry between the sexes along the coast of the Sepik provinces is reported not only by Hogbin but also by Mead (1935, 1938–1949) and B. Blackwood (1951). It was further confirmed (personal communications) by some recent ethnographers who studied the region with this kind of question in mind: Kathleen Barlow and David Lipset (Murik Lakes), and Nancy Lutkehaus (Manam). Ms. Lutkehaus noted that man/woman relationships follow this pattern of near equality and strong rivalry along the whole coastal area, stretching from Wogeo Island to the mouth of the Sepik River.

24. This study abounds in convincing insights about man/woman relations among the Iatmul. Hauser-Schaeublin used female informants to a far greater extent than did Bateson, and she concludes that while men wish to make a clear and emphatic distinction between masculine and feminine spheres, women pursue a "synthesis." At the same time, Iatmul institutions expressing uterus-envy are much stronger than the corresponding Orokaiva institutions. This is not to say that (RH) correlates directly with the degree of uterus-envy in a culture. Rather, I argue that societies having strong sex competition tend to have elaborate institutions expressing uterus-envy (cf. Mead 1949). (RH) is never more than one of the forms such institutions may take. It is not known why this form is taken rather than another, and I do not believe that any objective factors determine the choice of particular forms in institutions serving a particular need in any given culture.

7 Laurent Serpenti

The Ritual Meaning of Homosexuality and Pedophilia among the Kimam-Papuans of South Irian Jaya

INTRODUCTION

Kolepom* is a low-lying island on the south coast of West Irian. In the rainy season the island resembles an inland sea, and only a few small places remain dry. In the dry season it is a vast muddy swamp. Vegetation is limited to innumerable varieties of reeds and rushes.

The population of approximately 7,000 people is distributed unevenly over twenty-five villages scattered over the swamps. Communication between the villages is limited almost exclusively to the period of the wet season, when small dugouts can be used. Even then, it takes three or four days to cross the island from the district capital Kimam, in the east, to Kalilam in the west. The inaccessibility of the swamps explains the relatively late introduction of colonial administration and missionary activity.

*Prince Frederik Hendrik Island.

292

Agriculture, the chief means of subsistence, has developed to quite a high level. All agricultural ground as well as the ground needed for dwelling houses has to be artificially obtained. The choice of seed plants, the composting of the soil, and the restoration of the level of the island are matters of constant concern. Each plant is separately planted and tended (Van Heurn 1957). Nevertheless, in such unfavorable natural circumstances, the food situation remains most precarious.

The dwelling island or *patha* is basic to the social organization of the village. A patha generally consists of the nuclear families of a father and those of one or more of his real or adopted sons, or the families of a number of brothers. If the patha-group grows too large, one or more of the families may build a new island, usually in the vicinity. Dwelling islands that are genealogically connected in this way form a territorial group of a higher order, called *kwanda*. In small villages, there are only two kwanda, which are then designated as *paburu* (village-sector). In the more populous villages, the paburu consists of two or even more kwanda. A distinct feature of social organization is the fact that the village-sectors oppose one another in a ceremonial and antagonistic relationship. This bipartite division exists also on the level of the paburu, where the constituent kwanda form two rival groups.

Marriage-exchange, preferably exchange of sisters, takes place between the kwanda. In practice the kwanda is exogamous, but the paburu need not necessarily be so, except where the kwanda is identical with the paburu. In view of the prevalent virilocal residence, the kwanda gives the impression of being patrilineal. People do not, however, reckon kinship in a patrilineal way: kinship groups have a bilateral character. The significance of local and kinship groups is seen most clearly in the feasts marking the different stages in the period of mourning. When a person dies, his closest relatives are not allowed to appear in public, except when covered from head to toe in a plaited hood. The gardens of the deceased are, from the moment of his death, taboo for everyone in his paburu. The fruits from the gardens, especially the coconuts, are carefully preserved to be handed over to the ceremonially opposite village-sector at the next mortuary feast. At each successive feast more gardens are closed and, as the period of mourning progresses, all the gardens of the paburu fall under the taboo.

293

When the dry season comes, following a person's death, as many islands as possible are planted with yams. There is a very close connection between yams and men, which is expressed clearly in a myth associated with the origin of yams. In this myth, the planting of yams is equated with the interment of a person whose rebirth, in the form of a yam, occurs at the same time as the harvest.

It is at the final mortuary feast that the greatest exchange of food takes place between the two constituent sectors of a village. This feast is generally known as *ndambu*. The feast has acquired a highly competitive character—sometimes to such an extent that the ritual nature of ndambu is subordinate to the competitive elements (cf. Mauss 1954).

ATTITUDES TOWARD SEXUALITY

Rules and regulations regarding sexual behavior on Kolepom are complex and sometimes seem paradoxical. Only by studying the underlying conceptual framework is it possible to grasp their fundamental meaning.

Sexual behavior is an important matter which can never be taken for granted. It pervades all aspects of life because of its influence on matters of paramount importance for survival. There is a considerable difference in belief between male and female sexuality as far as the meaning and function of sexuality are concerned. Female sexuality is potentially dangerous for men and for society, as is most clearly demonstrated in the myth of Koné.

Koné is a woman who has no husband and who therefore tries to molest men whenever possible. When the women are out fishing and a man is alone in the house, she may come to tempt him. The man tries to pull off the hood (the mourning cape) she is wearing over her head, which is, however, impossible since it is part of her body. The man then recognizes her and will take to his heels with some excuse or other. Traditionally he used to go straight to the *burawa*, the bachelor's house, and tell the men there that Koné had invited him. It is very dangerous to have sexual intercourse with Koné, for with her vagina she cuts off the man's penis, to take home with her.

Once upon a time a young man wanted to find out if what the

men said about Koné was true. When Koné came to visit him and lay down, he said, "Wait a moment, I am very hot, I will have a bath first." He went outside and cut off the sprout of a banana tree. Returning to Koné he put this sprout into her vagina and ran off to the burawa. When, later the men went to have a look, the sprout was cut through. Nowadays Koné lives somewhere in the old village-sector of Bomerou, behind a tree. No man will ever pass this tree alone, for fear of being raped.

Occasions are numerous in which sexual intercourse is forbidden or at least undesirable. They center mostly around typical male activities; for instance, before a wrestling match, before a hunting expedition, or while making a drum or a big canoe. If one loses during the match or the hunt, the spoils are disappointing; a common reproach is that the person in question had had intercourse the night before. Not only is intercourse strictly forbidden while making a drum or a big canoe, women are not even allowed to touch these items.

The prohibition on heterosexual intercourse is most rigidly enjoyed during the planting period of ceremonial crops. It applies to all who have planted yams. A man is not allowed to accept food from any woman except his wife, for fear she has had sexual intercourse. A planter does not even chew betel with a nonplanter because the latter may have had sexual intercourse. The sorcerer who prepares the "medicine" for the promotion of the growing crops may have a dream that one of his clients has had sexual intercourse. This dream invariably results in communal questioning; and if someone pleads guilty, it results in a severe warning or beating up. Sexual intercourse is not only harmful to the crops but also to the trespasser himself, who runs the risk of becoming physically weak or short-winded, or of developing pains in his chest or sores on his penis.

The fear of heterosexual intercourse in crisis situations sometimes leads to a general avoidance of women. During the planting season, for instance, the woman is not allowed to sit in the man's place; at night she must sleep in a different part of the house. Formerly, special houses were built in which women stayed day and night until this ban was lifted. Women are especially dangerous during menstruation. In the western part of the island, women still reside in a separate menstrual hut during their periods. They are also instructed to stay away from the yam fields, for their presence might have an unfavorable influence upon the growth of the crop. During the planting season, moreover, a menstruating woman should be generally avoided at all costs.

The second period of sexual abstention is the period after childbirth. Now the crisis situation centers around the woman—and her husband is potentially dangerous, threatening her easy delivery and the health of the child. Everywhere on the island the husband is prohibited from seeing his wife during or shortly after her confinement, not even to come near her. Other men, too, are strictly prohibited from approaching her.

As long as the navel string has not fallen off, both husband and wife are subject to strict rules of taboo. The birth process is considered unfinished and, especially during this time, the man's actions may greatly influence the child's health. He is not allowed to leave the house or to do any heavy work outside. In native belief, he is not allowed to touch water because that would make the child "cold"; nor may he see the child lest it grow old too quickly. He must keep away from people who have planted taro or yams, for that contact might sap his wife's vitality and eventually cause the infant's death.

Even after the umbilical cord drops off, the man should avoid all places and opportunities in which he could meet with evil influences. Should he approach such places too closely, he is also endangered, apart from the danger the man represents for his child's health and for the woman. Sexual intercourse is strictly prohibited for the time being: the man would be sexually using "the child's road," (birth canal) thus depriving the infant of its chance to get safely through the difficult early period of its life. Every care must be taken not to damage its bond to its mother.

CHILDREN'S FEASTS

The successive feasts that are given for the children must be regarded as stages in the process of loosening the ties with their mother. This process is especially significant for boys. The number and ritual salience of girls' feasts are limited to occasions marking biological transitions, as, for instance, with appearance of the first pubic hair, menstruation, and consequently the first wearing of the *tjatowa* (grass pubic covering).

When the infant is about two or three months old, the feast called *warowonèjere* is celebrated. The child is carried to the threshold of his parents' house, where he is held by a woman helper. The mother stays inside, near the door, but she is not visible to visitors. At this feast the husband thus sees his newborn son for the first time and sees his wife again following the birth.

The second feast is celebrated when the boy-child starts crawling around. The child is carried through the village on the shoulders of his mother's brother or by another man whose child is ceremonially held in the same way by the first child's father. It is significant that at this stage the ritual action is no longer performed by a woman, but by one of her male relatives. From then on the child is allowed to go where he pleases in the village and neither of his parents are subject to restrictions (including prohibitions on sexual intercourse). Ideally it is the child's MB who performs the ritual; and, from that time on, a lifelong joking relationship exists between them. This joking relationship is, however, sometimes socially inherited, so that in actual practice it sometimes is not the MB, but the FMB or another relative who is in charge. More important is the fact that he is a member of the opposing paburu. In this and subsequent feasts, it is also significant that celebrations always take place during the final feast for the dead.

The next phase in the social development of the boy is precipitated by the phase in which he starts walking. The potential danger to the child remains but is eventually diminished enough that the taboo on eating ceremonial crops is lifted. After the child has eaten ceremonially of the yam, the parents are also allowed to eat feast crops again. The feast in which the underlying conceptions regarding the boy's physical and mental development are most clearly expressed is the feast of the shaving of his hair, called *munawarre* (*muna*, hair, *warre*, doing away). The age at which this ritual is performed varies from approximately four to six years. The ritual action is meant to remove the last remnants of the child's birth and his remaining associations with the womb, because his first hair is the same he had when he first emerged from his mother's womb. As long as the child is small, he cannot do without the tie

297

to his mother, so cutting his hair would mean exposing him to great danger. Because of this, when the feast is celebrated at an early age, a small tuft of hair is sometimes left on top of his head so that the physical separation between mother and child is not perceived as being too sudden. Eventually it has to be removed since this hair may become a hindrance to his subsequent growth, for it "pulls" the child back, as it were, to the womb. The hair is shorn by the same relative who is in charge of the rituals during the earlier children's feasts.

The shaving of the hair not only marks separation from the mother, it also starts the process of progressive association with the males, culminating in ritual entry into the bachelor's house some years later. By breaking off the ties with his mother, the child's well-being and growth is now primarily the father's responsibility. The man who cuts the hair must give the mother a canoe, a paddle, and a string of dog's teeth, in part as payment for "the pain and trouble of providing birth," and in part as compensation for "handing" the child over to its father. The father is obliged to supply a pig which is laid on top of the other accumulated feast food. The child is then placed atop the pig and stays there while his hair is cut with a sharp bamboo knife. The child's links to his mother, and his responsibility toward her later, are symbolized by the fact that the hair is not allowed to drop directly onto the ground. The hair must fall on the food, preferably on the most valuable item, the pig, in order to emphasize that the child should always remember to give her food whenever she is in need of it. Afterward, the hair (at least in the eastern and northern villages) is placed in a sago tree, which becomes from that moment the unalienable property of the boy, and at the same time reminds him that he should later plant sago trees for his mother's use. A direct ritual reference to the bachelor's house is implied also in men's explanation of the shaving ritual, to the effect that the new hair is now stronger and can bear easily the hair lengthenings that boys have during their stay in the bachelor's house.

Subsequent feasts are all more or less repeats of the munawarre feast: those for the piercing of the earlobes, the nostrils, and the nasal septum. The holes are made to wear the ornaments that signify the growing boy's status as a man in the community; for example, the pig's bone through his septum shows that he is a headhunter. The blood that flows from the piercing is supposed to be womb blood that must be removed symbolically. These ceremonies proceed in the same way as the previous ones. The same relative also performs the ritual procedure while the boy sits on top of the food, allowing the boy's blood to drop on it. The feasts following the munawarre feast, however, are no longer celebrated in any of the villages, not only as a result of the missionaries' disapproval but no doubt also because they were always considered to be of minor importance.

BURAWA, THE BACHELOR'S HOUSE

During my fieldwork there were no longer any overt sexual manifestations of the bachelor's house. This void was due to government and missionary measures aimed at eradicating, as completely as possible, all sexual customs and beliefs that in one way or another were connected with the burawa. From the beginning of missionary and government interference, this aspect of Kolepom culture was regarded with disfavor (Fikkert 1928). From the Dutch government's point of view, such disfavor was mainly because Kolepom culture was thought to be strongly influenced by the neighboring Marind-anim; in the Dutch government's opinion, this referred to the rapid spread of venereal granulomae as a consequence of promiscuous sexual intercourse (during rituals) which could cause sterility and consequent extinction of the population— as had almost happened earlier to the Marind-anim (Van Baal 1966).

The Roman Catholic mission has always held rather negative attitudes toward sexuality in general, and to those aspects of sexual behavior that deviate from the strict monogamous, marital pattern of Western culture, in particular. Many a missionary expressed the opinion that, in newly Christianized societies, the obvious and ineradicable deviations from the rules of Western societies should be avoided and prevented. This attitude explains to a certain extent their intransigent efforts to wipe out all cultural manifestations, as, for instance, traditional dances and games, which in one way or another could revive ritual sexuality. The scanty information that gradually became available concerning rituals and ceremonies in the bachelor's house provided all the more reason for both missionaries and government officials to persist in their attitude. Any past attempts of the natives to reinstate the bachelor's house, such as were made in the village of Teri in 1961, were nipped in the bud. Although middle-aged and old men could still provide me with reliable information, for they had all passed through the various stages of the bachelor's house, I was not able to personally attend any ceremonies to verify my information. Moreover, as a result of the above-mentioned government and missionary attitude, people tended to be secretive, especially on these subjects, for fear of imprisonment or other kind of punishment. Information is therefore rather scanty and, on important points, incomplete, which means that we have to look into the whole of our ethnographic data for support of evidence when certain data are insufficient.

In some respects there is considerable variation in customs regarding the bachelor's house, between the swamp villages in the central and northern parts of the island, on the one hand, and in the western villages, on the other. Even within these broad categories, though, there are numerous other variations I shall not describe in detail because they are of minor importance.

The age at which boys enter the bachelor's house varies considerably in all villages, since it is dependent upon the simultaneous celebration of the final feast for a dead person. On this occasion a number of boys of varying ages, from about ten to fourteen years, are admitted. (Sometimes the boys are even younger.) The entry in the bachelor's house is nowhere dependent on visible signs of biological transition from boyhood to adulthood. Yet, the fact that admission into the bachelor's house always takes place during the final mourning feast is in no way coincidental, as we shall discuss later. The final feast consists of a competitive feast sequence (*ndambu*) in which the handing over of the ceremonial yams to the opposite village-sector is the most important part (see Serpenti 1972). Afterward there is a competitive dance between the village-sectors until shortly before sunrise. At this feast, the ban on sexual intercourse with women is lifted. During the dance, promiscuous intercourse takes place with the women who participate in the dancing.

The scanty information available on this dance leads to the

conclusion that there were few sexual rules to be observed except for the prohibition of incestuous intercourse (cf. Van Baal, chap. 3). Informants in the western villages were quite clear on the point that all women were sexually available to all men. When entering the house in which sexual intercourse took place, men had to be informed of the corner their female relatives slept in so that they would take a woman in another corner who was not in any way related.

The first reports of missionaries and government officials mention the custom of "testing" sexually the marriageable girls. According to informants, the intention was to see whether the girls could stand the test. If they felt ill after intercourse, it was proof that they were not yet suited for marriage. It is possible that this trial took place during the promiscuous sexual intercourse of the ndambu festival.

As the dance draws to an end in the early morning hours, the boy is prepared by his older relatives for departure. His face is painted in the same way as a dead man's: using betel juice, two curved lines are drawn from the eyes over the cheeks to the mouth, and short lines are added below the eyes. No variations are permitted, nor is clay or any other paint used. Two or more dugouts are joined by covering them with sago leaves. On this raft the collected food is piled, with a pig on top. The boy initiate is placed on top of the pig, as in the foregoing children's festivities. His female relatives, especially his mother, start wailing and sing the usual mourning songs; they scratch their foreheads and jump into the water to cover themselves with mud. They clasp the boy's legs, caress his face, and move his arms up and down, as it were, to make him live again. This is the usual mourning behavior when somebody has died. In the meantime, the men constantly pour sago over the boy's head and back. This practice is done, according to informants, to ensure that the boy will grow to be a great cultivator. Curiously enough, however, such was also done with the headhunters when they came back from a successful raid. The ritual use of sago, including the placing of the boy's first hair into a sago tree, is still unclear, the more so because sago has probably been a recent introduction on the island, and its significance in other rituals is rather slight.

In the same way as during burial, when the corpse is placed on a similar raft, the women are driven away by the rowers. The rowers belong to the ceremonially opposed village-sector, as is the case also with the people who, during the burial procedure, handle the corpse and dig the grave. Slowly and solemnly the vessel moves toward the dancing place where the people are still dancing. On its arrival, all the men who accompany the raft form a long line and proceed slowly toward the dancing place, with the boy in front. The rhythm of the drums is now accelerated. A man from the opposite village-sector steps forward and suddenly throws a mourning hood over the boy's head. At the same moment, all the drums cease immediately and the dancing comes to an end. The similarity with burial is striking because as soon as someone dies, no drum sounding occurs anywhere until the final feast of the dead. The boy is now taken straight to the bachelor's house. There is little reason to doubt the conclusion that the admission into the bachelor's house is perceived as the boy's ritualized death.

In the western villages where the procedure of admission is different, the same symbolism underlies the ceremony. A prominent part in the ceremony there is the use of the bull-roarer. The instrument is called *yet,* which is also the name of the mythical figure (Yet) it represents. He is, in stature, a kind of superman with a white skin and an extremely long beard. He has a wife and no children. Although he can produce noise (the bull-roarer sound), he cannot speak like ordinary men. Periodically, a large amount of food should be collected for Yet, which he then swallows at once. After the men have called him to come and eat, he returns to his conjugal bed somewhere in a hole in the ground. This procedure happens also when the boys are admitted to the *yetörendör,* the house of Yet. On the island where the food is collected, the men gather with their bull-roarers. In the meantime the young men who are to be initiated stay in a house at the other end of the village, together with their female relatives and MB (*nawa*). At noon, the men start moving slowly in the direction of this house, simultaneously swinging their yets to produce a terrific howling and screeching noise. The women and boys are supposed to believe that Yet is on his way to the house to devour the boys. The women are frightened or pretend to be so, and they are supposed to weep and lament at the loss of their children. When the men arrive at the house they knock three times at the wall. The MB takes hold of the boy and brings him outside while covering the boy's eyes with his hands, for he is not yet allowed to see the bull-roarer. The women are, as a matter of course, not allowed to go or look outside. The MB, other men, and the boy enter a number of dug-outs, while the food is collected and a temporary shelter for the boys is built. Upon arriving, the men swing their bull-roarers to produce an ear-splitting noise; and when the boy's fear has reached a climax, the MB suddenly removes his hands from the boy's eyes so that he finally sees the object producing the sound.

The seclusion of the boys, seen as a ritual death, is initiated and executed by the men. As a consequence they are now responsible for transforming this death into new life, as they do in performing the mourning rites, which aim at a ritual rebirth by accomplishing a transformation of the deceased into a new kind of spiritual being. Similar to the way in which the men were dangerous to the women and infant before, during, and after childbirth, so, too, are the women dangerous to initiates after they have entered the bachelor's house. From then on the boys are not permitted to see any woman, nor are they allowed to go into the water (except in the western villages), or to eat foods taken from the water. In general, the initiates are subject to the same taboos that apply to a pregnant mother. If the boys want to relieve themselves, they must do it during darkness and otherwise hide themselves with the mourning cape so that they cannot be seen by women. The women are not allowed to approach the bachelor's house. In the villages, even eating utensils, being closely associated with women, are carefully kept in a corner of the bachelor's house. The boys must not go near them, lest their teeth drop out and they remain weak all their lives.

The father and the MB are not allowed to see their wives during this time of ritual seclusion, and most definitely cannot have sexual intercourse with them, since that might have a serious effect on the boy's health, making him ill or old before his time.

In the bachelor's house the boys are given a place in a corner that is so narrow that they can not sleep with their legs stretched out. Their posture resembles that of a fetus. In the western villages, however, the boys are forced to sleep sitting up, with their arms and legs stretched "to make them straight limbed." The father and MB take turns watching all night to straighten out the boy's legs should he try to curl up.

(1) To accomplish the task of transforming "deceased" youths into "newly borns," the men use a very powerful medicine: sperm. It is man's life-giving potency, powerful and beneficial. When, for instance, an epidemic strikes the village and causes many deaths, as often happens, promiscuous heterosexual intercourse involving as many people as possible is organized in the village to collect large amounts of semen (probably by coitus interruptus). According to the information collected in the village of Bamol, very young girls are preferably selected for this sexual intercourse. Bamboos are cut, smeared with the sperm, and subsequently set on fire. The exploding bamboos, laden with sperm, frighten all the evil forces that threatened the village. To that end, long bamboo poles, higher than the houses, are smeared also with sperm and erected all around the village.

Sperm is, in a certain sense, the antipole of menstrual blood, the latter being harmful, potentially life-threatening, and female. No wonder sperm plays an important role in the process of rebirth of boys into manhood. Boys' rebirth is achieved in several ways.

At his entry into the cult house, the boy is placed under the charge and guidance of a mentor who is designated as his "adoptive father." This man is supposed to have regular homosexual intercourse with the boy to make him strong with the semen that is inserted into his body through anal intercourse. In the western villages, there is no doubt that the adoptive father is mother's younger brother—nawa—or someone who is placed in the same kinship category. Although information from other villages is less clear on this point, one can safely assume that the same pattern of relationship exists here. The MB has a special position toward his sister's children as a bride-giver in direct exchange marriage. They help each other in planting and harvesting, and they share food. A sister's son displays a conspicuous lack of respect toward his MB, even when there is a substantial difference in age. They play all sorts of pranks on each other, at which neither of them does or should get angry. This relationship is the only one in which the use of obscene language is also permitted, a privilege that is freely used.

In all the village groups, this joking relationship is continued with the sons of the MB. In direct exchange marriages, MBS is also father's sisters' son, which means that a reciprocal joking relationship exists between cross-cousins. Since this relationship may again be taken over by the children of cross-cousins, such joking relationships may be numerous and traditional, which explains the difficulty in tracing back such a relationship to its original nawa-model in some villages (Serpenti 1965:140).

The homosexual adoptive relationship in the bachelor's house exists primarily between two boys, both inmates of the house, but who differ in age and duration of stay. This difference means that the older boy cannot possibly be his real MB. In most cases, he is a real or classificatory cross-cousin. As long as this cross-cousin is older, he is still designated with the term *nawa*, and the same pattern of behavior is applied to him.

There is no indication that homosexual relationships are continued after the boys leave the bachelor's house. On the contrary, as youths grow older—in the last phase of the seclusion period—they perform these sexual duties toward the younger boys less regularly, and they cease them altogether when they secretly start meeting sexually with women. Nevertheless, a lifelong emotional relationship often results from homosexual relationships. I even had the impression that many an adoptive relationship originated, in fact, not so much from an adoptive agreement with the boy's father as from casual erotic experiences with the bachelor's house. In practice, the cross-cousin relationship is extended to such a degree that everyone who is not classified as a real or classificatory brother can be a homosexual partner in such relationships. As far as the eastern and northern Kolepom groups are concerned, however, the institutionalized form of their homosexual relationships on a regular basis is confined to the one mentor.

At their entry into the bachelor's house, the boys are painted black all over their bodies. This paint is sometimes a mixture of charcoal and coconut oil. According to some informants, however, sperm, not coconut oil, is used in the mixture. This paint should not be removed as long as the boys are designated as *munaka* (a term which is first used here in the bachelor's house). They are therefore forbidden also to go into the water during this period.

On the day of his entry to the cult house, the boy also receives

305

the hair lengthenings for the first time. The "mentor" is in charge of preparing and applying them. It is a rather painful operation, since the short strands of hair give little grip. The appendages for the munaka may only be made from areca or sago leaves. The material used for the hairdo, as well as the length of the appendages, distinguishes the several ritual grades in the bachelor's house. For the munaka, the appendages come down no farther than the ears. In order that the strands of hair can bear the plaited sago leaves, they are rubbed with sperm to make the hair strong, and sometimes the hair appendages are treated also in that way. In contrast to the western villages, where the hair lengthenings are used only as adornment during dance festivals, in the central and eastern swamp villages great importance is attached to the hair. The appendages are a sign of growing manhood. It is the "male" hair which grows in the bachelor's house, in contrast to the first head hair that originates in the womb. The reasons why the hair appendages (and, in relation to these, the munawarre feast) are considered so important in these villages is still unclear. It is true that these villages, more than the western ones, are influenced by Marind-anim culture, which valuates the hair. There are, however, many other borrowed elements from Marind-anim culture that do not seem to have acquired great significance (Van Baal 1966). In my view this custom fits well into the social thought of Kolepom people because, on the one hand, hair is a visible sign of biological growth, while on the other it is a part of the body that can be manipulated without harm for "growth."

Especially in the western villages, I had the impression that homosexual relations are considered very important. More men are involved, and sexual intercourse takes place more frequently than in the central and eastern villages. My information reveals that sometimes seven or more men have anal intercourse with the boy during the same night. In other villages, homosexual intercourse is not considered sufficient to make the boy strong. To ensure that the boy grows into a productive member of society, the most prestigious men in the villages are in charge of conveying to the boy their special qualities as a cultivator (warrewundu) or as a headhunter (pangi).

On the day of entry to the cult house, the mentor makes incisions (using a sharp piece of bamboo) for the first time in the boy's upper arms, upper legs, and abdomen. These wounds are rubbed with the semen of headhunters and cultivators in order to increase the initiate's strength. Another related idea is that the sperm penetrates the boy's body at the places where strength is most needed. The most distinguished headhunters rub the boy's right arm, a lesser one the left arm, while the cultivators are in charge of his legs and abdomen. The sperm-rubbing does not take place in the bachelor's house: the boys are taken to a nearby coconut island after sunset. For a couple of days the boys that have been treated in this way are not allowed to touch water, lest the sperm not fully penetrate them.

(2) For the purpose of arousing the men and producing the next needed sperm, a complicated system of reciprocal rights and obligations is set in motion. Betrothal is normally arranged at a very early age. At the time the boy goes to the bachelor's house, the girl betrothed to him moves into his parents' house. And from this moment onward the boy's father has authority over her. The boy is not allowed to see her, and in some instances does not even know who his fiancée is. Apart from her share in the domestic duties, she is also indispensable in making her future husband strong and vigorous by putting herself at the disposal of the village adult men, in order to stimulate ejaculation. While the boy is being incised, the older men go to the house of the boy's father. Striking the bottom of the canoe with a punting-pole is a signal to the girl. When she comes out of the house, she is taken by the waist and laid down in the canoe. She is not supposed to resist. The parents-in-law know that she is going to have sexual intercourse with the older men; however, they pretend to be ignorant of what is going on, for between father-in-law and daughter-in-law allusions to sexuality are strictly forbidden. It should be stressed here that in these and other cases of sexual license, incest rules are strictly observed. The girl is taken to the island where, on one side, the boy munaka is waiting, and on the other side, intercourse with the girl takes place. The sperm is collected in a banana leaf and brought to the boy. After rubbing it on his body, the boy is thrown into the air by the men. This is done for a group of boys. If they happen to fall on their feet, the boys are considered already strong. If, however, they fell on their knees or back, they still have to be rubbed many times.

Ethnographic information from several sources seems to confirm that the boy's fiancée's obligation to engage in sex with the men can be taken over by the boy's mentor's betrothed. In such cases the mentor, who himself has sexual rights over the boy, puts his betrothed at the disposal of the men to collect the sperm for rubbing his pupil. Previously (Serpenti 1965:164) I attributed this custom (of having the mentor's fiancée act as a stand-in) to sexual immaturity on the part of the boy's betrothed. In reconsidering the data, I am not so certain whether this is such a relevant factor. Information about the exact age of the girls after more than twenty years is difficult and essentially unreliable. The best indication consists of descriptions stating the girls were "very young." The first missionaries were in a better position to estimate the approximate age of the girls. They regularly made mention of schoolgirls who, for days on end, did not attend the mission school because they were sick after intercourse with a number of mature men. In his diary, Father Thieman (n.d.) mentions a number of girls (with names and exact age) who took part in sexual intercourse when they were no older than eight. It is not clear whether the age of these girls was derived from a birth register kept by the missionary. Even if it was an estimate, we can safely assume that the girls were not yet sexually mature, because the wearing of the pubic covering as a sign of sexual maturity was well known to the missionaries, which precludes mistakes on this point.

By the same token, informants could have been quite honest in telling me that the sexual duties of the boy's betrothed were taken over by the mentor's fiancée because of sexual immaturity in the former, due to the influence of a long and intensive mission influence which expresses abhorrence of these customs. Moreover, although the girl could be helped by another girl, for instance, her sister or the mentor's fiancée, the latter one need not necessarily be mature. This assistance was considered necessary because many men (ten to fifteen and often more, according to my informants) usually participated in the sexual activities.

Although we do not know how reliable the missionaries' information is on this particular subject, an indirect indication of the frequency of sperm collecting can be acquired from the observed nonattendance of schoolgirls. They were absent rather frequently, and the missionaries interpreted nonattendance as the consequence of illness from frequent cohabitation. However, a girl was not allowed to go outside or to work for three or four days after the intercourse took place, for she might otherwise (sympathetically in magical thought) cancel out the effect of the sperm in the boy (her betrothed).

Until now observers have believed that real intercourse took place, which means coitus interruptus. This could well be the case, although the nonattendance of schoolgirls cannot be taken as proof of it, for the girls were not allowed to go outside. Since the collection of sperm is the aim of the custom, the possibility remains that with the very young girls no real penetration took place, but, rather, that the arousing of sperm was achieved by masturbation or otherwise. An intriguing question in this respect is what place the testing of the girls had in this connection. If actual intercourse took place, the testing of the girls for marriage makes no sense, because they were already used for the purpose of sperm rubbing. It could well be that the custom was explained *as such* but, *in practice,* it was *identical* with the sperm-collecting procedure.

Another interesting problem is why, in a society where wife-lending and promiscuous intercourse were rather frequent, such very young girls were selected for the purpose of sperm rubbing. The answer should at least partly be found in the all-pervading gift-exchange system (Lévi-Strauss 1949, 1958; Mauss 1954). Sexual relations create rights and obligations just as exchanges of food do. As a matter of fact, a stream of "gifts" of a sexual nature is always counterbalanced by a stream of food. The father needs his daughter-in-law to make his son "strong." By the same token, the girls are indirectly responsible for the welfare of their future husbands. Even before marriage a man depends on his wife for his physical well-being, which gives the woman certain claims on her future husband. If, for instance, after his seclusion period, a boy runs away with another girl, the result will often be a fight between the two young women. A common reproach of the deceived girl to her rival is, for instance, "I have always been diligent and I have often had intercourse with the old men, so that my betrothed has grown tall and handsome. You have always been lazy, so your betrothed has remained small. Now you want to steal mine." A large share of the food collected by the boy's father for the feast of his entry is meant for the girl's father or foster father.

309

Another part of the food is earmarked for the men who took the boy to the burawa. This exchange of food merges into the usual exchange pattern between the village parts, since a return gift is made in the other village half, in which one or more boys are simultaneously taken to the *burawa*. The men who have rubbed the boy with their sperm are rewarded with stalks of *wati*, a strong intoxicant. However, since these men are usually the same men who assist the father in collecting the food—and this assistance should be reciprocated with wati—there is again a dovetail into a more complex reciprocal whole. This whole series of obligations is again part of the ndambu festival and consequently of the final mortuary feast in which large quantities of food are exchanged between the moieties.

Apart from its consequences for the intricate gift-exchange system, semen collecting raises another question: Why is it not the wives but the very young girls who are used for the sperm-rubbing ceremony? Here we have the interesting but purely speculative possibility that the females participating in the intercourse are not selected for sexual maturity but, on the contrary, the men have a preference for the sexually immature. One should bear in mind the precautions taken to prevent the boys from touching, seeing, or approaching mature women. The danger that women represent, in this respect, culminates the men's fear of menstrual blood. The "growing of the boy" during this period is paralleled by the "growing of the yam," during which all sexual intercourse with women is prohibited, evidently because of the detrimental effect of menstruation upon the growth and health of the ceremonial yam crop. Unfortunately, our data are too weak to corroborate the assumption that it is the *absence of menstruation* that makes young girls especially suitable for the producing of sperm used for the rubbing of initiates in the bachelor's house.

(3) The third way to provide the boys with the indispensable semen is to let them drink or eat it. To that end the collected sperm is mixed with sago or coconut. This mixture is also used to protect people in case of an epidemic. The mixture is then not only eaten or drunk but also used for rubbing the bodies of everyone, including women and children in the particular village-sector. In such cases, as many mature men as possible are involved in promiscuous intercourse in order to produce the necessary sperm.

The attitude of men toward the boy changes radically from the moment he enters the burawa. Before, people had been very indulgent toward children. Now obedience and respect are demanded of initiates, and any infringement of the ritual rules is severely punished, for instance, by beating him with burning sticks (while he is not allowed to brush the sparks away).

(4) In the western villages, where the custom of sperm rubbing does not exist, the initiates are awakened early before daybreak and then forced by the men to bathe in cold-water streams. Repeated in the evening as well, this is done to accustom the boys to early rising and to the cold. At about 8:00 A.M. they are given their only meal for the day. During the whole initiation period, they are forced to live on a starvation regime to harden them against periods of scarcity. The boys are instructed also in agricultural techniques and magic associated with agriculture. To that end they are given a small garden plot to work on. Myths and head-hunting tales are told, and they are taught how to behave before, during, and after head-hunting expeditions. They are instructed in how to have sexual intercourse with women, and what dangers they represent. They are told that to ward off all her evil influences, they have to rub the woman's body with sperm before copulating with her for the first time. In the western villages, the ritual seclusion period usually lasts no longer than one or two months. In other villages, however, the boys stay on in the bachelor's house for years.

From time to time, the hair appendages are renewed because they decay rather quickly. At the same time, they are lengthened until they reach halfway down the boy's back. On these occasions, the boy is again rubbed with sperm, including his hair and appendages.

(5) Apart from on these occasions, the boy can always take the initiative for having a sperm-rubbing ceremony performed on himself. It is not proper to ask the older men directly; therefore, he can use some customary signal, such as playfully throwing areca nutshells toward them, while casting meaningful glances in the direction of a nearby island.

After a year or more, when new boys are admitted in the bachelor's house, and during the final mortuary feast, the munaka are promoted to the next stage. This ceremony is called *mabukulu*.

At this occasion the boy is given a pubic covering for the first time. It consists of a large cone shell, called *mabu*. *Kulu* is the rope with which it is fastened. The initiates are now called *tjutjine*. The hair appendages are again renewed and lengthened; now they reach all the way down the boy's back. They are no longer made of areca or sago leaves but of a coarse type of reeds split lengthwise (called *tju*). Their bodies are painted to show that they are in the transition period between the lowest and the highest grade: the top half is painted red while the lower half remains black. The hair appendages are painted in both colors. As long as part of the body is black, the boys are not allowed to appear in public, and they are still obliged to wear the mourning cape. On the evening of the day the boy receives the large shell, however, he is led to the dancing place. On his arrival, a few men light up his face so that all who are present, including the women, can see him for a short time. The rest of the night the boy is allowed to participate in the dance. But before sunrise, he covers himself back up with the cape and returns to the burawa, where their dwelling place is now halfway between that of the *mabureede,* the initiates in the highest stage, who sit around the fire in the center, and that of new munaka, who sit in the corners. At this feast again the customary rubbing with sperm takes place.

The next feast is called *bapanda warre* (*bapanda,* mourning cape; *warre,* doing away), which means the casting away of the mourning cape. The youths are now less restricted in their movements. They are allowed some contacts with females, but they are not yet allowed to touch or be intimate with them. In this respect, however, there is a rather great distance between the ritual rule and social reality. Many informants have confirmed that during this period youths start having contact with the girls and having intercourse with them. This heterosexual coitus is connived at as long as it is kept secret and the relationship does not include their own betrothed. The mabureede initiates thus sometimes exchange female sexual partners. Youths are still prohibited to enter their father's house. And all contacts are still arranged through go-betweens. Except for betel and tobacco, these youths have no other food taboos. The hair appendages are again renewed, but they now only reach to their elbows. The large pubic shell is replaced by the small penis-cap that is worn by all adult men. The youths, painted red all over their bodies, now take their place in the center of the burawa around the fire. This is the last occasion on which the boys are smeared with sperm.

The youths are ritually fit for marriage and for leaving the burawa, after they pass a final ceremony, called *purakuru*. It requires them to wriggle their bodies through a narrow opening. To do so they wear a tight-fitting broad belt of plaited rattan. The belt is so narrow that it only just encircles the waist. Youths are scarcely able to eat. The boys have to lie down on the ground, and with combined efforts the belt is pulled up over their legs and buttocks. The "mentor" is especially charged with the protection of the youths' genitals, since this is a rather painful operation. Once it is in place, a tail of rushes hanging down to the ankles is fixed to the belt. After four or five days, it is removed and the long tail is replaced by the short one usually worn by adult men. Again, details and information are lacking to explain the meaning of this peculiar ceremony. Even if interpreted as a ritual confinement (which is speculative), the meaning of the tail of rushes remains obscure.

Nevertheless, the parallel with the mourning ritual is again striking and fascinating: before burial the dead man is painted black. His relatives from that moment on hide in mourning capes, which are also smeared with charcoal. All successive feasts mark progressively the stages in the transformation process that the spirit of the deceased is believed to undergo. This process culminates with the ceremonial opening of the deceased's grave. The bones are cleaned and special care is taken with the skull. The lower jaw is tied with rattan fiber to the skull. The whole skeleton is subsequently painted red. It is not quite clear whether coconut oil or sperm, or a mixture of both, is used for the cleaning and the painting. Elsewhere (Serpenti 1965:214) I argued that both the opening of the grave and the simultaneous opening of the yam plant mound should be interpreted as ritual rebirth. And the same holds for the seclusion period of the youths: they are "buried" black and "reborn" red at the occasion of opening the grave.

THE HEAD-HUNT

One more ritual will further clarify the conceptual framework underlying the interrelated initiation ceremonies and the customs

313

connected with head-hunting (see also Serpenti 1968). The mabureede have a very important task to fulfill: the taking of a head.
Ideally, it is not permitted to open the grave of any deceased person
until a head has been taken. The mabureede are entrusted to the
guidance of an experienced headhunter from the opposite village-
sector, preferably the same who was in charge of the proceedings
during the children's feast and the youths' entry in the bachelor's
house. The boy is protected by him and, during the attack in enemy
territory (Serpenti 1968), instructed by him on how to cut off the
victim's head. When the men decide upon a raid, promiscuous
intercourse takes place between the headhunters and the young
girls the evening before. The mabureede are smeared with the
sperm to protect them from being killed during the raid.

The man who had a youth under his care does not keep the
trophy for himself. Immediately after the head has been cut off,
the young man is ordered to drink of the blood dripping from the
head in order that henceforth he himself will be as courageous
and successful a pangi. The head is then put into a betel bag and
ceremoniously offered to the mabureede. He carries the bag home
on his shoulder and, on arriving in the village, he goes straight to
the grave of the deceased. There the head is fixed on a pole placed
on the grave. Other heads are likewise placed on other graves.
Now the festivities to end the mourning period can be started. In
this connection, it is relevant to note that the grave can only be
opened by the men who are accustomed to prepare captured heads.

Until recently, heads were placed on the grave of a dead man
on the occasion of the final rites, irrespective of whether a head-
hunt had been organized. By the time of my fieldwork, though, a
coconut substituted for the hunted head, and was put atop the
pile of collected food at the ndambu feast. Van Baal (1966:747–
748) remarks that, among the Marind-anim, the pole bearing the
heads, which is stuck into the ground, is supposed to represent a
fruit-bearing coconut palm. On Kolepom, people are acquainted
with the myth in which is told how the coconut palm grew out of
the head of a buried man. Thus, sprouted coconuts are planted
on the grave. These coconuts originate from the deceased person's
trees, which are cut down immediately after his death. As soon as
the shoots are long enough, it is time to conclude the mourning
period.

From then on the headhunter and his pupil stand in a very close and indissoluble relationship to each other. Among the *Kiwai,* a neighboring tribe, the mother's brother is charged with supervising the young man during the hunt. On Kolepom this is the same person who performed the rites during the children's feasts and the entry in the burawa, and who, theoretically at least, is the mother's brother. More important, however, is that he is a representative of the opposing village-half, so he can be easily classified as a mother's brother.

The mother's brother is the actual headhunter. He is supposed to offer the captured head to the boy under his care who, in his turn, acts for the headhunter when back in the village. Beside ordinary foods, the flesh of the victim also is prepared for the feast. The boys, who at this occasion are newly initiated into the bachelor's house, are rubbed with the human fat before being painted black with charcoal. The region of the boys' hearts is rubbed with the bloody heads so that the vigor of the blood will penetrate into their bodies. The inmates who are now promoted to be tjutjine have to swallow an eye of the head, which they are not allowed to chew. Henceforth they would be able to see where the enemy is hidden.

The grave is closed up again, and the pole that bears the heads on top becomes the center of the dancing place. While the *watjip,* the traditional dance, is progressing, promiscuous intercourse takes place between the headhunters and the young fiancées of their pupils. At daybreak the mourning garb, which until then are worn by the deceased relatives, are laid aside; and the collected food, including the flesh of the slain enemies, is handed over to the opposite village-part. The eating of human flesh is a privilege of the hunters and the inmates of the bachelor's house.

After the meal, people begin to clean and prepare the heads. This ritual is again attended with promiscuous sexual intercourse between the older men (experienced hunters in charge of the preparations) and the fiancées of the youthful owners of the heads. The sperm is collected for smearing the heads. This semen rubbing of the inmates of the bachelor's house, and the head-hunting ritual, are performed thus on the occasion of the final mortuary feast. It is probable that the collected sperm is used for smearing the captured heads as well as for rubbing the boys. According to Verhage

315

(1957:48), the sperm is also used for "washing" the faces of those initiated into the art of preparing heads. When the head has been smeared with sperm, it is painted red and black, and appendages are applied to the hair. The length of the hair appendages and the manner of painting resemble the adornment of the tjutjine in the bachelor's house. The head is subsequently hung from the ceiling of the bachelor's house. In some villages the head seems first to have been buried for a couple of days.

CONCLUSION

Many details of the customs related to Kolepom sexual behavior remain unknown. Nevertheless, the fundamental concepts of the Kimam regarding life and death can be used as a structural basis, or at least as an integrating factor, to clarify the interdependence of these various rituals.

The ndambu ritual, with its unmistakable potlatch character, is rightly perceived as a focal point of Kimam culture by participants as well as by observers. Until recently, however, too much attention was paid to the social structural elements, as, for instance, the dualistic character of a society and the concomitant acquiring of prestige and status in the community. This approach to the analysis of the ndambu ritual was obvious because the competitive element in ndambu sometimes becomes so dominant that reciprocal food exchanges between persons and groups or villages take place *independently* of their ritual basis.

The result, however, was that little attention was paid to the fact that all important initiation ceremonies and mortuary rituals are concentrated around this feast because of their underlying conceptual interrelatedness. The transition rites for the boys, the bachelor's house, the head-hunt, the planting and harvesting of the yams, the burial and the opening of the grave, the taboo on picking coconuts during the mourning period, the rules regarding sexual license, and sexual prohibitions—all these elements operate simultaneously in expressing one goal: the birth of life out of death.

In this cyclical conception of life, the roles of males and females are essentially different. Women produce life that is ultimately bound to die. They represent the principle that life leads to death. For men it is the other way around: they produce life out of death.

This complementarity of male and female roles in reproduction symbolically closes the life cycle. In the first generative process, men should not interfere; in the second, it is women who should be kept out. If the first process can be called "natural," the second one should be described as "ritual." It is understandable, therefore, why women in no way participate in men's rites, except insofar as they are an indispensable asset for the men to perform their rites effectively. Women should assist in producing the male life-giving medicine: sperm, without which the transformation process from death to life is impossible.

The dualistic structure of Kimam society is given a firm ritual basis because of the fact that all-important ritual functions have to be performed in sequence by the opposite village-sectors. To them also the ceremonial yams are given. In the system of reciprocal rights and obligations, the village-sectors handle each others' deaths in such a way that they are dependent upon each other for the creation of new life, represented by the presentation of the ceremonial yams.

8   Arve Sørum

Growth and Decay: Bedamini Notions of Sexuality

Ritualized male homosexuality, in conjunction with male initiation, has a central place among many ethnic groups of the Papuan Gulf area of Papua New Guinea and adjacent parts of West Irian (cf., e.g., Williams 1936*c*, Landtman 1927, Van Baal 1966). The cultural tradition of which these peoples are a part extends inland and can be traced as far north as the East Strickland Plain and the Great Papuan Plateau.

In the latter area, in which the Bedamini live, ritualized homosexual behavior seems to be significant in all ethnic groups. Ritualized homosexuality is not, however, part of Bedamini ceremonial initiation as such; but in their belief system, male homosexuality is of central importance, and it forms the basis of male initiation. The Bedamini ideology of sexual relations is similar to that of the neighboring Etoro (Kelly 1976), and it also resembles Kaluli notions on sexuality (Schieffelin 1976:123–128).

Kelly's (1976) excellent paper established a metaphoric relation between the Etoro domains of witchcraft, and sexual relations within a larger conceptual system, "in which life and death are complementary and reciprocal aspects of the transmission of life force" (Kelly 1976:51). In the symbolic field of sexual relations, the Etoro believe that acquiring semen means the acquisition of growth and vitality, while losing semen leads to weakness and, ultimately, death. This basic cultural premise is shared by the Bedamini as well. Focusing on ritualized homosexuality, I will elucidate the structure of Bedamini beliefs in this domain, which center on sexual relations in the context of social relations and cosmology.

Approximately 3,800 Bedamini (Biami) live in the Nomad River area of the Great Papuan Plateau between the Strickland River and the edge of the Southern Highlands in the Western Province of Papua New Guinea. Their territory, situated between 1,000 and 2,000 feet in altitude, is covered by tropical rain forest. Being a remote corner of the Western Province, administrative penetration of the area did not occur until the latter half of the 1960s.

In 1972, the Bedamini were scattered throughout an area of roughly 420 square miles in sixty communities, each containing between twenty and one hundred people living in one large longhouse. Longhouse sites are shifted every three or four years in connection with the clearing of new communal gardens. The economy is based on shifting horticulture and sago production; bananas and taro are the chief garden crops. Hunting, gathering, and fishing are significant, while pig husbandry is poorly developed. The clearing and planting of gardens are collective activities, though basically, each nuclear family is economically self-sufficient.

The population is organized into exogamous patrilineal clans, which are in turn subdivided into shallow patrilineages, the core of which is a group of adults descended from a common father's father. Neither clans nor their constituent lineages are interrelated in a genealogical framework. The agnatic status of clans and lineages, in relation to one another, is determined both by a tradition of patrilineal descent from a collectivity of common ancestors, and by common intermarriage with a third clan.

The Bedamini practice real or classificatory FZSD marriage, so a man can expect to receive a wife from the clans into which his father's sisters were married. Different sibling sets[1] within a clan are tied by shared matrilateral relations, in addition to common

319

clan membership. Clan fission follows the cleavages that occur between lineages with the least matrilateral relations in common. Relations with nonagnates depend on the particular pattern of intermarriage between lineages at any one time.

There is a dual division of the tribe which the Bedamini explicitly recognize. This division is between those with whom one's own clan intermarries, and those with whom one does not intermarry, categorized as *uda-lasu* and *fi*, respectively. The category fi includes all clans that are recognized as agnates. The duality is thus a result of the marriage system, and its form slowly changes according to de facto marriage transactions.

There is no political institution that embraces the Bedamini people as a whole. The longhouse is the largest political unit, but alliances are formed with nearby communities, with whom networks of agnatic relations are close or affinal relations are concentrated. Since a longhouse group consists of men from several agnatically interrelated clans, communities are exogamous in a statistical sense, but not in a normative one. Alliances are not between communities as such, but between certain of their constituent local descent groups.

Residence is virilocal, and a group of brothers, their wives, and children, form the basic residential unit. The clan that owns the land the community utilizes is usually dominant in numbers but not necessarily in terms of leadership, which is individually based on performative qualities such as fighting abilities and skills in oratory, rather than on clan membership and the control of wealth. Since Bedamini society is egalitarian and leadership limited, serious conflicts are resolved either through violence, spatial movements to remote garden houses for short periods, or by leaving the community altogether. These migrations result in an extensive and regular flow of people between communities.

The most prominent man of a community is the "fight leader." A reputation as a warrior enhances a man's social position. Warfare was an immediate part of life on the Papuan Plateau until administrative control was established, a fact that thoroughly affected many aspects of Bedamini culture.

The ritual and knowledge of Bedamini religion are clustered around two opposed, yet interrelated, themes. These are sickness/death, and growth/fertility. The first theme is expressed through a set of beliefs and practices connected with ancestral spirits, witchcraft, curing, and funerals (Sørum 1980:273–297). The second theme is most clearly expressed through male initiation, ritualized homosexuality, ritual formulas, and activities connected with the growth of plants and animals.

There are three categories of spirits: (1) nature spirits, (2) ancestral spirits (*æselibu*), and (3) *sagisu,* the offspring of ancestral spirits or of the union between a shaman and a spirit-woman. The nature spirits are believed to be innately evil and beyond human control, while ancestral spirits are both benevolent and dangerous, and humans can influence them. The ancestral spirits have their resorts in sacred spots of primary forest, but they may appear in animal form throughout the jungle.

Male shamans are the only ritual specialists. Their activities, as mediums and curers, are centered on the spirit seance, or *gesame.* Through them the shaman communicates with ancestral spirits— with the assistance of his personal sagisu spirits—which are able to possess him (Sørum 1980:273–297). Sickness and curing have a prominent place in Bedamini thought. Serious illness and subsequent death are nearly always attributed to witchcraft, the absolute reality of which imposes constraints on Bedamini perceptions that must be taken into consideration in understanding social interaction. Most deaths are attributed to male witchcraft, and it is believed that the male witch consumes the victim's liver, the seat of the soul. Serious illness is normatively attributed to female witchcraft, which is curable. The cure is performed by the shaman; it consists in objects being extracted from the body, and a subsequent spirit seance to return the patient's lost soul (æselibu), which is, moreover, the spiritual aspect of man that continues to exist as an ancestral spirit after death. The æselibu leaves the body during dreams and sickness; and the shaman's main task is to reinstate the soul inside the patient. If he does not succeed, the patient will die.

The Bedamini recognize that a child is conceived through sexual intercourse and insemination, but they believe that several acts of intercourse are necessary. Each time, a new part of the child is implanted by the male. The woman's womb is viewed as the temporary "house" of the child. Semen is thus regarded as an active

321

substance with the potency to produce growth; but the mother's blood is also a necessary, complementary substance for a child's physical maturation. The strong bones, *gasa,* are thought to be inherited from the father, while the soft tissues, *hū,* are inherited from the mother. Strength and endurance are associated with masculinity, and softness and weakness with femininity.[2] To express that a man is strong and courageous, for instance, a Bedamini says that "he has got bones." The soul is inherited in its totality from the father. A small child has no soul of its own, but shares that of its mother through suckling. The soul grows gradually in the child as it is weaned and removed from the physical influence of its mother. Both men and women thus possess substances that will ensure growth, but growth can only be initiated by men, since it is the semen, *ami,* that is actually planted in the womb (cf. Herdt, chap. 4).

Women give birth in a temporary bush shelter (*kagelobo-tiasu*) not far from the longhouse. After delivery they spend a few days there in the company of other women before returning to the longhouse. While married men know the facts of birth, young unmarried men claim that they do not know how a child is born: it is deliberately kept secret. But both sexes share in the cultural ideas of conception.

Before returning from the birth hut, a female baby is provided with a small string skirt. Male babies are not provided with any clothing, and, in fact, boys run naked until they are five or six years old. The reason for this difference is not so much modesty on the part of the women as it is the debilitating effects on young men of even looking at female genitals.

Bedamini, like the Marind-anim (Van Baal 1966:817), consider semen the essence of life. This basic quality of semen pervades their ideas on growth and life, decay and death. These ideas converge in ritualized male homosexuality. Immature boys do not possess semen, and they can mature only through the intervention of their seniors. Behind this conception is also the assumption that weakness in males will ensue from too much association with women, in particular through sexual intercourse. Boys have been breast-fed and have spent their first years in a predominantly female sphere of influence. The solution to this dilemma is to supply the boys with semen from the age of eight to ten years.

The insemination is managed orally, by having the boys manipulate and suck the penes of young unmarried men, an activity referred to as *sibi*. The young man who will be a boy's inseminator is selected by the boy's father, and he must belong to the opposite moiety, that is, to a group with whom the boy's clan intermarries. The inseminator will normally be a member of the clan(s) into which the boy's father's sister(s) married; he will be from a clan that the boy himself later may marry into.

Homosexual relations are *sema* (sacred) and a male secret, although I doubt that the men are able to conceal them completely from older women. Bedamini men thus are reluctant to discuss homosexuality, and it was not until the later stages of my fieldwork that I gained some insight into the matter. The act of penis manipulation and sucking normally takes place at riversides under the guise of having a bath. As far as I know, homosexual activity occurs strictly between two partners and is not performed within larger groups of men.

The most effective time for insemination is said to be when the moon is full. The moon is classed as male, and, by implication, it is associated with fertility and growth. In fact, the lunar cycle forms a concrete image of the whole process of growth and decay. The sun is classed as female. It is associated with weakening effects, since it dries the leaves and branches of felled trees and drains the energy from humans by making them sweat. This image of the sun is clearly based on an analogy with the negative female influence on males.

The final events of the initiation of young men into adult status are approximately timed to coincide with the advent of the new moon in the West (Sørum 1982). First there is a procession of novices from a bush hut in which they have been secluded for one day of ceremonial decoration. A decorated male dancer, called *kenonie* (lit. "new moon"), leads the procession back to the longhouse, where they are presented as a new group of adult males. The dancer has a representation of a vulva painted on his chest and a small crescent-shaped fragment of a pearl shell tied to his beard. The pearl shell is also termed kenonie. (A large crescent-shaped pearl shell [*su*] is one of a man's most precious possessions.) The message implicit in this ritual procession is clearly that the novices have been "reborn," or rather perhaps "matured," as the

323

result of ceremonial male influences.

The preparation for male adulthood is a long process dependent on the acquisition of semen, which finds its symbolic expression in the initiation ceremony. The idea that prolonged insemination of boys is necessary to make them grow is analogous to the Bedamini theory of conception, in that the fetus requires many acts of heterosexual intercourse. Van Baal (1966:493) noted the same analogy in Williams's (1936c:172) data from the Keraki.

All ethnic groups of the Great Papuan Plateau—the Bedamini, Etoro, Onabasulu, and the Kaluli—emphasize the necessity of pederastic homosexual activities for creating men, but their respective techniques of semen transmission differ (Ernst 1972, personal communication; Kelly 1976; Schieffelin 1976). The Bedamini and Etoro practice the oral insemination of young boys; the Kaluli practice anal intercourse; and the Onabasulu (who live between the Etoro and the Kaluli) practice masturbation and the smearing of semen on boys' skins (see Herdt, chap. 1).

Proceeding from the north to the south, there is symbolic inversion of practices of semen transmission. Kelly (1977:16) sees these differences as a means of intertribal and cultural differentiation. They are presumably also expressions of differing ideas about the acquisition of strength in general. The Bedamini link the practice of oral insemination explicitly with the acquisition of strength by eating food and drinking water, and they react vehemently to the Kaluli practice of anal insemination, which they consider polluting and dangerous, and on which they themselves have placed a strict taboo. The Bedamini say that if anal intercourse takes place, the stomach of the recipient of semen will swell because he becomes pregnant, and then he will die.

For males, life centers on the gain and loss of semen. In their early youth, they gain in semen, and grow as a direct result. Afterward, semen is mainly lost through copulation with women and by supplying it to boys. Consequently, weakness will gradually ensue, ending in old age and death, the ultimate decay. For the Bedamini, human death quite literally means decay, since the corpse is kept within the longhouse for up to a week (depending on the status of the deceased) before it is put on a platform behind the longhouse. On the platform the corpse is left to decompose until only the bones remain. It is significant that only men touch the corpse if it has to be carried, including (if the deceased is a male) its removal from the house to the platform. Handling the corpse is in all other respects mainly the task of women. The closest female relatives of the deceased arrange the position of the corpse inside the house, sit around it while mourning, and remove its fluids and decomposed skin. They also periodically sit in mourning beneath the platform, allowing the body fluids to drip down on them as a sign of their grief. Since death is associated with decay, only females can handle the corpse. Men, who are responsible for growth, cannot do so since it negatively affects their powers. It must be added, however, that these rules do not apply in cases of cannibalism following warfare and witch killings, for men are as much involved as the women in handling the victims (though of course the victims are consumed before any sign of decay).

The Bedamini males' theory of sexuality is given cosmic significance. It is believed that homosexual activities promote growth throughout nature, particularly in gardens, while excessive heterosexual activities lead to decay in nature as well as in social groups. The balance of these forces is dependent on human action. It may seem a contradiction for Bedamini to lend these notions such general significance, since semen is lost also through homosexual activities, and the birth of children is recognized as the result of heterosexual activities. However, the Bedamini stress that it is only heterosexual activities in *excess* of what they consider necessary for producing a child that have these negative consequences. Men are of course aware that growth in gardens and forests is dependent on the decay of vegetation. Analogically, all human growth presupposes that semen is lost by some males. Homosexual fellatio always has positive effects on growth, even if the benefactor is deprived of semen. The Bedamini do not seem, therefore, to experience any inconsistency in the cosmic equation of homosexuality with growth and heterosexuality with decay.

Finally, we must remember that this notion predominantly represents the male point of view. The degree to which women share these ideas is difficult for me to tell. Nor did Bedamini men have any clear views on women's thoughts about sexuality. The men do not know whether women engage in homosexual activities. They generally believe that girls mature without necessary additives, since growth for them is effected through their blood, and

325

suckling does not influence their strength. The neighboring Etoro men (Kelly 1976:47) and Kaluli men (Schieffelin 1976:124) express similar views about female growth and sexuality.

From a basic distinction between male and female, I have established two cultural oppositions—growth:decay, and homosexuality:heterosexuality—which are central to the sexual domain of Bedamini thought. I shall next look in more detail at general configurations of male/female relations and the shape of sexual imagery in Bedamini culture.

Longhouses are strictly divided between male and female sleeping quarters. Small children sleep with their mothers. The family jointly cooks food at its own fireplace in the communal section of the longhouse, often shared with the families of the husband's brothers. Garden houses, which are occupied for extensive periods by a household or by the households sharing a fireplace in the longhouse, provide a setting for more intimate family life than that of the longhouse. But even there the sexes have separate quarters. This spatial separation is generally reflected also in social interactions between men and women. Males have little knowledge of what interactions between women are about, and vice versa; and men, at least, try to keep the significance of much of their own interactions hidden from the women.

Yet, there are no indications in everyday life of intense sexual antagonism or sex anxiety. Certain proscriptions on interpersonal interaction must be observed by both men and women after copulation, particularly in relation to preparing and giving away food. A woman must never step over the possessions of men or expose her genitals to young men, on account of the debilitating effects of femaleness. There is little concern with menstrual blood. Women continue to reside in the longhouse while menstruating, though they do keep to their own quarters for a few days. Bodily wastes are regarded as polluting, regardless of sex, but they are not a matter of great concern. Persons as such are not polluting, and the two sexes can, to a large degree, mingle freely in everyday public situations. *Relationships* between the sexes have their harmful effects, however, since it is through heterosexual intimacy that males are exposed to the weakening principle they ascribe to women. The avoidance of too much intimacy between the sexes is the responsibility of men as much as of women. Thus, I wish to stress that it is the complementarity of the sexes that is emphasized, and it is upon male/female interaction that Bedamini focus interest, rather than on the harmful qualities of any bodily substance per se.

There is often a large age discrepancy between spouses. Women marry before puberty: but, since their husbands are then in their mid-twenties, leviratic widow marriages are common. In their second marriage, women are often more independent, owing to their prior life experience. Senior women's independent attitude toward their husbands may also be related to their economic position, for wives (and husbands) privately own the products of their separate plots in the communal garden, although they share food with each other in daily meals. Besides, the inmarrying women of a community usually are agnatically closely related to one another (because of the concentration of marriages between a few neighboring clans) and thus they can count upon mutual support. An older widow may in practice act as a household head, even if she has adult unmarried sons.

Marriage (*uda lamo,* "take woman," *uda imo,* "give woman") takes the form of symbolic bride capture. The bridegroom's local community stages a mock attack on the bride's longhouse, which in turn fakes a vigorous defense, before the bride is seized and the "attackers" withdraw. The girl-bride is not told that her future community is coming for her; certainly this experience must deeply impress a girl of ten. The next day, a marriage feast is held at the bridegroom's longhouse, after which large amounts of food are exchanged between the couple's respective clans. The bride-wealth is inconsiderable and, apart from the food, it consists of a few shell valuables, dog's teeth headbands, necklaces, and axes. More important than this bride-wealth is the norm of reciprocity underlying all marriage transactions: the wife-giver and wife-taker relation will be reversed in the next generation.

A man may also "capture" a wife through a fine performance as a ceremonial dancer. Young girls may be so impressed by the beauty and power of a dancer that they will elope with him (cf. Schieffelin 1976:171). If the successful dancer is later able to demonstrate a legitimate claim to the girl's family in terms of previous marriages between their two clans, the "romantic" union usually is legitimized. Love magic may be also used by both sexes to attract a spouse or a lover. Most magic involves the use of fragrant herbs, which are worn or hidden on a spot where the desired partner is expected to sit. Men believe also that it is through such magical procedures that female witches can force them into sexual relationships.

Polygyny is common, and about three-fourths of the senior men of a community have more than one wife. Additional wives mostly are acquired through widow remarriages. Divorce is rare, since marriage involves a necessarily continuous relation between groups. If we are to judge by the frequency of accusations, adultery is also common, and is strongly resented when discoverd by the cuckold husband. Almost invariably his anger will be directed at his wife, whom he will beat. Occasionally, a husband kills his wife when learning about adultery. Spouses have occasional quarrels which may take a serious turn if one or the other spouse resorts to physical violence. In either case, the woman is bound to lose the fight. The other inhabitants of the longhouse may intervene, joining the fight. In this way a marital quarrel is transformed into an intracommunity brawl among both men and women who take sides and use wooden clubs. But this fighting, though serious, prevents even more serious outcomes, since the fighting is kept within strict limits. Nonetheless, on the whole, relations between spouses are fairly peaceful and are characterized by mutual affection.

Sexual intercourse takes place in the bush. It is taboo within a house or in a garden, which is a rational derivative of the equation between weakness and heterosexuality. Intercourse is likewise forbidden when people are engaged in productive activities. The common explanation for strains in intracommunity relations, bad harvests, and other collective misfortunes is that people have engaged in too much sexual intercourse.

There are two interchangeable terms for penis, *ewa/gata,* just as there are two terms for female genitals, *gubi/gabe.* An erect penis is referred to as *holofai,* while *hade* means to "copulate with." All these terms are used by both sexes for swearing. *Ami-rabe* (semen-vagina), *gabe-habalo* (menstrual blood), and *gabe-gegebo* (vulva of pig) are also common expressions. Sometimes sexual expressions are more subtle, such as *erafia* (my sibling's); or *duliæme*, the name of the mother of the creator goddess Dunumini. The last exclamation alludes to a mythological scene: Dunumini cried out for her mother when wounded while trying to seduce an innocent boy. In fact, all swearing in the Bedamini language derives from the terms for genitals or heterosexual activities.

Sexual imagery drawn from nature and the spirit world appears in Bedamini thought. Examples: when a woodpecker lands on a tree, the penis of a male ancestral spirit is said to become erect. Footprints of a pig may be referred to as the marks of the vulva of an ancestral spirit-woman; while leaves of an appropriate form are thought to be manifestations of her genitals. The piercing sound of a cricket at sunset is a sign of sexual intercourse between a spirit-couple in the bush. Such are all concrete images, based on analogies of form and the tacit concept that events in the spirit world have their counterparts in the world of the living.

Sexual symbolism pervades the male ceremonies. Male dancers may have representations of the vulva painted on their chests and a large leaf resembling a penis (but referred to as "earlobe") fixed to the front of their loincloths. Even drums are seen as "male" and "female". To the "male" drums are tied the beak of a hornbill, a phallic symbol, whereas a vulva representation is incised upon "female" drums. Amusing farces performed by guests upon arriving at ceremonial occasions often have sexual content. Let me give a couple of examples. On one occasion, there were two men acting as witches: a "male" figure endowed with a large bamboo "penis" and a "female" figure with a slit unripe papaya placed between his thighs. The "female" witch lay backside down, the "male" on top, and they started simulating sexual intercourse while the onlookers, men and women alike, cheered. Then the couple moved through the longhouse, the "male" witch thrusting the bamboo penis toward his partner, while the inhabitants of the house shouted obscenities at them. On another occasion, a man dressed like a female dancer was chased around the longhouse by another man, impersonating an evil nature spirit. Such farces are much enjoyed as entertainment. A few men (but not necessarily always the same ones) dress like women at feasts, mostly imitating old ladies. (Women never impersonate men in this way.) A young man in female attire sometimes joins the group of young female dancers surrounding a drummer. But I do not think we should see male transvestism as a significant element of ceremonial life; it is rather viewed as comedy.

Many young and middle-aged men enjoy exchanging jokes about sex. Young men may cut images of vulvas into rocks and trees and consider it amusing that other men's wives see them. Sexual joking in particular is marked at spirit seances (Sørum 1980:276–279, 291). The joking is triggered by remarks by the spirit medium about sexual encounters in the spirit world. The listeners may start sticking glowing sticks in each other's crotches; or fake copulating with pillars; or shout for women in the direction of other long-houses; and so on. This behavior and its attendant verbal joking is referred to as *uda fofagisa* (longing for women), which implies that the performers are virile and strong. At spirit seances there is an all-male audience, and the sexual joking contributes to an atmosphere of camaraderie. Besides, the noise is supposed to scare witches that may threaten the sick person on whose behalf the seance is held.

The Bedamini label the relations between two persons after an object or an experience they have shared. Among such named relations are *gubinasu* (vulva sharer) and *hadesu* (copulation sharer). This labeling does not mean that the two men have copulated with the same woman, only that they have exchanged many jokes on the subject. The homosexual experience, which is secret, is never used as a label for any relationship. This void does not prevent men from joking about homosexuality when segregated or removed from contact with women. A common form of their sexual horseplay is to try to grab hold of each other's penis. *"Ti holofia?"* (you erect?), *"na-gini naha"* (give it to me to eat), and *"ti ewa mai"* (you have eaten cock) are all remarks that allude to homosexual activity. They are seen as jokes, given the appropriate context; but their meaning is always ambiguous, so they also may be intended as a serious offense. To leave no doubt as to the intent of the joking, both the joker and his partner bow their heads toward each other and shout "jyh!" This gesture is a message that a subsequent remark or an action is meant to be a joke.

While men and women rarely are intimate in public, relations between unmarried males are characterized by intimacy and physical closeness. They frequently hold hands, hug each other, and sleep together. But these actions do not in themselves imply a homosexual relationship. If near age-mates do have a homosexual relationship, it is viewed as their own private business, and it is not part of the ritualized homosexuality concerned with the insemination of immature boys. Relations among women are intimate and close as well, but they are already married and preoccupied with a household to manage. They also individually occupy separate small sections within the women's quarters, while young men lead a more independent life as a close group in the whole men's quarters. Children of both sexes are kept apart from early childhood on. Boys and girls do play together frequently until the age of seven or eight, but they can only have close relationships with others of the same sex.

Most young men experience an extended period of bachelorhood, during which there is no opportunity for heterosexual relations, except adultery, which is risky. Masturbation is negatively viewed because of its weakening effect. Homosexual relations are the only acceptable sexual outlet, a fact that cannot account for the existence of ritualized homosexuality but certainly does contribute to its importance in the male community.

I have now established an apparent contradiction between Bedamini ideas and action, that is, between men's concepts of sexual relations and their actual behavior in social life, which is overtly centered on heterosexual relations. On the one hand, men attribute a cosmic significance to the link between homosexuality and male growth, attributions that ultimately concern the vital interplay of life and death. On the other hand, heterosexual imagery pervades Bedamini conceptualization of the world and is equally essential to ceremonial life and ritual practice. Heterosexual relations are regarded as depleting of strength and thus harmful; still, men joke about the subject and show a great interest in, and desire for, sexual relations with women. Women have a debilitating effect upon men, but sex anxiety or antagonism is atypical of relations between husband and wife in everyday life.

First, men copulate with their wives and usually do not seem to suffer any immediate loss of strength as a result. As Kelly (1976:43) says of the Etoro, men can alleviate their private anxieties "by engaging in the very act that they fear." Second, the joking, and sexually charged behavior of many men on festive occasions, is nothing less than a message that reinforces their feeling of strength and manliness. They pretend that their vitality is so great that they do not fear the debilitating effects of femininity. Third, Bedamini men do not believe that abstinence will ensure eternal youth. Since subsidiary magical means exist for ensuring growth in gardens, pigs, and men, so the sun and other cosmic influences decrease strength. Bedamini social life is, then, based on the relation between male and female, which is reflected in cosmological imagery and ritual practice. Finally, heterosexuality and homosexuality are complementary opposites in Bedamini thought, for one cannot exist without the other.

Bedamini codifications of sexuality—and its projection into a cluster of idioms centered on the life cycle of living things—can be summarized by the following set of oppositions, which, I believe, represent the basic elements of this domain of sexuality in the Bedamini world view:

male : female :: homosexuality : heterosexuality :: growth : decay

At the core of ritualized homosexuality, we find a vital concern with fertility and growth. As men struggle with the mystery of life and female reproductive powers, they invent a mystery of their own, through which they are able to control the powerful effects of semen, the essence of life (cf. Herdt, chap. 4). By making this knowledge a secret, they make it more important; so secrecy is a meta-message to those who share in it that, on the cosmic level, they are in a relation of superiority to those who do not share the secret.

Bedamini ritualized homosexuality strongly feeds on an analogy with female reproductive powers but does not imply male envy of female genitals. Hage (1981:268–275) argues that in New Guinea, ritualized homosexual practices constitute, in conjunction with male initiation, a "subset of possible magical acts to induce male growth" that are correlated with an egalitarian type of social structure based on dual organization. Bedamini social structure, and the idioms associated with male initiation (Sørum 1982) and homosexuality, seem to exemplify this view.

The basic symbolic opposition between male and female in this cosmological scheme seems to be immutable. However, Ernst

(1978:193) shows that the Onabasulu see the sago grub/beetle (an important food) as encompassing the opposite cultural principles of maleness and femaleness, for the beetle is associated with the former whereas its larvae represents the latter. Each beetle goes through a process of transformation that includes both "male" and "female" stages. I do not know if the Bedamini share this view on the sago grub, but I find it highly probable, for the equation male:female::high:low (which forms the context for Onabasulu ideas on the sago grub) is of central ideological importance to both ethnic groups. Besides, sago grubs are important exchange items among both the Bedamini and the Onabasulu.

The other two oppositions of the symbolic set are definitely mutable. The one pole implies the other. The same man makes the transition from homosexual acts to heterosexual acts; similarly, the same object (e.g., plants) undergoes both growth and decay. On a more abstract level, my interpretation of Bedamini codifications of sexuality implies that homosexual relationships must lead necessarily to heterosexual ones, as growth must lead to decay. Thus, each element can be transformed into the other within a bounded, yet changing, system of metaphor linkage, and these transformations are necessary for the cosmic cycle to reproduce.

Kelly (1976:45, 47–48) argues that a fundamental premise of Etoro cosmology entails that increase in one part of the system must lead to depletion in another part. This cyclical notion implies that depletion is a precondition for growth, just as death is a precondition for life in a closed system. The Bedamini and Etoro share these fundamental cultural premises in the domain of sexual relations. The central themes of this symbolic domain seem to extend throughout the Papuan Plateau and, farther beyond, they apparently underlie a vast cultural tradition that is found throughout the Western Papuan Gulf area extending into Irian Jaya (see Herdt, chap. 1).

There is a basic dualism of inherently cyclic nature in this ideology, which is evident in Bedamini conceptualizations of their world. Through the decay of the felled trees of a garden, for instance, new growth arises; and the male moon dies and is reborn: it is weak when first appearing in the sky with the female sun but gains strength when the sun fades and disappears, a process analogous to the development of a male from infancy to adulthood.

Bedamini social organization is to a large degree constructed on marriage transactions and the resulting kinship relations they entail. The exchange of women is thus central to the Bedamini comprehension of their social universe, a fact that is reflected in their construction of reality through different domains of belief. The Bedamini practice of delayed exchange allows males a rightful claim to women from the clan(s) that "took" their father's sisters. The ideal spouse is FZSD, or her equivalent, suggesting that marriage transactions between two groups are repeated, at least in theory, every fourth generation.

The cyclic nature of this marriage system is based on a distinction between those with whom one does not marry and those from whom one takes women. The wife-taker must necessarily be transformed into a wife-giver in order to become a wife-taker again. Furthermore, this entails a necessary complementarity between wife-takers and wife-givers, since they cannot reproduce their groups without obligatory reciprocity. The marriage system directly involves ritualized homosexuality through the convention that the inseminator belong to a clan that is in a wife-taker relationship to the recipient. The exchange of women thus provides a model of and for Bedamini conceptual creativity in the domain of sexuality.

If the oppositions thus far identified in Bedamini beliefs about sexuality are represented, the following schematic set unfolds:

male	:	female
homosexuality	:	heterosexuality
growth	:	decay
strength	:	weakness
bone	:	tissue
moon	:	sun
wife-taker	:	wife-giver
agnates	:	non-agnates

This schema can easily be extended. For instance, the phrase "to grow" is derived by analogy from the term "to ascend" (*hedæbe*). Indeed, the terms are identical; and upward/high is associated with the male side, while downward/low is associated with the female side.[3] The above oppositions demonstrate once again the basic dualism of Bedamini conceptualizations. But this model is not one of static duality with fixed poles, or of resulting antagonistic social oppositions, for the opposites must of necessity be transformed into their counterparts. The system is trapped, so to speak, in a struggle of cosmic cyclical change. Despite continual changes in relationships between elements of the system, the system as a whole is static, since any halt in the cycles implies its breakdown. To clarify the ontological status of this construct, it is important to stress that it does not refer to an inclusive and consistent folk model. It represents the analyst's reconstruction of the patterns of Bedamini idioms and practices.

Ancestral spirits perform two types of dance ceremonies—called *gafoi* and *gosei*. These dances are performed nightly somewhere in the spirit world, and the Bedamini believe that should the ancestors stop dancing, the ground will shake and destruction will ensue. To keep the ancestors dancing, then, men must regularly stage these ceremonies as well. There is thus a mutual responsibility between ancestral spirits and living men that cannot be ended without catastrophic consequences. This view is analogous to the structure of idioms centered on human sexuality.

The Bedamini world view in its totality does not constitute a coherent whole. It consists of clusters of idioms, or domains of thought that can be related metaphorically to one another, or they may be associated with one another through sharing elements from different contexts (Kelly 1976; Sørum 1980; Wagner 1972). The context, which gives these domains their thematic ordering, is often established through a focal ritual, for action gives meaning to the structure of thought. Here, I have viewed ritualized homosexuality as providing such a focal point, through which a systematic arrangement of idioms has emerged, thus resolving the above paradox of growth and decay.

In closing, I wish to stress that I have mainly dealt with the male codification of sexual relations. My social status as a man barred me from studying the women's counterpart to the men's conceptual system. I do not mean to imply that men and women live in two different cultural universes, for, in general, men and women share the same cultural values and beliefs. Nonetheless, particularly in the sexual domain, secrecy and mutual ignorance prevail. Thus, it would be meaningless to talk about the Bedamini *people's* cod-

335

ification of sexual relations since interpretation of certain events, and the definition of the situation for various phenomena, must differ between the sexes. At least so long as men try to keep secret their vision of life and death.

NOTES

1. Parallel cousins are included in the sibling category. A sibling set, including patrilateral parallel cousins, form the core of a patrilineage.
2. Cf. Schieffelin (1976:117–134), on Kaluli stereotypes of male and female qualities and behavior, which are fairly typical of Bedamini notions as well.
3. Cf. Ernst (1978:193–194), on the male/female dichotomy that pervades many aspects of Onabasulu social organization and thought, with its associated opposition between high and low.

9 Shirley Lindenbaum

Variations on a Sociosexual Theme in Melanesia

The essays in the present collection comprise perhaps the most radical inquiry to date into the anthropological deconstruction of our notions of gender, sexual expression, and forms of social relatedness. More intimate in focus than the analyses of recent decades, which were primarily concerned with the symbolic worlds of Melanesian men and women (Lawrence and Meggitt 1965; Brown and Buchbinder 1976), they redirect our attention to the cultural and gender-specific nuances of sexual and emotional attachment and self-identity, explored earlier by Hogbin (1945–1946) and Read (1952, 1955). They encourage us to rethink "sexuality," to give it the same shifting historical sense that now accompanies the anthropological uses of "nature," "gender," or even "politics." Although sufficient evidence is not yet in to permit a definitive account of the connections that exist in Melanesia among fantasy, eroticism, sex roles, gender, and various forms of social existence, the information presented in this volume does suggest that it is time to attempt a broad synthesis.[1]

Our present state of knowledge concerning ritual homosexuality in Melanesia is still somewhat limited. There may be more information to come from areas such as the Great Papuan Plateau or the periphery of the Eastern Highlands; also, some data are unavailable because of certain pledges of trust between Papua New Guineans and certain anthropologists. In addition, some rituals involving homosexuality are evaporating with the present generation of adults, as Godelier's (1982a) account of the Baruya indicates; in other cases, the rituals are difficult to reconstruct from earlier reports, as Van Baal attests (chap. 3). More troublesome, perhaps, is our present confinement to the considerations of but one participant in a double discourse. The missing dimension concerns female/female interactions, noted but not investigated by several ethnographers in societies with documented male ritual homosexuality.[2] A greater impediment lies in an analytical method that proceeds with one sex at a time, when as this book demonstrates, gender is the mutual product of men and women acting in concert, whether it be in the form of cooperation or of opposition. Still, women's presence is ubiquitous, and much can be read about women's affairs from the imprint they have on the lives of men.

As Herdt's most valuable introductory essay shows, male ritualized homosexuality in Melanesia can be located in time and space. It is a recent or current phenomenon of the Lowlands and fringe areas of the Eastern Highlands, as well as of Eastern Melanesia. While Herdt's survey reliably reports its presence among perhaps 10 to 20 percent of all Melanesian groups, it should be noted that ritualized homosexuality does not represent a separate species of cultural behavior in the region. Indeed, as the chapters in this book indicate, there is a conspicuous sharing of symbolic themes, a sense of variation and permutation upon a common Melanesian fund of sociosexual behavior and social organization, both within and beyond the region in which ritualized homosexuality occurs.

This observation, however, challenges us to explain the presence of different forms of sexual expression and gender formation within a single cultural zone. Herdt addresses the problem by proposing that an early group of migrants brought with them a ritual complex subject to successive regional, social, and ecological transforma-

338

tions in response to local group adaptations. My own approach attempts to capture the dynamics of this adaptational process and focuses upon what I take to be evidence of the transformation of social systems in different regions at different times. In the following paragraphs, I will begin by exploring the nonrandom incidence of the cultural phenomena in question, and suggest that certain spatial continuities and discontinuities in social and symbolic forms provide an illuminating point of entry for the present investigation. Some regions in Melanesia have a cultural coherence that suggests small variations in social contexts, while others exhibit wider disparities in cultural forms as well as in social, political, and economic arrangements, and thus provide evidence of the social and historical forces that combine to transform a way of life. The most revealing approach is to observe ideas, behaviors, and social contexts as they change. The preceding chapters, and the Melanesian literature in general, afford examples of several such transitional moments; these are the basis for the analysis that follows.

Building upon small and then broader areal contrasts, I have sought to identify the factors that contribute significantly to the presence or absence of ritualized homosexuality in particular societies, taking note of differences in population size and density, in productive modes, and in certain forms of marriage. Sister exchange and the absence of bride-price emerge as crucial features of those cultural systems with ritualized homosexuality, which attempt to sustain egalitarian relations among affinal groups.

The analysis then shifts from spatial to temporal variation in social forms, in order to catch the sociosymbolic transformations that accompany the transition from ritualized homosexuality to cultures that cherish exclusively heterosexual relations. Semen emerges as the analogue of bride-price, a conclusion that leads to a more extended discussion of the nature of wealth in different cultures. It is suggested that important aspects of the psychodynamic change we are examining coalesce around the production, exchange, and consumption of key items of value, and that the shift in Melanesia from semen to pigs, shells, or feathers charts a shift in the organizational focus of intellectual, emotional, and productive energies around these body-produced or non-body-produced items.

Lowland and Highland societies are treated as ideal types in this

339

segment of the investigation, with the Eastern Highlands occupying an analytic midpoint. The production of "men" is seen to be the focus of cultural attention among Lowland groups, as is the production of "bigmen" in the Highlands. Ideologies as well as ritual activities serve to mask women's reproductive labors in the former region, and their productive labors in the latter. The social context is defined in which we find equality among affines, or the dominance of wife-takers, or of wife-givers.

The analysis turns then to gender ambiguity, which is a special feature of cultures with ritualized homosexuality, and explores the relationship of gender ambiguity to themes of sibling incest and erotic expression, as psychosocial correlates of the structure of sister-exchange marriage in particular productive modes. The expression of gender ambiguity, themes of sibling incest, and homoerotic expression all become muted in the great wealth-accumulating ceremonial exchange societies of the Western Highlands. A final section poses the idea that the urge to revise our present understanding of the cultural meaning of sexuality belongs to wider intellectual currents of our time.

THE CULTURAL GEOGRAPHY OF SEXUALITY

The nonrandom incidence of ritualized homosexuality provides the starting point for an analysis that attempts to illuminate the political and economic forces underlying changing ritual and social forms as well as psychosexual states. In some areas of Melanesia, variations in ritual elements (but one aspect of the total system) are such that different cultures within a region appear to be commenting one upon the other, quiet chamber music performances, with each group attuned to the sounds of their neighbors. Malekula and the Small Islands, described by Allen (chap. 2), form one such complex. Here, three neighboring areas share in using shark symbolism, hoaxes, and the importance of the male phallus in their rituals of initiation, yet the form of homosexual expression varies in each place. Among the Big Nambas, the power of the penis is manifested in highly organized homosexual behavior that occurs between senior men and youths. In the nearby Small Islands, however, the theme of anal penetration occurs only in the context of

the hoaxes perpetrated on novices held in seclusion following penile super-incision, while in West Aoba, a homosexual theme is
present merely in theatrical representation during secret rites of
initiation.

The Great Papuan Plateau forms another regional complex, consisting of the Etoro, the Bedamini, the Kaluli, and the Onabasulu.
All four tribes share similar views about the need for the insemination of young boys, but express some differences concerning
the appropriate mode of transmission. Thus, Etoro and Bedamini,
who are culturally and linguistically closely related (Kelly 1977:10),
transmit semen through oral intercourse, Kaluli through anal intercourse, and the Onabasulu through masturbation and smearing
of semen on the bodies of initiates. Since the members of each
tribe become men in different ways, they are culturally distinct
beings at a most fundamental level, as Kelly observes (ibid.:16).
Sørum (chap. 8) describes the Bedamini contribution to this regional "discussion."

The Marind-anim, as Van Baal indicates (chap. 3), were in many
ways the lead players in the Southwest Papuan Gulf complex, to
which the Kimam (Serpenti, chap. 7) appear to have been attuned.
Although the Sambia also belong to this latter complex, as Herdt
(chap. 4) suggests, the Anga-speaking groups do appear to have
gone off to practice in the next room. In this respect, they have
joined the flute players of the Eastern Highlands.[3] In all cases,
variations in the expression and elaboration of homosexual activities take the form of ethnic differentiation within a region.

If we raise our sights to include regions in which ritualized
homosexuality is not the appropriate male initiation experience,
and examine also the differences in other symbolic elements and
social forms, the spatial variations become more informative. From
this larger, Melanesia-wide perspective, the New Guinea Highlands emerge as a region in which ritualized male homosexual
experience is notably absent. In place of the exchange of semen
during male initiation, the ceremonial exchange of valuables (shells,
feathers, and pigs) is the center of attention, and where this form
of exchange becomes most elaborate, male initiation itself is absent. In this last region, most particularly in the Western High-

lands, cultural interest is directed at the making of men of status, rather than at the ritual forging of male identity—that is, at the making of big men, rather than at the making of men.[4]

From this perspective, the Eastern Highlands occupies an intermediate place, with no large-scale ceremonial exchange systems, a concern for "little" big men, and the existence of male initiation rituals in which homosexuality is a muted symbolic theme, not a behavioral reality. The social identity of males in this location derives from ideological, psychological, and social bondings, which include homoerotic elements, as Read (chap. 5) indicates.

It should be pointed out that by thus comparing these three regions (the Lowlands, the Eastern Highlands, and the Western Highlands), I do not intend to imply a view of unilineal progress from one stage of sexual expression, gender formation, or set of productive relations, to another. The analysis is placed in a framework which, I hope, points instead to the systematic interconnectedness of various aspects of these cultures, best illuminated at moments of historical transformation.[5] It is during such interludes that the relationship among the parts becomes visible. This calls for an anthropological approach equal to the complexity of the vision: a simultaneous evaluation of symbol, psyche, ecology, and sociopolitical relations (see Keesing 1982 for a similar attempt to combine these partial modes of interpretation in one analysis).

The broadest contrasts among Melanesian cultures emerge, then, from a comparison between the so-called semen groups of the Lowlands and the Highland cultures in which semen is not the ritualized stuff of life.[6] The comparison takes on a Lowland/Eastern Highland/Western Highland character[7] (see map 2), as well as a contrast between semen ingested, blood expelled, and a lack of concern for the input or output of body fluids as the necessary condition for the creation of male gendered beings. In place of a Lowland (and Eastern Highland) focus on body substances, we find in the Western Highlands an externalization of interest to the surface of the body itself (M. Strathern 1979). The Enga, for instance, have no rituals of male initiation, but the puberty rites for young bachelors require prolonged body and eye washings to nullify the stunting effects of unavoidable contact with clanswomen (Meggitt 1965b:127). Among the Western Highland Melpa also, where neither male initiation nor puberty rites occur, men decorate themselves with ceremonial valuables during intergroup exchanges that enable them to achieve full masculine adulthood. While the Melpa do not share the Enga view of the eye as an agent of corruption, they do give a special attention to decorating the head (Strathern and Strathern 1971) as a way of stressing the fertility and sexuality that attract women and valuables, thereby enhancing masculine "growth."

The transformation in ritual forms from Lowlands to Highlands is accompanied by the modification of a number of other factors.[8] The most obvious differences concern the size and density of populations in each region, and their different modes of production. (The Eastern Highlands complex will be mentioned separately as the discussion proceeds.) The societies in which ritualized male homosexuality occurs are often small in size and inhabit precarious environments, as Herdt (chap. 1) notes. The Etoro and Onabasulu, perhaps among the smallest, have populations of 400 and 430, respectively, in densities of fewer than 20 persons per square mile, while the larger Marind-anim and Kimam populations of 6,000 and 7,000 are still no rival for the Western Highlands Enga, who number about 50,000, with population densities in their central zone of 350 to 400 people per square mile (Meggitt 1967:24).

Highland societies are also based on the intensive production of sweet potato and domestic pig-herding, for which female labor is the fundament, whereas the smaller Lowland groups tend a different assemblage of crops—banana, taro, yam, sago, and coconut—accompanied by hunting and fishing, productive modes in which male labor is especially important. In this context, men derive status from goods produced by their own labor (Collier and Rosaldo 1981), and the accumulation by one man of many wives does not give rise to significant productive advantages, as it does in the Highlands. Indeed, Serpenti (1965:132) notes that since the first rung on the Kimam social ladder is determined by skill in the cultivation of male-produced ceremonial crops (yams and taro), polygyny offers no great benefit and is reserved only for the extremely industrious cultivator who can meet the demands on his root crops from his wives' numerous relatives.[9]

A most striking aspect of social organization in societies with ritualized male homosexuality concerns the overlap between marriage and homosexual relationships, as Herdt (chap. 1) notes. The pattern of marriage in most cases is that of sister exchange, with no payment of bride-price. In some places, other forms of marriage also exist, such as delayed exchange marriage with infant betrothal, said to be the normative preference for the Sambia (Herdt 1981:43), or the Bedamini and Sambia practice of real or classificatory FZSD marriage, in which a man expects to receive a wife from the clans into which his father's sisters were married (Sørum, chap 8). In all cases, a marked effect of structural and symbolic dualism exists between affinal groups (see Hage 1981), a pattern reinforced by the homosexual relationships among men. For, as Kelly notes of the Etoro, and as Herdt (chap. 4) hints for the Sambia, the ideal inseminator is a boy's sister's husband. Thus, the married sister and her brother have the same sexual partner (Kelly 1977:181–183).

Social relationships in these societies are characterized, then, by a kind of double affinity, by the return of a woman from a previously defined affinal group. This duplicated affinity is further heightened by semen transactions between actual or potential brothers-in-law. The rules of marriage and homosexuality thus combine in mutual support. One key to these overlapping structures surely has to do with the logistics of maintaining sister-exchange marriage in small populations subject to intermittent epidemics, and the difficulties of completing a complex marital exchange in the correct sexual sequence. Nature, as Thurnwald (1916:272) comments, does not dispose of the distribution of differently sexed children to one couple in such a systematic way. This situation is compounded by the danger of bride capture—for the Sambia a highly prestigious if rarely achieved means of acquiring a wife (Herdt 1981:44)—or by the running away of the bride, a feature of Kimam local group loss and gain (Serpenti 1965:128–129).

Some demographic remedies are available in delayed exchange marriage, or in the exchange between two lineages of a sister for a daughter, which is a feature of Baruya marriage (Godelier 1976:13). Kimam sometimes buy "sisters" from other groups in order to exchange them for wives, as do the Keraki (Williams 1940a:141), while the Banaro provide a corrective by killing the undesirable sex in successive births (Thurnwald 1916:272). This latter act of human engineering occurs perhaps in the absence of semen transactions, which in other societies give contractual strength to marriage agreements.[10]

The jural connotations of semen exchange (from the viewpoint of men) have been well described by Spencer and Gillen in their comments on the Arunta bridegroom-to-be in Australia:

> It frequently happens that the woman whose daughter is thus allotted to him may have a son and no daughter born, and in this case, without waiting on the chance of a girl being born, the man agrees to take the boy. . . . This establishes a relationship between the boy and the man, as a result of which the former has, until he (is circumcised) to give his hair to the man, who on his part has, in a certain way, to look after the boy.
>
> *(1927, 2:470)*

The prospective bridegroom "looks after the boy" by having sexual intercourse with him as though he were a wife, and by anointing him with semen (Layard 1959:106). In the eight-section sister-exchange marriage system of the Arunta, homosexual and heterosexual rights interweave, as they do among the Kimam and the Etoro, where a man relinquishes access to his sister but acquires access to a brother-in-law when the sister is given or promised in marriage (Kelly 1976:52). Thus, life force (as semen) flows between same-sex and different-sex partners, linking individuals and groups in complex chains of mutual dependency and obligation. It might be said that semen is a kind of covenant that keeps the sister-exchange system intact, one that is tied to the problem of maintaining a balance of personnel in small-scale communities. The transmission of semen is in some ways the characteristic affinal offering of bride-service societies, a gift of one's own labor, except that the prestation here is an internal transformation of the labor of others, forming one part of the complex reciprocities whereby affines maintain egalitarian relationships (Collier and Rosaldo 1981).

TEMPORAL VARIATION IN SOCIOSEXUAL FORMS

That sister exchange and ritualized homosexuality act in tandem may be seen in situations where the two systems are breaking down. Beardmore (1890) reports, for example, that homosexual anal intercourse and marriage by sister exchange were present among the Kiwai. By 1927, however, Landtman finds no trace of this homosexual activity, saying "I think it quite possible that the customs of the people, changing as they are, may have altered in this respect since Mr. Beardmore's time" (1927:237). Landtman (1927:245) comments, in addition, that although sister exchange is still the expressed ideal, bride-price marriage has begun to creep in, with a return gift from bride's kin to groom's kin.

Similarly, among the Kimam, Serpenti (chap. 7) notes the demise of the bachelor house with its attendant homosexual practices. The young man now stays at home before marriage, and his betrothed no longer moves to the house of his parents (Serpenti 1965:129). We may assume that these affines no longer have the same authority over the bride that they once had, including an early claim on her labors, sexual and domestic, an important shift in the social relations among affinal groups. Significantly, Serpenti (1965) tells us that sister-exchange marriage among the Kimam is also breaking down, supplanted by the new custom of bride-price marriage, a trend he attributes to increased interaction among villagers resulting from the Pax Australiana and to a larger marriage pool that provides more partners for young people. Kimam also show a recent dependence on European goods. Young men now work away from the island for a year or more to acquire these much coveted items, which subsequently circulate at home through bride-price exchange (Serpenti 1965).

These changes, documented among the Kimam and the Kiwai, illustrate the interdependence that exists between sister-exchange marriage and ritualized homosexuality, a relationship recently described also for the Baruya (Godelier 1982a:53). As the relations of production become transformed, and as different social configurations supplant the former social order, we see that whereas semen was the agent of social production in the societies with ritualized homosexuality, bride-price goods perform that function in "posthomosexual" social forms.

The Kimam and Marind-anim are two societies whose ritualized homosexuality depart most from the others described in this volume. Both societies inseminate their youths but give ritual emphasis also to the power of heterosexually-derived substances. Semen and vaginal fluid, mixed together, and produced by many men copulating with one woman—who may be the initiate's wife (Marind-anim) or betrothed (Kimam)—is an emulsion used for a variety of purposes. Sometimes rubbed on the boy's body to make it grow, the substance is employed also as a medicine, a ceremonial food, and as a fertility agent for new gardens. Marind-anim also view it as a lethal component of the sorcerer's concoctions. Both cultures encourage a ritual relationship between boys and their mother's brothers, who become their mentors and perhaps inseminators, although this relationship is only hinted at for the Kimam (Serpenti 1965:163). In both places, also, homosexual and heterosexual intercourse is associated with a complex exchange of food and labor.

Van Baal suggests that the elaboration of ritualized heterosexuality in a culture that gives central ideological place to the life-producing significance of male sperm may be attributable to the demonstrable failure of the fertility process itself. My own analysis would place more emphasis on the signs of change affecting significant sociosexual aspects of Marind-anim life, which Van Baal describes so well both here and in his earlier monumental work (1966). Prior to 1920, when the colonial government banned the great rituals, feasts, and associated sexual practices, Marind-anim was an expanding culture, spreading from the coast to the interior, as well as along the coast from east to west. The resulting widespread ritual and social organization of these communities seems incompatible with the narrow horizons of social forms that stem from sister-exchange marriage. Moiety organizations, once freed from the isomorphism of marriage exchange, provide the basis instead for broader regional integration.[11] As the marriage system shifts beyond the confined reaches of sister exchange, then, and as bride-price payments enter into relationships among affines, the exact and balanced reciprocities of the former marriage system take on a new shape. Gone is the sense of humility and indebtedness that wife-receivers feel toward those whose sisters they have taken in marriage, a structure of dutiful respect that never took the form of permanent hierarchy, veiled as it was by the reciprocal that each group stood ultimately as wife-giver and wife-receiver to the other. The dominance of wife-givers was also muted in each case by the importance of the sibling relationship, whereby a wife's elder brother continued to maintain an active interest in the life of his sister and her children after marriage (see Serpenti 1965:137).

The intrusion of bride-price into the marriage system, along with the demise of sister exchange, however, is a sign of significant social transformation. The counterbalancing aspects of reciprocal exchange wane, and wife-giving groups begin to hold a superior position. This principle seems to hold for areas in the Sepik region where sister exchange was formerly the rule,[12] as well as among the Kimam and Marind-anim. Moreover, the Imo rites of the Marind-anim, in which the ritualized hostility of men and women finds greatest expression, occur among inland tribes who are struggling to sustain sister exchange and moiety exogamy, a resistance no longer exerted by coastal groups whose Mayo rites project the image of the Mayo woman of motherly care. It might be suggested that these inland communities, facing the incipient affinal hierarchies of the new marriage arrangements entering their communities, may soon strike their affines with bride-wealth instead of pelting their women with excrement. This transition should be accompanied also by some distancing from the notion of semen as the sole agent of reproduction.[13]

For the Kimam, as we know already, the transformation is already further underway. Kimam youths temporarily leave the world of their elders to find new wealth and new wives outside the village. Moreover, at death, Kimam do not destroy European goods or put them in the grave, which is the fate of crops, fruit trees, and the everyday articles used or made by deceased men (Serpenti 1965:121). In the absence of sister exchange, imbalances develop in the relationships between marriage-affiliated groups. The accumulation of bride-wealth indicates a significant break also in the rebirth of life from death, which gave symbolic and behavioral integration to the egalitarian tenor of Kimam social life.

Schwimmer (1973:210) reports the Orokaiva sentiments on these matters, in a society where exchange and bride-wealth marriages now occur side by side. Orokaiva do not consider bride-wealth to be equivalent to the bride. Bride-wealth is a payment for the anger of the bride's parents and is accompanied by a humility that recognizes the lifelong indebtedness of wife-takers. In the Eastern Highlands, once again the pivotal case, bride-price marriage and the focus on European-derived wealth reaches slightly greater elaboration, and Fore men are uncertain whether bride-price or the woman represents the greater value (Lindenbaum 1979:136).[14]

This state of affairs changes dramatically in the Western Highlands, where superiority is gained not by giving but by taking more wives from others. The focus of interest shifts here from the women to the objects given in exchange, and the center of attention concerns the imbalance in bride-wealth, not the imbalance in women (Strathern and Strathern 1971:158). One accompaniment of this total sequence of transformation concerns the displacement of erotic interest from semen substance to shells, which are said to be valued for a tantalizing "brightness" that attracts both men and women (ibid.:20),[15] a matter discussed again in the next section.

One can thus trace the pattern of relationships among affines as they change from the dogged egalitarianism of sister exchange, to a sense of the dominance of wife-givers as bride-price enters the system and the social labors of men and women become realigned. As the exchange of ceremonial wealth increases, accompanied by further redefinition in the division of labor by sex, the worth of the items exchanged (women and bride-wealth) becomes culturally ambiguous. The dominance of wife-takers emerges, along with a focus on goods produced by women and men, the latter set, however, in behaviors and ideas that mask women's contributions to the production process. Institutions of homosexuality or heterosexuality express and orchestrate the total configuration.

FROM SEMEN SUBSTANCE TO ITEMS OF CEREMONIAL EXCHANGE

The shift from semen to bride-price transactions (or from bride-service to bride-wealth societies in Collier and Rosaldo's terms), is accompanied here by a widening of the distance between the exchange partners themselves. Local group exogamy is supplanted by an expansion in the scope of marriage prohibitions, which now direct the passage of women beyond the clan to affinal kin, who may later become ceremonial exchange partners.[16] The increased labor of women now underwrites the garden work to produce root crops for domesticated pig herds and for larger human populations; ideologies of patrilineal unity (on the whole) supplant a focus on affinal connectedness, and the idea that men create men gives way to the notion that men "give birth to" key wealth. That is, in place of the rituals involving homosexuality which generate

349

a semen substance to fashion "men," the ceremonies of Western Highlands groups pose the notion that men transact with a different currency of exchange (pigs and shells) which are the hallmark of "big men." Where the ideologies of the semen cultures "mystify" women's contribution to the reproductive process, the big men cultures give women's labor a different order of invisibility. In the Western Highlands, appropriated female labor and the products of female labor command increasing male attention.[17]

The two types of exchange system thus differ in a number of ways, most tellingly in the nature of the objects exchanged and the manner in which they are produced and transacted. Certain constraints exist on the expansion of an exchange system in which semen is the focal commodity. The potential for amplification here lies in an acceptance of semen substitutes, such as coconut, pork fat (Orokaiva), and sago (Kimam). Sambia sometimes replenish semen depleted in homosexual activities by the ingestion of various milk saps at later stages of the initiation cycle. But the loss of male semen in heterosexual intercourse is renewed always by the auto-ingestion of these tree saps. Thus, many semen substitutes exist, but all conversions to prime substance take place within the body.

The objects of bride-price transaction, and subsequently of ceremonial exchange (feathers, shells, and pigs), freed from this bodily constraint, introduce a greater variety of more durable wealth into the exchange system, although it should be noted that many of the new exchange valuables are worn ceremonially as body ornaments, predominantly by men. Moreover, the new valuables belong to a hierarchy of worth that is subject to a different order of conversion. The Enga exchange system, for example, restricts category leaps (among four classes of valuables) beyond conversion to a proximate class, with the aim of gaining ultimate control of a category 1 item for use in ceremonial exchange. An *individual* Enga, for instance, may be compensated for insult with a pearl shell, a cowrie necklet, or a conus shell, items from categories 2, 3, and 4, respectively, while *clans* participate in the Tee exchange with pigs or cassowaries, items belonging to category 1 (Meggitt 1971). A relationship thus exists between the worth hierarchy of the valuables themselves, the denotation of who should participate in exchange with them, and the occasions on which a transaction may occur.

The exchange systems of the Western Highlands have thus arrived at a new order of magnitude and complexity, both in the objects of exchange themselves and in the social engineering they may be used to effect. Pigs, the Enga prime category, are used by all social aggregates above the level of the individual (the lineage, subclan, and clan) and for all social purposes appropriate to the behavior of these groups. Melpa shells have achieved perhaps a greater level of mobility and are used as generalized media in a wide range of transactions (A. Strathern 1969b). Moreover, the pigs and shells used in these exchange systems are no longer generated solely by home production (as is semen), but are passed from partner to partner in financial transactions that increase the volume of interchange generated by one item and provide power to the men who gain dominance in these financial networks. (It may be in this sense, the prestige of the donor, that Sambia men who have given their semen to many initiates are said to experience a sense of increased strength [Herdt, chap. 4].)

In tracing the symbolic transformations that exist between ritual exchanges of semen substance and ceremonial exchange objects, the Sambia provide a remarkable piece of evidence, for the same term that applies to masculine decorations and ritual paraphernalia (such as feathers and shells) is also a secret pseudonym for semen (Herdt, chap. 4). It is particularly fitting that the evidence should come from the Sambia, who occupy a fringe area of the Highlands and who have but recently begun to keep pigs and grow sweet potatoes in the manner of the Highlanders, thereby stepping up the need for female labor. Thus, the shift from semen to shells records, objectifies, and is an instrumental turning point in the appropriation by men of the sexual and social labors of women. These data seem also to support some of the insights of Ferenczi (1913, 1914), and especially of Fenichel (1938), concerning the relationships among social institutions, sexual instincts, and wealth.[18]

The Melanesian material also indicates the ways in which media of exchange that are not bodies (women) or body products (semen) can undergo cultural elaborations which in turn will form a basis for the hierarchical positioning of those who accumulate or exchange them. The transformations we have been following exhibit, in addition, a shift from involuted forms of marriage and ceremonial exchange to more expansive chains of ritual and social connection (Rubel and Rosman 1978). Furthermore, we see at one glance the dynamic connections between psyche and social process to which Bateson drew our attention (see Keesing 1982:2–3).

GENDER AMBIGUITY AND CROSS-SEX SIBLINGS

It is of some significance that the objects of exchange are of ambiguous gender. Even Melpa shells, which women are forbidden to exchange and which may seem to have traveled a greater distance from bodily entanglement than the other items of transaction, still appear to have important masculine and feminine features. The value of shells is based partly on an appreciation of their brightness or iridescent gleam (Strathern and Strathern 1971:20). This luminosity, which gives shells their magical ability to attract further wealth, is enhanced by sprinkling the shells and their resin backing with fresh red ocher, a substance and color used for women's face painting, which stands symbolically for both women and consanguineal ties. That is, the red paint on these ostensibly male items symbolically acknowledges that while men appropriate and control shells, they depend on female links (and perhaps female labor?) to obtain them (Strathern 1979:535).

Gender ambiguity is a striking feature also of the plant, animal, spirit, and human world of the societies described in this volume. Indeed, the cultural tolerance for gender ambiguity in societies with ritualized homosexuality exceeds that of "heterosexual" societies. The Sambia, for instance, have an appropriate cultural category and social place for male pseudohermaphrodites (Herdt 1981), in contrast to the Melpa, where such individuals remain unmarried (M. Strathern 1972:199), and also to the Mae Enga, whose women abandon "demon children" in the bush (Meggitt 1965b), doing away with what they consider anomalous births. In societies with ritualized homosexuality, by contrast, key items of ritual and exchange play upon, even amplify, the symbolic dissolution of sexual boundaries. The sago grub, a beetle used by the Onabasulu in affinal prestations, for example, has a life cycle with both "female" and "male" stages. Grub prestations thus offer for reflection a meaning that is said to transcend their exchange, objectifying as a unity the disparately experienced aspects of the male/

female dichotomy and reaffirming its basic complementarity (Ernst 1978). The cultural codes of the neighboring Bedamini, for whom the sago grub is also an important exchange item, propose a similar nonbinary message that homosexuality leads inexorably to heterosexuality, as growth leads to decay in the cosmic reproductive cycle (Sørum, chap. 8). These authors tell of transformations of body substances within and between the sexes, of oppositions that are mutable, and of gender constellations that have particular powers of attraction.

The hermaphroditic pig, an animal with ambiguous external genitalia, is a focus of cultural interest on Nduindui (Allen, chap. 2), as well as on other small islands of the North Vanuatu group. Of greater interest, perhaps, the intersexed pig is valued on the islands where ritualized homosexuality occurs in symbolic rather than behavioral form. On the island of Malekula, where homosexuality is a highly institutionalized behavior, the hermaphroditic pig is of no ritual interest at all. Men turn their attention instead to male pigs whose upper canines are removed, allowing the lower tusk to complete one or two circles. Big Namba men of Malekula rise in rank as they sacrifice these pigs in elaborate rituals of masculinity, storing the circled tusk as a memorial of the event (Layard 1942). Having also knocked out the canines of their own women, men give ritual attention to an animal which, although near meatless, combines the image of the phallus and the vagina in a male body. A product of their own ritual intervention, it is a suitable symbol of sexual hegemony, compatible with the political authority of the hereditary chiefs of patrilineal clans, as Allen notes.

Malekula, however, presents some contradictory evidence for the present analysis, for although the creative powers of ambiguously gendered ceremonial items become muted here, in much the same way that Melpa delete direct reference to the feminine aspect of shells, this occurs in an area where ritualized homosexuality has developed in a manner unknown in other parts of Melanesia. Hereditary Malekulan chiefs exercise a monopoly on the sexual and social labors of many youths and many wives, a situation that would require a separate social and historical analysis for this Eastern Melanesian island region.

The theme of cultural hermaphroditism occurs also among the

353

neighboring Nduindui, who make erotic play of sexual "confusion" in the theatrical interludes of initiation. Male dancers turn their buttocks (as if they were women) toward a group of male and female novices, while singing songs to them in the manner of male seducers (Allen, chap. 2). The motif of a continuing feminine identity in male bodies is a subject of initiation discourse that goes well beyond the north Vanuatu region, as Allen observes.

Perhaps the most striking aspect of sexual fusion, with its potential for order or chaos, concerns the theme of the brother/sister pair, which occupies a prominent place in the present assemblage of essays. The primordial act of sexual separation is represented in social life by two men who exchange sisters, giving away that part of themselves that contains a "natural" fertility. Their reluctance to undergo this separation is expressed by the Baruya, whose myths of origin propose that humanity was born of a double incest (Godelier 1976:21).[19] Baruya are said to confess that at times, "when they really think about it, they would rather marry their 'sisters' with whom they grew up and whom they know well, than marry a girl from a different lineage and spend their lives with a stranger" (ibid.:20). Moreover, when a Baruya girl first menstruates, her fiancé declares, "You are no longer your father's, but mine. Look upon me as your older brother" (ibid.:19).

The theme of incest, in which two men vicariously fulfill each other's sister-incest desire, is said to form the psychological template for sexual development in societies with ritualized homosexuality and sister exchange (Layard 1959:105). The creative power of sibling incest is a message ritually enacted also in Nduindui initiation, where its awesome potency generates prestige for the ritual sponsor as well as for the participants (Allen, chap. 2).

Brother and sister seem at times to be treated as a single unit. What happens to one has a consequence for the other. Beardmore (1890) writes, for instance, of a ceremony among Kiwai and Mowat peoples in which a brother leaves the house of his father to reside in the men's house, where men anally copulate with him. At this time, his sister has a V-shaped cut incised above her breasts, a scar she is said to carry for life. This symbolic castration allows her brother to become a fertile being, differentiated from her, and the possessor of their inherited masculinity. The interdependencies of the brother/sister pair are conveyed also by the inseparability of marriage and initiation as an institutional complex. For instance, Herdt (1981) writes of the synchrony of marriage and the later stages of Sambia initiation. Kelly, too, notes that an Etoro father arranges his daughter's marriage (when she is five years old) and thereby nominates his son's inseminator, since these are ideally one and the same (Kelly 1976:52–53). Not only do initiation rituals thereby coincide with marriage ceremonies in the same communities, but the sister's marriage in many ways delivers to her brother an element of her own fertility.

The ritual severance of male/female siblings, once effected, results in an altered status for both. As soon as a young Baruya man is initiated and enters the men's house, for instance, his older sisters stop calling him "little brother" and begin referring to him as an "older" sibling (Godelier 1982a:15). From a balanced pair, a new hierarchy emerges, a status change the Bedamini express in the form of men's ceremonial acquisition of the genitalia of both sexes. A male dancer, leading the procession of initiates who are in transition to adulthood, has a vulva painted on his chest and a crescent-shaped pearl shell (said to be one of his most precious possessions) tied to his beard (Sørum, chap. 8). The pearl shell, a masculine symbol that we may now assume to be an objectification of his semen substance, speaks also to the symbolic elusion of human and social reproduction in indigenous discourse. The message of the generative power of male/female siblings is muffled in the Western Highlands, where initiation (among Enga and Melpa) is not part of the marriage-ceremonial exchange complex, and where the centripetal thrust of social and psychic attention is rent by marriage rules that broaden the range of kin with whom sex is prohibited.

HOMOEROTICISM

This brings us to the topic of erotic pleasure, not much discussed in anthropology, as Herdt (1982a, chaps. 1, 4) notes. Much has been written on forms of sexual antagonism in Papua New Guinea, but anthropologists have been less attentive to different kinds of pleasures and desires. The essays in this volume alert us to the importance of homoeroticism and heteroeroticism as formulative individual and social experiences. We appreciate the different qualities of sensual knowledge created at different stages of juvenile and adult life, from narcissism to erotism, at least for one gender. Moreover, the vision of male life cycles that expunge mother, often before puberty, but permit qualitatively different libidinal attachments to sister, should make us reflect upon what we have come to think of as "sexual instinct."

The erotics of everyday life in Melanesia derive also from notions of identity that are relational, not essential. Individual identity in these circumstances seems to require continual reproduction, made collectively and socially, rather than discovered, as we think, "from within." The tolerance for gender ambiguity diminishes as cultural themes direct erotic attention toward objects attached to the self, rather than toward treasured internal substances.

Read's essay describes with some refinement the psychodynamics of a world different from one in which semen and sister exchange define the paths of men, women, and affinally related groups. Gahuku-Gama age-mates, like Orokaiva dancers, uphold an ideal relationship that lacks a sense of hierarchy. The age-mate is a duplicate of the self, and initiation rituals aim at a psychosocial bonding that gives rise to a subjective sense of "shared maleness" among men who are bonded as affines. This phallic sense of being, however, appears to be accompanied by a special kind of sexual anxiety. Gahuku-Gama men believe that they should be the object of women's desires, yet they doubt that they are. Even armed with magical substances to draw women to them, they still find that girls frequently precipitate the breaking of a first betrothal, which deprives the men of their full masculine status. Moreover, Gahuku-Gama men think they are contaminated by sexual contact with women, a set of contradictions which appears to arise in the absence of the contractual assurance of receiving a wife by sister and semen exchange. Greater burdens are thus placed on young men to *create* an aura of masculine desirability, a task they share with fellow age-mates who face the same predicament. Men in these societies must call upon a set of emotional and cognitive sensibilities to create bonds among themselves, in much the way that men and women use notions of romantic love in free-choice marriages in Western culture. Homoerotic bonding thus provides men with one avenue of support, as does the idea that women are polluting, a notion that similarly sends men toward members of their own sex for the reinforcement of conflict-laden identities. It is significant that the notion that women contaminate men is not found in most of the sister-exchanging societies with ritualized homosexuality.[20] The age-mates of the Eastern Highlands, like the Orokaiva dancers (Schwimmer, chap. 6), thus join in a lifelong "embrace" that creates for them a sense of masculine presence, a politicosexual potency with which they attract and discipline their women.

Still, matters between men and women are not as simple as this "resolution" might make it seem. The "deep structure" of the male pair, Schwimmer reminds us, is really a triangle, with a female as the hidden third party, a message transmitted also by the paired *nama* flutes, which tell of a masculine authority that combines both masculine and feminine elements. The initiation process, too, begins with young males as quasi females, passing through changing relationships with their instructors to a definition of male gender that still combines both elements. Moreover, while the rites are designed to make boys into men, they do so in a paradoxical way, by "feminizing" them, as Allen (chap. 2) and others have noted. We are in a hall of mirrors, bound to become more dizzying when women's images of themselves, as well as of men, begin to refract among the rest.

The key Melanesian theme of a male being who incorporates his opposite is a message we have heard before at other times and in other places. The androgyne, primarily a male figure in India as well, is a creator whose completeness allows him to generate from within himself. As a theological image, the androgyne changes to accommodate the shifting currents of religious movement that give it life. The androgynous figures posed by Vedic and Puranic Hinduism, religions of hierarchy and caste, split apart in order to be creative. Various forms of Indian mysticism, by contrast, extoll a pro-chaos image in which the mystic merges with an undifferentiated godhead to realize his nature (O'Flaherty 1980). Images of the female-in-male or male-in-female are thus alive with psychological, ideological, and social import. Future studies in Melanesia may tell us whether women see themselves as merging or splitting beings, or perhaps both.

The present studies provide us, nevertheless, with some understanding of the nexus of sexual and social transformations that we see elsewhere at a distance and across greater expanses of time. By comparing a somewhat idealized view of the small-scale Lowland societies of Melanesia with the populous Western Highlanders (placing the Eastern Highlands for this purpose somewhere in the middle), and by viewing the systems as they change in time, we can begin to trace some of the symbolic/structural continuities and discontinuities that exist among them.

Procreation theories, and the degree to which people attend to them, provide an important clue for understanding these linkages. The semen and semen-blood models of reproduction (from the Lowlands and Western Highlands, respectively), as male ideologies of the reproduction of social life, occur in somewhat different contexts. Although the latter model assigns women a certain ideological place, we have seen that the dominant discourse has moved away from women's generative role in social reproduction, and women's labor contributions thereby become culturally invisible.

Procreation theories appear in contexts that differ as to the things being reproduced, as well as the means by which procreation is thought to be achieved. All objects that are exchanged mediate social interaction, thus shaping and becoming instruments of transformation. Semen and bride-price objects (which become the wealth of male ceremonial exchange) belong to a set of connections that bind individuals in differing ways to work processes, as well as to one another. Sister and semen exchange thus reproduce social systems that differ qualitatively from the ones generated by bridewealth. Centripetal or centrifugal marriage rules, as well as the interactions among affines as equals, inferiors, or superiors, are important components of these changing sets of relationships. So too is the male initiation complex, with ritualized homosexual and homosocial behaviors shaping gender constructs that elicit certain qualities of erotic attachment. Notions of identity forged in different social and relational environments parallel, in some sense, ideas of sexuality, for sexuality, like gender, is the social product of a particular era.

Different concepts of selfhood develop also when a cosmology is drawn from the body rather than from the external world. Moreover, when body parts and body substances are seen as essential constituents of personality, and where societies pay greater attention than do we to the physical bases of emotion (Read 1955), bodily experiences contribute to different modes of subjective knowledge. The inner states of individuals must differ, therefore, where people transact predominantly with parts of self rather than with representations of self.

The contributors to this volume present us with abundant material with which to reformulate a number of old assumptions. The story of homosexuality and heterosexuality in Melanesia is an account of the development of masculine identities and erotic states forged in ritual and familial environments we have little considered. We are offered data that is at once private and social, personal and political. The story is a chapter in the political economy of gender, as well as in the history of money, as psychic energies relinquish body substance in favor of more objectified forms of wealth with which to express and influence the sociosexual relations of production.

Future studies will build upon this venture and should furnish us with accounts of female identities, constituted by women (and men) in various ritual and secular contexts. Following the analysis suggested here, one line of inquiry might trace the connections linking the exchange of milk among women (Godelier 1982b:15) with the exchange of more objectified women-produced items, such as net bags, skirts, mats, banana-leaf bundles, and other forms of women's wealth.[21] Such an analysis would track the diminution of gender inflected onto the objects themselves, as they articulate with items that men exchange (resulting from male production or male appropriation), and would provide a fuller gloss on the psychosocial interactions of women and men in their everyday lives.

The present collection of essays nevertheless provides abundant new testimony for the current exploration of sex and gender which appears to herald the overthrow of those modes of thought whereby, we believe, we have obscured or misrepresented our bodies to ourselves. We now see that our tendency to think that nature is to culture as female is to male, as domestic and private is to political and public, does not hold for much of the world for much of the time (Rapp 1979). Deprived of their formerly invisible status as a grid through which to view the universe, these dualities lose the authority they once had over us. Moreover, it is as if the game will never end. All the components of the discourse are now seen to be culturally and historically constituted, not the least among them, notions about men, women, and sexuality, the fundaments of the entire edifice.

NOTES

1. An earlier version of this paper was presented at the City University of New York Graduate Anthropology Symposium on Gender Relations and Social Reproduction in November, 1980. I am grateful to Jane Schneider and other participants in the symposium for helpful comments on that occasion. I would also like to thank the following readers for their perceptive comments: Richard Shapiro, Pam Smith, Joyce Riegelhaupt, Annette Weiner, and John Lindenbaum.

2. See Herdt (chap. 1). Deacon (1934) reports lesbian relationships on Malekula, and Godelier (1982a:82) speaks of imitative sexual intercourse during Baruya female initiation. DuToit (1975) also reports women lying together in positions of intercourse. However, the institutionalized female/female erotic relationship is a historically avoided ethnographic topic.

3. Sambia belong to this Eastern Highlands flute complex in the sense that these phallic instruments, said to have been stolen from women, are key symbols in the male bloodletting initiation experience (Herdt 1982a, 1982b).

4. See Keesing (1982) on the sociopolitical context of the ritual forging of men. It is important to recall also that children in bride-service societies lead a rather untroubled, labor-free existence (Collier and Rosaldo 1981). The discipline of initiation comes as a severe corrective, turning juniors into productive adults. This contrasts with the Enga, among whom there is no initiation, and children lead a controlled existence, which includes gardening and pig herding.

5. See Rubel and Rosman (1978) for a structuralist reading of the process.

6. See Whitehead (n.d.) and Lindenbaum (n.d.) for earlier analyses utilizing this large-scale contrast.

7. Eastern Highland societies provide a symbolic turning point, in that they manifest an interest in both blood and semen (Sambia) or blood and flutes (Fore, Gahuku-Gama), the flute a symbolic penis that emits sound.

8. I would like to acknowledge here the value for the present analysis of Collier and Rosaldo's (1981) work on bride-service and bride-wealth societies as ideal types.

9. The Big Nambas of Malekula (discussed below) are in many ways an exception.

10. Banaro also observe a complex four-way exchange system. See also McDowell (1972) for a detailed account of the difficulty of adhering to the rules of sister exchange, again, in a society with no rituals involving homosexuality.

11. Compare Tuzin (1976:310) who describes a similar set of trans-
    formations in the Sepik region. See also Barth (1971) and Bulmer
    (1960–61) on ritual/ceremonial integration.
12. The Bedamini seem anomalous in this respect.
13. Similar historical transformations may underwrite the extreme
    forms of male/female hostility documented in the Eastern
    Highlands.
14. It is significant also that Fore men become "contaminated" by giv-
    ing bride-service to affines (Lindenbaum 1979:124).
15. A parallel analysis might examine hair, grown long and rubbed
    with semen and semen substitutes in the Lowlands, greased with
    pig fat in the Eastern Highlands, and severed by Western High-
    land men, who fashion it into wigs.
16. Rubel and Rosman (1978) provide a lucid analysis of the struc-
    tural transformations involved here.
17. Lindenbaum n.d. presents this view in more detail.
18. See Epstein's (1977) essay which asks why Tolai shell money
    (*tambu*) is so highly charged and is also called by the same name
    as that which is tabooed.
19. Compare references to incest origin myths among the Etoro, the
    Marind-anim, and the Kaluli, to which Schwimmer (chap. 6)
    refers.
20. See Meigs (1976) for further data concerning the contamination
    of men and women.
21. In some ways, the discussion is already under way. See Weiner
    1976, M. Strathern 1981, and Sexton 1982.

Bibliography

Allen, M. R.

1964   The Nduindui: A study in the social structure of a New Hebridean community. Ph.D. dissertation, Australian National University.

1967   *Male Cults and Secret Initiations in Melanesia.* Melbourne: Melbourne University Press.

1968   The establishment of Christianity and cash-cropping in a New Hebridean community. *J. of Pac. Hist.* 3:25–46.

1969   Report on Aoba: Incidental papers on Nduindui District, Aoba Island. Edited by C. Leaney. Vila, New Hebrides. Mimeographed.

1972   Rank and leadership in Nduindui, northern New Hebrides. *Mankind* 8:270–282.

1981   Innovation, inversion and revolution as political tactics in West Aoba. In *Vanuatu: Politics, Economics and Ritual in Island Melanesia,* edited by M. R. Allen, pp. 105–134. Sydney: Academic Press.

In press   Elders, chiefs and big men: Authority legitimation and political evolution in Melanesia. *American Ethnologist.*

Amelsvoort, V. F. P. M. Van

1964   *Culture, Stone Age and Modern Medicine.* Assen: Van Gorcum.

Ashley-Montague, M. F.

1937   The origin of subincision in Australia. *Oceania*
(–1938)   8:193–207.

Ashworth, A. E., and W. M. Walker

1972   Social structure and homosexuality: A theoretical appraisal. *Brit. J. Sociol.* 23:146–158.

Atkinson, J. J.

1903   *Primal Law.* New York: Longmans, Green & Co.

362

Augé, Marc
1982   *Genie du Paganisme*. Paris: Gallimard.

Baal, J. Van
1934   *Godsdienst en Samenleving in Nederlandsch-Zuid-Nieuw-Guinea*. Amsterdam: Noordhollandsche Uitgeversmaatschappy.

1963   The cult of the bull-roarer in Australia and Southern New Guinea. *Bijdragen tot de Taal-, Land-, en Volkenkunde* 119:201–214.

1966   *Dema, Description and Analysis of Marind-anim Culture*. The Hague: Martinus Nijhoff.

1970   The part of women in the marriage trade: objects or behaving as objects? *Bijdragen tot de Taal-, Land-, en Volkenkunde* 126:289–308.

1975   *Reciprocity and the Position of Women*. Assen: Van Gorcum.

1981   *Man's Quest for Partnership*. Assen: Van Gorcum.

1982   *Jan Verschueren's Description of Yéi-nan Culture*. The Hague: Martinus Nijhoff.

Bamler, V. G.
1911   Tami. In *Deutsch Neu-Guinea*, 3 vols. edited by R. Neubauss, pp. 489–566. Berlin: Verlag Dietrich Reimer/Ernst Vohsen.

Barker, T. N.
1975   Some features of Ai'i society. Ph.D. dissertation, Dept. of Anthropology, Laval University.

Barth, F.
1971   Tribes and intertribal relations in the Fly headwaters. *Oceania* 41:171–191.

1975   *Ritual and Knowledge Among the Baktaman of New Guinea*. New Haven: Yale University Press.

Bateson, G.
1932   Social structure of the Iatmul people of the Sepik. *Oceania* 2:245–291, 401–453.

1946   Arts of the South Seas. *Art Bulletin* 28:119–123.

1958   *Naven*. 2d edition. Stanford: Stanford University Press. (Orig. 1936).

1972   *Steps to an Ecology of Mind*. Scranton, Penn.: Chandler Publishing Company.

1978   Towards a theory of cultural coherence: Comment. *Anthropological Quarterly* 51:77–78.

Baumann, H. Van
1955   *Das Doppelte Geschlecht. Ethnologische Studien zur Bisexualitat in Ritus und Mythos*. Berlin: Dietrich Reimer.

Baxter-Riley, E.
1925   *Among Papuan Headhunters*. London: Seeley, Service and Company.

Beardmore, E.
1890   The natives of Mowat, Daudi, New Guinea. *JRAI* 19:459–466.

Beaver, Wilfred E.
1920   *Unexplored New Guinea*. London: Seeley, Service and Company.

Bell, F. L. S.
1935   The avoidance situation in Tanga. *Oceania* 6:175–
(–1936)   199, 306–325.

Berndt, C. H.
1965   Women and the "secret life." In *Aboriginal Man in Australia,* edited by R. M. and C. H. Berndt, pp. 236–282. Sydney: Angus and Robertson.

Berndt, R. M.
1965   The Kamano, Usurfa, Jate and Fore of the Eastern Highlands. In *Gods, Ghosts and Men in Melanesia,* edited by P. Lawrence and M. J. Meggitt, pp. 78–104. Melbourne: Melbourne University Press.

Berndt, R. M., and C. H. Berndt
1951   *Sexual Behavior in Western Arnhem Land*. New York: Viking Fund Publication no. 16.

Bettelheim, B.
1955   *Symbolic Wounds, Puberty Rites and the Envious Male*. New York: Collier Books.

Bieber, I., et al.
1962   *Homosexuality, A Psychoanalytic Study*. New York: Basic Books.

Blackwood, B.
1935   *Both Sides of Buka Passage*. Oxford: Clarendon Press.
1939   Life on the Upper Watut, New Guinea. *Geographical Journal* 94:11–28.
1951   Some arts and industries of the Bosmun, Ramu River, New Guinea. In *Suedseestudien, Gedenkschrift zur Erinnerung an Felix Speiser,* pp. 266–288. Basel: Museum fuer Volkerkunde.

Blackwood, P.
1981   Rank, exchange and leadership in four Vanuatu societies. In *Vanuatu: Politics, Economics and Ritual in Island Melanesia,* edited by Michael Allen, pp. 35–84. Sydney: Academic Press.

Bleibtreu-Ehrenberg, G.
1980   *Mannbarkeitsriten*. Vienna: Ullstein Materialien.

Boelaars, J. H. M. C.
1950   *The Linguistic Position of South-Western New Guinea.* Leiden: E. J. Brill.
1981   *Head-hunters About Themselves.* Verhandelingen van het kon. Instituut voor Taal-, Land- en Volkenkunde, no. 92. The Hague: Martinus Nijhoff.

Boswell, J.
1980   *Christianity, Social Tolerance, and Homosexuality.* Chicago: University of Chicago Press.

Bourdieu, P.
1977   *Outline of a Theory of Practice.* Trans. Richard Nice. Cambridge: Cambridge University Press.

Bowers, N.
1965   Permanent bachelorhood in the Upper Kaugel Valley of Highland New Guinea. *Oceania* 36:27–37.

Bremmer, J.
1980   An enigmatic Indo-European rite: Paederasty. *Arethusa* 13:279–298.

Brookfield, H., and D. Hart
1971   *Melanesia: A Geographic Interpretation of an Island World.* London: Methuen.

Brown, J. K.
1963   A cross-cultural study of female initiation rites. *American Anthropologist* 65:837–853.

Brown, P.
1978   *Highland Peoples of New Guinea.* Cambridge: Cambridge University Press.

Brown, P., and G. Buchbinder
1976   Introduction. In *Man and Woman in the New Guinea Highlands,* edited by P. Brown and G. Buchbinder, pp. 1–12. Washington, D.C.: American Anthropological Association.

Buchbinder, G.
1973   Maring microadaptation: A study of demographic, nutritional, genetic and phenotypic variation in a Highland New Guinea population. Ph.D. dissertation, Columbia University.

Bulmer, R. N. H.
1960   Political aspects of the Moka ceremonial exchange
(–1961) system among the Kyaka people of the Western Highlands of New Guinea. *Oceania* 3:1–13.
1970   Intensive ethnographic studies. In *An Atlas of Papua and New Guinea,* edited by R. G. Ward and D. A. M. Lea, pp. 92–96. Port Moresby: University of Papua New Guinea and Collins-Longman.

1971   Traditional forms of family limitation in New Guinea. In *Population Growth and Socio-Economic Change,* pp. 137–162. Research Bulletin no. 42. Canberra, Australia: A.N.U. Press.

Burridge, K.
1979   *Someone, No One.* Princeton: Princeton University Press.

Burton, R. V., and J. W. M. Whiting
1961   The absent father and cross-sex identity. *Merrill-Palmer Quarterly of Behavior and Development* 7:85–95.

Carrier, J.
1972   Urban Mexican male homosexual encounters: An analysis of participants and coping strategies. Ph.D. dissertation, University of California, Irvine.

1977   Sex-role preference as an explanatory variable in homosexual behavior. *Archives of Sexual Behavior* 6:53–65.

1980*a* Homosexual behavior in cross-cultural perspective. In *Homosexual Behavior: A Modern Reappraisal,* edited by J. Marmor, pp. 100–122. New York: Basic Books.

1980*b* The Omani xanith controversy. *Man* 15:541–542.

Chalmers, J.
1903*a* Notes on the Bugilai, British New Guinea. *JRAI* 33:108–110.

1903*b* Notes on the natives of Kiwai Island, Fly River. *JRAI* 33:117–124.

Chinnery, E. W. P., and W. N. Beaver
1915   Notes on the initiation ceremonies of the Koko, Papua. *JRAI* 15:69–78.

Chowning, A.
1980   Culture and biology among the Sengseng of New Britain. *J. Polynesian Society* 89:7–31.

Codrington, R. H.
1891   *The Melanesians.* Oxford: The Clarendon Press.

Cohen, Y. A.
1964   *The Transition from Childhood to Adolescence.* Chicago: Aldine Publishing Co.

Collier, J. F., and M. Z. Rosaldo
1981   Politics and gender in simple societies. In *Sexual Meanings,* edited by S. B. Ortner and H. Whitehead, pp. 275–329. Cambridge: Cambridge University Press.

Coppet, D. de
1981   The Life-Giving Death. In *Mortality and Immortality,*

    edited by S. C. Humphreys and H. King, pp. 175–204. New York: Academic Press.

Cory, D. W., ed.
1956   *Homosexuality: A Cross-Cultural Approach.* New York: Julian Press.

D'Andrade, R. G.
1966   Sex differences and cultural institutions. In *The Development of Sex Differences,* edited by E. E. Maccoby, pp. 173–203. Stanford: Stanford University Press.

Davenport, W. H.
1965   Sexual patterns and their regulation in a society of the Southwest Pacific. In *Sex and Behavior,* edited by F. A. Beach, pp. 164–207. New York: John Wiley.

1977   Sex in cross-cultural perspective. In *Human Sexuality in Four Perspectives,* edited by F. A. Beach and M. Diamond, pp. 155–163. Baltimore: Johns Hopkins University Press.

Deacon, A. B.
1925   The Kakihan society of Ceram and New Guinea initiation cults. *Folk-lore* 36:332–361.

1934   *Malekula: A Vanishing People in the New Hebrides.* London: George Routledge.

DeCoster, M.
1978   *L'analogie en Sciences Humaines.* Paris: PUF.

Devereux, G.
1937   Institutionalized homosexuality of the Mohave Indians. *Human Biology* 9:498–527.

Donaldson, M.
n.d.   Warfare, production and sexual antagonism: The political economy of pre-capitalist societies in the Eastern Highlands of Papua New Guinea. Unpublished MS.

Doucere, Mgr. V.
1934   *La Mission Catholique aux Nouvelles Hebrides.* Paris and Lyons: Emmanuel Vitte.

Douglas, M.
1966   *Purity and Danger.* London: Routledge and Kegan Paul.

Dover, K. J.
1978   *Greek Homosexuality.* Cambridge, Mass.: Harvard University Press.

Dumont, L.
1980   *Homo Hierarchicus.* Trans. M. Sainsbury, L. Dumont, and B. Gulati. Complete revised English ed. Chicago: University of Chicago Press.

Dundes, A.
1976 A psychoanalytic study of the bull-roarer. *Man* 11:220–238.
1978 Into the endzone for a touchdown: A psychoanalytic analysis of American football. *Western Folklore* 37:75–88.

DuToit, B. M.
1975 *Akuna, A New Guinea Village Community.* Rotterdam: A. A. Bakema.

Dutton, T. E.
1969 *The Peopling of Central Papua.* Pacific Linguistics Monograph 9. Canberra: Linguistic Circle of Canberra.

Eekhoud, J. P. K. Van
1962 *Ethnografie van de Kaowerawedj.* Verhandelingen van het kon. Instituut voor Taal-, Land- en Volkenkunde, no. 37. The Hague: Martinus Nijhoff.

Eliade, M.
1958 *Rites and Symbols of Initiation.* Trans. Williard R. Trask. New York: Harper Torchbooks.
1976 Spirit, light and seed. In *Occultism, Witchcraft, and Cultural Fashions,* by M. Eliade, pp. 93–119. Chicago: University of Chicago Press.

Ellis, H.
1929 Preface. In *The Sexual Life of Savages,* by B. Malinowski, pp. vii–xiii. New York: Harcourt, Brace & World, Inc.
1936 *Studies in the Psychology of Sex.* Vol. 2. New York: Random House. (Orig. 1910).

Elmberg, J. E.
1955 Field notes on the Mejbrat people in the Ajamaru District of the Bird's Head (Vogelkop), Western New Guinea. *Ethnos* 20:3–102.
1965 The Popot feast cycle. *Ethnos* 30 (supplement) 1–172.

Epstein, A. L.
1977 *Tambu:* Shell money in Tolai. In *Fantasy and Symbol,* edited by R. A. Hook, pp. 149–205. London: Academic Press.

Ernst, T. M.
1978 Aspects of meaning of exchanges and exchange items among the Onabasulu of the Great Papuan Plateau. *Mankind* 11:187–197.
1979 Myth, ritual, and population among the Marind-anim. *Social Analysis* 1:34–53.

Errington, F. K.
1974   *Karavar: Masks and Power in a Melanesian Ritual.*
            Ithaca: Cornell University Press.

Evans-Pritchard, E. E.
1970   Sexual inversion among the Azande. *American An-*
            thropologist 72:1428–1434.

Faithorn, E.
1975   The concept of pollution among the Kafe of Papua
            New Guinea. In *Toward an Anthropology of Women,*
            edited by R. R. Reiter, pp. 127–140. New York:
            Monthly Review Press.

Farquhar, J., and D. C. Gajdusek
1981   *Kuru: Early Letters and Field-Notes from the Collec-*
            tion of D. Carleton Gajdusek. New York: Raven
            Press.

Federn, P.
1952   *Ego Psychology and the Psychoses.* New York: Basic
            Books.

Feil, Daryl K.
1978   Women and men in the Enga Tee. *American Ethnolo-*
            gist 5:263–279.

Fenichel, O.
1938   The drive to amass wealth. *Psychoanal. Quart.* 7:69–
            95.

Ferenczi, Sandor
1913   The ontogenesis of symbols. In *Contributions to Psy-*
            cho-Analysis, 1916, pp. 233–237. Boston: R. Badger.
1914   The ontogenesis of the interest in money. In *Contribu-*
            tions to Psycho-Analysis, 1916, pp. 269–279. Boston:
            R. Badger.

Fikkert, D. H.
1928   *Bestuursmemorie van den gezaghebber D. H. Fikkert*
            over het tijdvak Oktober 1928–1933. Unpublished
            MS.

Firth, Raymond
1973   *Symbols Public and Private.* London: Allen and
            Unwin.
1981   Spiritual aroma: Religion and politics. Distinguished
            lecture for 1980. *American Anthropologist* 83:582–
            605.

Fischer, H.
1968   *Die Negwa: eine Papua-Gruppe im Wandel.* Munich:
            Klaus Renner Verlag.

Fitzgerald, T. K.
1977   A critique of anthropological research on homosexuality. *Journal of Homosexuality* 2(4):285–397.

Foley, M.
1879   Sur les habitations et les moeurs des Neo-Caledoniens. *Bul. de la Soc. d'Anth. de Paris,* ser. iii, 2:604–606.

Ford, C. S.
1960   Sex offenses: an anthropological perspective. *Law and Contemporary Problems* 25:225–248.

Ford, C. S., and F. Beach
1951   *Patterns of Sexual Behavior.* New York: Harper and Bros.

Forge, A.
1972   The Golden Fleece. *Man.* 7:527–540.
1973   Style and Meaning in Sepik Art. In *Primitive Art and Society,* edited by A. Forge, pp. 170–192. London: Oxford University Press.

Foucault, M.
1980   *The History of Sexuality.* Trans. by Robert Hurley. New York: Vintage Books.

Foulks, E. F., ed.
1977   Anthropology and psychiatry: A new blending of an old relationship. In *Current Perspectives in Cultural Psychiatry,* edited by E. F. Foulks et al., pp. 5–18. New York: Spectrum Publications, Inc.

Freud, S.
1961   The future of an illusion. In *The Standard Edition of the Complete Psychological Works of Sigmund Freud,* ed. and trans. J. Strachey, 21:3–57. London: Hogarth Press. (Orig. 1927).
1962   *Three Essays on the Theory of Sexuality.* Trans. J. Strachey. New York: Basic Books. (Orig. 1905).

Gajdusek, D. C., et al.
1972   *Annotated Anga (Kukukuku) Bibliography.* Bethesda, Maryland: National Institute of Mental Health.

Galis, K. W.
1955   *Papua's van de Humboldt Baai.* The Hague: Voorhoeve.

Gebhard, P.
1971   Human sexual behavior: A summary statement. In *Human Sexual Behavior,* edited by D. S. Marshall and R. Suggs, pp. 206–217. New York: Basic Books.

Geertz, C.
1973   Ethos, world view and the analysis of sacred symbols. In *The Interpretation of Culture,* by C. Geertz, pp. 126–141. New York: Basic Books.

Gell, A.
1975   *Metamorphosis of the Cassowaries.* London: The Athlone Press.

Gennep, Arnold Van
1960   *The Rites of Passage.* Trans. M. K. Vizedom and G. L. Caffee. Chicago: University of Chicago Press.

Geurtjens, H. M. S. C.
1934   *Op zoek naar Oermenschen.* Amsterdam: Roermond-Maaseik.

Gewertz, D.
1977   From sago suppliers to entrepreneurs: Marketing and migration in the Middle Sepik. *Oceania* 48:126–140.

Glasse, R. M.
1974   Le masque de la volupte: Symbolisme et antagonisne sexuels surles hauts plateaux de Nouvelle Guinee, *L'Homme* 14:79–86.

Glasse, R. M., and M. J. Meggitt
1969   *Pigs, Pearlshells, and Women.* Englewood Cliffs, N.J.: Prentice-Hall, Inc.

Godelier, M.
1969   Land tenure among the Baruya of New Guinea. *J. of the Papua New Guinea Soc.* 3:17–23.
1971   "Salt currency" and the circulation of commodities among the Baruya of New Guinea. In *Studies in Economic Anthropology,* pp. 53–73. Washington, D.C.: American Anthropological Association.
1976   Sex as the ultimate foundation and cosmic order of the New Guinea Baruya: Myth and reality. Godelier's translation of his paper in *Sexualité et Pouvoir,* edited by A. Verdiglione, pp. 268–306. Paris: Traces Payot.
1977   *Perspectives in Marxist Anthropology.* Trans. Robert Brain. Cambridge: Cambridge University Press.
1982*a*   *La Production des Grands Hommes.* Paris: Fayard.
1982*b*   Social hierarchies among the Baruya of New Guinea. In *Inequality in New Guinea Highland Societies,* edited by A. Strathern, pp. 3–34. Cambridge: Cambridge University Press.

Goodenough, W.
1971   The pageant of death in Nakanai. In *Melanesia: Readings on a Cultural Area,* edited by L. L. Langness and J. C. Weschler, pp. 279–290. Scranton, Penn.: Chandler Publishing Co.

Gourguechon, C.
1977   *Journey to the End of the Earth.* New York: Charles Scribner's Sons.

Gourlay, K. A.
1975   *Sound-Producing Instruments in a Traditional Society: A Study of Esoteric Instruments and Their Role in Male-Female Relationships.* New Guinea Research Bulletin no. 60. Port Moresby: A.N.U. Press.

Greenberg, J. H.
1971   The Indo-Pacific hypothesis. In *Current Trends in Linguistics. Vol. 8: Linguistics in Oceania,* edited by T. A. Sebeok, pp. 807–871. The Hague: Mouton and Co.

Guiart, J.
1952   L'organisation sociale et politique du nord Malekula. *J. Soc. Ocean.* 8:149–259.
1953   Native society in the New Hebrides: The Big Nambas of Northern Malekula. *Mankind* 4:439–446.

Haddon, A. C.
1890   The ethnography of the western tribe of Torres Straits. *JRAI* 19:297–440.
1891   The Tugeri head-hunters of New Guinea. *Internl. Arch. f. Ethnogr.* 4:177–180.
1917   New Guinea. In *Hastings' Encyclopaedia of Religion and Ethics* 9:339–352.
1920   Migrations of cultures in British New Guinea. *JRAI* 50:234–280.
1924   Introduction to *In Primitive New Guinea,* by J. H. Holmes, pp. i–xii. New York: G. P. Putnam's Sons.
1927   Introduction to *The Kiwai Papuans of British New Guinea,* by G. Landtman, pp. ix–xx. London: Macmillan & Co. Ltd.
1936   Introduction to *Papuans of the Trans-Fly,* by F. E. Williams, pp. xxiii–xxxiv. Oxford: Oxford University Press.

Hage, P.
1981   On male initiation and dual organization in New Guinea. *Man* 16:268–275.

Hallpike, C. R.
1977   *Bloodshed and Vengeance in the Papuan Mountains.* New York: Oxford University Press.

Hallpike, C. R., ed.
1978   *The Kukukuku of the Upper Watut,* by Beatrice Blackwood. Oxford Monograph Series no. 2. Oxford: Oxprint.

Handelman, D.
1979   Is Naven Ludic? Paradox and the communication of identity. *Social Analysis* 1:177–191.

Hardman, E. T.
1889   Habits and customs of natives of Kimberly, Western
               Australia. *Proc. Roy. Irish Acad.*, 3d ser., 7:70–75.

Harrison, T.
1937   *Savage Civilization.* London: Victor Gollancz Ltd.

Hauser-Schaeublin, B.
1977   *Franen in Kararau.* Basler Beitraege zur Ethnologie,
               vol. 18.
1977   Vom terror und segen des blutes, oder: Die emanzipa-
(–1978)   tion des mannes von der frau. *Wiener Voelkerkundige*
               Mitteilungen 24/25 (N.F. Bd. 19/20), pp. 93–116.

Heider, K. G.
1976   Dani sexuality: A low energy system. *Man* 11:188–
               201.
1979   *Grand Valley Dani: Peaceful Warriors.* New York:
               Holt, Rinehart and Winston.

Held, G. T.
1957   *The Papuans of Waropen.* The Hague: Martinus
               Nijhoff.

Herdt, G. H.
1977   The shaman's "calling" among the Sambia of New
               Guinea. *J. Soc. Oceanistes* 56–57:153–167.
1980   Semen depletion and the sense of maleness. *Ethnopsy-*
               chiatrica 3:79–116.
1981   *Guardians of the Flutes: Idioms of Masculinity.* New
               York: McGraw-Hill.
1982*a*   Fetish and fantasy in Sambia initiation. In *Rituals*
               of Manhood: Male Initiation in Papua
               New Guinea, edited by G. H. Herdt, pp. 44–98.
               Berkeley, Los Angeles, London: University of California
               Press.
1982*b*   Sambia nose-bleeding rites and male proximity to
               women. *Ethos* 10:189–231.
n.d.   The accountability of Sambia initiates. In *Anthropol-*
               ogy in the High Valleys: Essays in Honor of K. E.
               Read, edited by L. L. Langness and T. E. Hays.

Herdt, G. H., and F. J. P. Poole
1982   Sexual antagonism: The intellectual history of a con-
               cept in the anthropology of Melanesia. In *"Sexual An-*
               tagonism," Gender, and Social Change in Papua New
               Guinea, edited by F. J. P. Poole and G. H. Herdt. *So-*
               cial Analysis (special issue) 12:3–28.

Heurn, E. W. Van
1957   Toerneeverslag, 11 April–17 May, 1957. Typescript
               report.

373

Hiatt, L. R.

1971   Secret pseudo-procreative rites among Australian Aborigines. In *Anthropology in Oceania: Essays Presented to Ian Hogbin,* edited by L. R. Hiatt and C. Jayawardena, pp. 77–88. Sydney: Angus and Robertson.

1975   Introduction to *Australian Aboriginal Mythology,* edited by L. R. Hiatt, pp. 1–23. Canberra: Australian Institute for Aboriginal Studies.

1977   Queen of night, mother-right, and secret male cults. In *Fantasy and Symbol,* edited by R. H. Hook, pp. 247–265. New York: Academic Press.

Hogbin, I.

1945   Puberty to marriage: A study of the sexual life of the
(–1946)   natives of Wogeo, New Guinea. *Oceania* 16:185–209.

1951   *Experiments in Civilization.* London: Routledge and Kegan Paul.

1970   *The Island of Menstruating Men.* Scranton, Penn.: Chandler Publishing Co.

Hooker, E.

1968   Homosexuality. In *International Encyclopedia of the Social Sciences,* edited by D. Sills, 14:222–233. New York: Macmillan.

Hugh-Jones, C.

1979   *From the Milk River: Spatial and Temporal Processes in Northwest Amazonia.* Cambridge: Cambridge University Press.

Hugh-Jones, S.

1979   *The Palm and the Pleiades: Initiation and Cosmology in Northwest Amazonia.* Cambridge: Cambridge University Press.

Hylkema, S.

1974   *Mannen in het Draagnet.* The Hague: Martinus Nijhoff.

Ionesco, E.

1959   La démystification par l'humeur noir. *L'Avant Scène* 196 (May):43–45.

Kaberry, P. M.

1939   *Aboriginal Woman, Sacred and Profane.* London: George Routledge and Sons.

Karsch-Haack, F.

1911   *Das Gleichgeschlechtliche Leben der Naturvölker.* Munich: Seitz and Schauer.

Keesing, R. M.

1976   *Cultural Anthropology: A Contemporary Perspective.* New York: Holt, Rinehart and Winston.

1982   Introduction to *Rituals of Manhood: Male Initiation in Papua New Guinea*, edited by G. H. Herdt, pp. 1–41. Berkeley, Los Angeles, London: University of California Press.

Kelly, R.

1976   Witchcraft and sexual relations: An exploration in the social and semantic implications of a structure of belief. In *Man and Woman in the New Guinea Highlands*, edited by P. Brown and G. Buchbinder, pp. 36–53. Washington, D.C.: American Anthropological Association.

1977   *Etoro Social Structure*. Ann Arbor: University of Michigan Press.

Kinsey, A., et al.

1948   *Sexual Behavior in the Human Male*. Philadelphia: W. B. Saunders.

Koch, K. F.

1974   *War and Peace in Jalemo*. Cambridge, Mass.: Harvard University Press.

Kottak, C.

1974   *Anthropology: The Exploration of Human Diversity*. New York: Random House.

Landes, R.

1940   A cult matriarchate and male homosexuality. *J. Abn. Soc. Psychol.* 35:386–397.

Landtman, G.

1917   *The Folk Tales of the Kiwai Papuans*. Acta Societatis Scientarum Fennicae 47. Helsinki: Printing Office of the Finnish Society of Literature.

1927   *The Kiwai Papuans of British New Guinea: A Nature-Born Instance of Rousseau's Ideal Community*. London: Macmillan and Company.

1954   Initiation ceremonies of the Kiwai Papuans. In *Primitive Heritage*, edited by M. Mead and N. Calas, pp. 179–186. London: Victor Gollancz Ltd.

Langmore, Diane

1978   James Chalmers: Missionary. In *Papua New Guinea Portraits: The Expatriate Experience*, edited by James Griffin, pp 1–27. Canberra: A.N.U. Press.

Langness, L. L.

1967   Sexual antagonism in the New Guinea Highlands: A Bena Bena example. *Oceania* 37:161–177.

1972   Political organization. In *Encyclopedia of Papua New Guinea*, pp. 922–935. Melbourne: Melbourne University Press.

1974   Ritual power and male domination in the New Guinea Highlands. *Ethos* 2:189–212.

Lawrence, P., and M. J. Meggitt, eds.
1965   *Gods, Ghosts and Men in Melanesia.* Melbourne: Melbourne University Press.

Layard, J.
1942   *Stone Men of Malekula.* London: Chatto & Windus.
1955   Boar sacrifice. *J. of Analytical Psych.* 1:7–31.
1959   Homo-eroticism in a primitive society as a function of the self. *J. of Analytical Psych.* 4:101–115.

Leach, E.
1961   Two essays concerning the symbolic representation of time. In *Rethinking Anthropology,* by Edmund Leach, pp. 124–136. London: The Athlone Press.
1966   Virgin Birth. In *Proceedings of the Roy. Anth. Inst. of G.B. and N.I. for 1965,* pp. 39–50.

Leedan, A. C. Van der
1956   *Hoofdtrekken der Sociale Struktuur in het Westlijk Binnenland Van Sarmi.* Leiden: Ydo.

Leenhardt, M.
1979   *Do Kamo.* Trans. Basia M. Gulati. Chicago: University of Chicago Press.

LeVine, R. A.
1981   Foreward to *Guardian of the Flutes,* by G. H. Herdt, pp. xiii–xviii. New York: McGraw-Hill.

Lévi-Strauss, C.
1949   *Les structures élémentaires de la parenté.* Paris: Presses Universitaires de France.
1958   *Anthropologie structurale.* Paris: Plon.
1962   *La pensée sauvage.* Paris: Plon.
1969   *Tristes Tropiques.* Trans. J. Russell. New York: Atheneum.
1973   *Anthropologie Structurale deux.* Paris: Plon.

Levy, R. I.
1973   *The Tahitians: Mind and Experience in the Society Islands.* Chicago: University of Chicago Press.

Lewis, G.
1980   *Day of Shining Red.* Cambridge: Cambridge University Press.

Lindenbaum, S.
1972   Sorcerers, ghosts and polluting women: An analysis of religious belief and population control. *Ethnology* 11:241–253.
1979   *Kuru Sorcery.* Palo Alto: Mayfield Publishing Co.
n.d.   The mystification of female labours. Paper presented to the Conference on Feminism and Kinship Theory, Bellagio, Italy.

Lipuma, E.
1981   Cosmology and economy among the Maring of High-
            land New Guinea. *Oceania* 51:266–285.

Lloyd, R. G.
1973   The Angan language family. In *The Linguistic Situa-
            tion in the Gulf District and Adjacent Areas, Papua
            New Guinea,* edited by K. Franklin, pp. 31–111. Pa-
            cific Linguistics, series C, no. 26. Canberra: Linguistic
            Circle of Canberra.

McDowell, N.
1972   Flexibility of sister exchange in Bun. *Oceania* 43:207–
            231.

McIntosh, M.
1968   The homosexual role. *Social Problems* 16:182–192.

Malcolm, L. A.
1968   Determination of the growth curve of the Kukukuku
            people of New Guinea from dental eruption in chil-
            dren and adult height. *Arch. and Phys. Anthropol. in
            Oceania* 4:72–78.

1970   Growth, malnutrition and mortality of the infant and
            toddler in the Asai Valley of the New Guinea High-
            lands. *Am. J. of Clinical Nutrition* 23:1090–1095.

Malinowski, B.
1913   *The Family Among the Australian Aborigines.* Lon-
            don: University of London Press.

1927   *Sex and Repression in Savage Society.* Cleveland: Me-
            ridian Books.

1929   *The Sexual Life of Savages in North-Western Melane-
            sia.* New York: Harcourt, Brace & World, Inc.

1954   *Magic, Science and Religion and Other Essays.* Gar-
            den City, N.Y.: Anchor Books.

Marivaux, P. Carlet de Chamblain de
1732   *Le triomphe de l'amour* (Theatre, Tome II, Le Livre
            de Poche, 1966).

Marshall, D., and R. Suggs, eds.
1971   Anthropological perspectives on human sexual behav-
            ior. In *Human Sexual Behavior,* edited by D. Marshall
            and R. Suggs, pp. 218–243. New York: Basic Books.

Marx, K.
1977   The fetishism of commodities and the secret thereof.
            In *Symbolic Anthropology: A Reader in the Study of
            Symbols and Meanings,* edited by J. L. Dolgin et al.,
            pp. 245–253. New York: Columbia University
            Press.

Mathews, R. H.
1896   The Boro, or initiation ceremonies of the Kamilaroi
            Tribe, Part II. *JRAI* 25:318–339.

1900   Phallic rites and initiation ceremonies of the South
        Australian Aborigines. *Proc. Am. Philo. Soc.* 39:622–
        638.

Mauss, M.
1954   *The Gift.* Trans. I. Cunnison. New York: Free Press.
Mead, M.
1935   *Sex and Temperament in Three Primitive Societies.*
        New York: Dutton.
1938   *The Mountain Arapesh.* New York: American Mu-
(–1949) seum of Natural History Press, vols. 36–37, 40, 41.
1949   *Male and Female: A Study of the Sexes in a Changing
        World.* New York: William Morrow & Co.
1961   Cultural determinants of sexual behavior. In *Sex and
        Internal Secretions,* edited by W. C. Young, pp. 1433–
        1479. Baltimore: Williams and Wilkins.
1968   *Growing up in New Guinea.* Harmondsworth, En-
        gland: Penguin Books. (Orig. 1930.)
Meggitt, M.
1964   Male-female relationships in the Highlands of Austra-
        lian New Guinea. *American Anthropologist* 66, Pt.
        2:204–224.
1965*a* *Desert People.* Chicago: University of Chicago Press.
1965*b* The Mae Enga of the Western Highlands. In *Gods,
        Ghosts and Men in Melanesia,* edited by P. Lawrence
        and M. J. Meggitt, pp. 105–131. Melbourne: Mel-
        bourne University Press.
1967   The pattern of leadership among the Mae Enga. *An-
        thropol. Forum* 2:20–35.
1971   From tribesmen to peasants: The case of the Mae
        Enga of New Guinea. In *Anthropology in Oceania,*
        edited by L. R. Hiatt and C. Jayawardena, pp. 191–
        210. Sydney: Angus and Robertson.
Meigs, A.
1976   Male pregnancy and the reduction of sexual opposi-
        tion in a New Guinea Highlands society. *Ethnology*
        25:393–407.
Mikloucho-Maclay, N. N.
1975   *Mikloucho-Maclay: New Guinea Diaries 1871–1883.*
        Trans. with comment by C. L. Sentinella. Madang,
        P.N.G.: Kristen Press.
Mimica, J.
1981   *Review of the Kukukuku of the Upper Watut,* by Be-
        atrice Blackwood. *Oceania* 51(3):226.
Minturn, L., et al.
1969   Cultural patterning of sexual beliefs and behavior.
        Ethnology 8:301–317.

Mitchell, W. E.
1978 *The Bamboo Fire*. New York: W. W. Norton & Co., Inc.

Money, J., and A. Ehrhardt
1972 *Man and Woman, Boy and Girl*. Baltimore: Johns Hopkins University Press.

Moszkowski, M.
1911 Die volkersstämme am Mamberamo in Höllandisch-Neuguinea und auf den vorgelagerten inseln. *Zeitschrift für Ethnologie* 43:315–346.

Munn, N. D.
1973 Symbolism in ritual context: aspects of symbolic action. In *Handbook of Social and Cultural Anthropology*, edited by J. J. Honigman, pp. 579–612. Chicago: Rand McNally.

Murphy, R. F.
1959 Social structure and sex antagonism. *SWJA* 15:89–98.

Murray, S.
n.d. Introduction to *Cultural Diversity and Homosexualities*, edited by S. Murray. Unpublished MS.

Neuhauss, R.
1911 *Deutsch Neu Guinea*. 3 vols. Berlin: Verlag Dietrich Reimer.

Newman, Phillip
1964 Religious belief and ritual in a New Guinea Society. *American Anthropologist* 66, Pt. 2:257–272.

Nieuwenhuijsen-Riedeman, C. H. Van
1979 *Een Zuster voor een Vrouw*. Amsterdam: Anthropologisch-Sociologisch Centrum, Afdeling Culturele Anthropologie, Universiteit van Amsterdam.

Nimmo, H. A.
1978 The relativity of sexual deviance: A Sulu example. *Papers in Anthropology* 19:91–97.

O'Flaherty, W. D.
1980 *Women, Androgynes, and Other Mythical Beasts*. Chicago: University of Chicago Press.

Oosterwal, G.
1959 The position of the bachelor in the Upper Tor territory. *American Anthropologist* 51:829–838.
1961 *People of the Tor*. Assen: Van Gorcum.
1967 Muremarew: A dual organized village on the Mamberamo, West Irian. In *Villages in Indonesia*, edited by Koentjaraningrat, pp. 157–188. Ithaca: Cornell University Press.

Opler, M. K.
1965 Anthropological and cross-cultural aspects of homo-

sexuality. In *Sexual Inversion,* edited by J. Marmor, pp. 108–123. New York: Basic Books.

Padgug, R. A.
1979   Sexual matters: On conceptualizing sexuality in history. *Rad. Hist. Rev.* 20:3–33.

Panoff, M.
1968   The notion of the double-self among the Maenge. *J. Poly. Soc.* 77:275–295.

Parkinson, R.
1907   *Dreissig Jahre in der Südsee: Land und Leute, Sitten und Gebrauche im Bismarck Archipel und auf den duetschen Salmoninseln.* Stuttgart: Strecker & Schröder. (Trans. N. C. Barry, n.d.: I.A.S.E.R. Library, Port Moresby, Papua New Guinea.)

Parratt, J.
1976   *Papuan Belief and Ritual.* New York: Vintage Books.

Pettit, P.
1977   *The Concept of Structuralism: A Critical Analysis.* Berkeley, Los Angeles, London: University of California Press.

Poole, F. J. P.
1981   Transforming, "natural" woman: Female ritual leaders and gender ideology among Bimin-Kuskusmin. In *Sexual Meanings,* edited by S. B. Ortner and H. Whitehead, pp. 116–165. Cambridge: Cambridge University Press.

1982   The ritual forging of identity: Aspects of person and self in Bimin-Kuskusmin male initiation. In *Rituals of Manhood: Male Initiation in Papua New Guinea,* edited by G. H. Herdt, pp. 100–154. Berkeley, Los Angeles, London: University of California Press.

Pouwer, J.
1955   *Enkele Aspecten Van De Mimika-Cultuur.* The Hague: Staatsdrukkerij-en Vitgeversbedrijf.

Purcell, B. H.
1893   Rites and customs of Australian Aborigines. *Leit. fur Ethnol.* 25:286–289.

Rado, S.
1965   A critical examination of the concept of bisexuality. In *Sexual Inversion,* edited by J. Marmor, pp. 175–189. New York: Basic Books.

Rapp, R.
1979   Review essay: Anthropology. *Signs: J. of Women in Cult. and Soc.* 4:497–513.

Ravenscroft, A. G. B.
1892   Some habits and customs of the Chingalee Tribe, Northern Territory, S.A. *Trans. Roy. Soc. So. Aust.* 15:121–122.

Read, K. E.
1951   The Gahuku-Gama of the Central Highlands. *South Pacific* 5:154–164.
1952   Nama cult of the Central Highlands, New Guinea. *Oceania* 23:1–25.
1954   Cultures of the Central Highlands. *SWJA* 10:1–43.
1955   Morality and the concept of the person among the Gahuku-Gama. *Oceania* 25:233-282.
1959   Leadership and consensus in a New Guinea Society. *American Anthropologist* 61:425–436.
1965   *The High Valley*. London: George Allen and Unwin.
1980*a*   *The High Valley*. Columbia: Columbia University Press. (New edition; orig. 1965.)
1980*b*   *Other Voices*. Novato, Calif.: Chandler & Sharp.

Reay, M.
1959   *The Kuma*. Melbourne: Melbourne University Press.

Reik, T.
1946   The puberty rites of savages. In *Ritual: Four Psychoanalytic Studies*, pp. 91–166. New York: Grove Press. (Orig. 1915.)

Remy, J.
1862   *Ka Moolelo Hawaii*. Paris: A. Franck.

Reports
1901   *Reports of the Cambridge Expedition to the Torres*
(–1935)   *Straits*. 6 vols. Cambridge: Cambridge University Press.

Rickard, R. H.
1891   The Dukduk association of New Britain. *Proc. Roy. Soc. Vict.* 3:70–76.

Rivers, W. H. R.
1904   *Reports of the Cambridge Anthropological Expedition to the Torres Straits*. Vol. 5. Cambridge: Cambridge University Press.
1914   *The History of Melanesian Society*. 2 vols. Cambridge: Cambridge University Press.
1922   *Essays on the Depopulation of Melanesia*. Cambridge: Cambridge University Press.

Rochas, V. de
1862   *La Nouvelle Calédonie et ses habitants*. Paris: F. Sartorius.

Rodman, W. L.
1973   Men of influence, men of rank: Leadership and the graded society on Aoba, New Hebrides. Ph.D. dissertation, University of Chicago.

Rogers, S. K.
1975   Sirorata community: A report for the Papua Communications Project. Department of Anthropology, Université Laval. Unpublished MS.

Róheim, G.
1926   *Social Anthropology, a Psycho-analytic Study in Anthropology and a History of Australian Totemism.* New York: Boni and Liveright.

1929   Dying gods and puberty ceremonies. *JRAI* 59:181–197.

1932   Psycho-analysis of primitive cultural types. *Intl. J. of Psycho-Analysis* 13:1–224.

1945   *The Eternal Ones of the Dream.* New York: International University Press.

1950   *Psychoanalysis and Anthropology.* New York: International University Press.

1974   *Children of the Desert.* Edited by W. Muensterberger. New York: Basic Books.

Rosaldo, M. Z.
1974   Women, culture, and society: A theoretical overview. In *Woman, Culture, and Society,* edited by M. Z. Rosaldo and L. Lamphere, pp. 17–42. Stanford: Stanford University Press.

Royal Anthropological Institute of Great Britain and Ireland
1951   *Notes and Queries in Anthropology.* 6th ed. London: Routledge and Kegan Paul.

Rubel, P. G., and A. Rosman
1978   *Your Own Pigs You May Not Eat.* Chicago: University of Chicago Press.

Rubin, G.
1975   The traffic in women: Notes on the "political economy" of sex. In *Toward an Anthropology of Women,* edited by Rayna R. Reiter, pp. 157–210. New York: Monthly Review Press.

Schieffelin, E. L.
1976   *The Sorrow of the Lonely and the Burning of the Dancers.* New York: St. Martin's Press.

1977   The unseen influence: Tranced mediums as historical innovators. *J. Soc. Oceanistes* 56–57:169–178.

1982   The Bau a ceremonial hunting lodge: An alternative to initiation. In *Rituals of Manhood: Male Initiation in*

Papua New Guinea, edited by G. H. Herdt, pp. 155–200. Berkeley, Los Angeles, London: University of California Press.

Schwartz, T.
1973 Cult and context: The paranoid ethos in Melanesia. *Ethos* 1:153–174.

Schweder, R. and E. J. Bourne
1982 Does the concept of the person vary cross-culturally? In *Cultural Conceptions of Mental Health and Therapy,* edited by A. J. Marsella and G. M. White, pp. 97–137. Boston: D. Reidel Pub. Co.

Schwimmer, E.
1969 *Cultural Consequences of a Volcanic Eruption.* Eugene: University of Oregon, Department of Anthropology.

1973 *Exchange in the Social Structure of the Orokaiva.* London: Hurst.

1974 Objects of mediation: Myth and praxis. In *The Unconscious in Culture,* edited by I. Rossi, pp. 209–237. New York: Dutton.

1975 Friendship and kinship. In *The Compact,* edited by E. Leyton, pp. 49–70. ISER, Memorial University of Newfoundland.

1979*a* Reciprocity and structure. *Man* 14:271–285.

1979*b* Aesthetics of the Aika. In *Exploring the Visual Arts of Oceania,* edited by S. M. Mead, pp. 287–292. Honolulu: University Press of Hawaii.

1980 *Power, Silence and Secrecy.* Toronto: Semiotic Circle, Victoria University.

1981*a* *Les Frères-ennemis.* Quebec: Université Laval, Department of Anthropology.

1981*b* L'archaeologie des messages. *Anthropologie et Sociétés* 5 (3):137–156.

1981*c* Power and Secrecy. *Semiotic Inquiry* I:214–243.

1982*a* Irons of Identity. Unpublished MS.

1982*b* The taste of your own flesh. Unpublished MS.

Seemann, B.
1862 *Viti, An Account of a Government Mission to the Vitian or Fijian Islands in the Years 1860–61.* London: Dawson's of Pall Mall.

Seligman, C. G.
1902 Sexual inversion among primitive races. *The Alienist and Neurologist* 23:11–15.

Serpenti, L. M.
1965 *Cultivators in the Swamps: Social Structure and Hor-*

ticulture in a New Guinea Society. Assen: Van Gorcum.

1968 Headhunting and magic on Kolepom. *Tropical Man* 1:116–139.

1969 On the social significance of an intoxicant. *Tropical Man* 2:31–44.

1972 Ndambu, the feast of competitive growth. *Tropical*
(–1973) *Man* 5:162–187.

Sexton, L. D.

1982 Wok meri: A women's savings and exchange system in Highland Papua New Guinea. *Oceania* 52:167–198.

Shaw, R. D.

n.d. Young man, strong man, kinsman, shaman: Samo initiation, its context and its meaning. Unpublished MS.

Sillitoe, P.

1978 Big men and war in New Guinea. *Man* 13:252–271.

Simpson, C.

1953 *Adam with Arrows.* Sydney: Angus & Robertson.

Sonenschein, D.

1965 Homosexuality as a subject of anthropological inquiry. *Anthropology Quarterly* 38:73–82.

Sørum, A.

1980 In search of the lost soul: Bedamini spirit seances and curing rites. *Oceania* 50:273–297.

1982 The seeds of power: Patterns in Bedamini male initiation. *Social Analysis* 10:42–62.

Speiser, F.

1923 *Ethnographische Materialien aus den Neuen Hebriden und den Banks-Inseln.* Berlin: C. W. Kreidel.

Spencer, B. Sir, and F. J. Gillen

1927 *The Arunta.* 2 vols. London: Macmillan and Co.

Spiro, M. E.

1968 Virgin birth, parthenogenesis and physiological paternity: An essay in cultural interpretation. *Man* 3:242–261.

1982 *Oedipus in the Trobriands.* Chicago: University of Chicago Press.

Stephens, W. N.

1962 *The Oedipus Complex: Cross-Cultural Evidence.* New York: The Free Press.

Stoller, R. J.

1968 *Sex and Gender, Volume I: On the Development of Masculinity and Femininity.* New York: Science House.

1975 *Sex and Gender, Volume II: The Transsexual Experiment.* New York: Jason Aronson.

1977   *Perversion: The Erotic Form of Hatred*. London: Quartet Books.
1979   *Sexual Excitement: Dynamics of Erotic Life*. New York: Pantheon Books.
1980   Problems with the term "homosexuality." *The Hillside J. of Clin. Psychiatry* 2:3–25.

Stoller, R. J., and G. H. Herdt
1982   The development of masculinity: A cross-cultural contribution. *J. Am. Psychoan. Assn.* 30:29–59.
n.d.   Intimate communications: Methodological aspects of clinical ethnography. Unpublished MS.

Strachan, J.
1888   *Explorations and Adventures in New Guinea*. London: S. Low, Marston, Searle and Rivington.

Strathern, A. J.
1969*a*   Descent and alliance in the New Guinea Highlands: Some problems of comparison. *Proc. of the RAI for 1968*, pp. 37–52.
1969*b*   Finance and production: Two strategies in New Guinea Highlands exchange systems. *Oceania* 40:42–67.
1970   Male initiation in the New Guinea Highland societies. *Ethnology* 9:373–379.
1972   *One Father, One Blood*. Canberra: A.N.U. Press.
1979   Gender, ideology and money in Mount Hagen. *Man* 14:530–548.

Strathern, M.
1972   *Women in Between*. London: Seminar Press.
1978   The achievement of sex: Paradoxes in Hagen gender-thinking. In *The Yearbook of Symbolic Anthropology*, edited by E. G. Schwimmer, pp. 171–202. London: C. Hurst.
1979   The self in self-decoration. *Oceania* 49:241–257.
1980   No nature, no culture: The Hagen case. In *Nature, Culture and Gender*, edited by C. P. MacCormack and M. Strathern, pp. 174–222. Cambridge: Cambridge University Press.
1981   Culture in a netbag. *Man* 16:665–688.

Strathern, A., and M. Strathern
1971   *Self Decoration in Mount Hagen*. London: Gerald Duckworth and Co. Ltd.

Strehlow, C.
1913   *Die Aranda-und Loritja-Stämme in Zentral Australien*. 4,1, *Das Sociale Leben der Aranda-und Loritja-Stämme*. Frankfurt: Joseph Baer & Co.

Thieman, M. S. C.
n.d.   Diary notes. Unpublished.

385

Thurnwald, B. R.
1916   Banaro society: Social organization and kinship system of a tribe in the interior of New Guinea. *American Anthropological Association Memoirs* 3:253–391.

Tiger, L.
1970   *Men in Groups.* New York: Vintage Books.

Tripp, C. A.
1975   *The Homosexual Matrix.* New York: New American Library.

Trumbach, R.
1977   London's sodomites: Homosexual behavior and Western culture in the 18th century. *J. of Soc. Hist.* 11:1–33.

Turner, V. W.
1967   Betwixt and between: The liminal period in Rites de Passage. In *The Forest of Symbols,* by V. W. Turner, pp. 93–111. Ithaca: Cornell University Press.
1971   *The Ritual Process.* Chicago: Aldine Pub. Co.

Tuzin, D. F.
1976   *The Ilahita Arapesh.* Berkeley, Los Angeles, London: University of California Press.
1980   *The Voice of the Tamberan: Truth and Illusion in Ilahita Arapesh Religion.* Berkeley, Los Angeles, London: University of California Press.
1982   Ritual violence among the Ilahita Arapesh: The dynamics of moral and religious uncertainty. In *Rituals of Manhood: Male Initiation in Papua New Guinea,* edited by G. H. Herdt, pp. 321–355. Berkeley, Los Angeles, London: University of California Press.

Vanggaard, T.
1972   *Phallos.* New York: International University Press.

Verhage, A., M.S.C.
1957   Nota over het Frederik-Hendrik Eiland. Merauke. Unpublished typescript report.

Wagner, R.
1967   *The Curse of Souw: Principles of Daribi Clan Definition and Alliance.* Chicago: University of Chicago Press.
1972   *Habu: The Innovation of Meaning in Daribi Religion.* Chicago: University of Chicago Press.

Waterhouse, J.
1866   *The King and People of Fiji: Containing a Life of Thakombau with Notices of the Fijians, Their Manners, Customs, and Superstitions, Previous to the Great Religious Reformation in 1854.* London: Wesleyan Conference Office.

Watson, J. B.
1965   From hunting to horticulture in the New Guinea Highlands. *Ethnology* 4:295–309.

Weeks, J.
1981   *Sex, Politics and Society: The Regulation of Sexuality Since 1800.* London: Longman.

Weiner, A. B.
1976   *Women of Value, Men of Renown. New Perspectives in Trobriand Exchange.* Austin: University of Texas Press.

1978   The reproductive model in Trobriand society. In *Trade and Exchange in Oceania and Australia,* edited by J. Specht and P. White (special issue), *Mankind* 11:150–174.

1979   Trobriand kinship from another view: The reproductive power of women and men. *Man* 14:328–348.

1980   Reproduction: A replacement for reciprocity. *American Ethnologist* 7:71–85.

n.d.   Transformations in gender constructs. Paper delivered at the American Anthropological Association Meetings, Los Angeles, December 4, 1981.

Westermarck, E.
1917   *The Origin and Development of the Moral Ideas.* Vol. 2. 2d ed. London: Macmillan and Co.

Whitehead, H.
1981   The bow and the burden strap: A new look at institutionalized homosexuality in native North America. In *Sexual Meanings,* edited by S. B. Ortner and H. Whitehead, pp. 80–115. Cambridge: Cambridge University Press.

n.d.   The sexual substance symbolism of New Guinea. Paper presented to the Conference on Feminism and Kinship Theory, Bellagio, Italy.

Whiting, J. W. M.
1941   *Becoming a Kwoma: Teaching and Learning in a New Guinea Tribe.* New Haven: Yale University Press.

Whiting, J. W. M., and B. B. Whiting
1975   Aloofness and intimacy of husbands and wives: A cross-cultural study. *Ethos* 3:183–207.

Whiting, J. W. M., et al.
1958   The function of male initiation ceremonies at puberty. In *Readings in Social Psychology,* edited by E. E. Maccoby et al., pp. 359–370. New York: Holt.

Whitaker, J. L., et al.
1975   *Documents and Readings in New Guinea History: Prehistory to 1889.* Brisbane: Jacaranda Press.

Wiedeman, G. H.
1972   Homosexuality, a survey. *J. Am. Psychoan. Assn.* 22:651–695.

Wikan, U.
1977   Man becomes woman: Transsexuals in Oman as a key to gender roles. *Man* 13:665–667.

Williams, F. E.
1924   *The Natives of the Purari Delta.* Port Moresby: Government Printer.
1928   *Orokaiva Magic.* London: Oxford University Press.
1930   *Orokaiva Society.* London: Oxford University Press.
1936a   *Bull Roarers of the Papuan Gulf.* Territory of Papua, Anthropology Report no. 17. Port Moresby: Walter A. Bock.
1936b   Papuan dream interpretation. *Mankind* 2:29–39.
1936c   *Papuans of the Trans-Fly.* Oxford: Oxford University Press.
1939   Seclusion and age grouping in the gulf of Papua. *Oceania* 9:359–381.
1940a   *Drama of Orokolo.* Oxford: Oxford University Press.
1940b   *Natives of Lake Kutubu.* Oceania Monograph no. 6. Sydney.
1976   *"The Vailala Madness" and Other Essays.* London: Hurst.

Wirz, P.
1922   *Die Marind-anim von Holläendisch Sued-Neu-Guinea.*
(–1925)   Hamburgische Universitäte, Abhandlungen aus dem Gebiet des Auslandskunde, Reihe B, Band 6: Teile I und II; Band 9: Teile III and IV.
1928   Beitrag zur ethnologie der Sentanier (Hollädisch Neuguinea). *Nova Guinea Livr.* 3:251–370.
1933   Head-hunting expeditions of the Tugeri into the Western Division of British New Guinea. *Tijdschrift voor Indische Taal, -Land, -en Volkenkunde* 73:105–122.
1934   Beiträge zur ethnographie des Papua-Golfes, Britisch-Neuguinea. *Abhandlungen und Berichte der Museen für Tierkunde und Völkerkunde zu Dresden* 19:1–103.

Wurm, S. A., et al.
1975   Papuan linguistic prehistory, and past language migrations in the New Guinea area. In *New Guinea Area Languages and Language Study, Vol. 1: Papuan Languages and New Guinea Linguistic Scene*, edited by S. A. Wurm, pp. 935–960. Pacific Linguistics Series C, no. 38. Canberra: Linguistic Circle of Canberra.

X., Jacobus
1893   *L'amour aux Colonies.* Paris: Isidore Liseux.
1898   *L'Ethnologie du Sens Genital.* Paris: Charles Carrington.

Young, F. W.
1965   *Initiation Ceremonies: A Cross-Cultural Status Dramatization.* Indianapolis: The Bobbs-Merrill Co., Inc.

Zegwaard, G. A.
1959   Headhunting practices of the Asmat of West New Guinea. *American Anthropologist* 61:1020–1041.

Contributors

Michael R. Allen was born in Dublin, Ireland, in 1928. He received his B.A. degree from Trinity College, Dublin, and his Ph.D. from the Australian National University in 1964. Since 1963 he has taught at the University of Sydney, Australia, where he is an associate professor. He has conducted fieldwork in Aoba Island, North Vanuatu, and in Kathmandu, Nepal, working with the Newar people. He has lectured and given seminars on kinship theory, South Asia, Melanesia, the sociology of Hinduism and Buddhism, ritual, structuralism, and other topics. In 1982 he was visiting professor at the University of California, San Diego. His publications have appeared in many journals, and his books include *Male Cults and Secret Initiations* (1967), *The Cult of Kumari: Virgin Worship in Nepal* (1975), *Vanuatu: Politics, Economics, and Ritual in Island Melanesia* (1981), and *Women in India and Nepal* (1982).

Jan Van Baal was born in The Hague, Netherlands, in 1909. He studied at Leyden University, where he combined the study of Indonesian languages, history, and law with that of cultural anthropology under the direction of the late J. P. B. de Josselin de Jong. He graduated in 1934 as Dr. Litt. on the Religion and Society of Netherlands South New Guinea. He has served as an assistant district officer in South New Guinea and as an administrative officer in East Java and on the island of Lombok. After the start of World War II, he was captured and held prisoner by the Japanese on Celebes until August 1945. In the late 1940s he returned to active service on Bali, Lombok, East Sumatra, and then became adviser to the governor of Netherlands New Guinea in 1951. He was a member of the Dutch Parliament in 1952–1953. In 1953, he returned as governor of Dutch New Guinea, a post he held until his retirement in 1958. In 1959 he joined the Royal Tropical Institute in Amsterdam, which he combined with part-time professorships at the Universities of Utrecht and Amsterdam. In 1969 he became full professor of anthropology at the State University of Utrecht, from which he retired in 1975. He has also participated in various UNESCO activities. His publications have appeared in numerous journals, and his books include *Dema, A Description and Analysis of Marind-anim Culture* (1966), *Symbols for Communication* (1971), *De Boodshap der drie Illusies* (1972), *De Agressie der Gelijken* (1974), *Reciprocity and the Position of Women* (1975), and *Man's Quest for Partnership* (1981), a study of the anthropology of religion and ethics. He hopes to occupy himself more fully with his colonial past in the coming years.

Gilbert H. Herdt was born in Oakley, Kansas, in 1949. He received his B.A. from Sacramento State University, his M.A. from the University of Washington, and his Ph.D. from the Australian National University in 1978. From 1977–1979 he was a postdoctoral fellow in the Neuropsychiatric Institute, Department of Psychiatry, UCLA, where he was trained in psychiatry, sex and gender. Since 1979 he has taught at Stanford University, where he is an assistant professor. He has conducted field research in a large psychiatric ward in Northern California, and among the Sambia of Papua New Guinea. He has lectured and conducted seminars on symbolic and psychological anthropology, ritual, sex and gender, mental illness and culture, New Guinea, and other topics. His publications have appeared in several journals, and his books include *Guardians of the Flutes* (1981), *Rituals of Manhood: Male Initiation in Papua New Guinea* (1982), and *Intimate Communications: Method and Interpretation in Clinical Ethnography* (in preparation, with Robert J. Stoller).

Shirley Lindenbaum was born in Melbourne, Australia, in 1933. She studied English literature and received her B.A. from Melbourne University. She studied social anthropology at the University of Sydney, from which she received her M.A. in

1970. She has taught at City University of New York and has been at the New School for Social Research (New York) since 1976, where she is now associate professor. She has conducted fieldwork among the Fore of the Eastern Highlands, Papua New Guinea, and in Bangladesh. She has lectured and conducted seminars in ethnology, medical anthropology, religion, symbolism, Oceania, and South Asia, and has most recently become involved in research and government policy on health in Bangladesh. Her studies have appeared in many journals and as chapters of books, and she is the author of *Kuru Sorcery* (1979) and the coeditor of "Sorcery and Social Change in Melanesia," a special issue of the journal *Social Analysis* (1981).

Kenneth E. Read was born in Sydney, Australia, in 1917. He received his B.A. and M.A. from the University of Sydney. He earned his Ph.D. from the University of London in 1948. He was a research fellow at the Australian National University in the 1950s, and since 1958 has taught at the University of Washington, Seattle, where he is a professor. During World War II, Read began research, as a member of the Allied forces, with the Ngarawapum of the Markham Valley (1944–1945), in what was then the territory of New Guinea administered by Australia under a U.N. mandate. He has conducted fieldwork among the Gahuku-Gama, Eastern Highlands Province, Papua New Guinea (1950–1951), and has done extensive research in a "rough-trade" gay tavern in the early 1970s. He has lectured and conducted seminars on social structure, religion, Oceania, comparative ethics, and other subjects. His publications have appeared in many journals, and his books include *The High Valley* (1965), *The Human Aviary* (1973), and *Other Voices* (1980). He is currently at work on *Full-Circle*, an autobiographical account of his experience with the Gahuku-Gama based on recent field research in Papua New Guinea in 1981 and 1982.

Eric G. Schwimmer was born in Amsterdam, the Netherlands, in 1923. He received his B.A. from Victoria University of Wellington, New Zealand (1948), his M.A. (Anthropology) in 1965, and his Ph.D. in 1970, both from the University of British

Columbia. Since 1975 he has taught at Laval University, Quebec, Canada, where he is Professor Titulaire. He has conducted fieldwork in New Zealand and among the Orokaiva and related peoples in the Northern Province of Papua New Guinea. He has lectured on structuralism, ritual, semiotics, social structure, Oceania, and South East Asia. His publications have appeared in many journals, and his books include *The World of the Maori* (1966), *Exchange in the Social Structure of the Orokaiva* (1973), and *Les Frères-ennemis* (1981).

L aurent Serpenti was born in Maastricht, the Netherlands, in 1933. He received both his B.A. and his Ph.D. from Amsterdam University, the latter in 1965. He has been a senior research fellow at the Royal Tropical Institute in Amsterdam, an adviser to the Dutch Ministry on Foreign Affairs and to W.H.O., and is currently lecturing in cultural anthropology at the State University of Limburg, Maastricht, the Netherlands. He has conducted fieldwork in Frederick Hendrik Island, Irian Jaya, among the Kimam people, and in Northern Sulawesi, Indonesia. He has also advised on several research and development projects in Thailand, Indonesia, Bangladesh, and Papua New Guinea. His publications have appeared in several journals, and he is the author of *Cultivators in the Swamps* (1965).

A rve Sørum was born in Oslo, Norway, in 1945. He received his Mag. art. from the University of Oslo in 1976. He has been a research scholar in the Ethnographic Museum, University of Oslo, since 1978. He has conducted seminars and lectured on symbolic anthropology, ritual, human ecology, social structure, and Oceania in the Museum and elsewhere. Sørum has conducted fieldwork among the Bedamini of the Southern Highlands Province, Papua New Guinea, and among the West Toraja, in Sulawesi, Indonesia. His publications have appeared in several journals.

Index